T0364973

COMICS AND STUFF

NEW YORK UNIVERSITY PRESS
New York

HENRY JENKINS

NEW YORK UNIVERSITY PRESS
New York
www.nyupress.org

References to Internet websites (URLs) were accurate at the time of writing. Neither the author nor New York University Press is responsible for URLs that may have expired or changed since the manuscript was prepared.

LIBRARY OF CONGRESS CATALOGING-IN-PUBLICATION DATA

Names: Jenkins, Henry, 1958- author.

Title: Comics and stuff / Henry Jenkins.

Description: New York : New York University Press, [2020] | Includes bibliographical references and index.

Identifiers: LCCN 2019029645

ISBN 9781479852741 (cloth)

ISBN 9781479800933 (paperback)

ISBN 9781479831258 (ebook)

ISBN 9781479815173 (ebook)

Subjects: LCSH: Comic books, strips, etc.--History and criticism. | Material culture in art. | Material culture in literature.

Classification: LCC PN6710 .J46 2020 | DDC 741.5/9--dc23

LC record available at https://lccn.loc.gov/2019029645

New York University Press books are printed on acid-free paper, and their binding materials are chosen for strength and durability. We strive to use environmentally responsible suppliers and materials to the greatest extent possible in publishing our books.

Manufactured in the United States of America

10 9 8 7 6 5 4 3 2 1

Also available as an ebook

CONTENTS

Introduction

Comics and Stuff—Core Concepts

In May 2012, Pulitzer Prize–winning author Art Spiegelman and distinguished arts critic W. J. T. Mitchell sat down at the University of Chicago. Spiegelman has long deployed the cultural capital he gained through writing *Maus*, his landmark graphic novel, to advocate for greater artistic recognition for comics:

> In the 1970s I was reading Marshall McLuhan. He pointed out that when something is no longer a mass medium, it has to become art or it dies. And I was realizing comics even in the 1970s were beginning to wane from their glory years—when they were truly a mass, mass medium. And I thought of it very literally as a Faustian deal that had to be made with the culture, and it was a fraught one and a dangerous one. . . . I figured it was necessary for comics to find their way into libraries, book stores, universities, and museums, because otherwise there wouldn't be an apparatus that could sustain what had been sustained by Sunday newspapers and pamphlet comics and things like that in the later part of the century. It was a Faustian deal because the medium gets tainted by its aspirations

> towards legitimacy, and I was part of the taint. (Mitchell and Spiegelman 2014, 21)

Spiegelman's "Faustian deal" provides the context for this book.

Whether the shift is from a mass audience to a hipster audience or from a popular audience to an "art world" readership, comic books are now often described as "graphic novels." This problematic term describes changes in physical format—from stapled magazines ("floppies") to hardbound books—and publication schedules—from periodicals to self-contained volumes. It also marks shifts in aspiration, the lowly comic book becoming the elevated novel, and the recasting of genre entertainment toward realistic, historical, autobiographical content. The emergence of an academic field of comic studies is a visible indicator of these shifts—graphic novels can be taught in literature classrooms, for example, whereas few would have taken traditional comic books into such spaces, unless they were smuggled under the desk. This next section covers familiar territory for comics fans and scholars. But I've found that readers newer to the format appreciate this background to understand the claims this book will make.

Ultimately, I explore the relationship between comics and material culture—what makes comics an important medium for reflecting upon people's relationships with stuff? Formally, graphic storytelling places a distinctive emphasis upon mise-en-scène, putting everyday objects on display, setting them into motion, and deploying them as core metaphors for thinking about our relationship with the past. This book is about what graphic novels that reflect on everyday life tell us about the ways people make meaning and manage identity through their relationships with stuff—that is, the accumulated things that constitute our familiar surroundings. *Comics and Stuff* seeks a conversation between two emerging fields—one focused on the study of comics and the other focused on the study of stuff (as understood within anthropology, sociology, economics, literary studies, and art history).

From Disposable to Durable

In *Breakdowns: Portrait of the Artist as a Young %@#*!* (2005), Spiegelman recounts how his father influenced his taste in comics. Disdainful about how young Art "waste[s]" his time and money, Art's father brags that he can buy many more comics for the same money. Dad finally brings home some old EC horror and crime comics, dumped on the market in the wake of psychiatrist Fredric Wertham's Senate testimony linking such comics to juvenile deliquency. As Spiegelman puts it, "I had never seen comics like these before. . . . I fell head over heels into a dangerous adult world of violent, sexually charged imagery" (n.p.). This story offers an origin myth for Spiegelman's work as a curator, critic, and educator who shaped which comics were passed to the next generation. These comics were "trash" because they were seen as containing bad art and worse ideas, as being inappropriate for youngsters, and because they were designed to be tossed after being read. As generations of fans and critics since have attested, the EC comics were also art—works that experimented with new visual strategies, that introduced morally complex situations, novelistic characters, and socially resonant themes, and that had recognizable auteurs.

In his book *Rubbish Theory: The Creation and Destruction of Value* (1979), Michael Thompson distinguishes among rubbish, which has no value and thus is quickly discarded, like packaging and branding materials; the transient, whose value decreases over time and thus has a limited shelf life; and the durable, designed to last and gain value through the ages. Both the durable and the transient occupy what he describes as a "region of fixed assumptions," whereas "innovation and creativity arise within the region of flexibility," a no-man's zone between the two (8). Much as Raymond Williams grounded cultural studies in a focus on dynamic processes rather than fixed categories, Thompson stresses that appraisals shift over time: "We are all familiar with the way despised Victorian objects have become sought-after antiques; with Bakelite ashtrays that have become collector's items; with old bangers transformed into vintage motor cars" (9).

Thompson (1994) seeks to move economics from a focus on scarcity as a determinant of value toward an emphasis on negotiations as people reappraise objects' cultural and economic value: "The secondhand car dealer is successful to the extent that he is able to delay the transfer of an item from the transient to the rubbish category; the antiques dealer is successful to the extent that he is able to emphasize the durability of an item" (273). Both operations involve border crossing and Thompson emphasizes the cultural power that shapes who gets to make their appraisals stick: "Those people near the top have the power to make things durable and to make things transient, so they can ensure that their own objects are always durable and that those of others are always transient" (273). In Thompson's account, power, economic value, and cultural hierarchy are mutually reinforcing, shaping our relationships with the stuff of everyday life. One might want to push him toward even greater fluidity in the status of objects, paving the way for even greater negotiations over value and meaning, but his conceptual framework allows us to ask such questions.

For most of their history, comics were widely understood as rubbish—you read them and discarded them—and they were printed on pulp paper that decomposed over time. So, at the most basic level, saving comics meant gathering the material and preserving it in formats that could be passed to future generations—comic strips were put on acid-free scrapbook paper; floppy comics were backed by cardboard, placed in plastic envelopes, stored in long boxes, and rarely, if ever, touched again. Spiegelman sought to change the cultural status and, secondarily, the economic value of comics. Institutions that had supported comics across the second part of the twentieth century—the print newspapers with their Sunday supplements or the brightly colored floppies sold through specialty shops—were faltering. The costs of paper, ink, shipping, and storage were increasing; readerships for printed matter were declining. Comics, as Spiegelman notes, were moving from a mass medium in the midcentury to a fringe medium by the 1980s. This shift was accompanied by a gradual narrowing of subject matter, an abandonment of many genres that were in production when comics enjoyed more widespread readership and a focus on superhero stories that retained their hardcore fans. To survive, comics needed to claim a much larger terrain, to expand what stories they told. And doing so required negotiation with potential gatekeepers, ranging from humanities departments to the shop clerks who determine which new books to showcase for their customers, from newspaper critics to podcasters and bloggers, from art curators to respectable publishing houses. A recent explosion of books of comic criticism documents this process of reappraising which comics mattered and why (Beaty 2012; Beaty and Woo 2016; Chute 2017).

As Thompson (1994) notes,

> The rubbish to durable transition is an all-or-nothing transfer. An object cannot gradually slide across from one category to the other as is the case with the transient to rubbish transfer. The transition involves the transfer across two boundaries, that separating the worthless from the valuable and that between the covert and the overt. Things may drift into obscurity but they leap into prominence. For an item to cross these boundaries it must begin to acquire value and it must emerge from its obscurity. . . . Since it has become visible it must also discard its polluting properties. (26)

What Spiegelman calls his "Faustian deal" involved trading the vibrancy of comics as a lively arts tradition for the respectability and durability that came from inserting the "graphic novel" into contemporary art and literature. Graphic novels would now be purchased in bookstores, checked out of libraries, and displayed proudly on bookshelves, works that would be reviewed by serious critics, discussed on public radio, and studied in the university classroom. In recent years, a growing number of artists who are female, queer, and people of color, have found their way into comics, embracing this new freedom to expand whom comics speak to and for. Damian Duffy (2010), for example, has written about the ways that black artists have participated in the "guerilla hustle and grind of independent, small press, self-published and online comics" as they lay the foundations for "the art and culture of self-determination" (8). Many of these artists still struggle to be recognized and embraced by the critical establishment that has grown up around this medium, though writers like Rebecca Wanzo (2020) and Hillary Chute (2010) have demonstrated that these new artists can trace a legacy of comics that had been marginalized and forgotten over time.

The collector culture that developed around comics prolonged their shelf life by protecting them from being touched and tossed. We might imagine two kinds of collectors—speculators who stressed the economic value of preserving comics, and buffs who emphasized the comics' personal and cultural meaningfulness. The speculator market depended on comics' disposability and thus their scarcity: every parent who threw out his or her kid's comics increased their value for those who kept them. And as comics became an enduring medium, it also became a durable medium—that is, comics were published in formats meant to last. On the level of format, comics had to become books, and on a cultural level, comics had to become novels.

The result, Mitchell and Spiegelman (2014) suggest, is a "tug of war between the vulgar and the genteel" (21) that has informed the most innovative work in the comics medium. For Spiegelman, rebranding comics as "graphic novels" gives too much ground to the genteel. For many, the term represents a form of putting on airs—"the literary equivalent of calling a garbage man a 'sanitation engineer'" (Raeburn 2004, 110) or describing a "hooker" as "a lady of the evening" (Neil Gaiman as cited in Bender 1999). So *Maus* and many other graphic novels are shaped by tensions between the respectability that comes from assimilating realist conventions and the vitality that comes from incorporating more vernacular elements—for example, dealing with family memory and public trauma through the funny animal book. Alongside *Maus*, the established canon of graphic novels includes Alison Bechdel's *Fun Home*, Chris Ware's *Jimmy Corrigan*, Marjane Satrapi's *Persepolis*, and John Lewis and Nate Powell's *March*, each adopting its own strategies for gaining cultural respectability while retaining what's most vital and liberating about the comics tradition.

From Comics to Graphic Novels

Spiegelman's Faustian deal was only one possible path forward for comics. In *Understanding Comics* (1993), Scott McCloud argued that comics were not a genre limited to men in capes, but rather a medium that could tell all kinds of stories in all kinds of styles for all kinds of audiences: "There are NO LIMITS to what you can fill that BLANK PAGE with—once you understand the PRINCIPLES that all comics storytelling is built upon" (5). Within this expansive notion of the medium, McCloud traces comics' historical roots to the Bayeux Tapestry, Trajan's Column, Egyptian hieroglyphs, and the Maya codices. McCloud's *Reinventing Comics* (2000) offered a blueprint for how comics artists could reinvent their medium for the digital age: "the page is an artifact of print, no more intrinsic to comics than staples or India ink. Once released from that box, some will take the shape of the box with them but gradually, comics creators will stretch their limbs and start to explore the design opportunities of an infinite canvas" (222). McCloud suggested that comics creators should embrace digital tools for producing their work, deploy digital distribution to reach the reader, employ micropayments to enable readers to pay for their work, and use all of this to get rid of the gatekeepers. For McCloud, then, the future required the dematerialization and digitization of comics.

To some degree, McCloud's future *has* arrived: a substantial percentage of today's comics readers prefer to digitally download their comics, though because the same content is sold both ways, the constraints of the printed page still determine their final form. Many younger artists make web comics, and in the process, comics are developing greater diversity in terms of theme and genre (since they do not have to fit into the categories by which comic shops organize their content) and in terms of who creates and reads comics (since readers can discover them via search engines and social media posts). The digital comics movement has made print an *option* rather than a given (Kashtan 2018).

There is another sense in which comics have been dematerialized: as comics content transforms into intellectual property repurposed across multiple media platforms. The superhero genre dominates the output of mainstream publishers such as DC and Marvel, moving into other media—from blockbuster movies to highly rated television series to top-selling video games—even as the readership for superhero comics has declined sharply. The top two comics publishers function as "research and development" divisions for major media companies—DC for WarnerMedia, Marvel for Disney—where, because of their lower production costs, they can combine the stability created by the longest-running characters in contemporary popular media—Batman and Superman comics have been published continually since the late 1930s—with the potential to experiment thematically or stylistically.

The term "comics," then, encompasses at least two totally different spheres of publishing: one dominated by major media conglomerates, the other driven by more traditional book publishers. Let's consider, for example, which comics were selling best in September 2015. According to Diamond, the comics distributor that supplies US specialty shops, ninety-two of the top-one-hundred-selling comics were superhero titles, with most of the other top-selling comics linked to media franchises (*Star Wars*, *The Walking Dead*, and *Fight Club*). Because so many of the top-selling superheroes have already been brought to the big or small screen, many top titles are marketed around a release in another media. Ninety-one of the top one hundred sellers were published by either DC or Marvel, with Image's *Walking Dead* the only title not by the two majors to break into the top twenty sellers. However, if we look at the graphic novels on the *New York Times* Best Sellers list (based on bookstore sales) over this same period, a different pattern emerges. Among the top ten sellers in paperback and hardback, only one is a superhero title (*Batman: The Killing Joke*, also the only work published by DC or Marvel) and only one title (*The Walking Dead*) overlaps with the Diamond list. Eleven out of the twenty titles were written by women; five were written by Raina Telgemeier (*Drama*, *Smile*, *Sisters*, and two *Baby-Sitters Club* books). The overwhelming majority included some depiction of everyday life, including such perennial sellers as *Fun Home*, *Maus*, and *Persepolis*. Comics are a curious case where "mainstream" titles are increasingly niche and "alternative" titles are increasingly mainstream. In practice, there is a third, intermediate category—works purchased as "graphic novels" through the comic book shops. Superhero stories exist here beside other genres, including fantasy, space opera, and crime/noir. In September 2015, the top-selling titles in this group included *Saga*, *Descender*, *Chrononauts*, *Mad Max: Fury Road*, *Fade Out*, *The Walking Dead*, and *Lady Killer*.

The works this book discusses are the offspring of Spiegelman's Faustian deal—works intended for print (with one exception, *Bayou*) and conceived as graphic novels. This book brackets those other two paths forward—McCloud's digital future and superhero IP in a converged media industry. They are both important stories, essential for understanding the current state of comics, but they are not the stories this book explores.

Of course, focusing on graphic novels does not necessarily put us on stable ground. Comics critic Douglas Wolk has quipped that what distinguishes a comic book from a graphic novel is "the binding" (Rogers 2008), but this *is* an important distinction. Graphic stories were printed and sold as books throughout the twentieth century, and these works were sometimes called "graphic novels," though the contemporary use of the term traces back to the 1978 publication of Will Eisner's *A Contract with God and Other Tenement Stories*, a self-contained book that dealt with everyday life in the Jewish tenements of New York City in the 1930s (Levitz 2014). Today, a story arc from the larger serial publication of a superhero comic sometimes is described as a graphic novel when it is published in bound form, whereas others reserve the term for a work conceived with a discrete beginning, middle, and end.

Adopting the term "graphic novel" signaled a movement from epic stories involving larger-than-life battles between mythic heroes toward more realistic stories in everyday-life settings. Some works discussed in *Comics and Stuff* incorporate elements of magical realism (*Daytripper*), fantasy (the Waldo stories), horror (*Bayou*), or whimsy (*Wimbledon Green*), but for the most part, they represent a tradition within the graphic novel depicting the practices of everyday life.

Tracing the moments each of my case-study artists entered the field can help to identify the multiple generations that have shaped today's graphic novels. Kim Deitch was part of the underground comics movement of the 1960s—a movement to free comics from the constraints of the Comics Code and to embrace the era's counterculture. That these comic artists, led by R. Crumb, could explore previously taboo subjects reflected their ability to publish outside of the mainstream comics industry—often attaching themselves to publishers associated with the alternative press or concert posters—and to distribute their work through so-called head shops rather than drugstores and newsstands. By the 1970s, female cartoonists wanted to escape from the "boys' club" ethos of underground comics. Joyce Farmer was one of the editors of *Tits & Clits*, while Carol Tyler was embraced by Aline Kominsky-Crumb and became part of the Twisted Sisters collective. (In both cases, it would be decades before their life situations allowed them to complete book-length works.) Bryan Talbot also began working in comics during the underground period as part of a parallel movement in the United Kingdom. These various underground comics movements opened the door for autobiographical comics, which allowed artists to share their own personal experiences, a tactic important for female artists embracing the larger feminist movement's consciousness-raising practices.

By the 1980s, the underground movement had largely run its course; the head shops were closing, often under legal pressure, but also due to shifts in the marketplace. Comics specialty shops emerged as the primary outlet. A smattering of artists were self-publishing, breaking free from the narrowing range of genres embraced by DC, Marvel, and other mainstream publishers. Art Spiegelman played a key bridging function as an editor: first through *Arcade* (launched in 1975), which he co-edited with Bill Griffith, and later with *Raw*, which he co-edited with Françoise Mouly. *Arcade* represented the last gasp of underground comics, whereas *Raw* signaled the arrival of something new, often described as "alternative comics." Charles Hatfield (2005) explains the difference: "Though driven by the example of underground comix, many alternative comics cultivated a more considered approach to the art form, less dependent on the outrageous gouging of taboos (though that continued too, of course) and more open to the possibility of extended and ambitious narratives" (x). While it is hard to define *Raw*'s unifying style or theme, the effort to deconstruct and redeploy archival images, especially classic comics, was one important throughline. For example, *Raw* volume 2, number 1, included an installment of Spiegelman's *Maus*; Charles Burns's "Teen Plague" (the blueprint for his later *Black Hole* graphic novel), which uses iconography from 1950s horror comics to explore adolescent sexual panic; Kim Deitch's "Karla in Kommieland," which rereads the politics of the McCarthy era through the image bank of early television cartoons; and Ben Katchor's "The Smell of Exterior Street," which explores his ongoing fascination with forgotten New York. The alternative press movement provided another way forward for the creative and political impulses that had shaped underground comics—local weekly, often tabloid, papers, aimed at the counterculture or the LGBTQ communities. Kim Deitch, Derf Backderf, and Alison Bechdel, among others, developed ongoing comic strips, syndicated across a national network of alternative newspapers, refining their skills and building their reputations, before publishing graphic novels.

Drawn & Quarterly and Fantagraphics also emerged to support the alternative comics movement. Seth, Joe Matt, and Chester Brown were all part of a Toronto alternative comics scene, and their works are published by the Montreal-based Drawn & Quarterly, which began operations in 1990. The publisher organizes anthologies showcasing international and emerging artists, and prints graphic novels by established artists. Mimi Pond's *Over Easy* also was published by Drawn & Quarterly, where the artist has landed after a career that included writing scripts and doing animation for *The Simpsons* and other television series, and publishing cartoons and other humor in *National Lampoon, Seventeen,* the *Village Voice,* and the *Los Angeles Times.* Fantagraphics was founded by Gary Groth in 1976; initially the publisher of the *Comics Journal,* it began to publish its own comics titles in 1982, starting with the Hernandez brothers' *Love and Rockets,* and later, such key alternative comics titles as *Eightball* (Daniel Clowes), *Acme Novelty Library* (Chris Ware), and *Hate* (Peter Bagge).

David Mazzucchelli moved from early work at DC and Marvel to publishing his own graphic novels through more conventional book publishers—Avon in the case of *City of Glass,* his graphic adaptation of a Paul Auster story, and Pantheon in the case of *Asterios Polyp.* Fábio Moon and Gabriel Bá—brothers and oft-time collaborators—began in Brazil's independent comics scene before being recruited by Dark Horse and Image; their *Daytripper* was published as a limited series for DC's Vertigo imprint. Jeremy Love was recruited as part of DC's Zuda webcomics initiative, where his *Bayou* series won critical attention, and he has gone mainstream, writing for the *G.I. Joe* franchise. Each illustrates ways that DC and Marvel have monitored alternative comics publishing and recruited talent they think might appeal to their base.

The commercial success of graphic novels has attracted mainstream book publishers. Scholastic is a particularly aggressive comics publisher for the young adult market. Scholastic's success has been facilitated by its strong partnerships with teachers and librarians, who have come to see graphic novels as vehicles for getting young people to read. Those entering comics publishing today can take for granted all of the ground gained by the alternative comics movement, including a strong infrastructure to support their publication and distribution. Emil Ferris, thus, came "out of nowhere" in early 2017, having gone to art school and paid her dues as a commercial artist, only to publish a massive and spectacular graphic novel, *My Favorite Thing Is Monsters,* with critical support from Spiegelman, Bechdel, Chris Ware, and others. And, after a lifetime of publishing single page cartoons in the *New Yorker,* Roz Chast's first graphic novel became an instant bestseller and critical darling. While the underground artists liberated themselves from industry constraints, and subsequent generations of alternative comics creators sought literary respectability, these writers take as given that comics can tell all kinds of stories, and are further broadening their readership.

Of course, this narrative places American comics publishing at its center, reading comics in Brazil, Canada, and the United Kingdom primarily in terms of how they enter the US market. But as we do so, we need to recognize that comics have different histories elsewhere in the world (for a useful overview, see Mazur and Danner 2014). In Japan, comics (manga) remain a mass media read by all genders and ages. If the superhero genre dominates US production, no single genre exerts that kind of influence on manga. The introduction of manga in translation into the US market coincided with these other efforts to expand the content and readership of domestic comics. The European comics tradition, by contrast, has often enjoyed elite cultural status, respected as an art form; numerous museums and festivals are dedicated to comics amid a much stronger tradition of academic research.

Pulling back, we can identify the graphic novel with a range of significant shifts:

Format: From floppy comic books to the bound book
Distribution: From the comics specialty shop to the bookstore and library
Readership: From hardcore "comics fans" (mostly male, mostly in their teens and twenties) to the "reading public" (now much more diverse in gender and age)
Cultural status: From popular culture to middlebrow culture
Genre: From the superhero saga toward a much broader array of popular genres and especially stories of everyday life

My goal here is not to trace these shifts, a task being addressed by other scholars. Nor is my goal to justify why we should critically engage with the contemporary graphic novel—from my perspective, that battle has already been won. Rather, my aim is to explore some key themes that emerge when we take these graphic novels seriously on their own terms. As graphic novels focus on everyday life, they are increasingly exploring consumer and material culture and reflecting on issues of nostalgia and historical memory. I hope to contribute a new conceptual and methodological vocabulary for thinking about graphic novels.

Collections and (Re)collections

A key element of this approach involves critical engagement with the literature around collectors and collecting, especially insofar as these practices connect to larger logics shaping the place of "stuff" in everyday life. While in earlier times collectors pursued objects that were already durable and held great value and prestige, more contemporary collectors often ignore questions of exchange or use value, or even cultural status, forming their collections from "the cast-offs of society, overtaken by technological advance, used and disposable, outmoded, disregarded, unfashionable" (Blom 2002, 165). These objects are often selected according to idiosyncratic criteria, though choices may also be subcultural, as niche communities form around shared interests. The objects in a collection, Blom argues, "mean something, stand for something, carry associations that make them valuable in the eye of the collector" (166). We might, thus, distinguish the collection from the archive, which, as writers like Diana Taylor (2003) note, has institutionalized status. The contents of an archive are "enduring materials" to be preserved and protected, "supposedly resistant to change" (19). Entering the archive requires a mobilization of cultural capital by either the institution or the individual curator. These are the people who, according to Thompson's account, have the power to make their value judgments stick, to ensure that their stuff remains durable rather than ephemeral. The concept of the ephemeral emphasizes disposability and perishability, the arbitrary nature of what survives. John Johnson, a collector who specializes in works of the 1940s, defines the ephemeral as "everything that would normally go into the waste paper basket after use" (Grainge 2011, 2), while Mary Desjardins (2006) talks about "throwaways not thrown away" (40).

Within the realm of comics, few exercise the cultural capital Spiegelman commands and, thus, few have his capacity to transform yesterday's "trash" into the contents of a "treasury," archive, or canon (Jenkins 2015). As Jeet Heer (2010) notes, comics creators, like other artists, seek instruction and inspiration from their own tradition. Whereas elite artists may find exemplars in museums and libraries, comics creators are forced to "educate themselves in the history of comics by scrounging through used book stores" (4). The comics tradition, until recently, was preserved within personal collections, whereas Chris Ware (Heer's focus), Spiegelman, and others helped to construct the archive for future generations, and thus to shape the meta-narrative—what Heer describes as "a pedigree and lineage" (4)—concerning the medium's history. Spiegelman, Ware, Lynda Barry, and others feel compelled to construct another meta-narrative to situate their work within comics' historical trajectory. Bill Watterson (1989) described a topsy-turvy progression within newspaper strips:

> Amazingly, much of the best cartoon work was done early on in the medium's history. . . . Comic strips are moving *toward* a primordial goo rather than away from it. . . . Most readers today have never seen the best comics of the past, so they don't even know what they're missing. Not only *can* comics be more than we're getting today, but the comics already *have been* more than we're getting today. (n.p.)

Watterson uses comics' history to contrast the constraints imposed on today's working artists, constraints that eventually led him to abandon his *Calvin and Hobbes* strip. Watterson's complaint that the best work of comics' past was no longer accessible concerned many other comics enthusiasts: if we are to make the case that comics can publish diverse content, we must make older, varied works more available.

Spiegelman, Ware, Seth, and other artists became collectors to insure their own access to these works. As critics and curators, they needed to be strong advocates for comics that deserved to be republished. Through this process, they identified the traditions within which to situate their own creative output. Here, for example, is how Spiegelman (1997) connects 1930s sex comics with the 1960s underground boom: "The Tijuana Bibles weren't a direct inspiration for many of us; they were a precondition. That is, the comics that galvanized my generation—the early *MAD*, the horror and science fiction comics of the Fifties—were mostly done by guys who had been in turn warped by those little books" (97). So he's tracing a chain of influence—from Tijuana bibles to the "vulgar modernists" to the "underground comics" and then, beyond, to *Raw* and today's alternative comics. Much like the auteurist critics who shaped film studies in the 1960s, Spiegelman and his contemporaries are rescuing works from undeserved neglect.

The first generation of collectors turned curators—represented in Heer's account (2010) by Bill Blackbeard—relished the work of "realist illustrators," such as Hal Foster, Milton Caniff, Alex Raymond, and Jack Kirby, who created the adventure comics of the 1930s and 1940s. Ware, as Heer notes, has been especially associated with comics artists that depict everyday life, such as Frank King and Gluyas Williams. Spiegelman's writings focus primarily on two moments—the emergence of the comic strip in the early twentieth century (Winsor McCay, Lyonel Feininger, and George Herriman) and the postwar era (Will Eisner, Harvey Kurtzman, Jack Cole, Basil Wolverton, and Bernard Krigstein). The first he understands as a period when the conventions of modern comics were still taking shape: "the first decade of comics was the medium's Year Zero, the moment of open-ended possibility and giddy disorientation that inevitably gave way to the constraints that came as the form defined itself" (Spiegelman 2004, n.p.). The second was a period when comics experimented with more mature themes and a more self-conscious relationship to mass culture. More recently, Spiegelman and Mouly (2009) have proposed a third core group (Sheldon Mayer, Walt Kelly, John Stanley, and Carl Barks), artists who created children's comics in this postwar period and thus shaped his generation's earliest encounters with the medium. Spiegelman's taste has helped to define the priorities of publishers such as Fantagraphics and Sunday Comics Press who are reprinting classic comic strips. And minority artists are also engaged in this search for lost ancestors. See, for example, Damian Duffy and John Jennings's *Black Comix* (2010), which seeks to reclaim the history of African American independent comics, or Trina Robbins's *A Century of Women Cartoonists* (1993), which traces a tradition of female contributions to comic strips and comic books that paved the way for the women's underground comics movement.

Often, these collector-artists' anxieties emerge in the pages of their graphic novels. In *Spent* (2007), Joe Matt devotes several pages to his practices as an avid collector of Frank King's *Gasoline Alley*. We see him take bundles of comic strips cut from vintage newspapers and full pages from Sunday comic supplements, and glue them onto acid-free paper, all the while grumbling about the time and money he has given over to this obsession and bragging that he has been able to assemble "the entire run of over forty years right here." Matt's publisher, Drawn & Quarterly, would eventually reprint the daily *Gasoline Alley* strips, under the editorship of Jeet Heer and Chris Ware. Seth, Matt's close friend, has similarly advocated for the largely forgotten Canadian artist Doug Wright, dedicating nine pages of his graphic novel *The G.N.B. Double C.* (2011) to exploring Wright's observational humor about suburban life (56–64). Seth would later curate and design Drawn & Quarterly's reprint of Wright's

Little Nipper series. In *Projections* (2012), Jared Gardner identifies an archival impulse shaping works by Ben Katchor, Kim Deitch, and Chris Ware, and as we will see, the mindset of the collector informs many more graphic novelists who create collecting stories—stories by, for, and about collectors, depicting the process of sorting through older cultural materials and deciding what remains of value for the present.

Stuff

The revaluing of comics can be understood as an extension of larger logics shaping how today's consumer culture operates. Contemporary culture is awash with "stuff." Since the Industrial Revolution, shifts in mass production and consumption have dramatically increased how many material goods enter our lives. This stuff is often discussed in terms of its disposability in a world where, we are told, nothing is made to last. Yet there has also been a sentimentalization of everyday life, which results in people holding onto things that have outlived their usefulness because these materials remind us of other times ("the good ol' days"), other people ("the dearly departed"), or aspects of ourselves. Consequently, we can't easily separate our "belongings" from our "sense of belonging."

When we use the phrase "and stuff" in everyday speech, we mean something vague, something like "etc." "Stuff" often becomes a sign of faltering confidence as we dribble off midsentence. However, this fascinating phrase links the material world of things and the emotional "baggage" we attach to them. In this book, "stuff" will refer to material culture, but also to the emotions, sentimental attachments, and nostalgic longings that we express—or hold at bay—through our relationship with physical objects. Objects can be singular and distinctive—one of a kind—or generic—shared with many in the same culture. Just as preexisting mental categories can be mapped onto stuff as a prosthetic memory, those meanings and memories may persist beyond the duration of particular artifacts, may be abstracted and mapped onto the larger landscape.

For the most part, the process by which we ascribe meaning and value to our stuff remains unconscious and invisible, the backdrop for our everyday lives. As Bill Brown writes in his foundational essay, "Thing Theory" (2009),

> As they circulate through our lives, we look through objects (to see what they disclose about history, society, nature or culture—above all, what they

> disclose about us), but we only catch a glimpse of things. We look through objects because there are codes by which our interpretive attention makes them meaningful, because there is a discourse of objectivity that allows us to use them as facts. A thing, in contrast, can hardly function as a window. We begin to confront the thingness of objects when they stop working for us: when the drill breaks, when the car stalls, when the windows get filthy, when their flow within the circuits of production and distribution, consumption and exhibition, has been arrested, however momentarily. (140)

Brown's observation that things assert themselves when they stop working in anticipated ways represents the tug toward materiality that shapes so much work on this topic.

You will hear much across this book about dust, grime, rust, and other examples of decomposition and decay. Like the rest of us, these creative artists pay attention to stuff when things start to break down, when we acquire or dispose of things. *Comics and Stuff* often deals with that transitional moment, when something that seems destined to turn into dust and ashes gets rescued, reappraised, reappreciated, and reclaimed.

Yet if a thing can be singular, stuff is always multiple and multiplying, not a meaningful object but a collection or at least an accumulation of items; stuff thus forces us to think about relationships and practices. We might also distinguish stuff from commodities, a term for goods read first and foremost in terms of economic relations. Stuff, on the other hand, can be meaningful on affective levels regardless of its exchange value. Craft and folk traditions within female and minority communities generate a wealth of meaningful stuff, often from raw materials discarded from the processes of mass production. In *The System of Objects* (1996), Jean Baudrillard makes a productive distinction between "utensils" defined through their functionality and "possessions" defined through their meaning: "What is possessed is always an object abstracted from its function and thus brought into relationship with its subject. . . . Such objects together make up the system through which the subject strives to construct a world, a private totality" (91–92).

Stuff (2010), written by the British anthropologist Daniel Miller, begins with this disclaimer: "Don't, just don't, ask for or expect a clear definition of 'stuff.' . . . To try and determine the exact criteria by which some things would be excluded from stuff as perhaps less tangible, or too transient, would be a hopeless exercise. . . . This is a book about the variety of things that we might term stuff, but nowhere in this volume will you find any attempt at a definition of that term" (1). Rather, Miller demonstrates his understanding of stuff through concrete examples demonstrating how people live in relation to their accumulated objects. Miller writes about the "somewhat unexpected capacity of objects to fade out of focus and remain peripheral to our vision and yet determinant of our behavior and identity" (51). Stuff is hard to study, the anthropologist suggests, because people's relationship to stuff often takes place behind closed doors: "Families are created in bedrooms and sometimes divorced there. Memories and aspirations are laid out in photographs and furniture. Yes, peering into the wardrobe you may be accused of voyeurism, of a lack of respect for privacy" (109). In *Comics and Stuff*, I am interested in stuff that artists put on display. We may not notice it the first time we read these books, but this stuff is not drawn by accident.

Another of Miller's books, *The Comfort of Things* (2008), takes us inside thirty households, all along the same London street. Miller uses ordinary objects and everyday practices—ranging from the family dog to Christmas ornaments—to document material culture at work. Miller's approach in the book is more descriptive and narrative than analytic: he constructs portraits of people and their stuff. There is an order to things: "They put up ornaments; they laid down carpets. They selected furnishing and got dressed that morning. Some things may be gifts or objects retained from the past, but they have decided to live with them, to place them in lines or higgledy-piggledy; they made the room minimalist or crammed to the gills. These things are not a random collection. They have been gradually accumulated as an expression of the person or household" (2). For him, people's relationship to these everyday objects might best be described as a cosmology or an aesthetic, something akin to Pierre Bourdieu's habitus. People are making meaning of themselves and their lives via what they accumulate and display: "The aesthetic form that has been located in these portraits is not simply a repetitive system of order; it is above all a configuration of human values, feelings, and experiences. They form the basis on which people judge the world and themselves. It is this order that gives them their confidence to legitimate, condemn and appraise. These are orders constructed out of relationships, and emotions and feelings run especially deep in relationships" (Miller 2008, 296).

Miller's work can be understood as part of a larger cross-disciplinary conversation about material life, described variously as stuff, things, objects, goods, materiality, or consumer culture. Archeologists (e.g., Hodder 2012) use these understandings of how people relate to things to reconstruct earlier times and places; anthropologists (e.g., Lemonnier 2012) use them to understand the structures and norms of everyday life in diverse cultures; consumer researchers (e.g., McCracken 1988b, 2005) use them to make sense of purchasing decisions and to anticipate desires and demands; art and literary scholars (e.g., Brown 2003) use these concepts to explore how artists have told stories about characters' relationships with their possessions. One strand decenters the human and personifies the object. I am more drawn to a second strand that calls attention to everyday social and cultural interactions, to the ways we map meaning and memory onto our material surroundings. Ultimately, I am interested in how humans use art and narrative to reflect upon their relationships with stuff.

Stuff represents feelings, memories, ideas, associations, and identities given material form, objectified so they can be shared with others. Stuff plays a vital role in the construction of identity and the performance of self, shaping how we see ourselves and are seen by others. Our characteristic ways of relating to stuff are thus shaped by the ways we are differentiated around gender, race, sexuality, class, or generation and, more generally, through the social construction of taste. Some stuff is thrust upon us, as in, for example, the ways young girls are gifted dolls intended to prepare them for feminine roles in society, and some stuff is handed down to us, as those with limited means often buy stuff at thrift stores where the selection is minimal and the fit sometimes arbitrary. Much stuff outlives the moment of its creation, encapsulating and perpetuating old ideologies, such as white supremacy or female inferiority, as though frozen in amber. So we can read people—both individuals and societies—from the objects they possess and through struggles over their possession. As archeologist Ian Hodder (2012) explains: "If it was not for things there would be no society. It is through our joint production, ownership, exchange, transfer, keeping, disposal of things that we enter into society. It is on our obligations and duties towards each other with respect to things that societies are stretched and strained. The forms of society are intimately related to the ways in which we handle objects and transform them into something meaningful and necessary for ourselves" (26).

Unlike previous generations, the stuff that matters most to us is often not a matter of inheritance, heirlooms and legacies. Rather, they are frequently elective purchases, items we've chosen because they reflect our own identities, values, and lifestyles. Thompson (1994) has argued that we can learn much about the class status of an individual by looking at what they throw away: "a poor man, since he has few possessions, can afford to discard very little; a rich man will be able to discard much more" (269). In affluent societies, more items become rubbish, but the opposite is also true: since it takes labor (and space) to hold onto things with no immediate practical value, affluence also determines what gets collected and displayed. When something is handed down, it bears moral and material obligations. One might imagine a highly mobile society to be relatively unencumbered with stuff, but curiously, as American society becomes more mobile, there is also a tendency to retain reminders of the places where we have lived and the people we have known. Even those aspects of the past we preserve are more a matter of personal preference than cultural or familial obligation, as becomes clear when we see people selling generations worth of family photographs on eBay, where they are purchased by collectors who are interested in them for different reasons. The selection and display of stuff reflects the gradual development of emotional attachments: we regard our stuff as "belongings" as we develop a stronger sense of ownership over ready-made objects we assimilate into our life worlds.

Much writing about consumer culture assumes that the alienation of production extends into consumption—that our stuff never really belongs to us because it is produced and sold by corporations whose interests are radically different from our own, that these ready-made objects will always lack the significance that comes from things we've made with our own hands or inherited from previous generations. Writers looking at nineteenth-century literature (e.g., Brown 2003) have surfaced a core theme concerning whether we are possessed by our possessions; instead, today, we might ask in what sense our belongings belong to us. These objects are never going to be fully adequate to the feelings and memories we ask them to contain: our objects let us down, but the human activity of mapping meaning onto objects remains a central aspect of contemporary experience. Our personalities assert themselves at every level, shaping what objects we acquire and how we acquire them, what uses we make of those goods and how we display them, how they relate to other stuff we acquire, how much stuff we assemble, and what stuff we get rid of, when, and why.

One might identify different strategies for managing our relationship to stuff, ranging from a minimalist and unsentimental attitude that stresses cutting down clutter, through the pack rat or collector for whom assembling stuff shapes personal and collective memory, to hoarding as a neurotic and dysfunctional relationship to stuff. These alternative relationships to stuff are performed across countless television programs that dramatize the assignment of value (*Antiques Roadshow*), the display of stuff (various home decoration and interior design series) and the war against clutter (*Hoarders*). Complex rituals of ownership and possession are performed, for example, through a genre of YouTube videos that feature consumers, often children, describing their feelings and perceptions as they "unbox" desired objects. The result is a constant turmoil over what to do with material goods that pass in and out of our lives. Such choices are at play in every consumer purchase but the stakes become clearer when we deal with things we collect from the past, whether personal—the goods we carry with us from childhood—or collective—what we preserve from past generations.

New media platforms, such as eBay, have only accelerated this process, creating a world where "nothing is ever lost," as one eBay advertisement promised. Anything can be recalled and reclaimed if you are willing to pay the asking price. These networked exchanges (and the consolidation of knowledge communities around them) result in particular configurations of interests. As Will Straw (2007) explains, "The internet . . . provides the terrain on which sentimental attachments, vernacular knowledges, and a multitude of other relationships to the material culture of the past are magnified and given coherence" (3). While much of the rhetoric around new media assumes the displacement of past practices, Straw argues that digital platforms also alter our relationship to the past, encouraging the growth and intensification of collector cultures.

Collectors are, put simply, people who know stuff—who recognize its value, understand its history, and appreciate its meaningfulness. Collecting is a material practice, but it is also a structure of feeling and knowledge. Collectors gather stuff; collectors own stuff. But collectors also desire stuff; collectors know stuff; in fact, collectors know stuff about stuff. Miguel Tamen (2001) describes collectors as "friends of interpretable objects," suggesting:

> All over the world, different groups of people gather around various bits and pieces of the same world, attributing to them intentions, dispositions, and even languages. Some of these activities appear to be, to me at least, a little eccentric . . . but this may only mean that I am not a member of certain groups. . . . There are no interpretable objects or intentional objects, only what counts as an interpretable object, or better, groups of people for

> whom certain objects count as interpretable and who, accordingly, deal with certain objects in recognizable ways. (3)

By this account, cultures, subcultures, fan groups, even religions, can be defined through the particular sets of meanings they map onto stuff they perceive to be meaningful. In this contemporary context, anyone may collect, any object may become meaningful, and any interest can coalesce into a community of "friends," though not everyone has the authority to make their assessments stick or the power to pass along their ascribed meanings. In *A Sense of Things: The Object Matter of American Literature* (2003), Bill Brown identifies a range of nineteenth-century texts that address such questions as "why and how we use objects to make meaning, to make or re-make ourselves, to organize our anxieties and affections, to sublimate our fears and shape our fantasies" (4). *Comics and Stuff* asks similar questions about contemporary consumer culture through the analysis of these graphic storytellers and their works.

Comics and Stuff

Art, like anthropology, offers a vehicle through which we become conscious of our relationship with material culture. Art historian Norman Bryson (1990) has argued: "Since still life needs to look at the overlooked, it has to bring into view objects which perception normally screens out" (87). Bryson contends that still life painters focused on mundane domestic details that would get lost in works with greater scope; the still life brings things close, rather than working on an epic scale, and focuses on things that might not have been documented through any other means. Bryson makes an important distinction between megalography (i.e., "the depiction of those things in the world that are great—the legends of the gods, the battles of the heroes, the crises of history") and rhopography (i.e., "the depiction of those things which lack importance, the unassuming material base of life") (61). Still life grew in prominence in early modern Europe precisely at the moment when art shifted from monumental works for grand publics toward those bought and sold by private individuals. Something similar is taking place when we seek to understand contemporary graphic novels. Throughout most of its history, American comics were megalographic—hyperbolic battles between good and evil, with superheroes functioning as the contemporary counterparts of the ancient gods and heroes at the center of classical paintings. Yet many graphic novels now focus on everyday personal experiences, whether rendered through autobiographical or novelistic writings -- a turn toward the rhopographic. Whereas paintings dealing with the practices and products of ordinary experience were seen as humbling or democratizing, the ability of comics to do "more" than tell stories about "men in capes" is emblematic of the medium's new artistic ambitions.

Comics can help us understand stuff for three key reasons. The first we've already discussed at some length: comics' status as material culture is undergoing dramatic shifts, from a disposable medium to a more durable one. Graphic storytellers have been embedded in collecting culture, as they sought access to older comics and educated the public about the cultural traditions from which their work emerged. This collector mentality leads to a particular emphasis on the roles that seemingly mundane or ordinary objects play in our everyday lives—their hidden meaning and unsuspected value. In this way, we can see the creators of graphic novels as negotiating between the values and meanings ascribed to artworks in the curatorial space and the values and meanings ascribed by collectors to objects in our everyday lives.

Second, many graphic novels take the practices of everyday life as their subject matter; they often contain and transmit collecting stories. Collecting stories are stories told by, for, and about collectors, or stories that are deeply shaped by collecting practices, knowledge, and structure of feeling. Today, comics are giving especially vivid expression to a culture preoccupied with the processes of circulation and appraisal, accumulation and possession. Comics trace the trajectories "stuff" travels: characters want stuff and stories put stuff into motion. These comics take us into the living room, the parlor, the bedroom, and the kitchen—the places where Miller suggests we might learn the most about our interactions with stuff. Comic artists, thus, are developing new representational and narrational strategies that, consciously or not, express a historically specific set of feelings about material culture.

Let's briefly consider the role that stuff plays in one celebrated graphic novel—Daniel Clowes's *Ghost World* (1998). From the opening panel, the book defines its adolescent protagonists through their tastes and purchases: "Why do you have this?" Enid asks her friend, Rebecca, before launching into a blunt dismissal of the "trendy, stuck-up, prep-school" values embodied in a mass-market teen magazine (9). Across the book, the two girls try on identities, often through their interactions with retail establishments: the book's most iconic image shows Enid wearing a fetish mask she purchased when she browbeat a neighborhood boy into taking her into a porn store. These two young women express themselves often through their camp appreciation or snarky dismissal of suburban life. Most of the objects that pass through their hands are consumed as kitsch. Yet there are several moments that show a more sentimentalized relationship to stuff.

The first centers on a yard sale where Enid is selling her unwanted possessions, but refuses to allow a young man to purchase a particular figurine: "I don't want him to buy any of my sacred artifacts, anyway. . . . I can't bear the thought of some jerk with a trendy haircut buying 'Goofy Gus'!" (15) Moments later, though, she wanders off, seemingly indifferent to its fate. "What about your stuff?" Rebecca asks, and Enid responds, "Fuck it—Leave it there! I don't want any of that shit." Yet Enid soon comes racing back, tears in her eyes, to recover the figurine, left among the overturned boxes. "Thank God!" she says as she clutches this "sacred artifact" to her chest. The episode suggests a mental conflict, a desire to be perceived as unsentimental and yet a desire to hold onto childhood things. By *Ghost World*'s end, Enid will go through this same process with Rebecca, walking away from her closest friend to go off to college, seemingly indifferent to her fate, but this latter scene again suggests deeper feelings are at play.

As Enid prepares to go off to college, she makes a pilgrimage to familiar places in her neighborhood, looking through old photograph albums and sharing stories with Rebecca, and going to a secondhand record shop in search of a children's song, "A Smile and a Ribbon," that made her happy when she was little. Following an unrewarding and degrading sexual encounter, she returns home to find that her father has dug out her old phonograph with the childhood favorite sitting atop the stack. She hunches over, sobbing, as she plays the beloved recording (figure I.1). Enid dismisses her father as clueless, but this moment suggests that he understands his daughter more deeply than she suspects. In both cases, childhood objects carry memory and meaning, showing aspects of Enid's life that she often shields from the world: these are among the most intimate and emotionally powerful moments in a book often cited for its cynical tone. Many readers will have "sacred artifacts" that touch them in ways they can't explain.

Third, comics have particular affordances that encourage the reader to scan the landscape, to pay attention to the mise-en-scène. Across this book, I will explore the relationship of comics to a range of other representational practices that people in earlier times have used to display and showcase their accumulated materials (from cabinets of curiosities to scrapbooks). While I

FIGURE 1.1. Enid collapses when she discovers her father has recovered a record and record player from her childhood. Daniel Clowes, *Ghost World* (1998). © Daniel Clowes. Courtesy of Fantagraphics Books.

am interested in comics and graphic novels as representing a particular set of media practices, I am less invested in constructing medium-specific arguments than in mapping comics within a larger continuum of visual and textual practices, including many that similarly require multiple modalities. Many of these earlier forms—illustrated novels, for example—have not received their due because they do not fit neatly within existing cultural hierarchies. In some ways, what is distinctive about comics is their capacity to absorb and deploy so many different visual strategies in the service of storytelling or, more generally, exposition (as illustrated by the essayistic *Alice in Sunderland.*)

Because comics take place in a completely fabricated world, everything is there by design. Whatever we see in a comic's panel was drawn to serve some purpose, even if readers are not necessarily meant to notice it. Some artists imagine new stuff that has little or no real world referent, but most copy stuff, using images or physical objects as references; as such, they spend time tracking down the "right" stuff, interacting within online networks, "friends of interpretable objects." And what is drawn, no matter how fanciful, takes on its own reality, a point to which I will return in chapter 2. The literary critic Elaine Freedgood (2010) talks about how readers, especially those trained in academic protocols, often overlook the rich details that run through nineteenth-century fiction:

> The Victorian novel describes, catalogs, quantifies, and in general showers us with things; post chaises, handkerchiefs, moonstones, wills, riding crops, ships' instruments of all kinds, dresses of muslin, merino, and silk, coffee, claret, cutlets—cavalcades of objects threaten to crowd the narrative right off the page. These things often overwhelm us at least in part because we have learned to understand them as largely meaningless: the protocols for reading the realist novel have long focused us on subjects and plots; they have enjoined us not to interpret many or most of the objects. (1)

Yet why place so many objects within view if we are intended to read past them in the case of the Victorian novel or "overlook" them in the case of the contemporary graphic novel? Surely, the conspicuous display of labor involved in such detailed representations requires more respect from the critic. Perhaps, as Freedgood finds to be true of Victorian novels, the authors use some of these background details to suggest larger cultural patterns or historical traditions.

Perhaps this stuff is meant to be read as a clue into the often unstated motives that shape the character's actions, and perhaps this stuff makes a key contribution toward the "reality effect" upon which such depictions of everyday life depend. In some cases, reading this stuff depends on ordinary cultural literacies, the same skills one might use to read someone's worldview from their bookshelves. And in other cases, reading this stuff requires the specialized but shared knowledge of some collector culture. And in still other instances, stuff gets read metaphorically—requiring a step outside the emotional realm of a particular character to conjure up the author who is using certain objects as a device to comment upon the action. So reading stuff opens the text to multiple levels of interpretation.

FIGURE 1.2. "Madge" sees the cafe for the first time as an outsider. Mimi Pond, *Over Easy* (2014). © Mimi Pond. Courtesy of Drawn & Quarterly.

In some cases, graphic artists encourage us to read their stuff through the lens of a particular occupational group—as for instance, the ways Derf Backderf's *Trashed* teaches us to see things from the perspective of a garbage collector, as discussed briefly in chapter 8. Consider, for example, Mimi Pond's *Over Easy* (2014), a memoir of the artist's experiences working in a Northern California diner amidst the counterculture of the early 1970s. In the first chapter,

FIGURE I.3. The cafe as experienced by a more seasoned waitress. Mimi Pond, *Over Easy* (2014). © Mimi Pond. Courtesy of Drawn & Quarterly.

she enters the Imperial Cafe as a young art student, recently forced to drop out because of overextended student loans, searching for a new space to draw. She explains, "I'd decided not to go to Dave's, an untouched monument of a 1950s diner. I have filled sketchbook after sketchbook with drawings of the customers there, their fat butts crawling over the edge of the stools. I have drawn the coffee pots, secure in their Bunn-o-Matic stations. I have drawn the napkin dispensers and I have drawn the waitresses" (10). Pond reproduces some of what she has put down in these sketchbooks, and when she meets Lazlo, the Imperial's manager, she attempts to trade one of her drawings for a meal. As Lazlo takes her on a tour of the spaces that are normally hidden from public view, we see them first through the eyes of an outsider, but later, as he hires her, we see them through the eyes of a waitress.

Pond communicates this shifting perspective, in part, through two full-page images. In the first (figure I.2), we see what "Madge"—as Lazlo swiftly nicknames her—sees as she first steps foot in the cafe—a view from the doorway, showing a waitress entering the space from the kitchen: the largely empty space encourages readers to scan the shelves, walls, and countertops, absorbing as much detail as we can, noticing everything from the patterns on the linoleum floors to the arrangements of the glasses, plates, and salt shakers, from the animal heads and clocks on the wall to the locks on the door separating the public areas from the kitchen. Pond maps this particular space and its aesthetic.

The second (figure I.3) shows the same space from the opposite direction. Here the focus is on the people and their activities, organized in various social clusters, eating their food, sipping their drinks, paying their bills, reading their newspapers, and studying the menus. And the chaos and clutter is amplified by her text, which describes the soundscape, "a solid, symphonic groove of rattling, clinking, steaming, frying, and nonstop chatter" (37). The second image is as disordered as the first was ordered, but both reward scanning. If the first image shows us the space as a customer would see it as they first enter the establishment, the second shows us the space as a worker might experience it looking out from the kitchen doorway.

As Pond takes us into the kitchen, she shares her first experiences cleaning the mess left behind all of the food preparation, scenes that stress the materiality of everyday objects. She depicts "enormous stock pots with charred bottoms sitting in the sink" (53), and narrates her encounters with "the greasy, honeycomb-patterned rubber" mats that the fry cooks stand upon all day (54): "I have to stick my fingers through the holes to get a grip. Gunk wedges under my nails. I meet with resistance. It seems almost cemented to the floor. I pull some more, and slowly, making a suction-y sound, it gives, leaving little hexagonal cakes of compressed food and grease underneath on the floor. . . . I stagger slightly, holding this big, unwieldy thing by its length. It's like a big, horrible tongue, trying to curl itself around me" (54–56). Here she conveys a wealth of sense details, drawing not only what she can see, in this case, for the first time, but also communicating the weight of the mat as she struggles to drag it outside to hose down. Comics offers Pond unique affordances for representing her induction into the ranks of the working class, including shifts in scale from small details (such as the cream pitchers or the arrangement of food on the plate) to splash pages depicting the entire space, from the juxtaposition of details within a single image to the staging of comic action across multiple panels, from stylized representations of the fashion associated with different subcultures who eat at the cafe to typographic configurations shaped like the swirling cream on top of her coffee. Across this chapter, the cafe is contrasted with the suburban Craftsman home where this middle-class girl grew up, or the art school where she most recently did her work, making clear that nothing in her past has prepared her for the experiences she will have working at this cafe. By the time this first chapter is over, readers know inside and out the setting where most of the book's subsequent action will occur and will have undergone a transition similar to the one experienced by the art student turned coffee house waitress.

In short, comics are stuff; comics tell stories about stuff; and they display stuff. Pond's *Over Easy* illustrates all three. As the book cover reminds us, this graphic novel was a Pen USA Award winner and a *New York Times* bestseller, both markers of the medium's shifting social status. *Over Easy* narrates a story that depends heavily on the material practices associated with a particular time and place. And Pond depicts the equipment with which her characters work as a means of capturing their particular knowledge and routines.

Reading *Daytripper*

Let's consider a more extended example of the ways comics deploy stuff to map the inner lives of their characters. From the start, *Daytripper* (Moon and Bá 2011) implies that there may be more to its lushly colored yet diffusely drawn images than meets the eye. A foreword, written and drawn by Craig Thompson (*Blankets*), introduces the book's authors/artists—Fábio Moon and Gabriel Bá, twins, born and raised together in Brazil, who have established a remarkable collaboration. Thompson argues against focusing on the themes of death and mortality that dominate the surface of this text: "there's far more happening in these pages—pondering the past, wishing for the future, but existing foremost in the EXPERIENCE" (n.p.). And in the book's closing pages, Moon returns to this issue: "Firmly based on reality, the most difficult thing wasn't trying to create a world that would look real. No, the hardest thing was creating a world that would feel real. Every reference, every photo, every color and every character, everything was made to try to reproduce feelings. A feeling that you were alive, happy, lonely, afraid or in love. We wanted the feeling that life was happening right there, in front of every one of us, and we were living it."

Daytripper asks us to imagine multiple possible lives as they might have been experienced by Brás de Oliva Domingos, an obituary writer and the son of a famous novelist, who struggles with his sense that he is not really living the life he had intended. Each chapter ends with the character's death—and with it, some hint of the never-realized possibilities should his life stop at that particular moment. Through this challenging narrative structure, we map the core relationships in Brás's life, including those with his parents, his best friend, his work associates, and his two lovers. Throughout, there is a strong emphasis on life choices, especially on the degree to which people find it impossible to value their immediate sensations and impressions. The book's protagonist has lived his entire life through a fog of regret, only coming to fully understand who he is—or what he wants—seconds before he dies (again and again).

The protagonist observes in the opening chapter, "Isn't it strange how we always seem to remember trivial things from our lives and yet we so often forget the important ones." Part of his craft as an obituary writer is bringing his subjects back to life for their loved ones through his acute attention to details that might otherwise be overlooked. His writing identifies what a person's life meant to those around them, the very thing he has such difficulty identifying in his own life. Brás's restlessness and inattention is contrasted with the artistic perceptions of his best friend, Jorge. As Jorge snaps photographs of the objects he finds on the shelf of a gift shop in a rural beach town (figure I.4), Brás's date shares her first impressions: "I don't know where he works or what he does, but I know he's living this moment, and absorbing all that this place has to offer him. . . . I'm sure if I could see his pictures, that through his camera he's telling what he sees. *That's* what he wants. It's through his photos that he tells us his dreams." Through such passages, Moon and Bá are also telling us how to read their images. *Daytripper* returns multiple times to Brás's living quarters, with some pages structured as a tour of the places where he lives and works. In each case, readers encounter the character at moments of contemplation: nothing much happens narratively, so our eye is drawn toward the empty spaces the protagonist moves through without really seeing them. The color washes and the fuzzy rendering of background details give the images a dreamlike quality.

Daytripper's characters become aware of their surroundings only when things they once took for granted disappear. For example, issue 3 depicts the breakup of Brás's romantic relationship: his lover is drawn in one panel as if she was already starting to fade, leaving Brás alone in the empty apartment they shared. A pair of bikini bottoms, hanging limply from a clothesline, conveys his sense of loss (figure I.5). In an essay on the cinematic object, Lesley Stern (2004) discusses how framing objects for the screen adds greater emotional significance to what is being depicted: "In materializing these objects the cinema invests them with pathos, renders them as moving" (411). Stern plays with two senses of moving—as in the concept of moving images and in the idea that something may be emotionally moving—and for her, the two are closely linked. She's interested in cinematic gestures that are ephemeral, like cigarette smoke or blowing leaves, which convey something fragile about the passing

FIGURE 1.4. Jorge sees things from the perspective of a photographer, translating stuff into images. Fábio Moon and Gabriel Bá, *Daytripper* (2011). Courtesy of Vertigo.

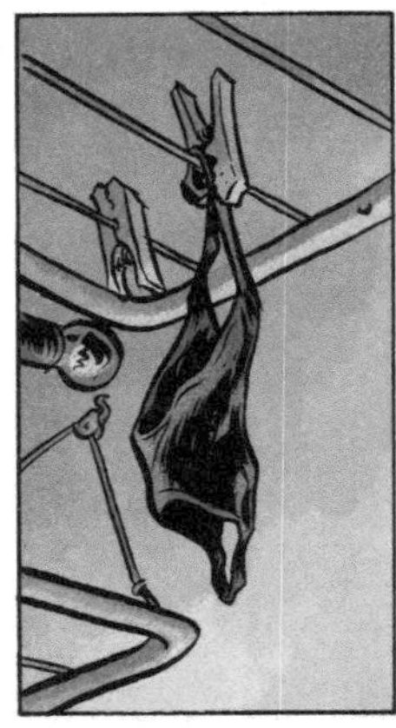

FIGURE 1.5. The bikini bottoms abandoned by a departing girlfriend become an object of nostalgia and regret. Fábio Moon and Gabriel Bá, *Daytripper* (2011). Courtesy of Vertigo.

FIGURE I.6. This image of a widow, wallowing in her dead husband's clothes, provokes a multisensory response. Fábio Moon and Gabriel Bá, *Daytripper* (2011). Courtesy of Vertigo.

of time. Consider, for example, the hypnotic sequence in *American Beauty* where viewers (and characters) watch video footage of a plastic bag "dancing" on the wind, a sequence one of the teens describes as the most beautiful thing they have ever experienced. Yet comics can gain that same poignancy through static images, through objects removed from temporality. We stare at the bikini bottoms with the same obsessive gaze as Brás himself.

While Brás appears on almost every page, given how the novel centers around his choices and responses, chapter 8 gains emotional power from his absence, showing what his wife, Ana, and his son, Miguel, do when he is on the road promoting his novel, and ending with how they respond to his death. Across two pages, we see Ana, who has been in denial, finally accepting her loss by gathering things that remind her of him—for example, a discarded pack of cigarettes—or listening to trivial voicemail messages. Perhaps most powerfully, we see her curled up on the sofa, wallowing in his old clothing (figure I.6). In *Home Bodies* (2010), James Krasner talks about grief as an embodied emotion, expressed by an altered relationship to our physical surroundings:

> When we lose the ones we love, we mourn them, in part, by continuing to feel the vitality of this intervening space as the dilation of our body image, and we know terrible confusion when the space turns out not to be between two bodies but only around the edges of ours. Why do the grief stricken yearn for the beloved's touch? It is not so much . . . that they recognize the impossibility of ever touching as that they continually expect that touch, and even fleetingly feel it. (33)

Laura U. Marks (2000) writes about "recollection-objects," that is, objects which gain emotional force because the artist invests them with the weight of memory, whether personal and idiosyncratic or more universalized. These things mean more—and more deeply within the story context—than they would without the emphasis the artist places upon them, gaining significance and resonance through acts of framing (what we are encouraged to look at) and narrative (what memories are shared through the depicted actions). Marks is interested in how "recollection-objects" operate within transcultural stories immigrants or exiles tell about the world they left behind. For its authors, now working in a US context, *Daytripper* is grounded in Brazilian culture: "[T]he way our characters relate to each other is Brazilian and the way we want to portray emotions, it's completely related to the way we live in São Paulo and the way we relate to our friends and family and . . . it's how we perceive life. We couldn't fake it—it would be like a story of Brazilians living in New York or a story of Brazilians pretending to be Torontonians." Marks suggests that the power of visual representation in such cases is often strengthened by filmmakers (or here, graphic artists) evoking other sense memories, such as those around taste, smell, or touch. The image of the widow wallowing in her late husband's worn clothing suggests both the tactile (things that once touched his body) and the olfactory (the smell of his body that may linger in his old clothes).

While Marks's focus is on cinema, others have suggested that comics, because of their varying degrees of stylization and detail, are especially effective at exploring the nature of human memory. For example, the cartoonist Chris Ware, whose works often focus on how humans relate to familiar objects, suggests, "A cartoon is not an image taken from life. A cartoon is taken from memory. We are trying to distill the memory of an experience, not the experience itself" (Sattler 2010, 206). Ware contrasts the experience of reading a comic, where images still depict something concrete and material, and reading prose, where ideally the reader stops seeing the words on the page and enters into the realm of their own imagination. Ware continues, "there's sort of this strange thing that can happen in comics, where your own memories and imagination can be called up, and at the same time you're sort of having sort of a visual experience" (213). Comics, thus, combine the objective and subjective, often through the evocative power of mise-en-scène.

A third such moment comes when Brás visits his father's house, shortly after the powerful patriarch's death (figure I.7). The obituary writer finds himself contrasting the space of the great author's study as he remembers it as a child and as he experiences it now: "Even though it was a big room, Brás' childhood memory kept the study ten times bigger. It could've been because he was such a small boy or because everything related to his father seemed

FIGURE 1.7. Each object takes on new significance as Brás visits his father's house, shortly after the powerful patriarch's death. Fábio Moon and Gabriel Bá, *Daytripper* (2011). Courtesy of Vertigo.

grand." As he looks at scattered papers or piles of books, observing an overturned coffee cup or scattered ashes from cigarettes his father had recently smoked, Brás describes his fascination with imagining what his father might have been doing in that study. In his reverie, Brás overlooks the copy of his own novel on his father's desk. In the closing chapter, *Daytripper* returns to that book: Miguel, now an adult, has discovered a half-finished letter inside, where the long-dead patriarch shared for the first time his recognition of Brás's adulthood and offered some reflections on what fatherhood meant to him. This passage closes the novel, as Brás, following his father's example, accepts his own mortality and recognizes the fragility of the life he has been living.

In this book, which again and again depicts its protagonist's death, *Daytripper* ponders the things we never really notice or value until it is too late, the things we leave behind for those who mourn our loss. *Daytripper* focuses on everyday life at its most precious and, in so doing, turns toward mundane details suddenly rendered meaningful to the characters because of this sense of loss. This focus on the meaningfulness of the material world is part of what gives this melodramatic text its poignancy.

What Comes Next

Comics and Stuff, thus, is interested in understanding the shift in historical consciousness brought about by changes in how we access and discuss "things" from our personal and collective past. What does it mean to live in a world where in theory we could reclaim every toy and every comic our parents ever threw in the trash? What does it mean that, at a time when little is made to last, we are choosing to hold onto our childish things much later than previous generations did? What changes as we develop expert discourse around objects that previous generations held in cultural contempt? And how is the assessment of our relationship to such materials bound up with the larger project of establishing the critical standing of graphic storytelling?

Does this fascination with stuff lead to particular formal practices? Do particular affordances of comics shift how we regard mise-en-scène? Does the recurring interest in material objects lead artists to make particular choices in their form and content? And, in return, as comics attempt to ground themselves in everyday life, what might the stories we tell about collecting and discarding stuff suggest about the "social life of things"? Do these stories offer a different glimpse into our everyday affect and ordinary material practices than can be gleaned through anthropological or sociological analysis?

Each of the discussed storytellers is actively and consciously reflecting on this stuff—both the material objects and the functions they play in our lives. The stories they tell embody their personal and idiosyncratic passions as collectors but also reflect differences around gender, race, and location that often determine what kinds of stuff matter, what histories objects evoke, what identities they express, and what work is involved in processing stuff. So, for example, male graphic storytellers often tell stories about collecting, while female graphic storytellers are apt to tell stories about themselves as the bearers of family history, or at least to understand their collections as embedded in interpersonal relationships. White storytellers often have the privilege to romanticize earlier moments of cultural history, remaining untouched by historic discrimination, whereas minority artists often look with horror on older cultural materials they need to displace in order to construct alternative futures for themselves. As we position the work of white male artists in relation to that of women and artists of color, important differences emerge in how they think about, with, and through stuff.

Having worked through some core concepts that underlie these analyses, this book explores the relationship between comics and stuff through a series of close readings of particular artists and their works, discussing how their texts engage with the culture around them. In each case, I attempt to reconstruct and recontextualize the interpretive frame that makes these material objects meaningful to these authors and these characters. In some cases, these interpretive frames reflect their fascinations as fans and collectors, drawn to particular kinds of popular culture as keys by which they make sense of themselves and the world around them. For one author, say, Bryan Talbot, the key interpretive frame may require us to deal with wonder cabinets or the music hall tradition, where for another—say, Emil Ferris—it takes us into the "monster culture" of the 1960s. In some cases, particularly for many of the female creators I discuss, these meanings are more personal, speaking to the dynamics of their particular families, mapping the most significant relationships in their lives. In many cases, these interpretive frames are closely related to the objects they draw on their pages, often the possessions that help define a particular character, but in a few instances (especially Emil Ferris and Jeremy Love), these interpretive frames take on a life of their own and the "stuff" itself fades into the background, while the "things" they obsess about become metaphorical as much as they are material. In most cases, the stories remain grounded in "reality," but some enter into a shadow world where a character's fantasies shape how they respond to the meaningful objects they surround themselves with. Comics are often linked to fantastical genres, but here, fantasy enters the texts at the level of enchanted objects (especially the fantasy of toys brought to life), which invites another way of exploring what it means for our belongings to become meaningful or expressing the recurring fear that we are becoming possessed by our possessions. These interpretive frames help, in each case, to define the artists' personal identities (their individual obsessions as fans and collectors), but are also shaped by larger social identities surrounding gender, sexuality, race, and so forth.

To get at these interpretive frames, I deploy a methodology that combines visual analysis with narrative and thematic analysis, following the stuff, looking at specific rituals and practices that grow up around material culture. The degree to which these analyses depend on close readings of specific frames or panels differs from chapter to chapter: my approach is more concerned with mise-en-scène than decoupage, with moments of display within panels rather than the breakdown of story elements across panels. Philipp Blom (2002) has emphasized the relationship of collections to narrative: "Every collection is a theatre of memories, a dramatization and a mise-en-scène of personal and collective parts, of a remembered childhood and of remembrance after death. It guarantees the presence of those memories through the objects evoking them" (191). Blom anticipates this book's interest in narrative and mise-en-scène as the core sites of analysis, as those spaces where the meanings attached to "interpretable objects" are most clearly at play. One of the risks in focusing on mise-en-scène is that these analyses can be misread as purely descriptive, but my goal here is to call attention to interpretable objects—whether they are central to the narrative or existing on its margins—that might have escaped the reader's notice, because we so often read past such things in our search for metaphors or narratives. Here I am trying to reframe these objects in relation to the interpretive frames that give them meaning to the artists and their characters, to resituate them within Blom's "theater of memories."

While each chapter is relatively self-contained, the juxtaposition of these diverse examples will offer a better understanding of how graphic novels explore contemporary culture's conflicted relationship with the past. In particular, I am interested in what makes our relationship to "stuff" meaningful as I work through different kinds of relationships to stuff—those tied to collecting and accumulating, on one hand, those tied to culling, sorting, and discarding on the other. This structure traces a movement from what is to be kept (and those who have the cultural power to make their judgments and interpretations stick) toward what must be discarded (at a personal and cultural level) so that we can get on with our lives. These concerns are gendered: male artists seem especially nostalgic for worlds that seem to be vanishing before their eyes, whereas women bear particular domestic responsibilities for dealing with the process of letting go of family members and their belongings after they pass away. I speak to narratives by "graphic women" and artists of color across all three sections of the book, though the relative emphasis on gender or race differs between the different discussions, given that these artists' interests as fans, collectors, and family members cannot be simply reduced to their race and gender.

Chapter 1 drills into some visual strategies that link comics back to earlier artistic forms, such as the still life, which depict everyday objects and practices. The subsequent chapters are organized into two sections: "Collecting Stories" considers four authors—Seth (chapter 2), Kim Deitch (chapter 3), Bryan Talbot (chapter 4), and Emil Ferris (chapter 5)—whose work reflects their particular fascinations as collectors. Seth's primary interests are in the history of comics, Deitch's with animation, popular music, and various spin-off products. Talbot and Ferris have somewhat more ambivalent relationships to collecting: Talbot describes himself as an "accumulator" whose primary interests are in Victorian and Edwardian culture, and Ferris's young protagonist collects images in her sketchbook and transforms everyday objects into the monster toys she cannot otherwise afford. "Object Lessons" explores stories that deal with materials passed between generations. C. Tyler taps scrapbooks as female writing to reconstruct the impact of World War II on her family's history (chapter 6); Joyce Farmer and Roz Chast depict the process of letting go of dying relatives' belongings (Chapter 7). Chapter 8 explores the question of the residual as it relates to comics, considering the current moment as one where we are collectively confronting what should be done with troubling artifacts from historic forms of racism as we prepare for a hopefully more inclusive future. Jeremy Love's *Bayou*, the work of an African American storyteller, reconstructs the racist imaginary of the Jim Crow–era South, appropriating and resituating elements from Walt Disney's controversial film *Song of the South*. Here artifacts that manifest racist ideology are brought back to life, become subjects rather than objects, forcing us to consider whether we possess or are possessed by our possessions. And an epilogue reflects back on the project as a whole.

The texts and artists I write about were selected because they are works I respect and admire, because they shed light on diverse strategies for displaying and narrating stuff, and because these artists have enjoyed limited critical attention at a time many worry that the canon of comics studies is becoming too narrow and too rigid. (For that reason, I am not saying much here about Art Spiegelman, Chris Ware, or Alison Bechdel, artists whose work fits this book's themes, but who have received extensive scholarly attention elsewhere.) I was also drawn to these artists and texts because they spoke to my own passions, interests, and experiences. Whatever other differences exist here (including those around race and gender that need to be acknowledged up front), there were some common concerns that made their stories meaningful to me. Like Mazzucchelli and Seth, I share a fascination with midcentury American modernism, living as I do in a 1930s art deco department store building in downtown Los Angeles that has been converted into loft space. Like Seth and Kim Deitch, I collect comics, animation, swing recordings, and tie-in products from across the history of American popular culture. *Alice in Wonderland* has been a key bit of cultural capital that I have shared with so many friends, colleagues, and students, so Bryan Talbot's work spoke to me immediately. And my dissertation on American vaudeville gave me a point of comparison with Talbot's discussion of music hall comedy. My generation came of age alongside the monster culture of the 1960s, and so for me, as for Emil Ferris, one of my favorite things is monsters. C. Tyler's depiction of her mother and father reminded me of my own parents, roughly of the same generation, with my father sharing her father's obsessions with his workroom and my mother sharing her mother's crafts and holiday decorations. And like Joyce Farmer and Roz Chast, I have dealt with the aftermath of my parents' passing and the disposing of their belongings. Finally, like Jeremy Love, I grew up in Georgia and have "mixed" feelings about *Song of the South*, a marker of my own identity as a child that provokes troubling responses from me as an adult. My grandmother took me to see the film at Atlanta's Fox Theater, where it had premiered some decades before, and she showed me the walled-off section in the back where black audiences were required to sit during the segregation era. In whatever ways Disney's film romanticized the relations between whites and blacks in the Reconstruction South, that moment also made me confront a different set of realities. Love and I would have encountered this text from different sides of a color barrier, but because it is part of a shared history, his depiction of these characters touched a raw nerve. Like all of these writers, I struggle to walk that thin and slippery line between collector, packrat, and hoarder. I am not bringing these autobiographical perspectives explicitly into the discussion, but they shape the knowledge I tap, and the insights I produce, as I engage with these texts.

1

How to Look at Stuff

From Still Life to Graphic Novel

Transitions in the status of comics impact their physical form (from floppy monthlies to bound books), their narrative structures (from comics to graphic novels), their cultural status (from "rubbish" to durable), their readership and distribution (from specialty shops to bookstores and libraries), and their underlying genres (a diversification from the superhero saga to a wider array of different kinds of stories, including many more stories focused on everyday life). As comic artists and readers confront such shifts, their collecting and curating practices identify and recover their artistic ancestors, demonstrating the medium's potential by showing the broader range of things it has done historically. The result is a large-scale sorting process: artists, publishers, critics, and readers determine which comics should be preserved for future generations.

Such shifts impact the form and content of contemporary comics—as comics depict daily life, they do so with an awareness of the promises and problems brought about by our access to older materials. Comics share stories exploring everyday encounters with objects—they use humans' emotional connection with things to visualize their interior lives (as in, for example, the tensions around the transitions associated with adolescence in *Ghost World*, or the process of mourning in *Daytripper*). Comics place stuff on display, encouraging us to look more closely at their mise-en-scène (as we saw in *Over Easy*).

In this chapter, I will explore how the visual strategies of comics encourage readers to adopt a particular relationship to their mise-en-scène. I am less interested in what makes comics unique as a medium and more interested in identifying specific affordances that shape how we read the meaningfulness of everyday objects from their images. Comics are scannable—or readers can stop to scrutinize a single panel. Often comics fans report that they read through a book the first time very quickly so they have an intense, immersive experience, and then they step back and read the book more slowly to fully absorb and reflect upon its visual practices. This urge to scan the comics image goes back to the origins of comic strips in American newspapers, as I will discuss in relation to Richard F. Outcault's *Hogan's Alley*. Second, comics are flippable—readers can move back and forth through them, comparing images scattered across the book. Here I will be attentive to a series of panels in Mazzucchelli's *Asterios Polyp* that use the state of the protagonist's apartment as an indicator of his shifting mental state during the course of a romantic relationship. Seeking to better understand how and why these visual strategies carry such social and affective weight, I read them in relation to the still life in early modern Europe and to cinematic mise-en-scène.

I will go more deeply into visual analysis here than in other chapters of this book that have a more thematic or narrative focus. My goal is to use stuff to bridge between formal analysis of these artists' varied representational strategies and cultural analysis of the processes of meaning-making surrounding the represented objects, often drawing on shared cultural knowledge and specific forms of fan expertise to read what kinds of objects are depicted and the roles they play across the various stories. In both cases, insights will emerge from our efforts to "follow the stuff," to trace the character's and author's relationship with meaningful objects.

Reconsidering the Still Life

I suggested in the introduction that the digital has led to new systems for appraising and circulating goods, new configurations of knowledge and interest, new communities of fans and collectors, and thus new forms of historical consciousness. Comics, as an expression of this new sensibility, might be expected to engage with negotiations around meaning and value. Comics are not in and of themselves a new medium, any more than paintings were a new medium in early modern Europe. In both cases, these established forms proved vital for capturing and conveying larger shifts in economic and social life. For the purposes of comparison, I want to consider what art historians tell us about the still life in early modern Europe, as a then-emerging genre focused on domestic details. I will not be exhaustive in tracing the history of the still life nor original in analyzing the paintings I consider, as I am not an art historian. But I want to summarize some claims made by art historians in order to illustrate how visual culture responds to material culture.

The early modern period (which spans from the end of the Middle Ages until the beginnings of the Industrial Revolution) was marked—at least among those for whom these paintings were produced, traded, discussed, and appraised—by the experience of "over-abundance," as the opening of new trade routes and the expansion of colonial power brought new wealth and the formation of the middle class. As Norman Bryson (1990) explains, "Dutch society was in the curious position of having acquired an immense surplus of national wealth, but with few cultural traditions that permitted its expenditure" (99). The Dutch and the Flemish spent their fortunes less on public monuments than on improving domestic life, and the purchase and display of paintings was part of this process. The still life emerged not from church or state sponsorship but from private patrons buying paintings to decorate their homes, resulting in a shift from projects promoting nation building toward a growing fascination with everyday life.

Writing about early modern Antwerp, Elizabeth Alice Honig (1999) describes new genres that represented the display and trade of goods. The painters depicted the marketplace as a cornucopia, with tables piled high with fruits, vegetables, flowers, and meats from all parts of the globe. Bryson (1990) notes that what might seem to the modern eye a painting of a flower arrangement often depicted as many different kinds of flowers as possible, often flowers grown at different times of the year or that originate in different geographic settings, again creating a fantasy of plenitude. The items displayed in still life paintings:

> come from a new and greater space, of trade routes and colonies, maps and discoveries, investment and capital . . . which bring to the table the porcelain of China and the carpets of the Near East, and the shell which

> lyrically sums up the wealth of the merchants of the sea. As with the flower paintings, the objects speak of oceanic distances and trade, and this sense of breaking the confines of regional or local space, of flying out towards the far corners of the globe, disrupts the unity and coherence of the tactile, domestic space of the table. (128)

Such paintings assumed viewers could appreciate what was being represented and the skills the artists brought to their tasks, knowledge which was becoming more widespread in a culture that was becoming more educated and affluent.

In *Ways of Seeing* (1972), John Berger argues that still life paintings were a central means by which people in early modern Europe expressed their relationship to possessions: “Oil paintings often depict things. Things which in reality are buyable. To have a thing painted and put on a canvas is not unlike buying it and putting it in your house. If you buy a painting you buy also the look of the thing it represents” (83). The early capitalists, Berger suggests, used paintings to display things they owned (or hoped to own). Painting technique captured the materiality of the depicted objects:

> What distinguishes oil painting from any other form of painting is its special ability to render the tangibility, the texture, the lustre, the solidity of what it depicts. It defines the real as that which you can put your hands on. . . . Every square inch of the surface of this painting, whilst remaining purely visual, appeals to, importunes, the sense of touch. The eye moves from fur to silk to metal to wood to velvet to marble to paper to felt and each time what the eye perceives is already translated, within the painting itself, into the language of tactile sensation. (87)

So, for the artist and the viewer alike, such works required discernment, their appreciation of the finer aspects of the material world, their appraisal of the value of things and their enjoyment of their sensual properties.

If Berger ascribes materialistic values to these paintings (part of his iconoclastic effort to debunk the sacredness of classical art), subsequent critics see these paintings as adopting more varied attitudes. Bryson (1990) writes, for example, “Dutch still life painting is a dialogue between this newly affluent society and its material possessions. It involves the reflection of wealth back to the society which produced it, a reflection that entails the expression of how the phenomenon of plenty is to be viewed and understood” (104). These representations may be critical of those who overvalue their possessions, perhaps moralistic toward a culture perceived as losing track of what matters, or reassuring in the face of disruptive change. Such paintings are part of a larger process of "working through" this new relationship to "stuff" in Dutch and Flemish society.

Scanning the Yellow Kid

Similarly, literary critic Bill Brown (2003) has made the case that the nineteenth-century American novel provided a vital medium for considering the consequences of the Industrial Revolution, which "changed daily life by, on the one hand, increasing industrial employment and thus the purchasing power of the working population and, on the other, exponentially increasing the number and kinds of goods for sale" (5). The key phrase here is "for sale"—this era saw an enormous increase in marketing discourse. The department stores in major cities and the mail order catalog everywhere enabled a profusion of new consumer goods.

This increase in the "stuff" the average American owned was accompanied by a new anxiety about "being possessed by possessions." European visitors to America during this period suggested that the inhabitants of a new country with limited cultural traditions sought to acquire distinction through what they could buy rather than through aristocratic birth or pedigree. Goods, newly produced in the country's factories, took center stage, often alongside handcrafted objects brought by immigrants from the old country. Newly affluent Americans went on a "buying spree," acquiring materials from Europe that they could then display (or, as often, simply store) in their Gilded Age mansions. The richly detailed descriptions that characterized American prose in the late nineteenth century represented the "textual residue" of this accumulation and display, while the period's great novelists, such as Stephen Crane, Mark Twain, Frank Norris, Sarah Orne Jewett, Henry James, and others, spoke to "the slippage between having (possessing a particular object) and being (the identification of one's self with that object)" (13).

A logic of "display" shaped the period's visual culture. Brown notes, for example, a shift in the late nineteenth century in the ways museums displayed objects—away from rows of artifacts in cases and toward tableaus that inserted those objects into narrative contexts. Department stores constructed stories around the goods they were selling, encouraging the public to understand items in regard to lifestyles rather than as one-off purchases. This new visual culture—whether the catalog descriptions of goods or their depictions in advertisements, posters, and signage—juxtaposed words and images.

The first American comic strips, such as Richard F. Outcault's *Hogan's Alley* (the home of the popular Yellow Kid character), appeared in newspapers during this same era, reflecting the desire to attract new classes of consumers. Scott Bukatman (2012) argues that the introduction of comic strips represented one aspect of a larger project to increase the newspapers' visual content: "The comics were not the only feature to utilize the new color rotary presses, and nearly every page of the supplements splashed bold, florid titles across the page, with sumptuous illustrations that provided a welcome respite from the tightly packed type of the news sections. There was also a sense of continual plenitude and surprise—anything might happen with the turn of a page: fact, fiction, fantasy, fashion, fun" (8). Keep in mind the massive size of the period's newspaper page. Photographs and paintings depict youngsters sprawled on the floor, unable to hold the newspaper's large and drooping pages—so they laid it flat and hovered over the comics.

While many observers have faulted Outcault for not appreciating the potential of frames to structure attention, his densely detailed compositions encouraged readers to scan and search the image, taking in information gradually, constructing their own interpretations of the relationships between the many dynamic elements at play. Outcault's comics are the opposite of the still life, which depicts a world of objects emptied of human activity: his comics are teeming with activity, yet they encourage a similar attentiveness to detail.

One's first impressions of "What They Did to the Dog-Catcher in Hogan's Alley" (*New York World*, September 20, 1896) (figure 1.1) is of sprawl and confusion—a decentered composition with many things occurring at the same time. Readers may miss some of the devices that contemporary comic artists use to focus our gaze. The title tells readers to pay attention to the dog-catcher (and what happens to him), the narrative basis for the page, but it may take some time to piece together the logical sequence of events. The image captures a single moment but hints at what came before and what follows. So there is the dog-catcher laying on the ground in what is more or less the image's center, surrounded by angry children and barking dogs, at the receiving end of kicks, bites, strikes, and brickbats. Other details suggest the prospect of greater harm to come, such as the ax in one kid's hands. For the most part, the eyelines of the characters are all directed toward the felled dog-catcher. One young boy

8 THE WORLD: SUNDAY, SEPTEMBER 20, 1896.—COMIC WEEKLY.

Made It a Coincidence.

"Look here!" he began as he entered the corner drug store at 10 o'clock in the evening. "I am tired of this sort of thing and propose to end it."

"You refer to life?" queried the clerk as he moved towards the soda fountain.

"I do, sir! Under present circumstances it is not worth the living. Let it end right here and now! You have poisons?"

"Oh, of course—a large, fresh stock."

"Arsenic, strychnine and so forth?"

"Yes."

"If it wasn't for my wife I'd live on," said the caller as he picked up a bottle of Florida water and sniffed at the end of it. "She'd drive a saint to his grave."

"I see."

"When she sees my dead face she may regret her line of conduct. I tell you, it's an awful thing to drive a good man to suicide."

"What syrup will you take?" queried the clerk as he rinsed a glass.

"Syrup? I want poison! No one asked you for soda-water."

"I know; but you see your wife was in here half an hour ago. She said she was also tired of life."

"She did, eh? Sure it was my wife?"

"Oh, yes. She also wanted poison to end her career. Said if it wasn't for you she'd try and live on, but you were such a mean cuss that she'd rather die."

"And my wife said that?" persisted the other.

"Every word of it, sir; and I didn't know but you might want to make a curious coincidence of it."

"How—how do you mean?"

"Why, she finally decided to take sarsaparilla soda and live on for a few days. Shall we say sarsaparilla and curious coincidence?"

"Well, you know"——

"But under the circumstances?"

"Well, then, under the circumstances I'll take the same as she did and live on, but she must look upon this as a great moral warning—a great moral warning, sir! Yes—sarsaparilla and plenty of water in it!"

He'd Done His Duty.

He had done his duty.

He smiled with conscious pride. His chest puffed out, and he trod the earth with elate footsteps.

His very air convinced those around him that no dipterous insects could find any lodgment on his person.

He had done his duty.

A glow irridated his countenance, and at times he laughed aloud.

Twice or thrice he roared with jollity.

He had done his duty, and was proud of it.

"Say," he said to some of his acquaintances who had met him at the steamer landing, as they repaired to a nearby saloon, "them Custom-House inspectors is blind as beetles! Did I do 'em? Well, watch me!"

Unbuttoning his vest he disclosed several layers of silks. From his pocket he extracted about half a dozen diamonds of the first water, and he passed around samples of some cigars of which, he said, he had a thousand more at the bottom of his trunks.

He had done his duty with a vengeance.

FIGURE 1.1. The cartoonist creates a sense of simultaneity and chaos within this single-frame comic strip. Richard F. Outcault, "What They Did to the Dog-Catcher in Hogan's Alley" (*New York World*, September 20, 1896). Courtesy of the Billy Ireland Cartoon Library and Museum.

has leaned over the balcony so far that he has fallen off the side, but he may not be noticed at first because doing so requires readers to go beyond the tight circle of ruthless youngsters to the building behind them and the various adults observing, without supporting, the authority figure in his duties.

A closer look at these children's faces suggests something else—a multicultural urban population. To be sure, Outcault draws on the period's racial and ethnic stereotypes to depict characters meant to be read as black, Chinese, Irish, and Jewish, but they are united in their resistance to the authorities.

Looking further into the background, readers may also notice several other parts of the puzzle: first, the dog-catcher's wagon, smashed and ablaze, and then beyond it, a young boy chasing two newly liberated pups down the street after a second man who seems to be part of the dog-catching operation. These details provide a chain of narrative events—what happened before the depicted moment—and thus place the page into a larger context.

So far, I am ignoring perhaps the most prominent figure—the Yellow Kid himself. The Yellow Kid stands out, in part, because he is, well, yellow. Here, as in many of the other Outcault panels, the Yellow Kid plays no active role: he has turned away from the dogcatcher. As Scott Bukatman (2012) notes, "the Kid is the center, but he is not the central figure. There is no center, no site where everything comes together" (9). His shirt makes ironic commentary, with a note indicating that the pocket is "full of rocks," suggesting he could join the fray at any moment.

For Jens Balzer (2010), what's striking about Outcault's work is "the interweaving of words and images within one space" (22), often organized around the Yellow Kid. Yet, as Balzer points out, text takes many forms here. While some have seen the words on the Yellow Kid's shirt (and on the girl's yellow hat) as a prototype for a word balloon or thought bubble, Outcault was already using these devices—see both the parrot in the cage and the falling boy for examples. There are also large blocks of generally unrelated text—not fully integrated into the cartoon, but not totally separate from it either, given that the image bleeds through.

Notice the great variety of signage, some related to the story (as in the dog-catcher sign on the burning truck), much of it unrelated (signs for hotels and boarding houses, a flier for the "Park Row Songster" laying on the ground). Such dispersed and diverse signage is typical of Outcault's word-image relations—part of the dense urban landscape he is depicting, part of the tension between middle-class constraint and working-class resistance that is his core theme. Balzer writes, "there are signs hanging, lying, or standing everywhere, every one intent on proclaiming, proscribing or prohibiting something" (24). These proliferating signs suggest the explosion of advertising and promotional culture in American cities: nothing in Outcault seems more hyperbolic than what is shown in turn-of-the-century photographs of Times Square (figure 1.2), part of what Ben Singer (1995) has described as the "hyperstimulation" of the early twentieth-century urban experience. Look at the layering of images and signs that surround New York City's Palace cinema.

Thierry Smolderen (2007) argues that Outcault's dominant visual strategy (which he calls "swarming") responded to the demands an expanding print culture was placing on people still getting accustomed to the rigors of reading: "Images of disorganized crowds . . . are the graphic artist's answer to an overwhelmingly textual culture: they can be read and deciphered—but in a

FIGURE 1.2. The cluttered signage and visual culture surrounding New York City's Palace Theater parallels the dense text and mise-en-scène in early comic strips. Courtesy of the US Library of Congress, Photographic Collection.

winding, serpentine and wanton kind of way" (n.p.). Outcault's dense images emphasize simultaneity—many things are taking place at once, multiple elements pull at our attention, people are brought together sometimes in cooperation and sometimes in conflict as they negotiate this shared space. Reading the Sunday funnies allowed Outcault's readers to rehearse and refine their skills at interpreting their urban surroundings.

For Smolderen (2014), there is nothing inevitable about the movement from these dense, cluttered single-panel comics toward the breakdown and organization of action across multiple simpler panels, since the goal ultimately is to capture attention from the reader and not necessarily shape it toward particular ends:

> The editor working for the yellow press, like the fairground barker . . . does not have to defend a coherent view of the world. He combines competing attractions, innovates when opportunity arises, or recycles old tricks. Like the newsboy who shouts the headlines in the busy street, he works with a quickly changing public which, by its reactions, selects the most promising variants. . . . An attraction doesn't need to say anything meaningful; it merely needs to attract. (104)

Smolderen's primary example of "swarming" in Outcault's work is "The Residents of Hogan's Alley Visit Coney Island" (*New York World*, May 24, 1896) (figure 1.3). The dog-catcher page is structured around an event and its consequences. This page is structured around a location. The attack on the dog-catcher provided much greater unity, whereas here there are many different centers of interest, each suggesting disasters about to happen, as in the people being dumped from the hot air balloon, those clinging to the spinning Ferris wheel, those bouncing out of the roller-coaster cars, and those about to be flung from the speeding merry-go-round, all suggesting technological processes gone awry. Despite such compelling events, many characters are looking elsewhere—about to enter the Seaside Museum & Vaudeville show, climbing out of the surf, walking off the edge of the frame. As Smolderen (2007) explains, "Outcault is transforming the printed page into a modern playground" (n.p.); Bukatman (2012) adds, "the single image does not demand any particular 'order' to its apprehension: the reader is free to explore the panel" (12).

There are strong parallels to other forms of visual culture that were emerging at the same moment. Something like what Smolderen calls "swarming,"

FIGURE 1.3. A classic example of "swarming" in early twentieth-century comic strips. Richard F. Outcault, "The Residents of Hogan's Alley Visit Coney Island" (*New York World*, May 24, 1896). Courtesy of the Billy Ireland Cartoon Library and Museum.

for example, might describe a famous sequence from *Tom, Tom, the Piper's Son* (Edwin S. Porter, 1905), a film central to Noël Burch's (1990) distinctions between early cinema practices and the "institutional mode of representation" (essentially what everyone else calls classical Hollywood cinema). Here, as in the Coney Island example, a fairground offers competing tugs on viewer attention (including actions in both the foreground and background), requiring readers to distinguish among a densely clustered set of characters. The screen is packed with activity, so much so that Burch notes spectators may well miss the key narrative action—the stealing of the pig—which is given no greater attention than the hawking of wares or the antics of the acrobats. Burch argues that the film invites a "topographical reading . . . that could gather signs from all corners of the screen in their quasi-simultaneity, often without very clear or distinctive indices immediately appearing to hierarchise them, to bring to the fore what counts, to relegate to the background what doesn't count" (154).

Tom Gunning (1986) refers to this period as the "cinema of attractions," a phrase inspired by Sergei Eisenstein's "montage of attractions," which, interestingly, connects the concept of the "attraction" (any sensual device for grabbing the viewer's attention) back to its origins in circuses and fairgrounds. Gunning's cinema of attractions invites a fascination with the affordances of the still emerging medium, may involve a direct address to the spectator, and pays more attention to creating remarkable spectacles than to developing complex characters or stories. Outcault's comics also tap the reader's interests in new technological practices (in this case, color printing processes) and, even more so, the scale of the newspaper page; the spectator is directly addressed by the Yellow Kid, who, like the "showmen" in Gunning's account, acknowledges our interest, and readers are encouraged to trace their own path across the image, rewarded by multiple attractions.

For Eisenstein, the origins of his concept of montage in theatrical practice—and in particular, the fairground—leads him to a recognition that juxtaposition may involve elements that are visible simultaneously as well as those that occur sequentially, an insight sometimes lost by subsequent interpreters of his theory of montage. For Eisenstein, these juxtapositions might, for example, take the form of layered superimpositions, or, in his later thinking especially, a greater focus on long takes and movement within the frame. Attention to these aspects of Eisenstein's work might help deconstruct too simple a distinction between montage- and mise-en-scène-focused approaches; as we will see in this chapter, we may similarly observe simultaneous and sequential constructions coexisting within the core vocabulary of the comics medium.

FIGURE 1.4. Similar "swarming" strategies organize Pieter Bruegel's *Children's Games* (1560). Courtesy of the Kunsthistorisches Museum in Vienna.

For Smolderen, Outcault's reliance on "swarming" links him to a range of earlier artists, including "Bosch, Bruegel, Jacques Callot, Hogarth, Cruikshank (among many others)," who sought to convey various forms of collective experience through often cluttered and decentered compositions. In an analysis of the Dutch master Pieter Bruegel, Rick Altman (2008) describes what he calls "the space of multiplicity" (191). We can see many techniques at work in *Children's Games* (1560), which is strikingly similar in its content to some of Outcault's images, cataloging popular children's pastimes (figure 1.4). Bruegel selects a vantage point that hovers over the crowded streets below, whereas Outcault characteristically stays close to the ground, looking up from the perspective of a small child. Much like Outcault, Bruegel disperses his characters' gazes, further reducing the chances of any one point becoming a center for attention. Instead, viewers mentally cluster the actants, deciding who is playing with whom, and what activities they share.

FIGURE 1.5. As in Bruegel, Outcault depicts a range of children's games and activities. Richard F. Outcault, "Opening of the Hogan's Alley Athletic Club" (*New York World*, September 27, 1896). Courtesy of the Billy Ireland Cartoon Library and Museum.

The contrast between Bruegel and Outcault is clearer when comparing "Children's Play" with "Opening of the Hogan's Alley Athletic Club" (*New York World*, September 27, 1896) (figure 1.5), where, again, a group of children is involved in a range of games and pastimes. In Outcault, there is a much stronger sense of frontality, with many characters looking toward the viewer. While Bruegel's image avoids words altogether, Outcault's is crammed with signage.

If the cramped quarters of the "Hogan's Alley Athletic Club" invite readers to anticipate possible intersections between the different activities, those potentials are more fully realized—and toward greater comic effects—in "An Old-Fashioned Fourth of July in Hogan's Alley" (*New York World*, July 5, 1896) (figure 1.6). Here the young men fire roman candles that impact the clusters of people gathered on the balconies and fire escapes, while other firecrackers are chasing the dogs toward the frame edges. Readers can imagine breaking

FIGURE 1.6. The trajectory of the fireworks links together diverse spaces. Richard F. Outcault, "An Old-Fashioned Fourth of July in Hogan's Alley" (*New York World*, July 5, 1896). Courtesy of the Billy Ireland Cartoon Library and Museum.

this action down analytically and sequentially at the cost of this strong sense of simultaneity.

Critical dismissal of Outcault rests on the idea that his work constituted a dead end, a belief that breakdowns are fundamental to the aesthetics of modern comics and that the fragmenting of space, the directing of reader attention, and the construction of a more complex page layout, all embodied by the early work of Winsor McCay, represented the path forward. While definitions of comics as "sequential art" focus on the relationship between panels (and the interpretive work performed across the gutters), this focus on inviting the reader to scan the image for meaningful or emotionally rewarding details prefigures, for example, Jack Kirby's hyperbolic splash pages. Splash pages are most often a full page, or sometimes two-page spreads, and are designed to grab the reader's attention and to establish the story's time, space, and animating activity.

Harvey Kurtzman and Will Elder pushed the comic potentials of Outcault's "swarming" practices as far as any graphic artists have before or since, as suggested by this splash page from a 1980 *Little Annie Fanny* comic (figure 1.7). Consider the sheer density of this image—there are probably more than a hundred characters here, representing distinctive types, personalities, and activities (the exception being a cluster of identical Jerry Brown supporters). Little Annie Fanny is the central figure, who helps to articulate the relationship between the reader and the action. She stands in a clearing slightly off center and remarks on the action. Her red, white, and blue outfit works much like the yellow shirt of Outcault's protagonist to attract attention, momentarily, before competing elements disperse attention across the rest of the page. As in Outcault, there is a profusion of texts—many word balloons, but also other variants. Kurtzman and Elder were famous for their so-called chicken fat gags, throwaway gags scattered across the image, there to be recognized (or not) by the reader, as an added amusement. As with Outcault (or Bruegel), readers' ability to parse this cluttered image requires chunking and clustering, anticipating points of potential conflict. And, also as in Outcault, there is a tension between an ordered event (the nomination of a presidential candidate) and disruptive activities.

A preoccupation with sequentiality has led comic studies to overlook simultaneity as a competing, often complementary principle. One involves juxtaposition *across* images, and the other juxtaposition *within* a single image. One is disciplined by the panel structure, while the other opens a greater space of free play. The splash page suggests that these two modes can coexist within the same work—offering a moment of digression or contemplation amid an experience otherwise dominated by the plot's advance. Such moments encourage readers to spend more time scrutinizing images. Such practices can occur in any sufficiently detailed panel where the mise-en-scène holds our attention longer than required to convey narratively salient information.

We might see Outcault's emphasis on visual and textual density, rather than breaking down the scene into a series of panels, as emerging from the display practices of early twentieth-century America, as reflecting the aesthetic concerns of the late Industrial Revolution. Yet, as these later examples suggest, this desire to produce images that can be scanned and scrutinized becomes an essential building block of comics as a medium, just as sequentiality and juxtaposition are. Comics encourage us to pay close attention to the characters in the context of their surroundings and, through this, to pay attention to their material objects, much as we might while looking at a still life painting.

FIGURE 1.7. "Chicken fat" gags encourage readers to scan the cartoon image, much as they did with early comics. Harvey Kurtzman and Will Elder, *Little Annie Fanny* (1980).

1.8

1.9

1.10

Flipping through *Asterios Polyp*

By way of comparison, let's consider the way images of "stuff" may function within a contemporary graphic novel—in this case, David Mazzucchelli's critically acclaimed *Asterios Polyp* (2009). *Asterios Polyp* has been widely discussed in terms of its eclectic visual style and ambitious themes. There are certainly moments here that tap into Bryson's megalographic tradition (including an extended sequence depicting Orpheus's descent into the underworld), images that convey the self-mythologizing of an architecture professor who has become a legend in his own mind, despite the fact that none of the buildings he has designed were ever built. But the book remains grounded in the rhopographic, in the everyday details of Polyp's evolving relationship with his on-again, off-again lover, Hana. Critical response to *Asterios Polyp* has rested on Mazzucchelli's experimentation with abstraction and symbolism, as he seeks alternative ways to represent his protagonist's emotional and spiritual life (Duncan 2012). I will focus on some of the less iconic, more realistic elements in the book—specifically a series of images that situate the characters in relation to their surroundings and belongings. Here a book organized around the idea of juxtaposition and sequentiality encourages modes of reading organized around scanning and flipping.

Our first introduction to the architect comes through a three-quarter-page rendering of his cluttered living room: clothes slung across the furniture, Chinese takeaway boxes on his coffee table, papers strewn about the floor, and rain pouring through half-open windows—all suggest neglect (figure 1.8). The next page reveals other details from the apartment, including a sink full of dishes and a desk covered with overdue bills, before finally introducing an unshaven, weary-eyed Polyp, lying in bed, watching old sex tapes, and playing with his cigarette lighter. These few pages offer a portrait of a man in free fall. Polyp is

FIGURES 1.8 – 1.12. David Mazzucchelli's *Asterios Polyp* (2009) encourages us to read the character's emotional state from the disheveled mise-en-scène. Hana's first impressions of Asterios's apartment (1.9). Hanna tries to integrate her stuff into Asterios's modernist apartment (1.10). The two lovers are already pulling in different directions (1.11). The force that will disrupt their romance is first introduced (1.12). © David Mazzucchelli. Courtesy of David Mazzucchelli.

roused from his stupor as lightning hits the house, a fire alarm sounds, and he is forced to evacuate, hastily grabbing a few select belongings, before the entire apartment bursts into flames. The rest of the book will give us a much fuller sense of who this man is, what brought him to this state, and how he undergoes a personal redemption.

Throughout the book Mazzucchelli offers six depictions of Polyp's living room, always the same size, always framed from the same perspective, each representing a different moment in his life. These are among the most detailed renderings in a book otherwise noted for its abstraction. Most furniture remains the same, yet minor differences here shed light on the character's life. Because the story begins in medias res and advances through digressions, the reader is forced to reconstruct the sequence. The earliest image shows Hana visiting Polyp's apartment for the first time, suggesting its state before she entered his life: the room is immaculate, free of clutter, personal embellishments, or, arguably, life (figure 1.9).

A second view (figure 1.10) shows us Hana moving her boxes into Polyp's space, with a primary focus on an ornate Japanese trunk, a *tansu*, that had belonged to Hana's parents. One wonders how any of this stuff is going to fit! Two other versions (figures 1.11, 1.12) depict a more fully integrated apartment, demonstrating the melding of their two rather different sensibilities, showing signs of life and change (including different arrangements of flowers) on top of the static elements that signal the protagonist's conservative lifestyle. And finally, there is an image (not reproduced here) of fire engulfing the space.

These images are separated (on pages 4, 12, 86, 155, 189, and 224, although the pages are unnumbered in the book), yet they are most meaningful when read against each other, with the reader flipping back and forth across the book. Kent Worcester (personal correspondence) has coined the term "flippability" to describe formal practices that exploit these particular affordances of comics and graphic novels. The term focuses attention both on comics as material objects that readers can flip through, and on the reading practices that distinguish a graphic novel from other media. Certain visual patterns emerge not through the juxtaposition of panels within a single page but rather from our mental juxtaposition of images many pages apart. Readers find themselves wanting to flip back and forth, trying to see each of these images at the same time, to measure what has changed and what has remained the same in the intervening sequences. Such nonlinear reading practices are, to be sure, not unique to comics. Historians of the book might note that other printed texts, including scripture, dictionaries, encyclopedias, and reference works encourage a similar flipping back and forth on the part of the reader, and nonfiction texts more generally may be read from the perspective of the index rather than the table of contents. But this flipping practice is fundamental to comics, something consciously built into their visual strategies.

These images of Polyp's apartment encourage readers to both scan the individual image for hidden detail (much like Outcault's earlier comics) and to flip across the book to make meaningful comparisons, tracing continuity and change over time. The contrast between figures 1.8 and 1.9, for example, gives a much clearer sense of the disarray in Polyp's life: the careful stack of books in figure 1.9 contrasting with the trash and empty bottles, the pile of books on the sofa, and the mound of newspapers stacked next to Hana's *tansu* in figure 1.8. Similarly, the glass table in figure 1.9 is replaced by a kidney-shaped table (in figures 1.11 and 1.12) that reflects Hana's more fluid style. We can see the different uses of plants and flowers (between figures 1.11 and 1.12), suggesting Hana's evolving ways of inhabiting the space, again in contrast with the withered plants that are another sign of Polyp's depression in figure 1.8. The paintings hanging askew on the wall in figure 1.8 contrast with the perfect arrangements in figure 1.9, as does the state of the blinds and the windows; the shades are hung at precisely the same height across all of the other images of this space. While the *tansu* is marked as personally significant to Hana when it first arrives (figure 1.10), she nevertheless leaves it behind when she breaks up with Polyp (figure 1.8). The table, whose aesthetic was so alien when first introduced, remains after her departure. Stacks of newspapers appear for the first time in figure 1.12 at the end of their relationship, though they remain in figure 1.8, implying a habit Polyp has acquired.

These details offer a more naturalistic rendering of the book's core idea—that our relations with other people can and often do shape how we see ourselves and the world around us. Consider a key line early in the novel: "It's possible for someone to freely alter his own perception of reality in order to overlap with that of another." Despite this comment, the book is often interested in the different subjective experiences characters may have of the same spaces. See, for example, the ways Mazzucchelli fragments the space of Kalvin Kohoutek's apartment (figure 1.13): each of the characters is in their own mental space.

Daniel Miller's *Stuff* (2010) suggests how an anthropologist might describe this same process of a couple integrating their belongings:

> Moving house allows for a kind of critical realignment of persons with their possessions. When moving house they discard some of their stuff but, in contrast to the house itself, many other possessions move with them. As such, moving house allows people to reconstruct their personal biography as represented in memories of associated objects and thereby the sense the family has of itself. Certain relationships with other people get discarded along with the objects that memorialized them, while others come to the fore and are used prominently in the decoration of the new home. So people have a chance to, as it were, work on and repair the way they represent themselves, and their own histories to themselves, and to the world, in accordance with how they now want to see themselves. (97)

Each panel here represents a moment when the characters reassess their self-representation through the eyes of someone else, again with the exception of figure 1.9, which suggests Polyp's total disinterest as he descends into self-absorption. Through these images, Mazzucchelli achieves something akin to what Orson Welles accomplishes in the breakfast table sequence in *Citizen Kane*, tracing the ebb and flow of a relationship via the ways two characters interact within a shared space.

Another way to look at these images is as still life painting—that is, as formal compositions centered on everyday objects. Scott Bukatman (2014) has argued that stasis is as much characteristic of comics as sequentiality and that

FIGURE 1.13. This page conveys the diverse perspectives the characters bring to Kalvin Kohoutek's apartment. David Mazzucchelli, *Asterios Polyp* (2009). © David Mazzucchelli. Courtesy of David Mazzucchelli.

certain artists—his examples are Chris Ware and Mike Mignola—emphasize stasis in their visual strategies. He writes, "The slowing down of the reading process, the elevation of observational detail over action, a sense of deliberateness, an enframing of the moment, and an evenness of pace: all open comics to the exploration of the mundane" (117). Much the same can be said about *Asterios Polyp*: the techniques encourage readers to scrutinize these images, much as one might read a still life painting or Outcault's early comics. Yet as Bryson (1990) notes, the still life involves a particular relationship to narrative: "The law of narrative is one of change: characters move from episode to episode, from ignorance to knowledge, from high estate to low or from low to high. Its generative principle is one of discontinuity: where states are continuous, homeostatic, narrative is helpless. But still life pitches itself at a level of material existence where nothing exceptional occurs: there is wholesale eviction of the Event" (61). Still life, Bryson tells us, is "the world minus its narratives or, better, the world minus its capacity for generating narrative interest" (60). My analysis of *Polyp* emphasizes the narrative dimensions of these images—so far, only in terms of the ways they fit within a series, depict shifts in the space over time, and connect to changes in the characters' lives. Bryson himself acknowledges that while the exclusion of the human form is "the founding move of still life," that situation "would be precarious," "a provisional state of affairs," as if "all that were needed to destroy it were the body's physical return" (60).

In practice, as Bryson notes, the stillness in the classic still life was often threatened by the introduction of details that imply temporality. For example, Dutch and Flemish artists might include figures of domestic animals, such as the dog whose barking posture hints at more immediate concerns in this Jan van Kessel painting from the mid-seventeenth century (figure 1.14). The still life also often operated in relation to other genres of painting. Consider the even-handed balance between domestic life and dramatic encounters in Diego Velázquez's 1620 *Christ in the House of Mary and Martha* (figure 1.15), which treats the preparation of food by the household servants as being of equal or greater interest than Jesus's visit. As we will see, there's a similar tension in many of the compositions in *Asterios Polyp* between the display of interior decorating and human activities, again involving a play between foreground and background.

Mazzucchelli is certainly interested in the ways that Polyp resists change; his lack of spontaneity and the rigidity of his thinking are recurring themes. Ultimately, though, *Asterios Polyp* is about the protagonist's capacity for reinvention

FIGURE 1.14. Early modern still life paintings often included elements that conveyed a sense of vitality and movement (as, for example, the dog and cat included here). Jan van Kessel the Elder, *Still Life with Fruit and White Dog* (mid-seventeenth century).

and self-discovery, once he escapes his fixed confines. Even in depicting his domestic space, Mazzucchelli anchors the images to specific moments. Figure 1.8 is devoid of human figures, but not necessarily human activities. Much as a classic still life might show a bowl of fruit bursting open from its ripeness (thus communicating a sense of the fragility of the moment being depicted), the flower that has shed its petals suggests decline from a more perfect state. Many other details—for example, the grocery bag abandoned in the middle of the floor or the jacket flung across the chair—suggest previous activities, whereas the accumulating newspapers hint at the passage of time.

Read retrospectively, figure 1.8 is striking for the absence of human figures, whereas the other images in this set include people moving in and out of the space, with word balloons that suggest their active perceptions of the state of the room. Figure 1.9, thus, captures Hana's first impressions of the space (and by extension, her early perception of its occupant). "Wow. Modern," she says, as

FIGURE 1.15. This painting splits its focus between details of domestic life and a depiction of a biblical encounter. Diego Velázquez, *Christ in the House of Mary and Martha* (1620). Courtesy of the National Gallery, London.

Polyp helps her remove her jacket. In figure 1.10, we see Polyp unwrapping the trunk while Hana unpacks a box, as they discuss how the pieces might fit together. "There are so many straight lines in here, I thought this would be a nice change," she says in a subsequent panel as she puts down a kidney-shaped coffee table. Providing some context, Hana names the *tansu* and tells her lover, "It's the trunk my parents used to carry their things on the ship from Japan." (This focus on family and ethnic tradition stands out here because, elsewhere, the novel hints at the friction between Hana and her parents—she feels they never fully supported her ambitions and that she is always overshadowed in their eyes by her brother.) Figure 1.12 includes the presence of a third party, the pompous and pretentious Willy Ilium, whose entry as an artistic collaborator and Hana's would-be romantic partner signals the beginning of the end of her relationship with Polyp. Hana pours Willy a glass of wine as her cat looks on expectantly, again signaling a specific moment rather than a generalized impression. And in figure 1.11, the word balloons hint at competing activities: Polyp wants to go to an art show, whereas Hana prioritizes her work, and again Mazzucchelli includes details—Hana adjusting her hat, Polyp playing with his lighter—that convey activity.

Of course, this being a comic and not a series of individual images, the actions often extend across the gutter. Mazzucchelli uses these compositions as the equivalent of establishing shots, introducing the characters and the space at the opening of a new sequence, and then inserting these moments into the story. So, for example, Hana's first introduction to the apartment in figure 1.9 is followed by Polyp preparing her dinner (where the discovery that she is a vegetarian forces him to quickly alter his carefully planned menu—a rare moment of improvisation). The unpacking of boxes seen in figure 1.10 sparks a fight in which Polyp dismisses Hana's coffee table as the work of "just a . . . pseudo-somebody" in contrast with his choices, all the work of top midcentury modernist designers. In that exchange, Hana challenges Polyp, "What if you had to leave suddenly and you could only take three things—what would they be?"—a hypothetical he refuses to address: "I don't think in terms of three." His actual response to this challenge emerges in the opening sequence as he grabs his cigarette lighter, his watch, and his pocket knife as he flees the burning building. Polyp sheds each object across the story: giving the lighter to a bum on a bus, giving the watch to a boy in Apogee—the town where Polyp resides for a large portion of the book—and returning the pocket knife to Hana in the closing scene. The clash of plans in figure 1.11 provokes an intense argument. The watchful cat in figure 1.12 leaps onto Willy in the next panel, spilling his wine on the apartment's pristine floors. So even if we see these panels as encouraging us to linger, they operate in relation to a narrative pull, often connected with a shift in Hana and Asterios's relationship.

Mazzucchelli depicts the living quarters or working spaces of several other characters in similar three-quarter-page compositions. For example, the asceticism of Polyp's midcentury modern furniture contrasts sharply with the overstuffed chairs, the flouncy drapes and tablecloths, and the native crafts and other bric-a-brac associated with the Goddess, who hosts him during his time in Apogee (figure 1.16). While the static nature of Polyp's domestic arrangements suggests an underlying if unstated logic, the Goddess relies on feng shui, saying, "This is the most auspicious arrangement I could come up with, so I advise you not to move anything." Given all that we have learned about Polyp, it's hard to imagine him feeling "at home" in this setting, yet stepping outside of his familiar environment allows him to discover new possibilities within himself and pay closer attention to the people around him. More than a hundred pages (and many events) later, Polyp has changed nothing in the Goddess's original configuration.

Mazzucchelli also contrasts the relatively recent clutter and trash around Polyp's apartment (figure 1.8) with the layers of paper, especially sheet music,

FIGURE 1.16. The Goddess discusses the feng shui of Polyp's living quarters. David Mazzucchelli, *Asterios Polyp* (2009). © David Mazzucchelli. Courtesy of David Mazzucchelli.

in the workspace of the composer Kalvin Kohoutek (figure 1.13). Here the old sweaters draped across the bookcase and easy chair give the room a warm, "lived-in" quality. If Polyp strips his quarters of any signs of his personal or professional life, Kohoutek's room overflows with his interests: sheet music is not only scattered and stacked on every flat surface, but also framed on the wall and organized into binders on his bookshelves.

We also learn a great deal about Hana through brief glimpses into her spaces. In some ways, Polyp's first visit to her studio is intended to parallel Hana's first visit to his apartment, with characters forming impressions based on aesthetic

FIGURE 1.17. The organic shapes of Hana's sculpture contrast with Asterios's geometric bias. David Mazzucchelli, *Asterios Polyp* (2009). © David Mazzucchelli. Courtesy of David Mazzucchelli.

criteria (figure 1.17). Her use of more fluid shapes and repurposed materials contrasts with his geometric focus. At first, he appreciates her work and her worldview—"These are really strong"—but he is reading them almost entirely through his own frameworks: "I can see you're grappling with the reconciliation of opposites. There's this palpable tension between order and change, the concrete and the imagined, man and nature, the rational and the irrational, humor and horror, fragility and fortitude." She discusses these relationships in very different terms, but he overrides her, setting up what will become a core tension in their relationship. And, of course, given the changes she brings to their shared quarters, we should not be surprised by the robust plant life in her own space.

When Polyp returns to Hana's studio after the couple has lived apart for some time, aspects of his perspective have been absorbed and transformed into her art: the sculpture follows more geometric logics, yet her studio still feels like a greenhouse. This is Hana's world, suggesting how much she has also grown during their time apart, but he can find room for himself within it—in part because they both seem to be moving toward a middle ground, a more flexible lifestyle that eluded them before.

Mise-en-Scène in Film and Comics

Throughout this chapter, I have identified distinctive visual strategies of comics via comparisons with other media—with still life painting as practiced in the early modern period, with the promotional culture of the late nineteenth and early twentieth centuries (including fairgrounds, advertisements, catalogs, and newspaper graphics), and in relation to cinematic practices. I am not so much interested in making a medium-specific argument for comics as I am in showing points of overlap across media, trying to break down the idea that what makes comics unique is the notion of the breakdown—the organization of the page into panels and gutters, insisting that a focus on mise-en-scène as depicted within a single image may also be an important dimension of the language of comics. Our analysis of *Asterios Polyps* shows how Mazzucchelli deploys frames that are intended to be scanned and pages that are intended to be flipped, which may be used to shed insights into the characters through depictions of their stuff. To build upon this example, I will dig deeper into the ways space has been conceptualized in film studies, comparing this to some early work in theorizing comics.

Film studies might describe the above analysis as mise-en-scène criticism. "Mise-en-scène" literally means "putting on stage," and sometimes describes those things—props, costumes, setting, lighting—that people would see if they visited the set. Here mise-en-scène has more to do with elements of setting as imagined or drawn from reference photos. V. F. Perkins was a key figure among a generation of British film critics writing during the post–World War II period who placed an especially strong emphasis on the interpretation and evaluation of mise-en-scène as a key to understanding character psychology and authorial style. Perkins ([1972] 1991) stressed the importance of mise-en-scène choices that enhanced narrative verisimilitude: "The primary function of decor is to provide a believable environment for the action. Thereafter—and only thereafter—the director is free to work in, and on, the setting so as to develop the implications of its relationship to the action" (92). When filmmakers bring mise-en-scène under their conscious and creative control, Perkins argues, "space itself becomes charged with meaning" (94).

Perkins's *Film as Film* finds its most compelling examples among a group of American filmmakers, such as Alfred Hitchcock, Nicholas Ray, Otto Preminger, and Vincente Minnelli, working in melodramatic genres during the postwar period. Perkins, for example, contrasts the ways Ray uses "upstairs" spaces in his films *Johnny Guitar* and *Rebel Without a Cause* to express family conflicts:

> In *Johnny Guitar*, upstairs represents isolation. The heroine Vienna, a saloon owner, attempts a rigid separation of public from private life; the former is lived on the ground floor of her establishment amid the drinks and the gaming tables, the latter in her upstairs retreat with its more delicate and feminine decor. . . . *Rebel Without a Cause* uses upstairs to point to the failure of a man through his weakness as both husband and father. His son is shocked and hurt to find him, aproned, outside his bedroom and on his knees. He is timidly mopping up the mess he has made by dropping the supper tray he is bringing to his wife. The location of the sequence reinforces the performances to make us appreciate the young man's anger and anguish. (90–91)

Where this expressive use of mise-en-scène is achieved, Perkins writes, "the spectator does not have to strain to make the required connections; his day-to-day experience provides the necessary background. In the Western hemisphere, at least, upstairs carries automatically the suggestions of privacy, rest, fantasy and male dominance which Ray employs" (91). Ray, as a filmmaker, deploys our knowledge of everyday practices in order to help us read the characters' worldviews from their physical spaces.

Often, for Perkins, the details that matter are those that reside just on the threshold of consciousness, details viewers may or may not notice depending on how closely they observe the characters' surroundings. Perkins and other mise-en-scène critics are especially interested in exploring the ways filmmakers may redirect our attention so that spatial elements that once seemed peripheral become central to our interpretation: "Direction can determine which objects and actions can be seen as foreground and which as background. By controlling the balance between the elements, by creating a coherence of emphasis, it can control the priorities of significance and so shape the movie's themes" (184).

The issue of directorial control versus the spectator's interpretive and perceptual freedom informed the period's core critical debates. André Bazin, a key influence on the mise-en-scène critics, constructed an ethical argument that prioritized the long-take, deep-focus aesthetic associated with the Italian neorealists, where any element in a shot can command our attention and where elements gain meaning through our ability to see the entire context. Bazin contrasted the ways spectators can scan the frame, making their own observations and interpretations, with the careful structuring of attention created through analytical editing in the Hollywood tradition or in Soviet montage.

So far, comic studies has been dominated by the assumption that meaning in graphic storytelling is generated through breakdown and juxtaposition, with Scott McCloud (1993) drawing explicitly on Soviet theories of montage to account for how panels may be combined to communicate different meanings. This stylistic emphasis explains the prioritization of, say, Winsor McCay, noted for his expressive framing, over Outcault, who is associated with a much denser, less structured visual presentation. Smolderen's concept of the "polygraphic" nature of comics, his emphasis on "swarming," the dispersed gaze, the unmoored reader, and juxtapositions among multiple forms of representation contrast sharply with more classical conceptions of comic design, such as those put forward by Will Eisner's *Comics and Sequential Art* (2008): "In sequential art the artist must, from the outset, secure control of the reader's attention and dictate the sequence in which the reader will follow the narrative. . . . The most important obstacle to surmount is the tendency of the reader's eye to wander" (40). For Eisner, breaking the action into discrete segments through framing allows the artist to focus attention onto narratively salient details, a process he calls "containment." I use the term "classical" to describe Eisner's model because of strong parallels with the ways analytic editing informs classical Hollywood cinema: focusing attention and decreasing distraction.

In *Understanding Comics* (1993), McCloud makes the potentially productive claim that comic artists shape the speed with which a reader moves across the pages by the visual density of each panel: a panel that includes a simple, iconic image can be moved past fairly rapidly as readers are eager to discover what happens next, whereas a denser composition may require readers to slow down and pay more attention. *Asterios Polyp* illustrates this principle: Mazzucchelli adopts diverse visual styles, some dense and detailed, some more abstract or symbolic, each making different cognitive demands, each constructing different temporalities.

Eisner and McCloud arguably overemphasize the importance of breakdown to comics. Certainly, the flow of information across sequential panels is a distinctive element of comics, but there can also be meaningful juxtapositions within a single panel (as we've already shown here). Perhaps most importantly, these two forms of juxtaposition do not represent an either-or stylistic choice as debates between mise-en-scène and montage in cinema have classically constructed.

We can, thus, have something approaching a still life in a comic, which, retrospectively, gets pulled back into the narrative flow. Consider, for example, the opening splash page from Bryan Talbot's *Heart of Empire* (figure 1.18). Like some of the classical still life paintings discussed earlier, there are different genres at play in the foreground and background—a still life composed of figs and pomegranates coupled with a street scene, rich in architectural detail. The text adds some cues in terms of the image's temporal and geographic coordinates, while also hinting at future events ("Seven Days to Cataclysm"), even as juices from the newly sliced fruits drip down from the window ledge, a more subtle temporality characteristic of the still life tradition. The storyworld starts to take shape on the next page (figure 1.19), which introduces Cardinal Barberini, who has just lowered a needle onto a phonograph record, which he seems to be listening to with rhapsodic attention. A page later, a different framing reveals that rather than spiritual uplift, the initial facial expressions show his orgasm as he is receiving a blow job from a nun kneeling at his feet—a different image of juiciness. Each revelation invites viewers to recontextualize previous images. This example demonstrates that juxtaposition within the frame (in effect, a mise-en-scène-centered approach) and juxtaposition across frames (an approach grounded in montage principles) may be a false choice: the two can work hand in hand and either can focus our attention on the material objects that surround the characters.

This focus on meaningful details is central to the way Talbot approaches his work. Talbot is a worldbuilder who thinks through every element he puts on his page and can speak about each detail's larger intimations about the depicted society. And he draws implicitly and often explicitly on references to the material world—places he has been, buildings he has entered, things he owns. In this case, Talbot has shared that the phonograph depicted here is a windup Victrola that he personally owns. *The Graphic Novel Man* (Wall 2014), which documents Talbot's artistic practices, provides the backstory of one particular sequence from *Grandville Mon Amour* (2010), set in a steam factory and

FIGURE 1.18. This splash page introduces a focus on mise-en-scène reminiscent of early modern still life paintings. Brian Talbot, *Heart of the Empire* (1999). © Brian Talbot. Courtesy of Brian Talbot.

inspired in part by the windmill sequence from Alfred Hitchcock's *Foreign Correspondent*, which Talbot recalled having seen as a boy. As he began executing the set piece, he explains, "I suddenly realized I had no idea how this factory was actually laid out or what it would actually look like. I knew I wanted it filled with steampunk machines and contraptions, but the actual reality of the place, I couldn't quite grasp." A Google image search offered many different Victorian factories, leading him to discover that "this fantastic Gothic nave of a factory with governors and big wheels and pumps and huge pistons" was "just five minutes up the road" from his home in Sunderland (Wall 2014). Talbot photographed the apparatus with his digital camera and incorporated precise renderings into this memorable fight sequence. Such background detail comes at a painful cost: as his wife, Mary Talbot, explains, the artist's professional efficiency leads him to want to complete a page a day, but such intricately drawn sequences take several days to execute.

FIGURE 1.19. By the next page, action is broken down into panels, relying more on principles of decoupage. Brian Talbot, *Heart of the Empire* (1999). © Brian Talbot. Courtesy of Brian Talbot.

This close attention to detail, even in fully imagined spaces, such as those found in his Grandville books, encourages readers to actively invest their belief into more fanciful content. The Grandville series operates within an alternative

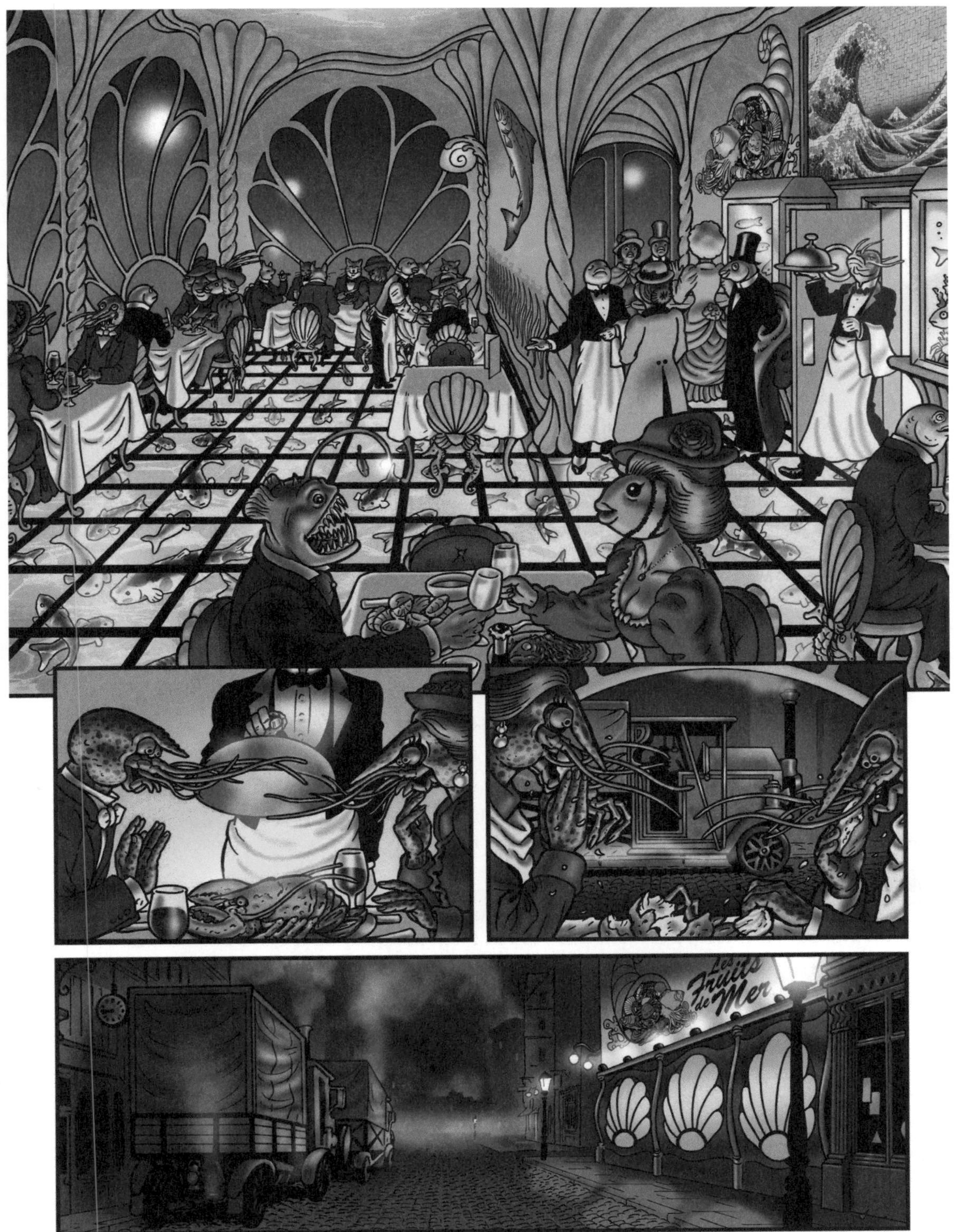

FIGURE 1.20. Detailed mise-en-scène brings a sense of plausibility even to the most fanciful of spaces. Brian Talbot, *Grandville Force Majeure* (2017). © Brian Talbot. Courtesy of Brian Talbot.

historical landscape in which Napoleon won and France remained the dominant European empire. Merging iconography from steampunk and French arcades, Talbot lovingly constructs environments that never existed, offering—across the five books produced so far—a range of different spaces, from brothels to cathedrals, from curiosity shops to artist studios, each made more plausible by his detailed renderings of specific furnishings. Moreover, inspired by the graphic creations of nineteenth-century French artist J. J. Grandville (known for his anthropomorphized animals), Talbot populates his imagined realm with diverse animal characters, all dressed and acting like humans.

Consider, for example, a page (figure 1.20) from *Grandville Force Majeure* (2017), which depicts an opulent seafood restaurant, where the waitstaff and guests alike are fish and crustaceans, although the men are depicted wearing top hats and the women wearing fashionable bonnets and gowns with plunging necklines. Talbot designs the restaurant's decor and furnishings in an appropriate art nouveau style, attentive to the ceiling fans, pots, and utensils when he draws the preparation of the food. There is something whimsical about the contrast between such realistically rendered spaces and the representation of the characters (for example, including cleavage on a fish woman). Part of the scene's wit centers around the multiple representations of sea creatures—realistic fish swimming beneath the glass floors, ornate and stylized fish and shells incorporated into the furnishings, anthropomorphized fish seated at the tables, and the seafood dishes served to the diners. Here we get a sense of why comics have so often been used to tell stories of superheroes or talking animals—because of this capacity to give our fantasies such concrete and convincing form. Charles Hatfield makes a similar argument for what he describes the "technological sublime" aspects of Jack Kirby's 1960s superhero comics, suggesting that the artist's renderings of improbable technologies "sold every concept, no matter how balmy . . . or how alien" (153–154).

And if comics artists can reproduce such surreal content with such vivid detail, then they can also construct aspirational spaces, where desired objects are brought together from diverse locations and again, rendered in an utterly believable manner. Reference photographs must have been used by Mazzucchelli for the design of Polyp's apartment, since, as fans online have identified, he fills the space with specific works of modernist furniture design, including Mies van der Rohe's Barcelona Chair, Marcel Breuer's Wassily or B3 Chair, a sofa by Le Corbusier, Eileen Gray's E1027 side table, George Nelson's Platform Bench, Isamu Noguchi's Prismatic Table, and Jean Prouvé's Em Table. Much as reading the rich detail in an early Dutch still life painting depended on social knowledge of the ways different kinds of goods had entered the Netherlands from other markets, the juxtaposition of these midcentury design classics can only be fully appreciated by someone who knows design history. Of course, unlike the patrons of the Dutch masters, the readers of the modern graphic novel can Google these objects online and read about their history. If reading Polyp's personality from his stuff depends on shared social knowledge through which we navigate everyday lifeworlds, reading Polyp's furniture in relation to these different designers requires connoisseur knowledge that may or may not be accessible to every reader. It is a nod from one collector to another. Such images invite our scrutiny and slow down the reading process.

Talbot's still life panel in *Heart of the Empire* has a timelessness that would be hard to achieve in a time-based medium, such as cinema, where the images advance at twenty-four frames per second. An interesting exception is the cellar sequence from Drew Goddard's 2012 cult horror film, *Cabin in the Woods*. As the characters enter into this creepy environment, their attention is drawn to the diverse array of cryptic artifacts; they identify some, but there are many more details than those the characters directly discuss. Many of the objects—from an old fortune-telling machine to a puzzle box—represent generic devices from other horror films, the kinds that summon demons, ghosts, and monsters. For a few brief seconds, different characters are drawn to these various objects, but when one of the girls reads from an old diary, the action converges around this particular choice, leaving viewers with a strong sense of the roads not taken. Once we've had a first encounter with the film, we can imagine going back to this moment and looking through things more carefully. We want to freeze the frame or slow-step through the sequence, discussing each element and speculating about which monsters they might summon. Such options are built into comics; artists often assume readers will focus more closely on compelling details or draw meaningful comparisons across a book. The DVD renders images both scannable (in the sense that viewers can freeze them to study them more fully) and, in a way, flippable (in that they can rewind or fast-forward, jumping around through the text in hopes of creating mental juxtapositions between narratively meaningful details).

There are certainly film sequences that contain some aspects of the still life—for example, the opening shots of Hitchcock's *Rear Window* (1954) encapsulate the troubled romantic relationship between the two leads (James Stewart and Grace Kelly)—one a news photographer who covers dangerous events (as shown by the smashed cameras and the photographs of cars bursting in flame), the other a fashion designer with strong roots in a particular art scene (as hinted at by the glamour photographs on the stack of magazines). Yet while the objects remain stationary, the camera is constantly moving, signaling specific connections between the artifacts.

The opening sequence from John Cromwell's 1944 melodrama *Since You Went Away* offers a much more elaborate exploration of material objects: the camera travels from the exterior of a typical American household, displaying a flag in its window that proclaims that someone in the family is serving in the military, across the interior space, revealing an empty chair, the sleeping family dog, a calendar and a draft notice both showing the same date, a sign recalling the couple's wedding trip, a pair of bronzed baby shoes, a family portrait of the mother and two adolescent daughters, all gradually hinting at the progression of the couple's relationship leading up to the moment when the husband departs for overseas service. Each new detail is accompanied by a new musical cue that ascribes emotional significance to what we are seeing. The story proper begins when the wife (Claudette Colbert) returns home, having dropped off the husband. As voiceover narration describes her longing for the absent husband, we watch her pick up and peer nostalgically at family photographs. As Peter Brooks notes in *The Melodramatic Imagination* (1995), melodrama works to externalize the character's emotions, mapping them onto physical coordinates that carry meanings and memories. Audience members experience what the characters feel; often those feelings get conveyed by music—which is what gives the genre its name—but also via mise-en-scène.

In classical Hollywood film, a range of devices can direct the viewer's attention to any element of the mise-en-scène that carries narrative salience: we will be shown what we need to know in order to follow the story. Bill Brown (2003) argues, however, that novelistic prose may describe things as if they were part of the background without fully directing readers' attention: "Indeed, differentiating between objects that are named and noticed, but hardly dwelt upon, on the one hand, and on the other, objects that are affectionately singled out and lingered over, establishes the foundation for constructing significant objects" (87). A comic artist may, if anything, have even greater flexibility to incorporate objects or settings that never become the conscious object of reader attention, but may convey an overall impression: there may be things hiding in full sight that readers overlook on first, or even subsequent, encounters, but that reward the sharp-eyed who scan the background. Seth has offered some perceptive comments on how space is constructed in comics as opposed to film: "There's some deep quality inherent in the still nature of comics that produces more a catalogue than a travelogue. I mean, when you're watching a film, the fact is that you don't stop to look at things, you can't pause and study the world in the same way you would when you're reading a comic. The fact is that much of the background is merely something the actors stand in front of, rather than a carefully calculated tableau composed by the artists" (Hoffman and Grace [2013] 2015, 206).

Summing Up

Throughout this chapter, we've explored how the affordances of comics as a medium—in contrast to film, the novel, and still life painting—encourage certain ways of engaging with mise-en-scène and, through this focus on the characters situated in their material surroundings, a particular interest in how humans relate to their stuff. Just as the still life painting in the early modern period, or literary and visual culture in the late nineteenth century, provided resources for audiences to reflect upon shifting material conditions, today's graphic novels represent a particularly powerful vehicle for thinking about how digital culture is intensifying the flow of old goods and artifacts through our lives, allowing us to hold onto or reclaim things that might once have been lost, allowing us to assemble collections or share insights with other collectors. As graphic artists expand their potential subject matter, these mundane encounters with stuff become a recurring interest.

As I've discussed the "stuff" of comics, I have focused both on the ways that graphic artists have sought to focus attention onto their mise-en-scènes and how those everyday objects bear memory traces of human relationships. It is the combination of the two—stuff and emotional baggage—that makes the study of artistic representations, such as graphic novels, useful as a means of mapping the personal and collective memories expressed by material culture.

COLLECTING STORIES

2

"What Are You Collecting Now?"

Seth and His Finds

"What are you collecting now?" asks Chet (a fictional character modeled after actual comic book artist Chester Brown) in a scene from Seth's *It's a Good Life, If You Don't Weaken* (1996). The fictionalized "Seth" responds by pulling books off his shelf: "I've got some GREAT stuff to show you!" (17). Chet's question conveys much: the act of collecting (gathering, researching, appraising, showing "GREAT stuff") is a normative part of their lives together, the basis of a homosocial bond between the two men. But the objects of their collecting passions are variable, both within the individual (Seth makes new discoveries) and also between the two (Seth and Chet collect different stuff.) What Seth ends up sharing with Chet—and with the readers of this graphic novel—is his discovery of Kalo, an obscure gag cartoonist who becomes the focus of Seth's obsessive search for more work, more information. As Seth exclaims in exasperation, "I don't understand you. This is some of the nicest cartooning I've ever seen. I'm NUTS about these guys! You're a cartoonist, why don't you like this stuff more?" (19). And later, when Chet himself finds a Kalo cartoon, he hesitates to explain why he was looking in a "cheesy" girly magazine, because he's afraid (justly, as it turns out) that his friend will laugh at his fascination with pinup artist Bill Ward. Throughout, the two pool knowledge and share resources, both informational and economic, even as they pursue their own interests and defend their own tastes. Their friendship is competitive, sometimes combative, but at the end of the day the shared experience of collecting brings them back together again. *It's a Good Life,* like so many of Seth's other works, is a collecting story—a story by, for, and about collectors.

A high percentage of comics creators (and a smaller but significant portion of their readers) are white, middle-aged, male comics collectors, so it should not be a surprise that many of their life stories deal with the pleasures of collector culture. The stories that emerge are often ripe with themes of homosocial bonding, competition, and male mastery, with collecting seen in part as a project of self-fashioning (a theme that especially resonates with Seth's works). This kind of collecting requires access to resources including disposable time, money, and space, all of which constitute a site of white male privilege in our culture. While many women share an interest in collecting at early ages, such interests are often discouraged as they grow older (a theme we will explore in chapter 3 in relation to Kim Deitch's collecting stories), both because of demands placed on women in the domestic sphere and because of the hostility they encounter in predominantly male sites of collecting, which sometimes have the spirit and atmosphere of a boys' club. In *Cult Collectors* (2014), Lincoln Geraghty protests how little critical attention has been directed toward collecting as compared to other fan activities, reflecting academia's ongoing discomfort with forms of consumption that cannot easily be reread as appropriation and remixing. As Geraghty notes, collectors often reconstruct the past and reinvent their own identities through their curatorial practices. Comics may be one place where collecting has been explored rather than dismissed.

Across the next two chapters, we will be considering two graphic storytellers whose work has been strongly influenced by their interests as collectors—Seth and Kim Deitch. Both are associated with specific interests—Seth with collecting old "paper," peripheral forms of printed matter, especially comic books and comic strips; Deitch with the history of American animation and of toys and other byproducts of media serialization. Each in their own ways places their knowledge and discrimination as collectors on display throughout their work: understanding their relationship with collecting is a key for unlocking other dimensions of their works, especially their focus on history and memory. This chapter is more focused on the psychological and social dimensions of collecting, whereas the next will consider how a collecting mindset impacts the formal construction of graphic novels. I will then consider two writers whose relationship to collecting is more challenging: Bryan Talbot shares his fascination with Victorian and Edwardian culture but characterizes himself as an "accumulator" rather than a collector, a perspective informing his formal and thematic choices in *Alice in Sunderland*. The protagonist in Emil Ferris's *My Favorite Thing Is Monsters* has a fannish interest in horror films, but she collects images, some mental, some she draws herself, rather than material culture—in part because she lacks the resources to do otherwise.

Collecting Stories

One reason why cultural studies has had some difficulty in dealing with collectors is a tendency to see collecting as consumer culture on steroids, whether understood through a Marxist lens as hypermaterialism or through a Freudian lens as fetishism, arrested development, and narcissism. Reading stuff as the manifestation of consumer capitalism isn't wrong—this is clearly an important part of how objects enter our lives in the twenty-first century—but starting there shortchanges other discussions we need to be having about stuff. As Daniel Miller explains in *Stuff* (2010): "Stuff is ubiquitous and problematic. But whatever our environmental fears or concerns over materialism, we will not be helped by a theory of stuff, or an attitude to stuff, that simply tries to oppose ourselves to it; as though the more we think of things as alien, the more we keep ourselves sacrosanct and pure. . . . Instead, this book tries to face up to stuff: to acknowledge it, respect it, and expose ourselves to our own materiality rather than to deny it" (5–6).

Seth as a collector/storyteller knows, respects, and values what anthropologists have argued about consumer culture more generally—that its practices and processes are meaningful, in the sense that they are full of meaning. Grant McCracken (2005) writes: "Goods . . . help us make our culture concrete and public (through marketing and retailing). They help us select and assume new meanings (through purchase). They help us display new meanings (through use). And they help us change meanings (through innovation). Goods help us learn, make, display, and change choices required of us by our individualistic society. They are not shackles but instruments of the self" (4).

Collecting involves material practices but also meaning-making practices. G. Thomas Tanselle (1998) reminds us, "Objects not only stimulate us to discover how they came to exist and what their original function was; they also tease us into probing their subsequent status and adventures" (12). Such questions generate quest stories, as collectors pursue prizes from one corner of the globe to another. Some of the best American movies—from *Citizen Kane* to *The Maltese Falcon*—are about collectors and collecting. Kane, for example, collects many things (including statues, zoo animals, and newspapers), but his dying words reference something of personal significance that has slipped through his fingers. In that context, the exchange of collected objects becomes one and the same with the exchange of stories. Mieke Bal (1994) tells us that "collecting is an essential human feature that originates in the need to tell stories, but for which there are neither words nor other conventional narrative modes" (103). And, perhaps, the best way to deal with those gaps is through using pictures to supplement what words cannot tell. For Bal, collections are stories rendered material, "telling objects." Such objects invite us to talk about their origins, their circulation, their exchange, and their use; these stories are shorthand for larger questions around identity, history, and memory.

As such, I will read Seth's graphic narratives as collecting stories intended to explain collecting as not only a meaningful activity but also as an activity invested in managing memories. Seth's obsessions as a collector are on every page of *It's a Good Life*, where the narration often talks about how things in his environment remind him of classic cartoonists and where the images depict characters scavenging through dime stores and used book shops. These references often foreshadow Seth's subsequent projects, such as reprinting the complete *Peanuts*, the formative works of John Stanley, or the comics of Canadian artist Doug Wright, all of which bear Seth's imprint as a curator and designer—or, for that matter, his commercial work designing covers for Criterion Collection DVDs. His fascination with the history of Canadian broadcasting yielded *George Sprott 1894–1975* (2009); a key character in *Clyde Fans* (2019) collects vintage postcards; and the eponymous protagonist of *Wimbledon Green* (2005) is "the greatest comic book collector in the world." "Nothing Lasts" (2013a, 2014) his most overtly autobiographical work, often describes his life in terms of items that pass in and out of his hands. Seth's own bibliophilic tendencies are on display in *Forty Cartoon Books of Interest* (2006), a series of short notes and commentaries on an idiosyncratic selection of artists whose work he recommends. "To know me is to know that I am a collector," Seth begins the book, acknowledging that above all he wants to share his "finds" with his readers. Seth's characters often work upon and work through prevailing stereotypes about collectors, yet because his graphic novels are so intensely

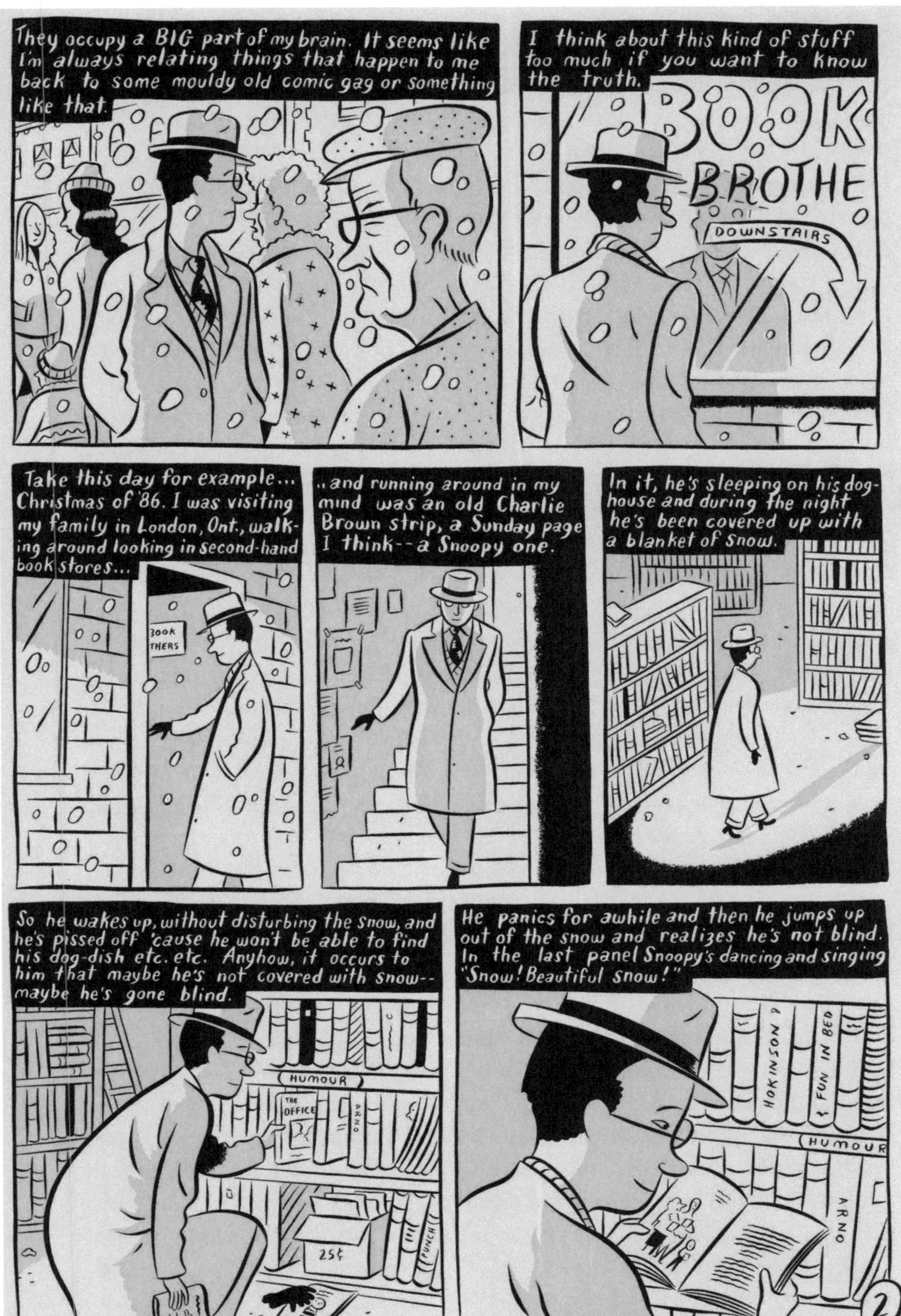

FIGURE 2.1. Seth's characters seem to be constantly window shopping, on the search for compelling "stuff." Seth, *It's a Good Life, If You Don't Weaken* (1996). © Seth. Courtesy of Drawn & Quarterly.

autobiographical (even though they are also highly fictionalized), these stereotypes shift meaning as they become representations of the "self" rather than the "other."

Seth's characters are obsessed with "stuff" in general and "paper" collectibles in particular: they devote their lives to acquiring, grooming, displaying, discussing, exchanging, and appraising ephemera. Many of their most intimate conversations center around their collections—for example, a scene in *It's a Good Life* where Seth is naked and in bed with his new lover but preoccupied with getting her to appreciate a new comic artist he's discovered (48–49). Seth's introspective comics often depict his characters moving through their environments, picking up objects, putting them down, peering into shop windows, all the while reflecting on collecting. In this example (figure 2.1), the protagonist is literally and figuratively in a world of his own: the only human figure in most of these panels, while even in the first panel he is drawn facing the opposite direction from the flow of the crowd. Here and on many pages of the book, his thoughts, conveyed through the text, have only a loose connection to his depicted actions. The words describe a *Peanuts* cartoon, discussing Snoopy's actions and dialogue, none of which are depicted on the page. We do not see Seth's eyes in any of these panels and his facial expression remains placid. There is something banal about the depicted actions, reflecting what Greice Schneider (2016) describes as a state of "ennui" or "aimlessness," an affective state very different from the character's own obsession with searching for and finding remarkable work by vintage cartoonists. Underneath, his characters lead lives of quiet desperation.

Decomposition and Recomposition

Longing without an Object

Clyde Fans (2019) depicts Simon, the more introverted of the two Matchcard brothers, as he wanders through his family home and the now closed family business. Simon recalls an old wooden box that his brother Abe had passed along to him when it no longer had a lid and was thus perceived to be worthless (figure 2.2). The box once contained "the little trinkets that are important in a boy's life," the childhood "treasures" that the adult Simon no longer fully recalls: "Time has mostly erased its contents from my memory . . . but somehow that box still looms large in my daydreams." He asks himself, "[W]hat Cracker Jack Prizes were in there? What Cigarette cards? Was there a Big Little

Book about 'something or other of the Mounties'?" The empty box remains, its contents scattered through the years, and Simon maintains a futile fantasy: "Sometimes I imagine that if I could just remember those objects, find them again and place them back in the box in just the right order, then (like a magic recipe) it would open up that time barrier and I'd be on the other side . . . in a better moment." Simon shakes his head, "how utterly, utterly stupid" (201-202). Rather than showing us the box, as he experienced it in boyhood, the visuals show Simon, working at an adding machine, going through receipts, an image that contrasts the boy's hopes for a magical life (in the text) with the adult's settling for something less (suggested by the downward twist of his lips). Through this juxtaposition, Seth suggests both the desire to escape and the humdrum reality the protagonist hopes to evade.

The boy's collection of childhood objects has often been emblematic of the collecting impulse—the story we tell to understand why some people carry that impulse into adulthood and others do not. Simon is a collector: he has been systematically acquiring and cataloging old postcards, in particular photo manipulations depicting outlandishly large objects or animals. No one collects in general: collecting is always particular. His brother Abe, who has a more pragmatic bent, is not a collector, though Seth connects Abe with another bundle of decaying papers (figure 2.3): "all the invoices, the purchase orders, the receipts buried in old filing cabinets or tied up and stacked in warehouses, fragile pieces of paper scattered over the province. Yellow bits of scrap with my name signed on them.

FIGURE 2.2. Simon recalls his lost treasure box. Seth, *Clyde Fans* (2019). © Seth. Courtesy of Drawn & Quarterly.

FIGURE 2.3. Abe reflects on another collection of papers—his invoices. Seth, *Clyde Fans* (2019). © Seth, Courtesy of Drawn & Quarterly.

Those fragments prove to the world out there that I once existed" (2019, 49). Seth depicts Abe as if he were almost entombed by his business records, surrounded by file cabinets, stacked leger books, and clipboards. Yet, however significant these records may have been in his working life, he sits with his legs spread and his head and body slumped, indifferent to his surroundings. A detail shot of the clutter on his desk shows some signs of recent activity, for Abe notes that he simply likes to sit here and think about the work he once did.

So what makes one pile of papers a collection and the other not, especially given that both embody memories of life accomplishments? Brenda Danet and Tamar Katriel (1994) argue that for an object to be collectible, it must be "reframed" as an "aesthetic object" (225), valued as a thing of beauty, as a vehicle for the imagination, and not according to purely functional or economic criteria. The items of a collection must be unique, distinguishable from each other. By both of those criteria, then, the nearly identical invoices are not a collection, but Simon's postcards are.

Abe struggles over what motivates his brother's collecting: "Perhaps it was busy work—something to fill up the hours, something to separate one long day from the next. I suppose we all, somewhat arbitrarily, pick something to give our lives meaning. Something to justify our existence" (2019, 76). That is, Abe understands collecting as work and only secondarily as play. But, most theories of collecting suggest that such practices are about signification, making distinctions that help people to assert control over the objects accumulating around them. As Eugene Rochenbeg-Halton (1986) writes, "We are mysterious creatures who mark our time on Earth through tangible remembrances. We transform time itself as it were, into tangible space through our makings and doings, personalizing our environment while objectifying ourselves" (188).

Through Simon's childhood box, Seth points to the arbitrary nature of what we keep and what we discard as we move from childhood to adulthood—an empty box, which once contained treasures, now devoid of contents, itself an object passed from one brother for whom it lacked use value to another who maintains a sentimental, almost mystical attachment to it. Why we collect such things, Seth proposes, is a secret kept not only from others, such as the uncomprehending sibling, but also from ourselves. The memory of once having collected something remains poignant and the promise of recovering lost objects carries some primitive notion of magical return to an imagined better time. "What if nothing was ever forgotten? What if nothing was ever lost?" asks one of the first commercials for eBay, which centers around an adult recovering a toy boat accidentally left behind on Cape Cod decades before (Desjardins 2006). Charles Foster Kane—another archetypical collector—dies crying out for his lost sled.

Recovering a lost past has been the dominant frame for thinking about nostalgia since Susan Stewart's *On Longing* was first published in 1984: "Nostalgia is a sadness without an object" (23). Like the contents of Simon's box, what we seek cannot be recovered (and in fact, was never ours to begin with); it remains decisively out of reach—an ideological and sentimental illusion. For Stewart, the collection involves the creation of a "hermetic" or "self-enclosed" world that protects the contents (and the collector themselves) from the ravages of time by removing them from circulation and use (151).

Seth has rejected the idea that he might be considered a "nostalgia artist," at least in so far as the phrase is frequently used to describe "a kind of Hallmark card sentiment that there is a golden past that you are yearning for." Speaking about his collecting impulses, Seth told one interviewer:

> I have no illusions about the superiority of the past. People have always been miserable and life has always been difficult. However, I can honestly say that I don't think much of this present time. Certainly, here in North America, things couldn't be cheaper, uglier, or more vulgar than they currently are (well, they could, and probably will be—in the near future). . . . While I personally have no desire to live through the Depression or World War II, I do think that culturally the quality of many things were superior, especially design. . . . You cannot look at a popular medium-priced radio or clock from that period and compare it with the same popular medium-priced item from today, and not come away convinced that things are just shittier today. (Miller [2004] 2015, 70)

Stuff was never perfect, it is simply worse now. Seth's collecting stories are a way of working through his own "muddled" thinking about past and present, a "muddle" that often boils down to a "structure of feeling" embedded within material culture, as opposed to the large-scale events (the Depression or World War II) that make history a bitch.

Seth the artist, as opposed to "Seth," the character, refuses to whitewash the past, often directing attention onto, for example, collectors invested in preserving racist or sexist representations. For example, when Seth catalogs Wimbledon Green's collection (figure 2.4), there's *Spooktown*, "beloved racist kid's humor comic, rare: $5600," suggesting this book is valued because its ideas about race would be unacceptable today (19). In such a context, a book can be "beloved" and "racist" in the same breath, suggesting a form of white male privilege that informs this particular collector culture: the collector's connoisseurship, which sees this shocking content as no more important than issues of short-lived and "ill-advised" romance comics or a free promotional giveaway, offers an alibi for returning to an era when social arrangements were more overtly organized around white supremacy. If things in the past were better crafted, Seth seems to be suggesting, we cannot so easily separate these objects from the social structures that shaped them. At the same time, Tom

FIGURE 2.4. Items in Wimbledon Green's collection are sometimes valued because of their racist stereotypes. Seth, *Wimbledon Green* (2005) © Seth. Courtesy of Drawn & Quarterly.

Smart (2016) suggests: "Perhaps projecting a raw sense of dislocation from what he imagines was a more stable past, he grasps at what he views as an understandable and simple value system. Beauty, courtliness, manners, self-expression, the dignity of manual work, an ability to express and understand nuance, community-mindedness and much more: all these values hold a profound importance to him. They are elements of a personal identity that gives him a sense of permanence in a world of flux and disruption" (79). So if the past represents horrifying social attitudes from which we seek to escape, those attitudes are also entangled with values Seth insists we preserve.

"Am I nostalgic? Can you feel nostalgic for an era you never lived in?" (Miller [2004] 2015, 70), Seth asks, before concluding that he sees the era of his own childhood as a transition point between the midcentury modern culture he adores and the contemporary junk culture he despises: a time when "the last vestiges of that old world . . . were still hanging around everywhere." He explains his collecting:

> Mostly I collect as a way of exploring the past. By buying the cultural objects (especially books, movies, and records) of the past you begin to get a deeper understanding of the times. There are so many surprises to be found. It's a constant process—there are so many layers of the past to dig through. . . . I just love the objects of the past and looking for them (and possessing them) brings me the most happiness in life. I like nothing better than looking through some dusty pile of magazines in an out-of-the-way store with the hope that something great is at the bottom of that unpromising pile. (Miller [2004] 2015, 69)

The core metaphors here are archeological: digging and sorting through dust, reconstructing a forgotten past. For the most part, Seth searches for objects produced, used, and discarded before he was born, but he also seeks to "recapture the feelings of childhood" by recovering some "totem" (again, an archeological or ethnographic metaphor): "Recently I tracked down a wrist-radio on eBay that I owned as a child. Holding it in my hands again was a beautiful moment" (Miller [2004] 2015, 70).

Two recurring images are worth considering more fully: first, the repeated references to digging through dust, and second, the idea of "holding it [the past? material objects?] in my hands." Both address the idea of memories embodied in a more material form. On the one hand, materiality makes memory more enduring—the objects of a collection constitute a form of prosthetic memory, carrying information about the past. Collections perform such memory work because we can read the memories from the objects, because we can hold the objects in our hands, and because the objects can be lost and recovered by subsequent generations. Yet the idea that the object will last is also partially an illusion: material culture is always in some state of decay; objects wear down through use or are displaced when they no longer command interest.

Gathering Dust

Dust is not dirt, as Mary Douglas (1966) understood it: not "matter out of place." Rather, dust is something that breaks off as the object breaks down. We can think of dust as what inevitably happens to older goods: we can't hold onto the past because it is coming apart in our hands. Seth is haunted by decay: "I think that the core narrative underneath any of my stories is the recognition that there is an underlying melancholy to life. An inherent sadness because everything is always moving into the past. . . . In my daily life, I'm always thinking about this process of things moving beyond your reach into the past" (Hoffman and Grace [2013] 2015, 220). In *It's a Good Life,* the protagonist describes aging plastic flowers, "you can barely make out their colours under all that dust" (41), and later lists things that make him sad, including "those little bits of broken glass at the bottom of the box when you're unpacking your Christmas ornaments" (42).

Carolyn Steedman (2002) describes dust as the opposite of waste, suggesting "nothing ever, ever going away" (166). Steedman notes that dust as a noun describes a substance (a pile of dust) and as a verb refers to two contradictory activities (to dust a room or to dust cookies with sugar) (160). Sometimes dust evokes destruction, signaling the breakdown of the material world, but, for Steedman, there is something generative about it. Seth and his other contemporaries trace—and thus preserve but also transform—objects from the recent past that capture their imagination. Seth's artwork is full of images of older consumer goods, sitting on shelves, stored in attics, accessible to the reader via his own creative output: "If I were to create a utopia, it would not be the past. It would be something incorporating favorite elements from the past—aesthetics from the past, ideas from the past" (Hoffman and Grace [2013] 2015, 219). The protagonist in *It's a Good Life* talks about the "evocative sadness for the vanished past" triggered by "the decay of old things." In "Sublime Neglect" (2013), Seth documents a struggle between "the man-made world and the everyday nature that has crept into it," resulting in evocative descriptions of rusted railroad tracks, an old brick wall "overgrown with weeds or crumbling with age," and a vacant lot "strewn with litter and detritus." Dust, rust, and weeds (each something new emerging through decomposition) creates new aesthetic value in the same way that scarcity increases a collection's economic value.

Considering dust as aesthetically valuable distinguishes it from the "kipple" described in Philip K. Dick's *Do Androids Dream of Electric Sheep?* As the radioactively damaged hermit John R. Isidore explains:

> Kipple is useless objects, like junk mail or match folders after you use the last match or gum wrappers of yesterday's homeopape. When nobody's around, kipple reproduces itself. For instance, if you go to bed leaving any kipple around your apartment, when you wake up the next morning there's twice as much of it. It always gets more and more. . . . No one can win against kipple, except temporarily and maybe in one spot, like in my apartment I've sort of created a stasis between the pressure of kipple and nonkipple, for the time being. But eventually I'll die or go away, and then the kipple will again take over. It's a universal principle operating throughout the universe; the entire universe is moving toward a final state of total, absolute kippleization. (65)

In Dick's novel, the whole world is falling apart, life dematerializes, and humans are incapable of protecting what they value. The replicants are now past their expiration date but refuse to give up life. Yet kipple—undesired and meaningless—accumulates, engulfing everything else. Collectors perform their own operations on kipple, since much of what they gather are things that others consider worthless—not much separates Simon's postcards from J.R.'s match folders. At the moment kipple becomes meaningful, it becomes collectible.

Dust operates in yet another sense, as something that obscures these objects' true value until they are rediscovered by collectors, archeologists, or "pack rats." Dust can be brushed aside; the object can be polished and displayed. In a surprisingly poetic passage in an otherwise prosaic essay, Michael Thompson (1994) describes what happens "when moths or rust corrupt or when thieves break through and steal; when an old master painting is slashed to ribbons, a Venetian glass goblet dropped and smashed into a thousand pieces, or a Georgian silver teapot over-warmed on the hot-plate and melted into a glistening lump" (273). This is where the anxiety of collecting lies—in the desire to arrest or even reverse this process, to preserve objects from normal wear and tear, to protect them from neglect, and to place them in a meaningful context where they can be appreciated and protected by and for future generations.

Without collectors, what survives seems random. Seth's *George Sprott* (2009) offers several examples: on the one hand, the recordings of Sprott's long-running television program, a beloved part of local broadcast history for a generation, get trashed when they lack material value for the television station. Yet his belongings are salvaged only because they are incidentally connected to something

FIGURE 2.5. The collector Owen Trade is depicted as a scavenger who nevertheless keeps certain memories alive. Seth, *George Sprott 1894–1975* (2009). © Seth. Courtesy of Drawn & Quarterly.

from the past that collectors see as worthy. The title character of "Owen Trade, Collector" is primarily focused on CKCK Television's horror show host, Sir Grisly Gruesome, but assembles objects from other on-air personalities. His collection (figure 2.5) contains various objects referenced throughout the book, including one bound notebook (out of many) of Sprott's lectures, a painting stolen from the program's set, and one canister of film, forgotten in the Coronet theater after one of Sprott's lectures. Across eleven tightly framed panels, Trade displays his finds, holding them in front of him—in the case of a painting, completely blocking himself from view. Rose Humbly, one of Sprott's few fans, had salvaged the letters from the theater's marquee, but not before two letters went missing: "someone broke into the warehouse. . . . Who would do such a thing?" (n.p.). Now her letters spell the somewhat appropriate, if offensive, word "crone." An observant reader will notice the missing letters—an O and a T—behind Trade (representing his initials) in this final sequence, though the collector denies that they have any significance: "just some letters I found." Trade sees himself as protecting Sprott's "legacy": "I Googled George the other day and got only one hit. Nobody under 40 even knows his name any more" (n.p.). But is it George's "legacy" if he is recalled on terms very different from his own? Here Seth has drawn Trade cut off from any of the objects he salvaged, dominating the frame, and stretching his arms wide to suggest his ownership over the entire project. Trade's collection involves a process of desentimentalization, as objects previously bearing Sprott's memories are attached to some other narrative—the history of the company where he worked, the story of a disrespected rival, or simply the collector's own experiences.

Holding Things

The opening of Seth's *Clyde Fans* (2019) is one long monologue represented as if through a single tracking shot across the spaces associated with the Matchcard brothers as Abe thinks aloud about the significance of printed matter and other objects in both of their lives. Some of what Seth depicts is utterly mundane—Abe scrubbing down his dentures or making and eating a soft-boiled egg—while others—old paintings and photographs, images from postcards, old letters—seem more promising when viewed through the eyes of a collector. Throughout, Abe hopes to read his reclusive brother from his possessions, believing Simon curated the environment where Abe will live out his old age:

> Simon prepared this place for me. It's true, he found no real satisfaction here. But somehow he put some of himself in every object in here. It's as if he chose them for the time when I would make my retreat inside these walls. The piles of books he left—almost like he planned a course of study for me. . . . And as I read each book, I linger over the thought that he turned these pages before me. . . . Only by infusing this whole place with the spirit of his lonely struggle could I ever come here and understand him. And find the contentment that the outside world never gave me. (73)

Here fraternal relations are mediated through things both brothers touched; the collection offers sanctuary from disruptive forces.

Abe's attempts to read his brother by flipping through the pages of Simon's collected books recalls Walter Benjamin's classic essay recounting his thoughts as he unpacks and orders his own books:

> [T]he books are not yet on the shelves, not yet touched with the mild boredom of order. . . . Instead, I must ask you to join me in the disorder of the crates that have been wrenched open, the air saturated with the dust of the wood, the floor covered with torn paper, to join me among piles of volumes that are seeing daylight again after two years of darkness, so that you may be ready to share with me a bit of the mood—it is certainly not an elegiac mood, but rather one of anticipation—which these books arouse in a genuine collector. (Seth 2004, 59)

Here, again, book collecting is associated with clouds of dust, though in this case, dust signifies the pleasure of being reunited with old favorites. This focus on materializing memory may account for why Seth stresses the tactile nature of the collection—objects you can put your hands on, as opposed to memories receding from your reach. Walter Benjamin ([1931] 1969) makes a similar connection: "One only has to watch a collector handle the objects in his glass case. As he holds them in his hands, he seems to be seeing through them into their distant past as though inspired" (60–61).

Benjamin discusses collecting as creating coherence from the "chaos of memories" (60). The mental frame the collector places around their collection is not simply a way of seeing the contents; it also can be abstracted and mapped onto the world. This is one of the first things that Seth's protagonist in *It's a Good Life* shares about himself: "[Cartoons] occupy a BIG part of my brain. It seems like I'm always relating things that happened to me back to some mouldy old comic gag or something like that. . . . It's silly but I swear, I can't do much of anything without—I mean, I can hardly say hello to someone without dragging Dr. Seuss, old Bemelmans or the inimitable Mr. Schultz into it" (2–3).

Yet the same collectible objects can generate multiple mental frames, depending on the individual collector's motivations—Seth situates his fascination with old cartoons in a larger history of comic strips; his hero masters everything he can learn about the people who produced these works, and that same search for encyclopedic knowledge motivates Simon's investigations of postcard artists and publishers. Those same cards could carry distinctive personal memories that speak to the times and places where they were gathered or they may generate meanings as the objects of a set. Naomi Schor (1994) writes about her own collection of postcards of Paris:

> With the exception of one or two real finds in my collection—whose acquisition was marked by a particular feeling of triumph—I would be hard pressed to say how I came by a particular card. When I opened my album or my storage boxes, time is not recaptured. . . . Postcards are organized in series, and their very seriality negates their individual mnemonic properties; what matters in the case of my postcard collection is not the contiguity between an individual card and the environment from which it was detached; rather it is the contiguity I restore between a single card and its immediate predecessor and follower in a series I am attempting to reconstitute, or the contiguity I create between cards linked by some common theme. (255)

For Schor, collecting postcards is less about preserving memory or mastering knowledge, and more about creating order by restoring a sequence disrupted as the postcards were scattered from their point of origin. Writing about baseball

card collectors, John Bloom (2002) argues, however, that constructing sets carries its own memories, quite apart from the specifics of what is represented, recalling practices that the men in his study associated with preadolescent pasts. For these men, collecting had been not simply a personal hobby but a homosocial practice, linking them with other boys with the same interests, and now with other men nostalgic for similar past experiences. While Schor speaks as a female collector, Bloom sees collecting as a distinctly masculine pastime, an issue to which we will soon return.

The Memory Artist

All of this is to say that collecting involves processes of framing and composition (perhaps recomposition in the case of men reassembling their childhood baseball card sets) that collectors use to hold the process of decomposition at bay; the collection gathers both things and their associated memories. The relationship between memory, collecting, and creative expression is the central theme of *Seth's Dominion*, Luc Chamberland's 2015 documentary about Seth and his work. Not unlike the comics, the film has several sequences showing Seth wandering around his home and office, showcasing his belongings. Seth freely acknowledges that his home is a work of the utopian imagination—"an art project" more than "a historical project": "I am just trying to make it the world I want to live in." Chamberland treats Seth's collecting as another dimension of his artistic vision.

Seth explains in the film's opening segment that his cartoons might best be understood as "memory drawings." Cartoons do not depict the world in detail, but rather provide "iconic images" that "stimulate in the reader their own experience." Cartoons encourage readers to add details from their own memories: "I can create a house and you can add the boards on it yourself." Seth compares memory to a "blueprint of a sensation": "You start to build the memory in your brain much the way you might start to move around toy figures in a diorama."

Seth's Dominion documents what Seth calls his "little hobbies" and "side projects"—his handiwork. Seth uses drawing, sketching, even carving rubber

FIGURE 2.6. Seth displays his Dominion, a model midcentury city sculpted from cardboard, one of the many memory arts showcased in the documentary *Seth's Dominion* (Chamberland 2015). Courtesy of the National Film Board of Canada.

stamps, to render his memories on the page. Seth may not be a nostalgia artist, but he is a memory artist. Such projects often take ideas from his sketchbook and reinsert them into the material world. The film takes its title from a collection of some fifty art deco buildings, each carefully crafted from cardboard (figure 2.6). Dominion City emerged from his sketchbooks, where he had designed the setting for some future (still unwritten) graphic novel. Seth found himself developing ever more detailed descriptions and histories of the small Canadian city's landmarks. Through the years, Seth incorporated some of these buildings as settings in his other graphic novels: he uses photographs of his cardboard sculptures to represent settings in *George Sprott* and Dominion is the city where Simon in *Clyde Fans* discovered his fascination with collecting postcards. Seth began to sculpt them, a practice he characteristically links back to his other interests:

> Having a collector's personality, I have long had a desire to "gather up" everything I like from the past. Obviously I couldn't bring home an old

> office tower or a deco apartment house. With old buildings, I had settled with snapping a photo, but now, through some form of sympathetic magic, I could actually take these places home with me. Not that any of the models are actual recreations of real buildings. Generally they are made up of whole cloth—or from recombinations of a variety of reference materials. Yet constructing the city and its past seemed to satisfy that longing to possess. I was collecting buildings—putting them in amber—saving them from the wrecking ball. (Seth 2010, 44)

Seth turns from photography back toward material practices as a means of preserving what he treasures about a fading world. Seth is now producing the objects he collects, thus bringing the process of performing and managing memory more fully under his own control.

In *Seth's Dominion*, the artist stages what gets described as a puppet show (more accurately, a toy theater performance) using figures he has designed and crafted. Seth's puppetry connects him to a much larger tradition of stop-animation artists, such as Jan Švankmajer and the Brothers Quay, who share his fascination with decay and decomposition, rust and dust, and who often create their art by manipulating aging objects. As Seth toys with his figures, we cannot help but recall his description of the ways people manage memories like "you might start to move around toy figures in a diorama." For Seth, this somewhat awkward form of puppetry offers another way for collectors to get their hands on things before their memories recede from reach.

Seth's Dominion moves from photographs and mental images to drawn images and imagined narratives to physical objects that can be displayed in museum galleries. *Seth's Dominion* parallels in interesting ways the project Orhan Pamuk initiated with his novel *The Museum of Innocence* (2009). From the start, Pamuk wanted to write a novel in the form of a museum catalog in which each object was presented to the reader, first as an example of a larger class, as a marker of the life and times of Istanbul at a moment of historical transition, as the bearer of collective meaning, and then, also, as operating within a particular narrative, a failed love story, a more personal memory. Pamuk wandered through thrift shops, seeking evocative objects. The novel's protagonist, Kemal, embodies collecting's most pathological dimensions—he is an obsessive, a stalker, an emotional cripple unable to move forward from a doomed love that destroys his life, a kleptomaniac who steals objects because they remind him of his beloved, and a fetishist who gathers stubs from his lover's every cigarette. Pamuk treats these practices as acts of curation—Kemal is assembling a museum to commemorate the love he maintained against all reason.

Pamuk assembled these objects, built his museum, and opened it to the public—a material extension of his fictional worldmaking. He also published *The Innocence of Objects* (2012), a museum catalog that artfully shifts between a meta-narrative about his work as the collector-author and the fictional narrative of Kemal's idiosyncratic museum. While many of these objects were already rescued and appraised by other collectors, others required the author to negotiate with hoarders: "They kept these objects without bothering to classify them, and their houses soon were filled up with mountains of paper and curios. . . . I always enjoyed breathing in their scent of dust, mold, and agedness" (49). *The Innocence of Objects* is a story told through words and pictures (in this case, photographs) that, like Seth's works, encourages Pamuk's readers to reflect on their own collecting:

> There is of course a strong bond that holds the novel and the museum together: both are products of my imagination, dreamed up word by word, object by object, and picture by picture over a long period of time. . . . The objects exhibited in the museum are described in the novel. Still, words are one thing, objects another. The images that words generate in our minds are one thing; the memory of an old object used once upon a time is another. But imagination and memory have a strong affinity, and this is the basis of the affinity between the novel and the museum. . . . The Museum is not an illustration of the novel, and the novel is not an explanation of the museum. (18)

The Innocence of Objects is a photographic and prose catalog of the museum and a transmedia extension of the novel. As these artists sort through everyday flotsam, they raise questions about the larger culture's archival impulses. If comics are to be saved, then why not cigarette butts? Why not postcards? Why not matchbook covers? And who should decide what passes the test of time?

Rituals of Collecting

So far, I've described a process of meaning transfer: that is, memories, associations, sentiments are transferred onto collected objects; by holding these materials in our hands, brushing off the dust, the rust, and the mold and polishing the silver, the collector calms what Benjamin calls the "chaos of memories." Grant McCracken (1988b) has described the various rituals consumers perform to take sentimental possession of the ready-made goods they purchase. By rituals, McCracken means shared social practices through which meaning is manufactured and identity managed. He identifies four basic sets of rituals:

- Exchange rituals refer to practices determining how we acquire objects. His examples concern transforming consumer goods into gifts—when gifts are given, what obligations gifts create, what values determine the choice of gifts, and so forth. As we extend this term to deal with collector culture, exchange rituals also concern the ways collectors make their finds and the ethical relations between collectors.
- Possession rituals determine how we develop attachments to things we have acquired. As McCracken explains, "consumers spend a good deal of time cleaning, discussing, comparing, reflecting, showing off, and even photographing many of their new possessions" (85). Such behaviors are often the most visible aspects of collecting culture—as with, for example, Seth showing off new "finds" to Chet in *It's a Good Life.*
- Grooming rituals have to do with how we preserve valued materials, especially the fragile materiality of cheap printed culture. Much of what I've said above about dust and hands speaks to this dimension, as do ongoing debates about how much value should be ascribed to objects that are pristine and untouched.
- Divestment rituals involve "letting go" of things we've collected when they are no longer personally meaningful or culturally significant. Such rituals play an especially large role in the narratives of sorting and culling, as I will discuss a bit later in this book.

In the following discussion, I focus on acquisition (exchange) and divestment rituals, but all four of McCracken's categories are useful for thinking about Seth's collecting stories.

Acquisition Rituals: Quests, Searches, and Finds

McCracken's original term here was "exchange rituals," because he understood this category primarily in relation to gift giving: "Attention needs to be given to the process of choice by which the giver identifies the cultural meanings they seek to pass along to the recipient" (1988b, 85). While the contents of a collection are sometimes given and received as gifts, collecting more frequently involves the collector in direct negotiations with others to determine what materials are to be acquired and on what terms. And such negotiations also involve the transfer of meaning, the construction of identities, and the establishment of social relations among participants.

Consider another of Seth's collecting stories, this one from *Wimbledon Green*. Sometime in the mid-1930s, Wilbur R. Webb, a pharmacist, begins "casually" reading some of the comics passing through his shop. Being a "meticulous sort" (31), he places each comic carefully into a suitcase after reading it, intending to reread these works, but because there is such a steady flow of fresh content, he never does. The suitcases, full of comics that have each only been touched once, accumulate, and because he lives alone, he faces no pressure to discard them. Web's hoard becomes a "find," the object of a collecting frenzy, which motivates the central plot of Seth's graphic novel. Wimbledon Green describes this moment of discovery (figure 2.7): "There was a diffused quality to the light—almost as though the air itself were dusty. A single shaft of sunlight shone through a tiny window and passed over my hand as I reached for the suitcase. . . . I snapped open the locks on the first suitcase. . . . Dust flew as I raised the lid. . . . I had just stumbled onto the lost entrance to El Dorado" (35–36). Across the page, Seth shows us the huge shaft of light streaming down upon the briefcase, ending with a pop of color as its contents are revealed: here, in this last panel, light radiates from the collection itself. Seth brings together the two images—dust and hands—traced throughout this essay, and with them, something else, captured by the shafts of light and the reference to El Dorado: the unattainable object, "the stuff that dreams are made of."

The "Webb Find" sets into motion the book's whimsical adventure yarn, as a colorful cast of collector characters barter, struggle, race, lie, cheat, and steal to get their hands on the treasured comics. The "Webb Find" is a "find" because its value is beyond question: there are contents here desired by any and all collectors, including many titles believed to have been lost (not unlike El Dorado's gold). The fact that these comics have been left relatively untouched only increases their value. One could imagine a world where the comics were divided among the various pursuers, each according to their own needs and interests. Not surprisingly, each collector wants them all. To be a "find," there must be a "quest"—the one validates the other.

A folk hero for consumer culture, "the greatest comic book collector in the

FIGURE 2.7. Wimbledon Green's "find" of a lost cache of comics echoes everything from *Citizen Kane* to Indiana Jones. Seth, *Wimbledon Green* (2005). © Seth. Courtesy of Drawn & Quarterly.

world," Green offers a hyperbolic version of the collector's capacities for consumption, acquisition, and discrimination. Bruce of Comic Ark tells us, "He could determine a comic's publication date just by the position of the staples" (15); another dealer notes Green's ability to distinguish the scents of different publishers' newsprint (77). Like Uncle Scrooge or Richie Rich, Green can land anywhere and ferret out hidden treasures. Harvey Epp of the Comic Cellar explains, "[Green was] a real picker—working the Goodwills and back alleys and yard sales. . . . He was a genius at finding things. He just knew where to look. . . . You'd never be able to do that today—the books just aren't out there anymore" (22–23).

In his autobiographical comic "Nothing Lasts," Seth describes how he acquired the childhood nickname "Back Issues." Young Seth tells his bemused classmates that he can look up an obscure horror film actor by digging through his old monster magazines. Seth digresses into a long rumination about the "unavailability of information in that era" as opposed to the "labyrinth of internet connections" (2014, n.p.). There was little information to be found at his local library about who drew the comics he loved: "Answers came by serendipity alone." Instead, he "mentally filed away" such questions "awaiting the day an answer would arrive, usually much later, and most likely by sheer chance" (n.p.). Kim Deitch, another comics collector/storyteller, constructs narratives in which online searches are central to his collecting stories. For Deitch, such interactions open old secrets and buried knowledge, allowing him to find unsuspected connections between objects, people, and places. For Seth, the web's easy answers devalue his collecting skills: "When you discover something off the beaten path, you can kind of make it your own" (Hoffman and Grace [2013] 2015, 175).

Being a gifted collector requires discrimination: the collector must appropriately value what they find. Here, again, Wimbledon Green is depicted as a collector of remarkable abilities. The fictional comics critic Art Stern explains, "The other customers of the store seemed shallow and crass. Men of poor taste seeking out old comics in a vain attempt to buy back their childhoods. Or empty speculators hoping to cash in on some collecting trend. Most of them quite lacking in knowledge. . . . Not Wimbledon Green. . . . He really seemed to know things. To understand!" (Seth 2005, 42–43). But Stern's admiration for Green's "high standards" ends in disappointment when Stern stumbles upon his idol sitting in a fast food joint, eating "greasy chicken" and reading through "crummy superhero comics" with "a look on his face . . . of a pig in shit" (43). A collector's reputation rests on their appraising eye; a collector's hands should be dusty but not greasy, crummy, or shitty.

Each time a collector acquires an object, they place their reputation at risk: a collector is defined by what they collect and shamed when their choices are not validated. Collecting stories are often drenched with flop sweat: the storyteller seeks to demonstrate their mastery and expertise and, at the same time, confront uncertainties about the value of their activities. In "Nothing Lasts," Seth describes his anxiety about how his classmates would react to him still reading comic books, going through elaborate preparations to insure that he could swoop in, grab what he wants, and buy it, with minimal risk of being observed. Seth contrasts his timidity with the boldness of a "more popular boy" who walked into the store, a girl on each arm, and proudly purchased a bundle of comics. Why do some collectors, thus, draw stigma where others walk away untainted? Seth has "back issues."

Seth displays his own discrimination through a recurring interest in pastiche. Pastiche manifests itself in *It's a Good Life* through Seth's project of fabricating a classic midcentury cartoonist and producing eleven examples of Kalo's work as if they had appeared in the *New Yorker, Esquire,* and *Saturday Evening Post* at the peak of his career, and a range of cheaper, lowbrow humor magazines during his decline. Seth's Kalo adapts his style to his changing circumstances, the demands of different editors, improving his craft over time. During the series' original run, some readers were convinced that Kalo was an actual artist Seth was reintroducing to the world. Yet, beyond the Kalo cartoons, *It's a Good Life* is drawn in a clear line style evoking vintage illustrations and with a characteristically muted color pallette.

Another of his graphic novels, *The G.N.B. Double C.* (2011), also relies extensively on Seth's pastiche of different cartooning styles as he imagines an alternative history of Canadian comics. Seth includes an extended essay on the actual cartoonist Doug Wright (figure 2.8): "His panels were carefully crafted examples of deep space and rich observation. . . . The environment of his strip was clearly his own town, his own street, his own house. Wright was drawing the world I grew up in—Ontario of the 1960s and 1970s. Every carefully rendered detail is perfectly familiar to me" (58–59). Seth's compositions here are often slightly off-kilter to the narrative action, suggesting a trained eye scanning the backdrops of Wright's cartoons, looking for telling details, inviting us to appreciate his visual style almost in the abstract. Seth might be describing his own techniques, which similarly situate his characters against a rural or suburban Canadian landscape at once familiar and nostalgic. *It's a Good Life* contains many panels of landscapes, mostly suburban neighborhoods or forests glimpsed from the windows of a moving train. These spaces are largely empty of people but piled high with snow or drenched with raindrops, an elemental conception of Canada that differs from the congestion and clutter in the book's New York sequences.

Seth is also strongly interested in the social relations among collectors. As Bart Beaty (2011) notes, Seth, Chester Brown, and Joe Matt constitute a particular artistic community or friendship circle, based at least for a time in Toronto. These artists are not simply real-life friends, they also depict their friendships across their works. For Beaty, these interlocking representations constitute reputation building, but such moments also address the ethics of collecting. The collaborative relationship between Seth and Chet throughout *It's a Good Life* contrasts sharply with the Coverloose Club in *Wimbledon Green*, an organization that seems to exist simply so the leaders can blackball rival collectors. Here the collectors engage in endless grudges—rivals, never friends—pursuing the same objects, doing any and every thing to get them.

If Seth's *It's a Good Life* assumes strong bonds between Seth and Chester, Joe Matt's *Spent* (2007) suggests the opposite—different expectations about how

FIGURE 2.8. Seth celebrates fellow Canadian comic artist Doug Wright for his observation of suburban life. Seth, *The G.N.B. Double C.* (2011). © Seth. Courtesy of Drawn & Quarterly.

collectors should treat each other can disrupt male friendships. The book opens with Joe and Seth rummaging a used bookstore when Joe stumbles into a rare volume of the *Birdseye Center* comic strip: "I've been looking for that book for years," Seth proclaims, anticipating that Joe will bow to his prior claim, but Joe holds his ground. Seth is still grumbling as they exit the store: "You deliberately bought that book just to piss me off! . . . You wouldn't even know about it if I hadn't shown you my old newspaper clippings!" (10–11). Almost a hundred pages later, the two are still bartering over this book, and along the way, Joe has intentionally purchased other collections he knows Seth wants: "every man for himself" (92).

If such interactions seem juvenile, there are strong parallels to how Matt depicts his own collecting practices as a child in *Fair Weather* (2002), such as taking advantage of a price guide to cheat a less savvy pal or betraying a friend's secrets in hopes of convincing another collector to sell him a coveted comic. If *Wimbledon Green* constructs a folk tale about the world's greatest collector, Joe Matt often depicts himself as the world's scummiest collector. In this same spirit, Seth modeled unsavory collector Jonah in *Wimbledon Green* after his own familiar persona (his Harold Lloyd glasses, gray flannel suit, cloth hat, and close-cropped hair). Ashcan Kemp characterizes Jonah as an example of collectors as "self-deluded fops . . . pining for a time before they were even born." While Jonah prided himself on his sensitivity, he was "a rather hard hearted individual with no real sympathy for others" (65). Jonah steals other collector's prize objects, seeing himself as "a preservationist—freeing these comics from the wrong owners" (68).

It's a Good Life also depicts Seth's relationship with women as often endangered by clashing tastes: "All they've got to do is to tell me that they like crime novels or Marvel comics or something and they're out" (15). Not unlike Stern's dismay over Green's tastelessness, such revelations can shift taste to distaste and, in the process, destroy attachments that once seemed promising. Seth ponders why he is so much more accommodating of diverse tastes with his male friends than with his romantic partners, though here, also, conflicting ethical codes cause friction. In Seth's stories, women may sometimes—though often cluelessly—assist in his collecting adventures, but they are rarely themselves collectors.

Although it was published too late to be fully incorporated into this book's analysis, Carol Tyler's *Fab4 Mania: A Beatles Obsession and the Concert of a Lifetime* (2018) gives us some points of comparison in terms of how fandom and collecting might be represented in a more feminine context. Barbara

Ehrenreich, Elizabeth Hess, and Gloria Jacobs (1992) see Beatlemania as marking a particular peak in the postwar emergence of teens and preteens as a specific market category (with fandom performed through purchasing and displaying related paraphernalia) and, more than that, as "the first and most dramatic uprising of women's sexual revolution" (85), reflecting shifts in gender roles and a refusal of forms of sexual repression that anticipate other forms of resistance that emerge later in the 1960s. Most accounts of Beatlemania came from the outside, as adults projected their meaning onto the girls' behavior, but Carol Tyler, building on her childhood diaries, shows us what it felt like from the inside, exploring the social rituals and practices associated with being a young Beatles fan. Many of these rituals center around affective investments that help to define social status within a larger community: Carol and her friends are quick to identify people based on whether they have the proper appreciation of the Fab Four, and then distinguish themselves within their fandom based on which of the guys they prefer (linking their female bonding to the inculcation of heterosexual desire). As with Seth and his characters, collecting and trading cards plays a central role in this emerging subculture, though the emphasis here is on the social bonds created via these exchanges, as when Carol gives a poor girl some of her duplicate Beatles cards as part of her efforts to recruit her into her fan club. Trust issues do surface here between the young fans—the poor girl steals Carol's makeup and she has to work extra jobs to be able to replace it as she prepares for an upcoming concert. There is little interest here in who creates these cards, though, since they are primarily valued based on what they represent—the objects of her fannish desire—and not as collectibles per se.

These are artifacts that Carol and her friends live with rather than things to be protected from wear and tear, even if the artist herself is drawing heavily on things that survived from her own childhood—for example, playlists of top hits from a local radio station—as the resources from which she constructs her graphic novel. When young Carol steals the sleeve from a Beatles single belonging to one of her brother's friends because she covets the picture, she folds the picture up and carries it around in her pocket next to her heart, rather than pressing it onto acid-free paper as Seth and his compatriots might. Tyler offers several images of her bedroom, where countless images of the Liverpool lads, cut from magazines, are taped onto the walls or tacked to a corkboard to form a shrine (figure 2.9). Here the religiosity of her fandom is directly paralleled with the social and material practices associated with the Catholic school she attends.

Her relationship to these bits of paper is more often transformative than protective—she uses these images as she wishes, and when she cannot own the thing itself she makes what she needs, as we see when she crafts replicas of the Beatles' instruments to decorate her walls. She has no more worries about cropping one of these images than she does about folding gum wrappers to create an endless chain, another of her hobbies depicted in the book. Tyler's narrative stresses her emotional investment in these artifacts rather than their economic cost or value, narrating how they become the focal point for her relationships with her friends and family members (her confession of stealing the record cover represents the onset of a crush), rather than representing them as a site of competition or expertise. Collecting thus represents an extension of her fannish investments—a way of showing devotion—rather than becoming an end into itself.

And there are no "finds" here—with the possible exception of the initial record cover she purloins—because everything she collects is still widely available at a moment of mass excitement over the rising stars she adores. Tyler stresses the profusion of related materials available at the Beatles concert in Chicago's Comiskey Park: "There were men selling Beatles pins, books, pictures, packages, pennants, posters, oil paintings, punch balls, buttons, necklaces, bracelets, and rings" (224). Collecting Beatles stuff represents another aspect of the communitas felt by a stadium full of screaming girls, all connected to each other by their passions for the Fab Four. Seth's collection is what sets him apart; Carol's is what links her to so many other girls of the Beatles era. Seth and his friends represent their collecting practices as an extension of their connoisseurship, as a display of their expertise and mastery; Carol Tyler is unapologetic about the raw emotions involved with being a Beatles fan, much as Ehrenreich, Hess, and Jacobs argue that what these young women found liberating was "to

FIGURE 2.9. Carol Tyler worships before her homemade altar to the Beatles. Carol Tyler, *Fab4 Mania: A Beatles Obsession and the Concert of a Lifetime* (2018). © Carol Tyler. Courtesy of Fantagraphics.

abandon control—to scream, faint, dash about in mobs" (85). However aberrant they like to see their own behavior as, Seth and his friends have the room and resources to pursue their interests, whereas Carol and her friends are at the mercy of others—their parents, their teachers, their older siblings—to accommodate or at least tolerate their interests.

Divestment Rituals: Putting Away Childish Things

McCracken's divestment rituals involve "letting go" of collections, shedding parts of ourselves as we toss those objects that embody them. If choices about what to save reflect sentimentalization and aestheticization, letting go requires depersonalization and desacralization. McCracken (1988b) describes a process of "erasure" as the owner scrubs away memories associated with an item before they pass it along to another future owner. Bal (1994) argues that in the narrative of collecting, "the initial event is arbitrary, contingent, accidental," since it is only recognized retrospectively by being put into narrative: "collecting comes to mean collecting precisely when a series of haphazard purchases or gifts suddenly becomes a meaningful sequence" (101). By the same token, divestment occurs when the old frame no longer dominates our understanding of the collection.

In *Clyde Fans*, Seth depicts the moment when an aging Simon abandons his collection. As he is being harangued by Abe, Simon endlessly sorts his postcards, using them to limit engagement. Asking how many are "enough" postcards to own, Abe accidentally overturns a box, destroying the careful order in which they have been preserved. Simon brushes it off: "It's not important, Abe. Just old paper" (371). Abe promises to set things right—"nothing ruined"—but for the slump-shouldered collector, nothing much matters any more. The fascination has passed, he is disenchanted, just going through the motions. The term "disenchantment" conveys the sense of sympathetic magic that collectors sometimes ascribe to their objects, in turn suggesting that divestment involves "breaking a spell."

Prior to that moment, collecting gave Simon's life purpose. As Abe explains, "Simon put a lot of effort into piecing together a history of these novelty cards. Writing letters, gleaning information from old magazines and mail order catalogues. From what I gather he wrote many inquiring letters to the creators of those cards or to their living relatives. . . . Hundreds of carefully typed notes for his grand history of these men, their times, and their postcards" (Seth 2019, 78). The effort ends in disappointment, though, when a rival collector publishes his own history of this obscure genre, rendering Simon's lifelong efforts

FIGURE 2.10. Seth's boyhood toys shatter as he opens and shuts his drawer. Seth, "Nothing Lasts, Part Two," *Palookaville* 21 (2013). © Seth. Courtesy of Drawn & Quarterly.

pointless. Simon's book would have been what Benjamin described as a "magic encyclopedia," the sum total of what the collector knows about his collection, and thus the justification for all of the work involved—but Simon's collecting story has no such satisfying ending.

In "Nothing Lasts," Seth documents when and how he abandoned the objects that had been most meaningful to him as a child, seeing such self-deructive moments as stepping stones toward adult manhood. For example, as young Seth lost interest in model building (figure 2.10), those "models that had fallen from favor" landed in a particular dresser drawer; "Each time I opened or closed the drawer something would break. The damage only got worse as I crammed more and more models in there. Eventually, the drawer was filled only with small shattered pieces" (2013a, n.p.). By the final panel in this sequence, Seth draws the jumble of meaningful fragments in the drawer, including a tire and the head and shoulders of Frankenstein's monster, as well as fragments now beyond recognition.

In another passage, he recalls his "best loved toys": "Nothing special about them. A bland assortment of cheap stuffed animals. Haphazardly acquired. . . . Each toy invested with a life of its own, emotionally animated as only a child can. Their faces remembered better than any childhood friend, recalled clearer than any teacher from that time" (2013a, n.p.). As the character dismisses their significance, Seth's depiction of these toys is at once generic (allowing us to

FIGURE 2.11. Seth shoots the stuffing out of his toys. Seth, "Nothing Lasts, Part Two," *Palookaville* 21 (2013). © Seth. Courtesy of Drawn & Quarterly.

recognize similar characters from our own childhood) and yet highly particular (for example, a dog in a hat or a penguin). At once, he tells us that these toys do and do not matter, that for all their blandness, he felt great affection toward them. Yet, one day, the adolescent takes his stuffed friends from the attic, hangs them from a tree, and shoots them "all to pieces" with a pellet gun (figure 2.11): "It wasn't a meaningful act, just something to pass the time. Still, I can think of no more fitting event to signify the end of my childhood" (2013a, n.p.). Seth shows himself sprawled on the ground and taking aim at the toys in one horizontal frame, while he dedicates five panels to the fate of his stuffed friends. In the first panel, the penguin has a noose around his neck and the dog in the hat dangles by one limb; then, as the shots are fired, the artist depicts their destruction, the dog now decapitated with stuffing hanging out. However indifferent he claims he was at the time, this panel breakdown stresses the horror of the moment. These divestment rituals feel especially masculine in their association of maturity with a rejection of sentimentality, with a demonstration of toughness, and with acts of violence and destruction.

Seth demonstrates two ways that divestment occurs—gradually over time (models breaking) and dramatically in some grand gesture (shooting the stuffing out of his plush). Chester Brown, Seth's collector friend, tells yet a third story in *The Playboy* (1992): here his guilt-ridden character gets caught in an endless cycle of acquisition and divestment, as he struggles with his addiction to pornography. Chester, as an adolescent, purchases and then systematically destroys one porn magazine after another: ripping up the pages, burning magazines in the family fireplace, burying them in the woods far from his home, only to replace them yet again. Brown refuses, at least in the context of this particular narrative, to regard his habits as those of a collector, even as he demonstrates his own growing expertise (displayed by the artist's loving re-creations of specific covers) and even as he taps collector networks to acquire the issues he fetishizes. The *Playboys*, in this case, are abject—objects of desire and disgust, exacting a practice of mastery and shame.

How do we understand these graphic storytellers' depictions of collecting as a source of shame in a context where these artists are placing these same habits on bold display? What happens when these men, afraid to be seen in public buying comics, are stripped naked in their own publications? Underground comics have long celebrated their refusal of self-censorship and willingness to shatter taboos; they imagine themselves to set no limits on what they will share with their readers. Joe Matt depicts himself eating his own snot, taking a crap, smelling his underarms, jerking off, and spending all of his money on View-Master slide sets.

We can read these images as a disgusting yet "honest" display of our common humanity—aspects of how we relate to our bodies and our stuff that we do not talk about in public. Yet they may also be read as conveying a sense of failed masculinity that impacts how men see themselves, how they fail often to build trust and intimacy in their relations and how they use collecting as a means of working through and compensating for certain disappointments and losses. Collecting is constructed here as an alternative form of patriarchal power—masterful, expert, antisentimental, a means of controlling one's self and one's environment, a means of constructing a homosocial sphere largely defined outside, if not in opposition to, the feminine sphere of domestic entanglements. If these stories celebrate collecting as a site of male bonding, however tentative, they can do so only by defining women as outside the role of the collector, thus creating a homosocial world that recalls past days spent in each other's basements or tree houses, where boy culture escaped maternal control or the intrusion of sisters, where boys could be boys and now men could be men.

This is why it matters that these collecting stories are constructed by and for collectors. Some of these representations come precariously close to the negative stereotypes regarding fans and collectors prevalent elsewhere in the culture—portraying collectors as immature, emotionally stilted and socially isolated, coping with professional failures. Yet Seth and his friends show these collecting practices from the inside out, as representations of self and not simply of the *other*, and they do so alongside a broader range of representations of what it means to collect. Collecting is normalized, even as readers are encouraged to reflect on both constructive and destructive dimensions of these practices. These cartoonists often depict themselves as having little control over their collecting fever and little self-awareness around their own behaviors, yet as artists, they are the ones selecting what to place on the page and how to frame these self-representations. Their mostly male readers are encouraged to identify with such shared stories, although these depictions of their real-world friendships are as hyperbolic as Wimbledon Green's larger-than-life antics. All of this is complicated, messy, and contradictory, and that is perhaps its power, since these comics force readers to think through the ways in which these stereotypes do or do not apply to their own lives and, perhaps, the ways these stereotypes shape how these men relate to each other. Their shared shame as collectors, their open acknowledgement of their self-pity and social estrangement, draws them into closer identification with each other, even as they hold each other at arm's length. Such is sadly often the nature of male friendship.

Wrapping Things Up

I began this chapter by talking about collecting as amplifying the meaning-making practices Grant McCracken sees as central to the operations of a consumer society. Throughout, we've seen many examples of the exchange, possession, grooming, and divestment rituals that shape what it means to "own" an object produced and sold by others, how we come to think of our possessions as belongings. Such practices also relate closely with the process of decomposition (dust) and recomposition (getting one's hands on lost objects), which I described here as central to the psychology of collecting. Collecting, framed in this way, is a means of negotiating a space between past and present, and thus is closely associated with the process of artistic expression, as in the case of Seth— a memory artist who sees comics as vehicles for capturing his own memories, and mechanisms by which he can trigger his readers to tap their own memories. Seth's collecting stories are built around moments when a randomly encountered object initiates a collection, when collectors struggle over things they each desire, when cases get made for why some works are more valuable than others, and when people let go of stuff they once cherished.

Such transactions occur often without much thought on the part of the characters, yet Seth's comics encourage readers to reflect upon the meaning of everyday collecting practices. His comics offer an incredibly diverse array of collecting stories, some broadly comic, some pathetic, some introspective, but all taking collecting seriously as a way of life. Seth understands collecting as a set of social and cultural practices as people seek out, appraise, acquire, and display meaningful objects and as their relationship to those objects impacts their interactions with others. Seth regards his artistic practice as an extension of his collecting—seeing drawing as memory work that helps people to recall and process past experiences, seeing collecting and curatorship as creative processes through which we reconstruct rather than simply recover older forms of material culture. And the particular forms that collecting takes here are bound up with the assertion of particular gender identities through homosocial bonding and the marginalization or exclusion of women, through an emphasis on appreciation and mastery over other forms of emotional investment, and through stories of divestment that link rites of passage to acts of violence and destruction. All of this is no doubt what Seth meant when he asserted, "To know me is to know that I am a collector."

3

"The Stuff of Dreams"

Kim Deitch's Remarkable Displays

Chapter 2's discussion of Seth introduced the concept of "collecting stories"—that is, stories by, for, and about collectors. A key theme running through the chapter was the relationship between collecting and storytelling: the collector does not simply gather random items; the collection is held together by a mental frame through which the collector makes sense of the various pieces. This frame often includes an awareness of the history of these items and how this stuff entered their possession. The collector is driven to complete the collection and, in doing so, to complete the narrative that the collection expresses. Across Seth's books, I located recurring sets of images—in particular, clouds of dust (which hint at the material and ephemeral nature of the collected materials) and holding hands (which suggests their tangibility and accessibility)—as well as recurring events—in particular, those rituals through which individuals assert their own identities in relation to their belongings. In Seth's comics, the potential for friendship among collectors exists alongside unethical and antisocial conduct, hinting at the nature of homosocial bonding between straight men.

In this chapter, I will consider the graphic novels and underground comics of Kim Deitch, who is as deeply immersed in collector culture as Seth, and whose comics reflect his interest in early twentieth-century popular culture. Deitch tells collecting stories, but his aesthetic also depends upon moments where he directly displays the objects he collects.

Kim Deitch's biography straddles the histories of American animation (his father, Gene Deitch, was an important cartoonist, best known for his *Tom Terrific* series, his work with Terrytoons, and his later independent projects in Eastern Europe) and underground comics (Deitch was a regular contributor to the New York–based underground newspaper *East Village Other*, starting in 1967). One can learn much about Deitch by reading his current projects as a continuation of the underground comics movement—his sexually explicit, politically radical, and offbeat content; his recurring references to drugs, alcohol, and insanity; his tactical deployment of racial stereotypes; and his sometimes intense graphic style all owe something to R. Crumb and his contemporaries. He also borrows techniques from the 1920s and 1930s cartoons of the Fleischer Brothers (including anthropomorphic representations of animals and inanimate objects, a very rubbery anatomy, and "cartoonish" titling and lettering) and he pastiches earlier styles, such as the turn-of-the-century comic strip he created for *Alias the Cat!* (2005).

Within his graphic novels, Deitch depicts his wife, Pam, and himself as consummate collectors who deploy a range of digital technologies and networks to track down obscure artifacts, and, in the process, often find themselves pulled into strange conspiracies and exotic adventures. Like Seth, Deitch is shaped by his nostalgia for the early twentieth century—nostalgia not for his own past but for culture that was produced before he was even born:

> I feel I was born too late and missed out on most of good stuff first hand, much of which is now probably lost forever. I think I would just about sell my soul if I could experience first-hand the evolution of the movies. To a lesser extent, I feel the same way about radio. Consequently, I do not consider myself to be a nostalgic person. I feel that I was born in a world of great popular culture already in decline. There were still plenty of hints around of what had been, but the really good stuff had already come and gone. Somehow I felt that culturally we had already lost something of great value. I've had this feeling for just about as long as I can remember. I think the major unspoken theme of the creative work I do is an attempt to find and imitate some semblance of what I (we) have lost or missed out on. (Deitch 2011a, n.p.)

Like Seth, Deitch depicts this nostalgia not as a desire to return to simpler times (olden times are plenty sucky in his stories) but as reflecting a dysfunctional relationship with his own times. Near the end of *Alias the Cat!*, Waldo, Deitch's most famous character, calls the artist out: "I'd like to know why any of this, which is totally irrelevant to anything going on in the world today, should make any difference whatsoever to you! To me that's always been the problem with you! You're in the twenty-first fucking century asshole! Wake up and smell the coffee!" (n.p.). A typical Deitch story moves from autobiographical accounts of his own life into fanciful adventures involving time travel and alien visitation. Deitch has created a vast mythology of characters who represent different moments in the history of American popular amusements (from medicine and minstrel shows in the nineteenth century through to contemporary computer games and e-trade sites), embodying the ongoing tension between personal obsession and commercial motives that have shaped each new media form. In his introduction to *The Search for Smilin' Ed!*, Bill Kartalopoulos (2010) offers this description:

> Kim Deitch's body of work comprises an ever-expanding system of subjectively narrated intergenerational stories that refer to, elaborate on, qualify, and sometimes refute one another in a great meta-fictional tapestry spanning more than forty years of production. This may seem like a lot to lay on the present volume's cockeyed yarn about a kiddie TV show host from the 1950s, little grey men, the frog murderer of France, and a talking cat named Waldo. But *The Search for Smilin' Ed!* is a story that takes as its premise the existence of a world where such things can coexist in one room and on one page as surely as they do within the mind of this extraordinary cartoonist. (1)

Across this chapter, I will explore the idea that such diverse "things" can "coexist in one room and on one page," exploring the ways that Deitch's narratives assemble miscellaneous objects of interest to the author who hopes they are also of interest to his readers and then displays them in spectacular panels that overflow with fascinating stuff. I link Deitch's amazing displays back to an earlier art form, the cabinet d'amateur, which also spoke to and about collecting—in this case, in early modern Europe. Sometimes the objects Deitch displays constitute a carefully organized collection, sometimes they are an assemblage of assorted junk. Deitch's images are often citational—that is, they spur our own search for more knowledge and context and invite us to read them intertextually across his larger body of work. As such, these images, like those in the cabinet d'amateur, offer conversational resources by which collectors can display their knowledge to each other. As the chapter continues, I will focus on the liminality of desirable objects, particularly toys, using Waldo as my recurring reference point but extending outward to deal with a diverse array of other enchanted possessions. Deitch is interested in the promotional culture that surrounded animation from the start and the ways that these characters get internalized as figures of our personal and collective fantasies. In the process, they become enchanted, coming to life, becoming part of the identities of those of us who invest ourselves in them. Finally, I will close off this chapter with a comparison between Deitch and another artist, Henry Darger, who also is known for creating sprawling, mythological narratives inspired by things he gathered from the culture surrounding him and expressed through the interplay of image and text.

Collections on Display

Pam and Her Cats

Originally published as a stand-alone issue by Fantagraphics in 2002, "The Stuff of Dreams" was retrospectively incorporated into Deitch's graphic novel *Alias the Cat!*, which is in turn part of the expanded mythos he developed around the figure of Waldo the Cat. "The Stuff of Dreams" deals with how the artist and his wife acquired a stuffed Waldo doll at a mysterious flea market and learned some of the object's backstory from an old sailor, Keller: it is a shaggy dog or perhaps, under the circumstances, a shaggy cat story involving shipwrecks, volcanic eruptions, tribal rituals, and South Seas adventures. For the purpose of our analysis, though, the narrative will take a back seat to certain panels, where Deitch displays his collections, often in ways that are only loosely linked to the story proper.

For example, *Alias the Cat!*'s front matter (figure 3.1) includes a pencil drawing, which Deitch dedicates to "my best-pal and co-adventurer, my lovely wife, Pam," that depicts some of the items the Deitchs collected or consulted while researching the book. Front and center is a stuffed Waldo doll, a figure of Deitch's own imagination, while alongside Waldo are two other famous cats—a stuffed animal based on R. Crumb's Fritz the Cat and a Felix the Cat windup toy. Taken together, these two figures hint at Deitch's own influences. As

FIGURE 3.1. This still life drawing includes Felix and Fritz, two fictional cats who influenced the author. Kim Deitch, *Alias the Cat!* (2005). © Kim Deitch. Courtesy of Fantagraphics.

writers like Ian Gordon (1998) and Donald Crafton (1994) have documented, Felix was among the first pop culture characters to be licensed and marketed. Deitch enjoyed a strong affiliation with R. Crumb, who increasingly stands for the underground comics tradition as a whole. Deitch also lovingly recreated glamour shots of silent film stars, framed and hanging on the wall, as well as old paperbacks, pulp magazines, and record albums assembled on the shelf. In short, this is a self-portrait of a collector through the items in his collection—more focused on establishing the author's popular expertise than on adding anything specific to the narrative. And yet, the $1,000 price tag attached to Waldo's foot hints at what set the book's events into motion.

Once Deitch begins his story, he still pauses periodically to show off his collection. A cartoon persona directly addresses the reader (figure 3.2), explaining his wife's fixation with "black Halloween cats from the 1920's and 30's and old Felix the Cat toys" (n.p.), cataloging different examples from her collection. In anticipation of the story's darker elements, Deitch states that "this one

FIGURE 3.2. Kim Deitch displays his wife's collection of stuffed black cats, as she comments. Kim Deitch, *Alias the Cat!* (2005). © Kim Deitch. Courtesy of Fantagraphics.

FIGURE 3.3. "Pam Butler and All Her Cats" offers a portrait of a female collector and her collection. Kim Deitch, *Alias the Cat!* (2005). © Kim Deitch. Courtesy of Fantagraphics.

looks more like a demon from Hell that's been killed and stuffed"; on the same page, he tells us, "Good ones don't turn up that often and when they do, they come high" (n.p.), suggesting the lengths collectors may go for such objects. And, near the bottom, he hints at a spousal conflict about how much Pam spends on her interests. If figure 3.1 gathered multiple objects related only through Deitch's own eclectic interests, these items constitute a bounded collection, defined both thematically (all black cats) and formally (arranged on shelves and explicated by their owners).

Deitch closes "The Stuff of Dreams" with another image of his wife and her collection (figure 3.3). Given the degree to which collecting stories so often focus on the homosocial world of male collectors, a portrait of a female collector and her beloved objects is striking. Pam seems carefully posed here, one pet cat on her lap and another staring at her curiously from the sidelines. The cat collectibles running through "Stuff of Dreams" also often include images of the Deitchs' black and white pet cats, sometimes sitting in Pam's lap, sometimes climbing up the bookcases and brushing past the collectibles—much as early modern paintings might include images of cats, dogs, parrots, and even monkeys interacting with the objects on display. This formal portrait constitutes yet another genre through which to represent the couple's possessions. Here Pam has pulled the items around her in a different configuration, no less focused on displaying them for the reader, but this time, absent any explanatory text other than the title, "Pam Butler and All Her Cats." In between comes yet another kind of display—in this case, directly addressing the reader as a someone who might help them locate a missing element, providing a mailing address and an EarthLink address (actual? fictional?) where the reader might write if they do succeed in getting their hands on a Waldo doll. Each of these full-page images represents a slightly different representation of the Deitchs and their stuff and each establishes a distinctive relationship with the reader. In some cases, we are openly acknowledged, while in others, the characters are closed off from us. Some constitute still life drawings, whereas others resemble portraits. Some emphasize stillness, whereas others suggest motion. Some are realistic, whereas others are more broadly cartoonish.

The cabinet d'amateur, or gallery painting (figure 3.4), a genre of artworks that originated in seventeenth-century Antwerp, offers one rich point of comparison with Deitch's images of his wife's collection. These paintings depict the space of an art gallery, complete with curators and critics, engaged in intense conversations, gesturing toward and examining the displayed works. Often these galleries were more aspirational than actual: they depicted works that might be scattered across many collections, private and public, including some examples that did not really exist but are drawn in the style of popular artists of the period.

These gallery paintings emerged at the moment when collecting and connoisseurship were increasingly valued by the economic elite and learned classes. As Elizabeth Alice Honig (1999) explains, "The highly identifiable nature of the remade paintings was important for both artist and collector. The artist showed by this means his remarkable versatility; he was another Proteus, assuming the recognized styles of every great artist and inventing their works in miniature. For the owner of the fictive gallery, the collection of highly attributable (but unlabeled) images gave him the opportunity to show off his knowledge of Antwerp's art" (204–205). Such paintings were conversation

FIGURE 3.4. The cabinet d'amateur tradition displayed artistic virtuosity by replicating works by varied artists and genres. Anonymous, *Cognoscenti in a Picture Collection* (ca. 1620). Courtesy of the National Gallery, London.

pieces, judged in part by the quality of exchanges staged around them, and they became vehicles for constructing distinctions: "Taste and judgment were thus formed through interactions between collectors and their guests in a collective process of viewing, discussing, and consensus-building, voiced in the language of connoisseurship" (206).

Similar goals are at play in Deitch's more contemporary works. On the one hand, the artist uses panels that evoke the cabinet d'amateur as a way of demonstrating his own abilities to reference and reproduce key icons from twentieth-century popular culture. Deitch often dismisses his own artistic abilities in interviews, confessing that his animator father told him that his drawing style was too crude and too inconsistent for animation work. Comics' critics have similarly described his figures as primitive, stiff, and lifeless, awkwardly positioned within the frame. Yet Deitch often demonstrates his skills by rendering detailed drawings of film stills he can reasonably anticipate will be recognized by fellow collectors, and these representations are often accompanied by prose offering some detailed discussion of the value of original versus reprinted images or of various film formats in which collectors might encounter these materials (figure 3.5). Strikingly, the individual stills reproduced on this page may recall the panels of a comic, except there is no sequentiality: we do not understand the panels in relation to each other but only in relation to Deitch's self-representation as an expert collector assessing these materials. One could imagine a different composition, one where the stills were laid out on a dealer's table, much as the paintings are hung on the wall in the gallery paintings. It is as if Deitch has conjured them from his own memory, reflecting back on what he did or did not buy the last time he went collecting. Deitch knows his stuff, gaining increased credibility the more the reader knows about the artifacts being discussed. On such pages, he also directly addresses his collector readers, encouraging them to write him if they have leads, or offering to make trades.

The original cabinet d'amateur differed in significant ways from the still life paintings discussed in chapter 1. For one thing, the objects they depicted were themselves depictions, often containing a great deal of action—ships floundering on stormy seas, hunters and their dogs chasing game, farmers working their fields, battle scenes, or religious paintings. The same might be said of the movie frames or posters that interest Deitch. He represents different genres and stars—from silent slapstick comedies to B-movie westerns, from Clara Bow to Lon Chaney. Second, unlike still life paintings that are defined by the absence of characters and activity, cabinets d'amateur are full of human figures creating, curating, and conversing about the gathered materials. And the same could be said for most of Deitch's drawings—for example, Kim and Pam having a loving spat about how much she paid for an eBay purchase. The social interactions that might have originally occurred around the cabinet d'amateur are brought onto the comics page in the form of dialogue and narration,

FIGURE 3.5. Deitch demonstrates his skills as an artist by his skillful reproduction of classic movie stills. Kim Deitch, *Alias the Cat!* (2005). © Kim Deitch. Courtesy of Fantagraphics.

even as the readers are now dispersed, cut off from the original creator and from each other. We can imagine the effect if word balloons were to be added to *Cognoscenti in a Picture Collection* (figure 3.4), if the patrons depicted were shown complaining that the works were overpriced, calling out the original works being reproduced, grumbling about the subject matter or debating where they might find the landscapes being depicted.

Some of Deitch's images offer more complex glimpses into collecting culture: his two-page spread showing a convention for bottle cap collectors in "The Sunshine Girl" (2008b) (figure 3.6) includes Deitch himself, manning a booth as a guest artist, the creator of what a sign proclaims to be "the holy grail of crown caps, Sunshine Soda" (n.p.). Here he plays with the dispersed gaze discussed in relation to Outcault: Deitch positions himself front and center not unlike the Yellow Kid, but he does not directly address the reader and there are no word balloons, despite the presence of a range of signs and other text scattered across the space. The page's layout encourages readers to let their eyes wander down the rows of the dealers' space, examining objects for sale at the various tables. As with the Yellow Kid or, for that matter, the cabinet d'amateur, an initial sense of clutter gives way to an awareness of different clusters of interaction. The large white space surrounding the stage, where some kind of theatrics are occurring, contrasts sharply with the pools

FIGURE 3.6. Deitch depicts himself as one of the participants at a bottle cap collectors' convention. Kim Deitch, "The Sunshine Girl," *Deitch's Pictorama* (2008). © Kim Deitch. Courtesy of Fantagraphics.

of black ink elsewhere. A two-page foldout ([1976] 1989) in *Beyond the Pale!* (figure 3.7) depicts the death bed scene of Hollis Hale, a financier known for his "Teddy Beariana": His servants and family have gathered around, many of them dressed in bear costumes, as his "faithful valet" plays his favorite song, "a rare cylinder recording of 'The Teddy Bears Picnic'" (65). Deitch's detailed drawing captures everything from Hale's stuffed toy collection to sheet music and school flags depicting bears, from the bear patterns on his wall paper to the whimsical bears in his final daydream. Deitch might have had the cabinet d'amateur in mind when he took the time to draw the various teddy bear paintings lining the walls of Hale's apartment or depicted Hale's servants pampering the old man's fantasies. Yet Deitch does not stop with recreating a physical space, incorporating the mental images of Hale still in his striped pajamas being visited by woodland creatures at the "Teddy Bears Picnic." Here his dreamland, as is typical in Deitch's work, owes a debt to the Fleischer Brothers, especially with the singing trees and anthropomorphic animals. And the composition's business is amplified by various textual mechanisms, including multiple forms of annotations on the content of his collection. We can think of these texts performing

FIGURE 3.7. The death of Hollis Hale, noted collector of teddy bears. Kim Deitch, *Beyond the Pale!* (1989). © Kim Deitch. Courtesy of Fantagraphics.

the social rituals of a collector showcasing his collection to an invested visitor. In short, the objects that interest collectors in these images are not inert or isolated but rather read as part of a larger world, which includes the collectors themselves but may also include the fantasies that animate their interest in these materials.

Like Antwerp's artists, Deitch displays his virtuosity as much through his ability to fabricate plausible examples as he does by being able to reproduce real-world objects. It is certainly possible to spot some of the depicted items in photographs or videos of his workspace, suggesting that he is seeking inspiration from objects close at hand, and this helps to provide some real-world grounding for his otherwise fantastical stories. At the same time, some details are totally fabricated, referring not to real-world media history but rather to the expansive and ever-expanding fictional world at the heart of Deitch's stories. So an object may play a central role in one story and appear as a background detail in subsequent works, offering an intertextual linage for the alert and loyal reader. For example, one depiction of his work space in *Alias the Cat!* (figure 3.8) shows two reels of *Satan Town*, a movie he had referenced just a few pages earlier, but also the Urn of Chondra, a pot-smoking pipe that figures

FIGURE 3.8. Kim Deitch's desk displays objects associated with his other graphic novels. Kim Deitch, *Alias the Cat!* (2005). © Kim Deitch. Courtesy of Fantagraphics.

prominently in *The Boulevard of Broken Dreams* (Deitch and Deitch 2002). And the Chinese Worry Dogs, visible here, resurface in Deitch's *The Search for Smilin' Ed!* (2010).

"Stuff of Dreams" stands out because of its explicit focus on displaying and cataloging items from the Deitchs' collection, but in many of his other graphic novels, readers are encouraged to stop and scan a dense mise-en-scène, reading the depicted objects as shedding light on the characters, their lifestyles, and their worldviews. In *Shadowland* (2006), Deitch (figure 3.9) depicts a clown-faced barker pointing customers toward the freakish exhibits of a 1936 traveling dime museum (death masks, shrunken heads, embryos in formaldehyde, a taxidermied pig). The adjacent page (figure 3.10) represents the same showman, A. L. Ledecker Jr., in retirement, watching cartoons in his Sarasota home several decades later, with many of these same macabre objects integrated into his domestic space. Once readers discover the pattern, there's much fun to be had in glancing between the two drawings, trying to determine what has happened to the various objects and characters over the intervening years (another example of what chapter 1 discussed as scanning and flipping).

Deitch's graphic novels are full of detailed renderings of earlier forms of popular amusements—the interior of early movie theaters (*Shadowland* and *The Amazing, Enlightening and Absolutely True Adventures of Katherine Whaley*), the window display of a contemporary toy store (*The Boulevard of Broken Dreams*), or the ribald furnishings of a brothel (*Shadowland, Katherine Whaley*), to cite just a few examples. Each setting is scrupulously researched and vividly detailed, encouraging readers to pay attention to the particulars. And his fascination with animation history leads Deitch in *The Boulevard of Broken Dreams* to imagine what kinds of memorabilia might have accumulated in the apartment of Winsor Newton (modeled after Winsor McCay) during his final days or to speculate about what Disneyland might have looked like if it had reflected the more anarchic and anthropomorphic style of early Fleischer Brothers cartoons. Such pages are breathtaking in their extrapolations about what objects might have emerged if the history of popular culture had taken some different turns.

FIGURE 3.9. The sideshow attractions associated with the showman A. L. Ledecker Jr. Kim Deitch, *Shadowland* (2006). © Kim Deitch. Courtesy of Fantagraphics.

"Do Your Own Research"

Deitch's depicted objects are citational—they encourage us to go online, look up more information, and further flesh out his story's context. Consider, for example, a two-page spread in *The Boulevard of Broken Dreams* (figure 3.11) showing the cluttered living room of Ted and Nathan Mishkin. On the wall are photographs of the fictional protagonists in their prime and a poster for a vintage Waldo the Cat cartoon, *Dream Street*. The Mishkins are watching what appears to be that same cartoon on television with various degrees of inattentiveness (Ted has passed out; Nathan, still a boy, is holding a beer). Word balloons

FIGURE 3.10. The retired Ledecker still surrounds himself with the same artifacts. Kim Deitch, *Shadowland* (2006). © Kim Deitch. Courtesy of Fantagraphics.

reproduce lyrics from the 1932 Victor Young song "Street of Dreams," which the animated cat is performing, while there are old 78 records of classic crooner songs scattered around the room. Among them are Bing Crosby's own version of "Street of Dreams," as well as tunes performed by Russ Columbo and Paul Whiteman. Such old jazz standards were often incorporated into early sound era cartoons: Deitch is the kind of collector who could tell you in which cartoons these songs were featured. He recounts his fascination with these crooners in his short story "The Cop on the Beat" (2008c); Deitch (2011a) also developed a series of autobiographical multimedia essays for the online edition of *Comics Journal* recounting his life as a record collector. There he often embeds videos or sound files allowing readers to experience the referenced performances.

Even this focus on his record collecting tracks back to his father, who first developed his skills as a cover artist for the jazz magazine *Record Changer*. Deitch (2011b) writes about his father's record collection:

> Looking back on my dad's collection I was starting to realize that his pile was okay as a square-one for discovering all the great music of that bygone era, but it was merely the tip of the iceberg. . . . I was also coming

FIGURE 3.11. References to old swing performers encourage readers to do their own research. Kim Deitch, *The Boulevard of Broken Dreams* (2002). Courtesy of Pantheon.

> to the conclusion that music was only one small part of a great cultural renaissance that had been going on in the early part of the 20th century. . . . I began to realize that if I wanted to really be familiar with what I perceived to be "the good stuff," I was going to have to start doing my own research. . . . If you *really* want to consider yourself to be a well-informed individual, then my feeling is that it behooves you to *do your own research*. Beware of second hand sources, including me. There is still much out there that is undiscovered and overlooked. (n.p.)

So studying Deitch's displays can lead readers deeper into his story world or can lead them out again, encouraging them to discover some of his favorite old performers and songs or make new discoveries on their own. Few readers will identify all of Deitch's allusions, but it is for this reason that these comics generate active exchanges, online and elsewhere, as networks of people trace his references. If Seth celebrates the chance discovery or "find," Deitch's collector-heroes do active research: "ferret out the lead, track down the raconteur, find the lost film or the corpse or the missing matinee idol, and just you see if that doesn't put you on the trail of even greater mysteries, buster" (McCulloch 2004, n.p.).

Who Collects What?

The three interconnected stories that constitute *Alias the Cat!* (2005) are each initiated by a new set of discoveries: in the first segment, Pam falls for a stuffed Waldo doll she encounters at an old flea market and they end up plying the dealer with drinks to learn where the doll came from. In the second, Pam buys an old cat costume on eBay, and Kim becomes obsessed with tracing its origins back to a silent movie serial, which, in turn, has its basis in a real-world power struggle. While no prints of the serial survive, Kim discovers through an ad in *Moving Picture World* that an obscure New Jersey newspaper ran a comic strip depicting the film's events, and he is able to find bound copies of these newspaper issues, never microfilmed, again on eBay. The costume's owner regrets parting with it and seeks to buy it back for sentimental reasons, behavior Pam pegs as not following eBay community norms. Pam and Kim visit his apartment, admire other items in his collection, and in the process stumble upon an old Magneto tape made by the man's mother about her encounters with the mysterious man who created the *Alias the Cat!* serial. In Part Three, Kim tracks down the offspring of an obscure cartoonist who oversaw the *Alias the Cat!* comic strip. His discovery that she also did promotional comics for the Tiny Town Bakers (which he copied as a child in order to learn to draw) leads him to search for the New Jersey town where the bakery was located. And it is here that he finally encounters the mysterious Mr. W., whose influence shapes all of the preceding events.

Something curious happens along the way: Pam begins the book as the desiring subject—she wants the stuffed Waldo doll and the cat costume for her collection. But finding out their backstory becomes Kim's obsession; more and more, Pam gets pushed aside. She is satisfied to accumulate and display interesting items, whereas he is driven to the breaking point by his pursuit of knowledge. Deitch has said that this graphic novel was intended to be a collaboration with his wife, who is also an artist, but somewhere along the way he took over and completed the story on his own, once again pushing a female collector into the background. Pam's collection is on display; Kim's collecting dominates the action.

Pam is not the only female fan and collector central to Deitch's fictions. "The

Sunshine Girl" (2008a), for example, takes us inside the world of bottle cap collectors as seen through the eyes of Ellie and Sid Whaley. Ellie is the driving force of the story, but by the end she has abandoned her hobby to focus on her family and her religion: "Well, I guess it just comes down to what a person's priorities are. I will admit that, at the beginning, I was as swept up in it all as anybody. But over time . . . I began to think maybe there was something more to living than just having a bunch of things" (n.p.). "The Cult of the Clown" ([1972] 1989) begins with heiress Candy Crenshaw sneaking out of the house, dressed as a clown, on the way to a gathering of an underground community linked by its fascination with the circus. Her father, wanting to teach her a lesson, dresses as a clown himself, but ends up getting too deeply involved, resulting in his tragic demise. After his death, the father becomes a folk hero, embodying the rebellious spirit of the clown cult. In all three cases, female desire sets the story into motion, but the women pull back, leaving the men to follow their passions to their extremes and often to pay the price for their curiosity.

Throughout this book, I am interested in such gendered differences in the ways male and female graphic storytellers depict stuff. But I do not want to simply naturalize the differences, seeing men as using collecting as a form of self-fashioning and women as dealing with family inheritance, even though this pattern persists across many of the discussed works. Such depictions are culturally produced, and often at the expense of erasing or repressing the experience of female fans and collectors, as occurs in Deitch's stories. We are seeing emerge from female artists, such as Carol Tyler and Emil Ferris, alternative representations of female fandom that often depict material practices of transformational use rather than stressing collecting per se.

Cultural Discrimination and Popular Expertise

Honig (1999) has described the kinds of expertise and mastery at stake for those standing in front of the cabinet d'amateur: "Connoisseurship involves the ability to make judgments based on agreed notions of style, artistic personality and quality; it supposes a belief that the trained eye is capable of making those judgments and indeed that such training for the eye is even possible; it further necessitates a vocabulary with which visual judgments can be articulated and understood" (196). Honig is interested both in the ways that these art patrons were making distinctions that helped determine the marketplace value of paintings (and their painters) and the ways that patrons were making their own bids for social and cultural capital.

In early modern Europe, expertise was developed in reference to high culture, whereas pop culture expertise is the knowledge that matters most in Deitch's comics. He is working at a moment when the cultural and aesthetic status of these earlier forms of popular culture are themselves shifting, as critics are claiming that pulp texts deserve to be preserved and protected for future generations, much as we've seen comic books get redefined as graphic novels. In an essay strongly informed by Pierre Bourdieu's theories of habitus and cultural capital, John Fiske (1992) describes fans as exercising popular discrimination, using their ability to appraise cultural materials and recount media history as an alternative expertise and a source of subcultural capital. Fiske describes fandom as "an intensification of popular culture which is formed outside and often against official culture" (34). Fan expertise follows logics often taught through schools but applied to inappropriate objects, to works educational institutions assume do not require such close scrutiny or deserve such prestige. Fan knowledge, Fiske suggests, may not help them get a better job or an educational pedigree, but it can be the basis for status and prestige within the fan community itself.

Fans' popular discrimination may inspire local contestation over what forms of culture matter, since the objects of this knowledge are less rigidly defined than the canons of school culture. In "TV and Me" ([1977] 1989), Deitch depicts an uncomfortable encounter between a so-called expert who has written a book about television history and an organization of self-proclaimed "Couch Potatoes," each with their own idiosyncratic views about which television programs matter. Their questions and disputes keep throwing him off or violating his sense of what constitutes the medium's highpoints. Ultimately, the enthusiasts override the expert, reverting back to debating which reruns to watch.

If Honig describes the ways that knowledge and taste came to cohere around particular artists through mechanisms of formal education, Deitch depicts the disputes that surface when fans try to discuss forms of culture where everyone can reasonably claim a share of expertise. Yet television and other kinds of popular culture have been more fully incorporated into the realm of high culture since Fiske and Deitch wrote these accounts: the "graphic novel" rhetoric claims for comics an artistic and literary status otherwise lacking. If anything, the result has been an even more intense contestation as the academy often absorbs those works that look like texts already included in the curriculum—for example, works that stress their literary qualities or experiment with more abstract visual styles—while excluding those that are grounded in Bourdieu's popular aesthetic.

The Grey Ones, a tribe of alien beings depicted in *Shadowland* (2006) and *Smilin' Ed!* (2010), constitute perhaps the ultimate embodiment of this collector mentality. As one of the *Shadowland* characters explains, "These creatures have a curious attitude about human beings. They consider us a flawed species, but a highly entertaining one. And it's our folkways, the ways we entertain each other than they consider to be our saving grace. It's what they consider us to be particularly good at and a thing they were very interested in preserving" (n.p.). Deitch depicts the aliens sitting in front of several rows of monitors, watching videos that span the history of popular amusements—everything from opera singers to black-faced minstrels, from Hamlet to porn, all reviewed and reappraised from this otherworldly vantage point.

The Grey Ones have cameras everywhere, so they are able to capture not only mass media products that might otherwise be lost, but also local performances or the lived experiences of their favorite personalities, all of which provide them with pleasure and satisfaction. The aliens maintain an "underground archive of popular culture that honeycombs the Earth's interior" (n.p.), with everything their spies observe being beamed to orbiting satellites and then converted into "laser story chips." They rescue old films and records from destruction; they raid museums to salvage artifacts that would otherwise be gathering dust; they kidnap self-destructive stars and showmen, helping them to overcome their crises, and putting them to work producing original content for the aliens' amusement. Deitch loves to tantalize his readers by showing the aliens consuming media that is now well beyond our reach—for example, watching original performances of Shakespeare's plays at the Globe Theater—and making judgments that contradict established wisdom—"It's funny for all of his fame, Edwin Booth just doesn't seem to stand the test of time. On the other hand, this guy, Paul K. Dintenfass, who never performed Shakespeare anywhere but in Mother O'Rourke's Staten Island boarding house is still knocking 'em dead down here. Go figure!" (2010, n.p.). The Grey Ones value popular culture *as* popular culture, and thus their judgments come from a different place than decisions to pick graphic novels for academic syllabi.

Magical Objects

If Seth and his protagonists are interested in "paper," Deitch's stories center around promotional goods—especially, as we have seen, plush toys associated with the early history of animation. The unstable and uncanny status of such objects in Deitch's works suggest an unresolved tension—he cannot simply dismiss these promotional objects as a corruption of pure artistic expression. Having grown up in the belly of the beast, he understands that commerce is what enables creative expression and, besides, he has a real passion for these objects that makes them hard to resist. There is more to these toys than meets the eye. By tracing their origins, Deitch draws us into his wild conspiracy theories and grand adventure yarns.

Toys and Artifacts

When, in *Alias the Cat!*, Pam seeks to purchase the Waldo doll, the old salt protests, "Hey! It ain't no toy, see! This here is an artifact!" (n.p.). Keller uses this claim as a pretext to jack up the purchase price, but as the story continues, we discover that the stuffed Waldo was produced by the people of a South Seas island, who saw the big blue cat as a deity. Seeing a business opportunity, Waldo the Cat enslaves the islanders, forcing them to produce stuffed toys in his likeness on a primitive assembly line, which he plans to ship back and sell to the West. Eventually, Waldo is overturned, the dolls are stuffed into the mouth of a volcano to appease the islanders' traditional gods, and most of the dolls are burnt to a crisp when it erupts. As Keller explains, "Me and this old boy been through some times! Like you wouldn't believe!" (n.p.). And it is precisely because they do not believe the seaman's yarn that Kim and Pam find themselves digging deeper, trying to get their hands on more Waldo stuff and on more information that might resolve his status as plaything or sacred object.

As Brian Sutton-Smith (1986) reminds us in *Toys as Culture*, toys are designed to operate in their own realm of play, outside but on the borders of everyday reality:

> Toys . . . are in marked contrast with the everyday world which they represent, or to which they refer, or in which they have their existence. . . . This contrast has, throughout history, made them objects of special attention, even of awe. Sometimes that attention has been of a sacred or religious character, as when they are used as facsimiles of real life objects and placed in the tombs of the dead to accompany them into the next world; sometimes that attention has been of a magical character, as when they are used to gain power over others whom they are supposed to represent, in which case it is said that what one does to the miniature will happen to its source of origin. . . . Perhaps religious, magical or playful attitudes all

> share a perceptual sense that there is something different about miniature objects, which contrast so strangely with everyday life. (349)

Toys in our culture are often objects associated with childhood (which has historically been a time when we are allowed special access to the realm of the imagination).

Part of the scandal associated with collector culture is that adults are holding onto their toys beyond the permitted time of childhood play and fantasy. Deitch, as an animation buff, knows that the earliest cartoons were not targeted at children and many of the first generation of cartoon characters had to be gradually tamed, rendered accessible and appropriate for children, a process that, in turn, constrained what animation and comics could become for the better part of the twentieth century. Waldo, as the personification of that earthier style of early animation, actively resists becoming a child's plaything. As Deitch explains, "His edges can't be smoothed off—even by me" (Glenn 2010, n.p.).

Deitch's own ambivalent feelings toward mass culture products shaped *The Boulevard of Broken Dreams*, his tribute to his father's generation of animators. The story opens at a banquet held to honor Winsor Newton, "venerable cartoonist and animation pioneer" (n.p.), at the dawn of the sound era: the evening begins promisingly enough as Newton performs a famous stage act, where he seems to interact in real time with the animated figure of Milton the Mastodon (modeled after Winsor McCay's Gertie the Dinosaur), but things turn sour quickly, as the drunken and ill-tempered cartoonists ignore or disrupt the performance, having little sense of the history of their own medium. The angry old master turns upon the attendees: "You guys have taken the art I created and turned it into shit!" (n.p.). As the story continues, Newton is among a number of outspoken critics who object to the industrialization and sentimentalization of animation—the negative consequences of Walt Disney's rise to success. Deitch and his protagonist, Mishkin, prefer the more rubbery characters and more improvisational narrative structures, the dreamlike mise-en-scène and the vaudeville-style performances associated with the Fleischer Brothers, over the more rounded and childlike figures, the carefully scripted stories, and the stable worlds associated with Disney. Mark Langer (2011) notes that these different styles emerged from different models of the production process: "West Coast studios produced animated films in a rigidly hierarchical system that used the story department as a choke point to maintain production control. The more informal system used at the Fleischers' studios was determined by a management philosophy that encouraged polyphonic forms of expression in the finished works" (46–47). At the core, then, is a tension between artisanal and corporate modes of production, which stand here for a friction between the artistic motives driving the animators themselves and the commercial motives shaping the finished product.

Boulevard traces what happens to the Waldo character across these various transitions. As Charles Hatfield (2004) explains, "Waldo, once the randy, free-spirited embodiment of amoral playfulness, becomes the object of moralizing sentiments and bathos" (n.p). Waldo, himself, puts it in blunter terms, complaining that the new management is turning him into a "fuckin' pansy!" (n.p.). Waldo provides critical commentary on the changes his character undergoes, with each new incarnation justified as preserving or returning to the original spirit. By the 1950s, Deitch tells us, "Waldo's personality has been recast as stupid, treacherous, even rather effete and impotent. He's no longer a star but has a humiliating, supporting role as valet to a virile rat" (n.p.). The final indignity comes when Waldo and the other Fontaine Fables characters become the focus of a line of "Lil' Critters" plush toys on sale at the Toys'R'Fun! chain. An industry representative explains proudly, "Some promotion, huh? I see it as a kind of a creative melding of old and new. And hey, this Toys'R'Fun! deal is just the beginning. . . . Very soon Rocket Rat and Waldo will be walking around Disneyland along with Mickey and Donald" (n.p.). Yet the moral struggle here is less clear-cut than initially meets the eye, given that these various permutations and commodifications of the cartoon industry are precisely what generate the various cat collectibles Pam and Kim so proudly display in "Stuff of Dreams."

Such promotional extensions have surrounded animated characters from the beginning. Donald Crafton (1994) tells us that by the early 1920s, Felix the Cat, a model for Waldo, was "perhaps the most popular screen character, living or animated, except for Chaplin," a byproduct of his studio's "advanced marketing" efforts (317). As Crafton writes about Felix, "the screen character instigates a desire for the viewers to physically possess him. For children, the desire can be satisfied by a physical surrogate (the doll). For adults the desire becomes aestheticized, the character's movements and gestures invite identification and empathy" (321). If, as Crafton suggests, Felix thrives because of his vivid personality, because "unavoidably one sees Felix as a living being" (338), then children projected aspects of that living personality onto the dolls, while adults wanted to embody Felix's saucy "tomcat" personality. Those objects that bore Felix's likenesses were never simply commodities: they were vehicles through which fans sought greater contact with a personality that had no existence beyond what his animators put on the screen and what fans could convey through their domestic performances. Given Felix's commercial success, there were plenty of knockoffs, imitations, and unauthorized versions, explaining the many misshapen and mutant-looking toy cats on Pam's shelves. Felix also generated many on-screen imitators—a whole army of cartoon cats from many different studios—thus explaining why, in his youth, Deitch saw the cartoon cat as a genre trope rather than a singular personality. And Felix's success paved the way for Walt Disney's even more ambitious promotional strategies, which Deitch depicts as corrupting the art of animation.

Deitch the collector-turned-artist cannot resist showing us the prototypes Newton himself had developed to exploit Milton and his other creations across media platforms, including detailed renderings of Miltown, an amusement park the animator imagined "as far back as 1920" (n.p.), and such consumer objects as a mastodon that opens up into an elaborate bar service. Even at his most artistically ambitious, Newton still has the heart of a showman: "If one is to communicate with the masses, we must entertain as well as we elevate" (n.p.). There is no pure art, Deitch suggests, only different compromises an artist makes in order to continue to produce new work.

The mechanisms of promotional culture are treated more sympathetically in *Alias the Cat!* Here the anarchist Malek Janochek has constructed a silent era version of transmedia storytelling to alert his society to the dangers of militarization and to focus public outcry against the corrupt agendas of the local business leadership. Malek translates real events into the fodder for a movie serial, which then gets retold via a comic strip in the local paper and enhanced through his live appearances impersonating his protagonist. The cross-promotion is ultimately what allows Deitch to research the series, since comic strips, advertisements, and news stories survive as memory traces while the film itself was destroyed. Later in the same book, we see similar urges leading to the founding of the Tiny Town Bakers, with its promotional comics and tourist attractions helping to finance a utopian social community where "little people" can work and live together with dignity. *Alias the Cat!* shows how two different showmen deploy transmedia promotion as a means of fostering progressive politics, marketing alternative values via popular culture.

A similar scheme animates Charles Varney in Deitch's *Katherine Whaley* (2013). The philosopher uses stage spectaculars, public lectures, and, later, film serials as a means of promoting women's rights, eugenics, spiritual uplift, and moral enlightenment. Drawing on his deep knowledge of media history, Deitch links Varney's film project to Lois Weber's *The Hypocrites*, which deployed artistic representations of the naked female form as a means of directing attention toward her critiques of Gilded Age orthodoxies. Katherine Whaley sees performing in the buff as a small price to pay if it will put humanity on a better path for the future.

When Toys Come to Life

Sutton-Smith (1986) stresses the often transgressive nature of children's play: toys are designed by adults to communicate certain moral virtues or to achieve certain pedagogical goals, but what happens when they get into children's hands may be something different. "Whatever toys may have originally signified to their makers (in plastic or wood), when children play with them this signification is often destined to be betrayed. . . . Play's excitements derive from both following the cultural rules for behavior and defying the cultural rules" (251). Children project their "longings, furtive wishes, glorious dreams, hopeless fears that cannot be expressed in everyday arrangements" (252–253) onto their toys and through them, they work through their relationship with the culture around them.

Read in those terms, the stuffed Waldo may be understood as a toy, a plaything, a collectible but also more than that—Waldo embodies the deep-rooted fear that we may be possessed by our possessions. Waldo is both object and subject, animate and inanimate, living and dead, real and imagined, material and immaterial, and animal and human. Once Waldo gets ahold of you, he never lets go—and, often, Deitch's characters are driven to drink and ruin through this association.

The child psychologist D. W. Winnicott (1971) discusses toys, our "first possession"—"perhaps a bundle of wool or the corner of a blanket . . . perhaps some soft object"—as "transitional objects" by which the child negotiates his or her anxieties about separating from the nurturing mother and gaining some degree of autonomy. These objects are understood as at once "me" and "not me," as an extension of the self as much as they are objects, because the "first possession" is the object onto which the child projects their first fantasies, which become the basis, in Winnicott's account, of the creative impulse that leads to future forms of self-expression. In the ideal situation, Winnicott imagines the parents—explicitly the mother—as helping to facilitate the child's play, allowing them to assert ownership over these enchanted objects and giving credence to the fantasies that form around them. In this way, the toy comes to life, becomes "real" for the child: "It must seem to the infant to give warmth, or to move, or to have texture, or to do something that seems to show it has vitality or reality of its own" (7).

Lois Rostow Kuznets (1994) traces a genre of stories dealing with what happens when toys come to life, a tradition that includes children's classics, such as *Pinocchio* and *Raggedy Ann and Andy*, as well as more recent works, such as *Toy Story* and *The Indian in the Cupboard*. Kuznets identifies several key themes running through such fantasies:

> Toys, when they are shown as inanimate objects developing into live beings, embody human anxiety about what it means to be "real." . . . Toy characters embody the secrets of the night; they inhabit a secret, sexual, sensual world, one that exists in closed toyshops, under Christmas trees, and behind the doors of dollhouses—and those of our parents' bedrooms. This is an uncanny (in Freudian terms) world of adult mysteries and domestic intrigue. It can be a marginal, liminal, potentially carnival world. (2)

In Deitch's underground comics, Waldo was simply one among an army of similar cat characters from the early days of animation: the black cat proliferated, in part, because the animator could project onto such figures old minstrel show jokes and personas, because these figures could be quickly drawn, and because they depended on solid black ink and did not require complicated shading. In "The Lowdown" (Deitch 1992b, 30), Mishkin asks him why "you don't look like other cats"; Waldo tells him that he was born when the clown host of an early children's television show turned out to be a "jaded sex pervert" who had intercourse with a domesticated cat. And in *A Shroud for Waldo* (1992a), readers learn that the cat houses the soul of Judas Iscariot, born in true carnivalesque fashion from the loins of a pregnant hag. Waldo becomes an eternal demon, tormenting drunks, the insane, and the artistic—the only people who can see him or feel his influence. A mock character sheet for Waldo in *Boulevard* offers a benign but telling description: "The thing to keep in mind about Waldo is, he's all charm and cute on the outside, but inside he's pure devil!" (n.p.).

Showing Waldo's darker side, *Boulevard* also includes Mishkin's self-portrait with Waldo straddling his shoulders, pushing and tugging on his face (figure 3.12), leaving open the question of whether Waldo is a real being only Mishkin can see or simply further evidence of his mental distress. Here Mishkin's imaginary playmate when he was a boy has overstayed his welcome. As Ted's brother explains, "Waldo the Cat is practically a living creature to him" (n.p.). In Winnicott's account, the process of letting go of the "first possession" and first fantasy occurs gradually and without great trauma: "Its fate is to be gradually allowed to be decathected, so that in the course of years it becomes not so much as forgotten as relegated to limbo. By this I mean that in health the transitional object does not 'go inside' nor does the feeling about it necessarily undergo repression. It is not forgotten and it is not mourned. It loses meaning, and this is because the transitional phenomena have become diffused, have become spread out over . . . the whole cultural field" (7). But Waldo refuses to fade into limbo; Waldo persists despite adult maturation and commercial corruption, continuing to taunt those who might want to escape his influence. Waldo is "practically" alive, "almost" real, not quite a figment of Mishkin's imagination, not really something he has created, and certainly not something he fully controls. In that sense, Waldo is not a toy.

FIGURE 3.12. Mishkin's self-portrait, with a demonic Waldo attacking him. Kim Deitch, *The Boulevard of Broken Dreams* (2002). © Kim Deitch. Courtesy of Pantheon.

In *The Secret Life of Puppets* (2001), Victoria Nelson traces the way that archaic spiritual beliefs persist within contemporary popular culture, often in displaced or disguised form, so that "irrational" and spiritual beliefs long since rejected by much of the secular culture get expressed through uncanny objects in stories of the fantastic and the supernatural. She is interested in the ways puppets emerged from a history of idolatry: puppets were made in man's image just as man was made from God's image, whereas "their static, unchanging nature imitates the permanence of the immortal." She describes ventriloquism as an old priest's trick as the religious leaders achieved powerful effects by speaking God's truths through the mouth of a statue. As realism took over the realm of high art, these once sacred rituals continued to be performed as popular entertainment—including puppet shows for children—and with the rise of cinema, many of these same associations got projected onto animated characters, who became similar figures of enchantment. She writes,

> No one who either remembers or observes the hypnotic fascination that cartoon characters hold for children can doubt the enormous power of this twentieth-century "animation of images"; yet another form of simulacra, cartoons as a phenomenon give us a rare opportunity for understanding the gut-level magnetism that puppet shows exerted for untold earlier generations. . . . Puppets and ventriloquist's dolls held their own in vaudeville and other venues until midcentury, when they transferred successfully to American television in such characters as Howdy Doody and Kukla, Fran and Ollie, followed by the Muppets. (256–257)

Deitch's works retrace this history, restoring to cartoon characters, their toy likenesses, puppets, and dummies some of the archaic beliefs in the divine and the demonic that was their inheritance according to Nelson's cultural history.

By *Smilin' Ed!*, Deitch has created a whole pantheon of demonic figures who maintain friendships and rivalries with the big blue cat. Waldo encounters these various demons inside a museum dedicated to the early comics art of Richard F. Outcault, and he follows them down a laundry chute into the subterranean world where the Grey Ones preserve their collections. Here, Waldo learns more about the secret lives of toys. In this case, the focus is on Froggy the Gremlin, a puppet who, Deitch recalls, performed various kinds of mischief on *Smilin' Ed's Gang*, a short-lived children's show from the early 1950s. Most of the footage that survives of Froggy in action comes from a subsequent series starring Andy Devine. The gruff-voiced Froggy possesses an otherworldly capacity to scramble people's minds, turning their words against them so that they often engage in self-destructive behavior. The naughty and disorderly Froggy makes a fool, again and again, out of various authority figures, especially cops, teachers, professors, and other professionals, who are unlucky enough to cross his path. Such goofy segments produce giddy laughter among children precisely because of the ways Froggy confounds the adult order, because he refuses to accept his proper place, but such slapstick can also be the focus of discomfort and anxiety: children may seek to disassociate themselves from their unruly

FIGURE 3.13. Froggy stored in a display case alongside Howdy Doody, Kukla, and Ollie. Kim Deitch, *The Search for Smilin' Ed!* (2010). © Kim Deitch. Courtesy of Fantagraphics.

impulses and uncontrollable appetites. The child cannot be blamed for the pleasure she takes in forces that are beyond her control. In Deitch's story, the Froggy doll has been possessed by the soul of a homicidal maniac, Monsieur Froganard, who uses the character to lure and molest children. The Grey Ones now keep Froggy inside a glass case (figure 3.13), alongside other exhibits from the early days of children's television (including, as Nelson might have predicted, Howdy Doody, Kukla, and Ollie), bringing him out periodically so they can stage new *Smilin' Ed!* episodes, which they claim as a classic, even though it has been mostly been forgotten by Earthlings.

So what kind of thing is Waldo? A toy or an artifact? A god or a demon? A real personality or a product of Mishkin's fevered imagination? A commodity or a collectible? Something innocent or something transgressive? He is all of these things and much more at various points in Deitch's graphic novels, and thus allows the artist to explore some of the core contradictions and ambivalences in his feelings toward American popular culture. He helps to stitch the various chapters of Deitch's sprawling narrative together; as such, he is also an agent of history.

Deitch's Resources

Like Seth, Deitch does not regard his collecting stories as exercises in nostalgia. Kim Deitch often describes himself as a history buff, but if this is the case, he deals with alternative conceptions of history, ones not often taught in the academy. I recall my awkwardness in initially presenting this chapter when I was challenged by a noted historian of American animation who demanded to know what kind of account sees a giant blue cat as a primary driver of the genre's history. It's a legitimate question, if a bit overliteral. As I have been researching Deitch's work, I have continued to struggle with an answer that might satisfy this person. Deitch's works tell us much about the history of American popular amusements—that is, on the level of local details (his careful recreations of specific iconic images and objects from the past) and historical personalities (*Katherine Whaley* manages to work in references to Robespierre, the Deists, Lois Weber, the Jefferson Bible, the eugenics movement, John McCormick, Vernon and Irene Castle, William Randolph Hearst, Cecil B. DeMille, Eugene O'Neill, J. Edgar Hoover, Pablo Picasso, Winston Churchill, and many others). On this level, Deitch knows his stuff, but he is also willing to play fast and loose with his interpretation of the past, introducing strange conspiracy theories, challenging rationalist interpretations, treating history with the same transgressive pleasure he finds through the legacy of American animation, toys, and children's television.

Deitch practices what Carlo Rotella (2007) calls "Pulp History": "Pulp History is to the history taught and written in the academy as pulp fiction is to canonical literature: wilder, more eventful, less encumbered by the demands of verisimilitude, darkly suspicious of standard-issue cultural credentials as signs of intellectual timidity or even of complicity in some elite plot against regular folks" (11). As Rotella argues, pulp history follows the same urges as academic history—a desire to understand the past—but follows different disciplinary rules (some would argue, follows no rules) and speaks to different audiences. Pulp history, he argues, straddles the line between history and literature, capturing the imagination with explanations that would not prove convincing under other circumstances.

Deitch's history speaks certain truths about the human experience that cannot be found in any textbook, offering a counterhistory that provides insights without asking or expecting to be taken seriously. Consider what Deitch (2005) has said about his art: "To me that's the wild beauty of this comics thing. I can recreate the world MY way! Half remembered, half imagined" (n.p.). Autographical references, real-world artifacts, and historical figures all provide a kind of "reality effect" that makes the events seem more real, and yet, as the stories continue, we move further and further into the realm of the improbable, drawing less on textbooks and more on tabloid newspapers, plunging the reader into a world of secret cults, underground utopias, alien abductions, crackpot religions, sexual perversions, and demonic possessions. Just as Waldo exists in a liminal space where he is sometimes real and sometimes imagined, Deitch positions his stories in a world that is sometimes history and more often fantasy.

Michael Moon uses this concept of "pulp history" to describe a different artist in his 2012 book, *Darger's Resources*. Henry Darger, Moon's subject, was an outsider who produced incredible (in all senses) volumes of fantasy stories and artworks, working as a janitor by day and living a mostly isolated life. Darger's works were discovered by a neighbor following his death and have produced tremendous responses from the art world. Many of the initial scholars of Darger's work were fascinated by his solitude, his poverty, his untrained eye, and his oddness, all of which cut him off from the larger conversations of the culture around him. His stories about young and often sexually ambiguous girls, frequently drawn without any clothes, reflected the mind of a pedophile or perhaps someone so sexually innocent that he did not understand basic biology. Moon instead reads Darger as driven by a collector mentality, albeit lacking the resources (economic, social, or cultural) that other artists (here, though not in Moon's book, Seth and Kim Deitch) bring to their work. As Moon reminds us, Darger drew his resources from the proliferating pulp culture of the early twentieth century, especially the often disposable print forms of the comic strip, the newspaper ad, the catalog, the pulp novel, and the religious tract (all forms that Deitch has also referenced at one time or another):

> Dissatisfied with his ability to draw the human figure, Darger initially experimented with collaging photographs of children and soldiers cut out of newspapers and magazines, embellishing them with his own drawing. For most of his career, he traced the images of the children he drew, scavenging them from print sources of several kinds, getting them photographically enlarged to fit into the large-scale panoramic visual style he developed, and organizing them into groups in landscapes of his own devising that were themselves collaged from elements clipped from newspapers and magazines. (5)

Many accounts romanticize the image of Darger roaming the streets, picking up objects from the gutter, and bringing them home as raw materials for his art. But Moon stresses his active and conscious choice of materials and the ways that Darger's borrowed materials inspired his story structures and his underlying themes, insuring that, despite his social isolation, he still was engaging in a dialogue with the culture around him: "To deny Darger the elements of choice and discrimination that went into the formation of his vision is to impoverish him anew" (59). Darger's epic narrative, which rambles across thousands of pages, with characters disappearing and then reappearing again in new contexts, involves an imaginative play with intertextuality and metatextuality—that is, with the same kinds of postmodernist literary tricks that are often ascribed to Deitch.

What Darger produced could not be described as comics per se, since, by and large, his output does not draw on the visual vocabulary associated with the comics tradition, but we might describe these works as graphic novels, given that they combine words and images to tell a story that could not be fully expressed through a single modality. Deitch (2008a) himself has called for a broader definition of graphic novels, one more connected to the illustrated novels of the nineteenth century than to the comics tradition:

> So many of those books were originally very heavily illustrated and often in stylized, sometimes downright cartoony art not unlike what came later in comic books. Dickens acted as his own art director, hiring the artists and choosing the subject matter in his books that they would be illustrating. . . . Thackeray went him one better, often illustrating his own books. Originally *Vanity Fair* had one hundred and ninety illustrations done by Thackeray himself, sometimes dropped onto a page exactly where the situation Thackeray illustrated was being described—getting kind of like a graphic novel I would say. (n.p.)

Deitch's argument destabilizes cultural hierarchies—Victorian novels now regarded as great literary classics may be misunderstood if we separate the words from the images—but he is also making the case for more experiments in multimodal fiction. This discussion of the illustrated novel runs on the inside covers of *Deitch's Pictorama*, a collection of short stories by Kim and his two brothers (Simon and Seth), illustrated for the most part by the cartoonist himself. Deitch's most recent work, *Katherine Whaley*, can also be described as an illustrated novel, a more ambitious display of those same techniques. Darger developed his pictures in support of his literary prose, sometimes coming back and producing illustrations years after he first wrote the stories, and other times seeking inspiration in these images that would shape the narratives he was constructing. Darger, like Deitch, seems to be experimenting with what a storyteller can achieve working within graphic fiction.

My point is not to claim for Deitch Darger's outsider status; Deitch does a good enough job of that himself, often associating his own persona with intoxication, addiction, and mental illness, often drawing himself as pixie-eyed, dirty, and unshaven. Rather, I want to suggest that Darger in Moon's account, and Deitch in mine, embody the aesthetic potential of collector culture—the ways that often idiosyncratic frames and interests, an attention to the particular, and an appreciation of past materials can become the springboard for a particular kind of worldbuilding practice. In both cases, their artworks emerged from the desire to place the stuff they found on display. Both artists are associated with a kind of sprawl, a visual and narrative density that some find difficult to parse, but which speak of the common desire to show and tell everything about a world that would otherwise only exist in the confines of their own imagination. Both flirt with kitsch, and yet, there is a deeper meaning beneath the surface of their work, even if we don't always know how to put together the pieces or how to sort out fantasy from reality.

From his visual style to his narrative structure, Deitch helps us to understand what it might be like to look at the world through the eyes of a collector. Like the early modern painters and consumers of cabinets d'amateur, he displays his own artistic virtuosity and cultural expertise through his ability to reproduce and display works from many genres, creating images of collectors and their stuff. Like the Victorian novelists he admires, he crams his stories with meaningful (and sometimes enchanted) objects. And like the illustrated novel tradition he seeks to reclaim, Deitch is actively experimenting with the relations between words and images to explore alternative visions of what graphic novels might look like. In the next chapter, Bryan Talbot will take this fascination with collage aesthetics, borrowed resources, and the Victorian imagination one step further with *Alice in Sunderland*. If Deitch explicitly understands his creative project in relation to his collecting, Talbot claims a different aesthetic grounded not in collecting per se but in various forms of accumulation.

4

Wonders, Curiosities, and Diversions

Accumulation in Bryan Talbot's *Alice in Sunderland*

With a career spanning back to the underground comics of the late 1960s, Bryan Talbot is perhaps the most respected graphic artist working in England today, continuing to create British comics while his contemporaries Alan Moore, Grant Morrison, Neil Gaiman, and Peter Milligan were absorbed into the American industry. In *The Graphic Novel Man*, a 2014 Russell Wall documentary on Talbot's life and work, British comic book editor Dez Skinn describes Talbot as "the David Bowie of comics," stressing his shape-shifting capacity as he constantly redefines his style and identity across both alternative and mainstream publishing.

Many of Talbot's works share a fascination with the Victorian and Edwardian eras. His series on the time-traveling Luther Arkwright (1978–1987) was one of the first steampunk graphic novels, a genre that taps Victorian era imaginings of alternative futures, and Talbot has returned to steampunk with his more recent Grandville series (2009–2017), inspired by nineteenth-century illustrator and social satirist J. J. Grandville. *The Tale of One Bad Rat* (1995) deals with an abused runaway girl and her love for Beatrix Potter. *Alice in Sunderland* (2007), among other things, explores the circumstances that inspired Lewis

Carroll. *Sally Heathcoate, Suffragette* (2014) deals with the struggle of British women to earn the right to vote, and *The Red Virgin and the Vision of Utopia* (2016) explores the life and work of nineteenth-century French radical feminist Louise Michel. (The latter two were co-created with Bryan's wife, the feminist scholar Mary M. Talbot.)

In *The Graphic Novel Man,* Talbot traces this fascination's origins: when he was growing up, "there would be Victorian things under glass domes, there would be stuffed birds, there would be plaster Alsatians, in most people's houses at that time. . . . [I]t went out of fashion for a while in the late 1950s, I think, in favor of futuristic stuff. It was all based on atoms, atomic designs came in. And in the 1960s, of course, it became incredibly trendy—Victorian stuff" (Wall 2014). Much as Seth and Deitch discussed their childhoods in terms of transitions in access to popular goods associated with midcentury America, Talbot came of age alongside this dramatic shift in fashion: objects that were ever-present for one generation fell out of fashion with another, only to become trendy again. Not unlike Seth, Talbot admires "Victorian stuff" as a residual culture: "They made things to last then, they put care into things, they used to make things out of polished wood and brass and leather." Talbot's eyes open wide as he describes period technologies: "If you have ever been in the presence of a proper old steam train, it's noisy as hell and all of this steam comes out, it's like a big fire-breathing monster! It's an incredible thing! I mean, a modern little electric train, there's no comparison" (Wall 2014). Talbot's fascination with the materiality of Victorian culture mirrors what Rebecca Onion (2008) has said about steampunk more generally: "The steampunk ideology prizes brass, copper, wood, leather and papier-mâché—the construction materials of that bygone era. Steampunks fetishize cogs, springs, sprockets, wheels and hydraulic motion. They love the sight of the clouds of steam that arise during the operation of steam-powered technology" (139).

Reading *Alice in Sunderland,* Talbot's most challenging work, not so much a graphic novel as a graphic essay, is an overwhelming experience, in part because of its epic scale—whether judged by its three-hundred-plus page length or its chronological scope, which traces the history of a mining and shipping city in Northwest England from the Age of Reptiles and the era of St. Bede through to the present. Any single page of *Sunderland* is overwhelming: each page features dozens of images Talbot has assembled from archives—old photographs, documents, woodcuts, carved marble, stained-glass windows, film stills, cartoons, and book covers, all jockeying for our attention, each conveying separate bits of information. At its center is the story of Lewis Carroll, the author of *Alice in Wonderland*, who spent part of each year in Sunderland, though Talbot interrogates that story more than he narrates it. On the surface, the book-length essay reads as an obsessive argument for the priority of Sunderland over Oxford in understanding *Wonderland*'s origins. In the process, Talbot links Carroll to everything from ancient mythology to music hall comedy. *Sunderland* is a project in radical intertextuality, forging links between dispersed narratives drawn from both history and fiction, mapping them (literally) onto a highly localized geography. The book is structured as a tour, walking Sunderland's streets and rowing its waterways, as Talbot points out landmarks. And on yet another meta-level, Talbot connects comics to a much broader history of artistic practices that combined words and pictures to construct narratives, including a consideration of Carroll's illustrator John Tenniel, the Bayeux Tapestry, the Lindisfarne Gospels, William Blake, and William Hogarth.

Do not panic if you lose track of the "plot" in my discussion of *Sunderland*, which might be described as a hypertext in printed form. It progresses through associational or intersectional logic, making unexpected connections to details mentioned many pages before. Yet, Talbot insists, "*Alice* IS pure comics. . . . An interlinked website wouldn't work as a story. If there's anything at all that's clever about this book it's the structure hidden beneath the surface. It shouldn't be obvious to the reader but the order that the information is presented in is crucially important. It holds everything together. Clicking on things at random wouldn't produce a cohesive narrative, just a series of uncoordinated pieces. For anyone who has an attention span longer than that of a gnat, it would be very unsatisfactory" (Gravett 2008, n.p.).

Rather than exploring the hypertext analogy, this chapter will discuss *Sunderland* as a print equivalent of a cabinet of curiosities—a curatorial project that follows its own associative logic—accumulating and displaying a wide array of objects, often with the goal of creating a microcosm rather than collecting one-of-a-kind objects within a more narrowly defined genre to constitute a specific set or tell a singular story. Our earlier case studies of Seth and Kim Deitch might invite us to see a collector mentality behind Talbot's ongoing fascination and encyclopedic knowledge of the material artifacts of an earlier historical era. Across an afternoon-long interview, Bryan and Mary Talbot consistently denied that their relationship to material culture might be understood in terms of collecting: Bryan shared, "I don't really collect things. I accumulate things"; later, he told me, "I like bits and pieces and things. It's not a cataloged collection as such. Even many of the comics I have are not complete. I know collectors who actively go out and search out, you have to have every single one of everything. I am not like that. I pick up stuff and I hold onto it if I like it" (personal interview, June 2013).

The distinction Talbot makes between "collecting" and "accumulating" parallels important debates within the literature on material culture. In what remains perhaps the most widely cited definition, Russell Belk and his collaborators (Belk et al. 1990) tell us: "We take collecting to be the selective, active, and longitudinal acquisition, possession, and disposition of an interrelated set of differentiated objects (material things, ideas, beings, or experiences) that contribute to and derive extraordinary meaning from the entity (the collection) that this set is perceived to constitute" (8). Collectors actively search, they want to possess "every single one," and they "catalog" what they collect. Accumulators "pick up stuff" and hold onto what they like. Accumulators take pleasures in the parts, collectors in assembling the whole. Following Belk et al., Susan M. Pearce (1994) writes, "One of the distinctions between possessing and collecting is that the later implies order, system, perhaps completion" (158). Talbot made a similar distinction when he described an adolescent experiment with stamp collecting that lasted less than six months: "As soon as I realized I was never going to get everything, what's the point" (personal interview, June 2013). To some degree, the distinction is one of intentionality, what the collector is trying to achieve or even the perception that acquiring things constitutes an achievement. For Belk, Pearce, and many others, collecting is connected with classification—however interesting or valuable they may be in their own right, the collected objects are part of a larger set: "The collection as an entity is greater than the sum of its parts. . . . Accumulation is usually seen as the simple magpie act, the heaping-up of material without any kind of internal classification" (Pearce 1992, 158). The collector makes conscious choices that determine what she does and does not collect. As Susan Stewart ([1984] 1993) explains, "To play with series is to play with the fire of infinity. In the collection the threat of infinity is always met with the articulation of boundaries" (159).

This chapter explores what it might mean to read Talbot's *Alice in Sunderland* in terms of an aesthetics and logic of accumulation. Meaningful objects run through *Sunderland*, which explores how stories originate, circulate, and proliferate around compelling places and artifacts. Yet these points of interest are often seen as rare, distinctive, unique, and idiosyncratic, rather than as part of a larger set, and he offers multiple, often contradictory, interpretive frames for why these things matter. Talbot plays with "the fire of infinity," allowing many different possibilities to emerge and offering little meaningful closure. He calls *Sunderland* a "portmanteau comic," a phrase suggesting a trunk to be unpacked, as well as the potential of creating new meanings through association, both useful descriptions of his book's construction.

I want to read this particular assemblage in relation to the much larger history of cabinets of curiosities or wonder cabinets (using the two phrases interchangeably) for what they might tell us about how people have historically made meaning through the process of accumulation and found beauty within what one study describes as "the endless etcetera" (Daston and Park 2001, 266). Wonder cabinets were encyclopedic assemblages of fascinating materials, intended as microcosms of a larger world, that became popular during the early modern period. A cabinet, today, would refer to a piece of furniture, but at the time, these accumulations of fascinating stuff might fill an entire room. This chapter is about the "wonders" and "curiosities" that provide the raw materials from which Talbot builds *Sunderland*, or to draw upon a different set of vocabularies, the "diversions and digressions" of the British music hall tradition, which constitutes the book's other core conceptual frame. This idea of constructing a narrative from "bits and pieces and things" also informs Talbot's use of collage, a popular practice of the Victorian and Edwardian eras, a more avant-garde one today. The wonder cabinet, the variety show, and the collage each represent ways of displaying and interpreting heterogeneous materials, embracing the impulse to accumulate beautiful and curious things.

Sunderland as Cabinet of Curiosities

Bryan Talbot introduces his "cabinet of curiosities" late in *Sunderland*. He is recounting the story of his working-class grandmother, who has no nostalgia for the "good old days." When Bryan was sixteen, she summoned him and passed along a cherished item—a "brass knuckle duster," which Talbot carefully placed within his cabinet alongside other treasures he and his wife have accumulated through the years (260–261). Here's how Talbot describes its contents: "This cabinet is filled with ephemera. A figurine of Marilyn Monroe . . . a bust of Wagner . . . a Laurel and Hardy condiment set . . . a souvenir of the Great Exhibition of 1851 . . . a Richard Nixon campaign badge . . . a first edition of Chairman Mao's *Little Red Book* . . . lost empires . . . faded dreams . . . brief candles . . ." (262). The bulk of the page (figure 4.1) is occupied by a single image of the cabinet and its contents. Many items are so small in the picture that one might need a magnifying glass to identify them. Yet, just as the narration directs attention to select items, Talbot offers detail shots of some of the most cherished stuff, including many objects not mentioned in the narration. Following the impulse to locate each detailed item in the cabinet itself, I find my eyes moving from the margins to the center—another variant on scannability.

Talbot ends the page by directing attention onto a particular item: "Look at this . . . a Victorian pottery bust of Ally Sloper," and spends the next page explaining this character's place in the history of British comics—influenced by Charles Dickens's Mr. Micawber, offering a prototype for W. C. Fields and Andy Capp. We are drawn to the cabinet through personal history, we are lead out via a particular strand of popular culture, but, by implication, every object here has a story, perhaps multiple ones, some personal memories, some shared cultural narratives. The tension between the cabinet's accumulated display and the focus on individual contents mirrors the ways owners of such cabinets in earlier times presented them to their guests. Patrick Mauriès (2002) writes: "This was a private space, requiring a formal introduction in the ritual form of a visit . . . a display ceremony in which the cult of the object was celebrated, and its history, its origins, and its fabulous genealogy was unveiled to the faithful in a form of ecstatic communion" (66).

The contrast between the Talbots' cabinet of curiosities and Kim Deitch's drawings of his wife's collection of "black Halloween cats from the 1920's and 30's" suggests the difference between accumulation and collecting. Deitch specifies what Pam collects, including the ways that her category is flexible enough to incorporate some related items ("Old Felix the Cat toys" or Waldo memorabilia) but not others. We recognize at a glance what unifies the items in this collection but also can observe the diversity of objects, a play of theme and variation. The ordered shelves imply careful curation. By contrast, the Talbots' shelves are a jumble of unrelated items, each competing for attention, leaving no unifying impression beyond their plentitude. The cabinet's disorder overwhelms precisely so its curator can explicate its hidden structures and meanings. We know what Pam collects and why; the Talbots' cabinet is full of mysteries. Writing about wonder cabinets of another era, Lorraine Daston

FIGURE 4.1. (OPPOSITE) The Talbots' cabinet of curiosities houses a grab bag of popular culture artifacts. Brian Talbot, *Alice in Sunderland* (2007). © Brian Talbot. Courtesy of Brian Talbot.

This cabinet is filled with ephemera.
A figurine of Marilyn Monroe... a bust of Wagner... a Laurel and Hardy condiment set... a souvenir of the *Great Exhibition* of 1851... a Richard Nixon campaign badge... a first edition of Chairman Mao's *Little Red Book*...
...lost empires... faded dreams... brief candles...
Look at this...
...a Victorian pottery bust of *Ally Sloper*.
WILD WOODBINE
NIXON'S THE ONE!
HOWARD THE DUCK
NATIONAL BENZOLE
AMRUTANJAN

and Katharine Park (2001) ask, "What properties linked coral, automata, unicorn horns, South American featherwork, coconut shell goblets, fossils, antique coins, turned ivory, monsters animal and human, Turkish weaponry, and polyhedral crystals?" (266). One might similarly question what unifying logic links the objects within the Talbots' assemblage. The objects are not actually random—each has been carefully chosen, albeit often for unrelated reasons; each attracted the eye of the cabinet's owner and was placed on display so that it could boggle future guests: "The wonder they aimed at by the profusion of these heterogeneous particulars was neither contemplative nor inquiring, but rather dumbstruck" (273).

One might also productively compare Talbot's representation of his cabinet with an earlier depiction of a wonder cabinet—a painting by the Hamburg-based artist Georg Hainz created around 1666–1672, which Mauriès used on the cover of his book (figure 4.2). This particular cabinet was a product of the artist's imagination, but it samples the kinds of rare and precious materials commonly displayed—exotic shells, ivory, and precious jewels, some in their natural state, some hand worked by craftspeople; religious icons and relics; memento mori; clocks and other engineering accomplishments. Such curiosities often contained power—whether magical power (ascribed to them by earlier peoples), political power (as many of these items were part of the patronage passed down between generations), or economic power (the conspicuous consumption of expensive and exotic materials). By contrast, Talbot fills his cabinet with oddities that were originally mass produced and mass distributed, the accomplishments of the entertainment and advertising industries, made of cheap plastic and other industrial-age materials, holding sentimental value but not constituting great economic investments.

The historic wonders and curiosities often depended upon occult knowledge—either literally (in the case of "unicorn horns" or "dragon eggs" once believed to have had fantastical origins) or figuratively (in the case of objects that trace a network of hidden connections). Today's wonders often gain their "magic" from their association with popular media narratives and their "aura" from their age. Either way, these objects represent a point of entry—a rabbit hole, as it were—into a secret history where things and stories are complexly intertwined. Mauriès (2002) explains:

FIGURE 4.2. The traditional cabinet of curiosities assembled wonders from around the globe. George Haintz, painting of imaginary cabinet of curiosities (ca. 1666–1672). Courtesy of Art Resource.

"Through the revelation of hidden connections invisible to the uninitiated, and through the discovery of an essential affinity between objects far removed from each other in geographical origin and in nature, collectors offered their visitors a glimpse of the secret that lay at the heart of all things: that reality is all one and that within it everything has its allotted place" (34).

This focus on "hidden connections invisible to the uninitiated" and the discovery of "affinity" between objects of diverse origins aptly describe *Alice in Sunderland.* As our guide proclaims: "Our stories will revolve around our location. Our setting shall generate tonight's entertainment. In words and pictures, the alchemy of the comic medium shall conjure a vision of Sunderland in the crucible of your imagination. Over the millennia stories have revealed the magic in the places where they take place" (9). Talbot depicts Sunderland as the crossroads through which key figures of Great Britain's political, religious, and literary history passed. Consider, for example, one passage that manages to link multiple cultural figures through a single theatrical production: "In 1852, Tenniel appears in a charity performance of Edward Bulwer-Lytton's *Not So Bad as We Seem* . . . by a cast of distinguished amateurs at the Lyceum in Sunderland, a cast headed by Charles Dickens and Wilkie Collins. The backdrop is painted by Mackem Clarkson Stanfield, close friend of Dickens and painter of Jack Crawford nailing the colours on the mast at Camperdown. Dickens dedicates *Little Dorrit* to him. The backdrop of another piece is based on the print *The Distress'd Poet* by William Hogarth" (117).

At another place, Talbot catalogs the features of St. Andrew's Church, which he characterizes as the "cathedral of the Arts and Crafts Movement," encapsulating an entire artistic scene through the beautiful objects it left behind: a William Morris carpet, a Edward Burne-Jones tapestry, a MacDonald Gill wall painting, and Edward Schroeder Prior's architecture. For all of these intersections, the focus here is hyperlocal: Talbot is fascinated by the remarkable events and incredible accomplishments that occurred within a handful of miles of his own home on Bede Terrace. Talbot shifts between different levels of historical analysis—family, local, national, global, cosmic—sometimes even on the same page, yet Sunderland is where his heart lies, and one way or another, all of these stories are anchored to this particular geographic location.

Daston and Park (2001) tell us that "wonders" in earlier times were also "textual objects—things to think about and think with," and, moreover, things to write about, draw, paint, or otherwise represent to the world. Texts stand in for the host playing show and tell, "creating the background against which objects were coveted or appraised" (68). Shirley Teresa Wajda (2003) suggests that early picture books were often also described as cabinets, such as *The Cabinet: Containing an elegant collection of entertaining stories for amusement for boys and girls* (1818). Such books introduced children to "a world of things" via texts that "simultaneously fragmented, ordered, and miniaturized the world and privileged the sense of sight" (48). Such books encouraged children to explore, becoming collectors of interesting specimen, in pursuit of moral and intellectual enlightenment. *Alice in Sunderland* operates in a similar tradition, albeit for an adult reader. Children's picture books have much in common with graphic novels in their mix of words and images, even if they draw upon different visual conventions, have different cultural statuses, are produced on different grades of paper, and are circulated through different channels.

Moving forward, I want to focus not on the Talbots' actual cabinet of curiosities or its direct representation but the way that this logic of accumulation models Bryan Talbot's textual practices—Talbot uses *Sunderland* to assemble and interpret objects scattered about the surrounding countryside and even depicts objects that no longer exist or may never have actually existed outside the imagination of earlier residents. For Talbot, textual practices are themselves often material practices, as illustrated by his focus on the "lavishly illuminated Wearmouth Bibles" (78), which he tells us weighed seventy-five pounds apiece and used vellum made from the skin of fifteen hundred calves. Produced in the early Middle Ages, many such works were lost or destroyed, though one of them, missing for eleven centuries, was rediscovered in Florence in the early twentieth century (81). Or consider the fate of Jack Crawford, whose adventures produced wealth for local potters as the plucky hero was depicted on mugs, pitchers, and plates (38). Crawford's "pickled heart" may or may not have been preserved as a sacred relic (58). While some such stories originate in oral culture, they are handed down as material artifacts.

"Wonders" can be understood in those terms: objects that help us reconstruct stories that matter to us individually or collectively. Some of the depicted "wonders" have natural origins, including the fossilized trilobites Talbot locates in the People's Park (33), the toad whose bulging head full of diamonds was discovered by an eighteenth-century laborer (37), the "calcareous tufa dome, formed by water filtering through the limestone" that was unearthed several decades ago when "some old fisherman's cottages were demolished" (104), or the taxidermy walrus (42) brought back by Captain Joseph Wiggins in Carroll's times. Some "curiosities" reflect earlier moments in the region's social and cultural history—carved Celtic dragons still visible on the ruins of a tower built and destroyed in the era of Alfred the Great (82); a monster-headed brass door knocker on the outer doors of a great cathedral pierced by the arrow of a local sheriff trying to bring down an outlaw seeking sanctuary (284); the mummified remains of a deformed child believed to be buried underneath the floorboards of a local pub (222); a "genuine press gang cosh" once used to shanghai seamen (221); or an unexploded bomb left over from the blitz and discovered "just under five hundred meters from where I'm writing these words" (51). Talbot often inventories assemblages of seemingly random objects, such as "a child's collection of treasures discovered beneath the floorboards of the nursery [in the rectory across the road from a Croft church where Lewis Carroll's father once preached], including a thimble, a small white glove, a child's left shoe and a scrap of writing in Carroll's hand" (45), his description of the Venerable Bede's last possessions, "a few peppercorns, linen napkins and some incense" (77), or the relics once housed in the Cathedral of Durham in the fourteenth century, "bones of the Innocents slain by Herod, milk of the Virgin Mary, and three griffins' eggs" (285). Wonders, as they say, never cease, at least if you live in or near Sunderland.

Mieke Bal (1994) has argued for a fundamental connection between collecting and storytelling: "[C]ollecting is an essential human feature that originates in the need to tell stories, but for which there are neither words nor other conventional narrative modes. Hence, collecting is a story and everyone needs to tell it" (103). The objects of a collection, Bal suggests, might be described as "telling objects," and certainly the wonders we have been discussing here are filled with narrative possibilities. So far, so good, as far as Bal is concerned. But Bal stresses that the act of collecting involves "cutting objects off from their context" (105), transforming them "from thing to sign" (111). To some degree, this focus on decontextualizing the object would hold true for wonder cabinets—their exhibits were accumulated from all parts and made to stand in for worlds beyond the reach of the people who owned them. It may also be partially true for the objects in the Talbots' contemporary cabinet, which are shelved and locked away, where they may gather dust. But Bryan Talbot's *Sunderland* re-locates its meaningful objects, explaining where they've come from and where they've been, returning them to their time and place.

Talbot links Sunderland to everything from Chaucer to *Doctor Who* and Harry Potter, but, most especially, he makes the case that *Alice in Wonderland* emerged from stories Carroll heard there (such as the tale of the Lambton Worm, which may have inspired "Jabberwocky") and places he walked past every day (Lizard Lane). Talbot cites Michael Bute's local history, *A Town like Alice's* (1997), as inspiring him to dig deeper into Carroll's Sunderland experiences. Both Bute and Talbot debunk the popular idea that *Wonderland* emerged spontaneously as Carroll sought to entertain Alice Liddell and her sisters while punting near Oxford. Talbot (figure 4.3) summarizes his theory of Carroll's authorship:

> Carroll describes his methods of developing stories; he jots down ideas, scenes, fragments of dialogue as they occur to him over time—a laborious process that takes years. Therefore much of *Wonderland* includes scenes he's evolved on other occasions. . . . The story he unfolds on this boat trip is full of references to recent incidents that are personal and amusing to the girls at the time. These appear in the original *Alice's Adventures Under Ground* manuscript but are all expunged or changed for the published *Alice's Adventures in Wonderland* which doubles the page count, using material from earlier tales, and introduces some famous scenes such as the Mad Tea Party. It has become a different story. (270)

In this account, Alice's adventures did not spring fully formed but rather accumulated over time. Bute quotes Carroll saying as much: "As the years went on, I jotted down, at odd moments, all sorts of odd ideas, and fragments of dialogue, that occurred to me—who knows how—with a transitory suddenness that left me with no choice but either to record them then and there, or to abandon them to oblivion, and I think it must have been ten years, or more, before I succeeded in classifying these odds and ends sufficiently to see what sort of story they indicated" (5). And Carroll cannot be understood as *Wonderland*'s sole author. Talbot notes that *Alice*, not unlike a comic, required the close collaboration between Carroll and his illustrator, John Tenniel: "His words and John Tenniel's pictures unite in a single vision, a continually morphing world populated by gloriously insane characters, most of whom are now cultural icons" (27). The artist fleshed out the author's sparse descriptions, shaping how readers recall the iconic characters (Talbot's example is the Mad Hatter).

Thinking about Talbot and, by extension, Carroll, through the lens of the wonder cabinet invites us to reconsider why Carroll refers to the place Alice finds herself when she tumbles down the rabbit hole, swims across a sea of tears, or passes through the looking glass as a "wonderland." I suppose I always thought "wonder" referred to the childlike awe with which Alice and the book's young readers encounter these remarkable places, but we might also think of Carroll's creatures, including a baby that turns into a pig, a griffin, a Mock Turtle, and many other mythical animals, as "wonders" as the term would have

FIGURE 4.3. Brian Talbot depicts the precariousness of the traditional account of how Lewis Carroll came to write *Alice in Wonderland*. Brian Talbot, *Alice in Sunderland* (2007). © Brian Talbot. Courtesy of Brian Talbot.

been understood in the medieval and early modern periods. Like the items in a wonder cabinet, each character—the caterpillar with his hookah, Humpty Dumpty, the Mad Hatter, the Cheshire Cat—is unique, each occupying its own time and space. Curiouser and curiouser, indeed! Collectively, these characters and events reflect Mauriès's description of the wonder cabinet's contents as "liminal objects that lay on the margins of charted territory, brought back from world's unknown, defying any accepted system of classification . . . and associated with the discovery of 'new worlds'" (12). *Through the Looking-Glass* follows a gamelike logic, tracing moves on a chessboard, but *Wonderland* follows an associative logic assembled from "odds and ends" from hither and there, material accumulated over time but only retrospectively placed in a narrative frame. And the same may be said for *Alice in Sunderland*, whose meandering development masks an underlying structure with Talbot casting himself as the guide who unlocks Sunderland's hidden treasures and secret stories.

Sunderland as Music Hall Performance

From its opening pages, Bryan Talbot also frames *Alice in Sunderland* in relation to popular performance and theatricality, in particular the British music hall. The title page is constructed as a vintage playbill, promising "an entertainment including numerous interesting diversions and digressions," a show "devised and performed by Bryan Talbot, the Wigan Titwillow." The book's first twenty-nine pages take place in and around the Empire Theater, which Talbot describes as "a Palace of Varieties built when Edwardian Sunderland prosper with the fruition of the Industrial Revolution and gushes with civic pride" (11). The Empire, he also notes, was built near the site of a temple to the Norse god Thor. The centrality of this theatrical setting is suggested by *Sunderland*'s subtitle, "Or an Evening at the Empire," and he nods to the Empire in the closing pages with the suggestion that the whole experience may have simply been the stuff of dreams as Mary chastises her husband for falling asleep watching *Swan Lake* there.

Talbot's use of "diversion" reflects the word's double meaning—on the one hand, referring, according to Webster, to "an activity that diverts the mind from tedious or serious concerns; a recreation or pastime" (signaling the escapist function of popular amusements), and, on the other, "an instance of turning something aside from its course," an apt description of his meandering movement through space and time. The book's fascination with diversions expands from the Empire's professionals to the domestic amusements Carroll and his contemporaries performed for each other. At one point, Talbot writes about Carroll's childhood fantasy life: "From his father he inherits an early love of nonsense humor and spends his time devising innumerable games and stories for his siblings. . . . Carroll makes railway games in summer, intricate mazes in winter and entertains his family at night with magic tricks or plays in his puppet theatres. . . . His first writings appear in homemade family magazines, the fertile germinating ground for much of his later work" (44). By the time he met Alice and her sisters, Carroll could thus tap a repertoire of amusements, many of which influenced *Wonderland* and *Through the Looking-Glass*.

The music hall tradition also motivates *Sunderland*'s aesthetic of accumulation and association. People often describe variety shows as offering "something for everyone," but they might be better described as appealing to diverse tastes and interests, since the most loyal patrons enjoyed the constant shifting between different amusements rather than developing strong preferences for specific genres. The British music hall, much like the circus or American vaudeville, constructed a performance from individual acts, each foregrounding the virtuosity of "one of a kind" performers. The stage might be occupied by song and dance one moment, baggy-pants comedy the next, followed by a Shakespearian soliloquy. Talbot inventories the many unique personalities who appeared at the Empire, including Harry Houdini, Stan Laurel, Henry Irving, Charlie Chaplin, Harry Lauder, Chico Marx, W. C. Fields, Benny Hill, and Marlene Dietrich. But he pays particular attention to George Formby, the working-class British lad from the North, who became an international stage and screen success by playing his ukulele and singing "silly" songs with "mild sexual innuendo" (15).

Talbot's fascination with the "variety" tradition gives him license to deploy a broad range of techniques, including pastiches of earlier comic book styles and genres. As he explains:

> Pretty early on I decided to vary the style of comic storytelling to suit each story—something inspired by the Sunderland Empire being a "palace of varieties" and that the book had to be somehow a "variety performance"—but my approach as to which style I chose was purely intuitive—in that each story

dictated its own style so immediately that there was no question of me deciding between different options. The ghost story of THE CAULD LAD OF HYLTON was obviously meant for a 50s horror comic treatment [figure 4.4]. The story of Sunderland hero Jack Crawford—a national hero in the 18th century and the person who gave the phrase "to nail your colours to the mast" to the language by his actions was—what else?—to be done in a BOYS' OWN ADVENTURE style [figure 4.5]. THE LEGEND OF THE LAMBTON WORM, the longest self-contained story in the book—demanded an Arts and Crafts style, probably because the first time I came across it, decades before, was in a 1900s illustrated fairy tale book [figure 4.6]. Yes, I know that there were never any Arts and Crafts comics but I tried to write and draw it as if there were. (Holland, n.d.)

Each segment—a few pages each—becomes a set piece. Just as Talbot draws analogies between earlier art forms—from stained-glass windows, tapestries, and illuminated manuscripts to Carroll's collaboration with his illustrator—*Sunderland* also uses pastiche to suggest diverse comics' genres and styles.

FIGURES 4.4–4.6 (CLOCKWISE FROM LEFT). The Cauld Lad of Hylton rendered in the style of a 1950s horror comic. Jack Crawford's story depicted as a *Boy's Own* adventure story. Talbot imagines what an Arts and Crafts approach to comics might look like as he tells the story of the Lambton Worm. Brian Talbot, *Alice in Sunderland* (2007). © Brian Talbot. Courtesy of Brian Talbot.

Much as Talbot shows his virtuosity at mastering varied styles of comic art, the music hall performer's act often incorporated diverse performance skills. Much as variety performers shift identities across the performance, Talbot adopts three distinct personas—the Performer, who embodies the high-culture tradition; the Plebeian, who brings an earthier perspective; and the Pilgrim, who guides our tour of the surrounding countryside. The Plebeian constantly disrupts the show, taking a cellphone call, burping, snoring, heckling—"Oi! Dogbreath!" (14)—stepping out to the lobby for "a pint of bitter and a packet of cashew nuts" (130), and otherwise refusing to take anything at face value. The Plebeian is joined in these various disruptions by the ghost of Sid James, a former music hall performer and prominent cast member in the popular *Carry On* films. James passed away on the Empire stage, a fact that produced howls of laughter at the time because of Sunderland's reputation as a tough house where so many performers had "died" before.

Whereas middle class reformers succeeded in turning American vaudeville into "family entertainment," the British music hall retained a strong association with the working class. In *A National Joke: Popular Comedy and English Cultural Identities* (2007), Andy Medhurst describes its characteristic ideological stance: "Music Hall was often vibrantly vulgar, testing the limits of censorship and questioning the stranglehold of 'decency,' so often a code for attempts to foist the constrictions of middle-class propriety onto working-class lives; and music hall was also committed to celebrating the joys of leisure in those brief temporal spaces when work took a back seat to pleasure" (66). In his 1941 essay "The Art of Donald McGill," George Orwell found similar attitudes in the naughty cartoons reproduced on seaside postcards, a reference that bridges the music hall and comics:

> They stand for the worm's-eye view of life, for the music-hall world where marriage is a dirty joke or a comic disaster, where the rent is always behind and the clothes are always up the spout, where the lawyer is always a crook and the Scotsman always a miser, where the newly-weds make fools of themselves on the hideous beds of seaside lodging-houses and the drunken, red-nosed husbands roll home at four in the morning to meet the linen nightgowned wives who wait for them behind the front door, poker in hand. . . . Like the music halls, they are a sort of saturnalia, a harmless rebellion against virtue. (n.p.)

Talbot uses the Plebeian and the ghost of Sid James to enact the music hall's challenge to middle-class dignity and authority, encouraging skepticism about his account. Periodically, the two working-class characters challenge assertions with billingsgate insults and slang—"a load of cobblers" (131), "Codswallop" (131), "That's a porky if ever I 'eard one" (252), "a complete load of fetid dingo's kidneys" (272). My reference here to "billingsgate" alludes to Mikhail Bakhtin's writings about the medieval carnival and its influence on the work of Rabelais, whose storytelling was said to have absorbed the grotesque language of the marketplace. Bakhtin (1984), like Medhurst, celebrates the "vulgar" dimensions of this comic tradition: "men's speech is flooded with genitals, bellies, defecations, urine, disease, noses, mouths, and dismembered parts" (319). One might map the space between the sacred and the profane in the gap between Jack Crawford's pickled heart and the ghost of Sid James's "fetid dingo's kidneys." The two clowns consistently challenge intellectual pretensions—"'E's just showing off! Bloody poser!" (80)—and they apply the same irreverence to the other historical figures, with Sid James summing up the proliferation of Alice narratives with his characteristic leer, "This Alice puts herself about a bit, don't she?" (132).

The Performer, with typical dramatic flair, tells the spectators that one of the stories we will be told is "a total falsehood . . . a complete whopper" (25). Sealing the answer in an envelope, he challenges his audience to guess which one: "some of the stories are folklore—but are they authentic or invented?" (25). Ultimately, the challenge turns out to be a device to keep both Talbot and his readers on their toes. More than that, the device signals the prospect of multiple and contradictory versions of these many stories as well as the blurry lines between folklore and history. But, in the end, the envelope is empty. Astonishing though some of his associations may be, every event has some grounding in the social and cultural history of this particular region.

At one point, Talbot depicts himself as questioning everything he has written: "I don't live in Sunderland! Sunderland doesn't exist. I've made it all up!" (186). As an American reader, Sunderland was so far off my mental map that I had no clue whether it was a real place. I had been taking Talbot's details about local history and geography at face value. Ultimately, my fascination with this work took me to Sunderland, where, in the company of Billy Proctor, then a PhD candidate, we visited many of the depicted locations, using Talbot's graphic novel as a guidebook. Proctor, who had lived in Sunderland for many years, said the book taught him to see the city through new eyes and encouraged him to discover treasures on his own doorstep.

Sunderland had once been the "largest shipbuilding town in the world" and at the heart of Britain's coal mining industry, but the docks had been shut in the late 1980s and the last mine closed in the early 1990s, leaving Sunderland struggling with a dual economic and identity crisis. *Sunderland* references the city's ongoing revitalization and, in particular, its vibrant art scene; Talbot argues that Sunderland has been unjustly marginalized in the national consciousness. A sequence depicting his neighbors gathering together for a bonfire, a practice he links back to ancient fertility rites, allows Talbot to celebrate contemporary Britain's diversity: "The street's native Mackems who, as we've seen, already have a rich genetic history, have fellow residents from all over the world—from Mexico, Vietnam, Zimbabwe, Iran, India, Israel, China, Italy—and even Wigan" (159). In the same passage, he shares how his neighborhood, once in decline, has managed to "claw its way back up" into a hub that can sustain a community of residents from all walks of life. Later on, Talbot challenges the politics of racial and cultural purity deployed as a weapon by the political Right:

> As we've seen tonight, we are all descendants of immigrants: of the dark-skinned Picts and Indo-European Celts, of the multi-ethnic Roman soldiers and the merchants from Africa and the Middle East and the Gauls from France who come with them and settle here, of the mixed race English, Vikings, Danes and Normans, of the Irish and European workers, Belgians, Lithuanians and Jewish Poles, who flood here in the 19th century to power the Industrial Revolution. Their descendants are 100% Mackem. Historically every group of immigrants to settle here has enriched the country culturally and economically. (297)

Here Talbot pushes against the myth of Britain as a "tight little island" holding its own against the world. British culture as a whole, and many of its specific stories and cultural practices, were accrued over time at what Mary Louise Pratt (1991) might describe as "contact zones," contested spaces where cultures encounter each other on an unequal basis and often are altered in the process. *Sunderland* seems to embody many traits that Pratt has identified as "the literate arts of the contact zone," among them, autoethnography, critique, mediation, parody, imaginary dialogue, and vernacular expression (4). And Talbot is drawn toward other hybrid texts, for example writing about the medieval illuminated manuscript as "a multicultural mix of native art combined with influences from the Early Egyptian Christian church, Byzantine and Islamic calligraphy," which was born in the Northlands but soon spread across much of Europe (75). Sunderland functions as both a microcosm (sampling many moments from British history) and a palimpsest (representing the building up of a national identity as diverse cultures left their mark).

Much as he celebrates Britain's mongrel roots, Talbot celebrates popular culture as worthy of remembering alongside the city's high art and literary accomplishments. Not unlike the way the variety show tradition might incorporate opera or elocution and its performers might "send up" more respectable texts, Talbot often pits the high and the low against each other—as in sequences where Henry V's "Once More unto the Breach" speech is rendered in the broad physical humor of a *Mad* parody (18) or where James catalogs various Shakespearian characters he played in his *Carry On* vehicles (132). Throughout, Talbot cites moments when cultural materials travel across such divides, breaking down hierarchies—with *Alice in Wonderland*'s history of performance, including in porn movies, seen as a core example of such fluidity. Talbot himself sounds like the ghost of Sid James when he questions the ways certain educated elites have dismissed his own medium: "Some people believe that comics are somehow sub-literate precisely because they do employ pictures though they don't seem to apply this logic to painting, sculpture, movies, theater, opera or ballet, all of which use no printed words. Come to think of it, ballet has a lot in common with superhero comics, the story being merely an excuse, a framework to show off the artist's skill with the form" (194). *Sunderland* features extended expositions on the theory and craft of making comics as explored in relation to the Bayeux Tapestry and William Hogarth's prints. *Sunderland* is a spectacular example of what can be done when artists ignore arbitrary constraints.

Sunderland as Collage

Talbot's decision to use photocollage as *Sunderland*'s primary visual technique seems ideal given his interest in blurring the boundaries between high and low culture and his fascination with the persistence of residual elements from Victorian and Edwardian culture. In the twentieth and twenty-first centuries, collage has been associated with modernist movements—from Dada, surrealism, and futurism to pop art and contemporary remix. Yet in the nineteenth century, photocollage was a popular practice, more associated with feminine craft than with the art world.* In her book *Playing with Pictures: The Art of Victorian Photocollage*, Elizabeth Siegel studied photo albums created by women from the upper and middle classes, identifying diverse strategies for manipulating photographic images: "Playful, witty and at times subversive, the compositions flout both the conventions of nineteenth century photography and the restrictions of middle- and upper-class Victorian society. Producers of photocollage pasted cut photographs of human heads atop painted animal bodies, placed real people in imaginary landscapes, and morphed faces into common household objects and fashionable accessories with a casual irreverence. Wielding scissors, paste pot and paintbrush—alongside no small amount of humor—aristocratic album makers changed the original meanings of the pictures with which they played" (13). How remarkable that such aggressive remix practices emerged so early in the history of photography: any anxiety about playing with likenesses or preserving the original images was rejected in favor of the creative freedom these women granted themselves to transform personal photographs and cartes de visite for their own expression. In *Dreaming in Pictures* (2002), an extensive study of Carroll's own photographic practices, Douglas L. Nickel notes that Victorians did not understand photography as an absolute reproduction of reality (recognizing that important parts of reality, especially the spiritual, cannot be easily reproduced through such a mechanical process). Instead, they saw photography as a mixture of objective and subjective elements, requiring the active participation of the viewer to fully process. Much as a family member might bring personal memories to domestic images, the larger public might bring knowledge of the Bible or other literary texts to photographs that staged imaginary or symbolic scenes. And we might extend this focus on extratextual knowledge and "imaginative projection" (41) to think about how Victorians might have processed the assemblages of images in these collages.

One section of Siegel's book, "Curiouser and Curiouser," includes images where photographic characters confront outsized plants and animals, sit atop

*Talbot stresses another popular culture tradition of collage as inspiring his approach—Jack Kirby's deployment of the technique in his 1960s comics, especially Fantastic Four (Brower 2012). Kirby had been inspired by the ways Richard Hamilton had deployed elements of his comics and he repaid the compliment by bringing avant-garde practices into the commercial mainstream of American comics. Kirby most often used collage to represent the alternative and cosmic realities his superhero characters encountered. Kirby inspired subsequent artists, including Bill Sienkiewicz, David Mack, and Dave McKean, along with Talbot, to use collage in their comics (Jenkins 2017).

giant mushrooms, are enmeshed in bird's nests, saddle frogs, or are otherwise situated in fairy-tale settings. Replacing the heads on face cards with family members or depicting various personages playing croquet were also familiar genres. And *Playing with Pictures* contains one image (figure 4.7) where pictures of household children were pasted into Tenniel's illustrations, part of a wider pattern of visual and textual appropriations of *Alice in Wonderland* (Sigler 1997).

Carroll, an accomplished amateur photographer, deployed similar manipulation practices in his works (in particular, *Evelyn Hatch*, 1879). Carroll cut the figure of a naked child from her original surrounding, painted over the image and placed her against a painted backdrop, all photocollage practices that Victorian women also deployed (figure 4.8). Here, again, we can think about Nickel's observation that Victorians accepted photographic reproduction as incomplete, embracing hybrid production practices with the understanding that photographs might be read figuratively or symbolically.

The forms of intertextual knowledge that allowed Victorians to translate such composite images into a meaningful

FIGURE 4.7 (TOP). Victorian-era collage incorporates family members into Tenniel's iconic illustrations for *Alice in Wonderland*. Courtesy of George Eastman Museum.

FIGURE 4.8 (RIGHT). Lewis Carroll incorporated similar collage and painting techniques in his own photographic practice. Lewis Carroll, *Evelyn Hatch* (1879).

whole were shared widely among the educated classes of the period, who had frequent experiences of looking through images together. If the cabinet of curiosities was often the site of social interactions as their mostly male owners provided the backstory for the "wonders," these photo albums were often the focus of social interaction within a mostly feminine sphere. Looking through photo albums and relishing such constructed images constituted yet another form of play in a culture where amateur theatrics and domestic performances were still widely practiced—an analogy already suggested by the references to playing cards and other parlor entertainments within the collages themselves.

In an essay about the German collage artist Kurt Schwitters, Roger Cardinal (1994) draws an explicit parallel between collages and wonder cabinets: "As if to caricature the posturings of the rich connoisseur, the virtue of whose cabinet of curiosities is that it comprises exquisite artificialia and naturalia transported with great difficulty across vast distances, [Schwitters] . . . limits himself to artificialia that anyone can pick up for nothing, located as they are in the most banal and close-by of sites" (73). Though his collages are abstract and ultimately reject the storytelling impulse altogether, Schwitters might have found a kindred spirit in Talbot, given their shared interest in locating hidden treasures in "the most banal and close-by of sites." Talbot does not have to leave his own house to locate Sunderland's historical wonders. When he traces the history of the house's original owner, he finds that the man knew people with strong connections to both Carroll and Tenniel. A picture hanging in his dining room inspires his reflections on Hogarth's contributions to the graphic arts.

Comics critic Paul Gravett (2008) has stressed the appropriateness of Talbot's formal practices:

> The comics medium seems ideally suited to this project of presenting both the passage and simultaneity of time. Unlike the flickerings of film, comics can fix panel after panel of different moments to be read, re-read and related to each other. Apply this to a whole book, and you have a way to convey these various interrelated histories as they ebb and flow through time. On many pages, Talbot also experiments with a different, less rigid approach to the usual grids of panels. Building on traditional collage, he takes full advantage of the hi-tech options of digital cameras and Photoshop software to merge images, objects, maps, into a kaleidoscopic stream, giving his photographs a watercoloured softness. (n.p.)

Figure 4.9 demonstrates how medium meets message: across a two-page spread, the artist combines both cartoonish and realistic comics images, a pen and ink sketch, color photographs, a Roman map, a gold coin, and a mosaic. One is reminded of Mauriès's (2002) description of the cabinet of curiosities as "a miniature universe of textures, colours, materials and a multiplicity of forms" (12). The eclectic mix of material conveys the chaotic nature of British culture at a time when the land, not yet a nation, was occupied by "a disjointed gamut of independent Celtic tribes, most of whose chieftains quickly and shrewdly make alliances with the Romans" (71). This two-page spread uses some familiar comics conventions—in particular, panel frames of various thickness—even if the pages don't observe a classic grid. But there are no gutters in *Sunderland*, as Talbot blurs the boundaries between images. Figure 4.10 illustrates a more cluttered and chaotic use of collage practices, as he shows how the story of the Lambton Worm progressed from early pulp novels to contemporary genre fiction. Even within the panels in figure 4.9, the map bleeds into the mosaic, while the cartoon of the Roman armies is layered on top.

FIGURE 4.9. Digital tools enable Brian Talbot to incorporate diverse materials into his collages. Brian Talbot, *Alice in Sunderland* (2007). © Brian Talbot. Courtesy of Brian Talbot.

FIGURE 4.10. The accumulation and assemblage of collage are appropriate for *Sunderland*'s multilayered discourse. Brian Talbot, *Alice in Sunderland* (2007). © Brian Talbot. Courtesy of Brian Talbot.

FIGURE 4.11. Talbot creates a sense of vertigo as his protagonist falls down the rabbit hole, surrounded by the texts upon which his argument rests. Brian Talbot, *Alice in Sunderland* (2007). © Brian Talbot. Courtesy of Brian Talbot.

Mauriès notes a tension in cabinets of curiosities between plentitude ("every corner and niche filled to overflowing" [66]) and order ("a multiplicity of frames, niches, boxes, drawers, and cases" imposing a "system" upon the "chaos of the world" [12]). Comics have often been described in similar ways: decoupage, breaking down a scene into panels, can make the action much more legible by focusing attention. By contrast, Cardinal suggests collage decenters the viewer: "Some collages evince such centrifugal energy that it is impossible to gaze at them without feeling vertigo. The viewer's characteristic reflex is to abandon the search for compositional regularity and to take refuge in close scrutiny, pouring over the pictorial elements one by one, as if deciphering a text letter by letter" (83). In figure 4.11, Talbot intentionally creates such a vertiginous effect as various scholarly accounts of Carroll's life swirl around his protagonist, who is falling backward down the rabbit hole. Figure 4.3, discussed earlier in terms of its revelations about Carroll's authorship, adopts a more ordered structure, not unlike the geometric patterns deployed by some Victorian women.

Schwitters's collages use fragments of texts, often on scraps of salvaged paper, alongside other images—creating a tension between different modes of viewing: "Ordinarily, to read and to scan are separate ways of seeking meaning, for when we read, our eyes follow letters and words in linear sequence, and when we scan they dart about freely in search of pattern or gestalt. The fact that we want to do both at the same time, but cannot, may explain much of the singularity and mystery" (83). In *Sunderland*, text consistently receives priority, since there is a continuous flow of narration. Words here sometimes function as captions and sometimes as dialogue. Either way, text tells us what to pay attention to—and often why it matters—thus taming some of the more polyvocal dimensions of collage.

The collages, with their vivid colors and spectacular images, offer a field for exploration and play once the history lecture is done. Each page gathers "wonders," according to the book's aesthetic of accumulation, as Talbot assembles thousands of compelling images he wants to share. In some cases, as in figure 4.12, the accumulation is itself the message, signaling the diverse forms these retellings have taken rather than necessarily requiring each to be studied individually. Only in the book's closing pages, once Talbot has taught us how to make meaningful connections, does he provide a few collages where words do not dictate our reading practices.

FIGURE 4.12. The proliferation of images here suggests the diverse ways that *Alice in Wonderland* has circulated through the culture. Brian Talbot, *Alice in Sunderland* (2007). © Brian Talbot. Courtesy of Brian Talbot.

Final Words

I have used Talbot's claim that he is an accumulator and not a collector as a point of entry into understanding *Alice in Sunderland*, discussing the use of the cabinet of curiosities and the music hall performance as models for the work's narrative and thematic structures, and collage for its visual strategies. Each practice involves the display and elaboration of heterogeneous materials. Each plays with "the fire of infinity" and confronts the "endless etcetera," having less rigidly defined boundaries than other collecting and expressive practices. We could not reduce this book to a single argument, since it is at once an analysis of the influences that shaped Lewis Carroll's *Alice in Wonderland*; an account of the multicultural history of Sunderland—and through that history, a consideration of the ways stories accrue over time; a defense of comics; and beyond what we've discussed, an ongoing mediation about mortality and rebirth. Throughout, Talbot's prose suggests hidden connections between diverse figures, events, and locations, demonstrating that the same story might take diverse forms as interpreted by multiple artists over time.

The Talbots' wonder cabinet represents an accumulation of things—material objects drawn from the past and present of popular culture. The music hall represented an accumulation of performances. But the graphic novel, like the collage tradition upon which it depends, represents an accumulation of images—with the images standing in for the world of people and things, allowing a more fluid relationship to those "telling objects" that others might collect. In the next chapter, we will consider Emil Ferris as someone who also plays with images drawn from both popular culture and high art as she tells the story of a would-be collector who lacks the resources necessary to build a material collection and who instead draws the objects she wants to possess.

5

"Monsters" and Other "Things"

Emil Ferris's Transformative Vision

Kare (short for Karen), the young protagonist of Emil Ferris's *My Favorite Thing Is Monsters* (2017), owns few things (in terms of material possessions). Kare is being raised by a single mother in a low-rent apartment in Uptown Chicago in 1968. She lacks the resources that seem so immediately available to collectors in the works of Seth and Kim Deitch. They may grumble about how much they are paying for a new item, but ultimately they can fork over the cash. Ferris depicts Kare's sparse bedroom—a bed, some bedside tables, some lamps, a few scattered magazines, and a blob monster stuffed toy (figure 5.1). Another depiction reveals a dresser, an art print, a monster poster, a few hairbrushes, and a Dracula bank (figure 5.2). There is not much accumulation here, given her passions and interests. Ferris provides detailed depictions of other characters' stuff, often drawing stark contrasts between what some characters lack (Kare's friend Sandy celebrates her birthday in an empty closet) and what others collect (Mr. Silverberg's Egyptian replicas). Ferris details other family members' belongings—her mother's Christian icons or her brother Deeze's cluttered bedroom. So to play on the book's challenging syntax, What sort of "thing" is "monsters"?

In the introduction, I argued that stuff could refer to material objects we accumulate but also to the emotional "baggage," the meanings and memories these objects embody. The looseness of "stuff" allows the concept to assume both material and immaterial forms, sometimes in the same sentence. Consider, for example, this passage from John Powers's 2017 response to Ferris's work: "We see Karen's inner and outer world, which is just bursting with stuff—her gothic dreams, her family's story, the murder of Martin Luther King Jr., ruminations on race and class and gender, portraits of kinky sex in Weimar Germany, hand-drawn copies of classic paintings complete with art history lessons and even spectacular magazine covers for imaginary horror magazines with titles like *Ghastly*" (n.p.). I have been interested throughout with the concept of meaningful or "interpretable objects," reconstructing the frames by which comics artists invite their readers into their particular worlds and teach us how to make sense of the stuff that matters to them. In this chapter, I am interested in what happens when that interpretive frame takes on a life of its own without necessarily being embodied as material artifacts.

Of all of the writers discussed in *Comics and Stuff*, Ferris is the most interested in the immaterial nature of stuff. Monsters, she reminds us, are things most people can't see. As Kare explains, "There are lots of things we don't see everyday that are right under our noses—like germs and electricity and just maybe—monsters are right under our noses, too" (n.p.). For Kare, "monsters" are not "things," material objects, but rather "monsters" is a particular structure of feeling, a way of constructing her identity and making sense of her experiences. Monsters are at once a multiple (taking many forms, possessing many identities) and yet also a singular interest. As Ferris explained on NPR's *Fresh Air* (Gross 2017): "There are these metaphors in horror that are not metaphors at all. They're the truth. They're the truth we chose to look at through horror. I think Karen is seeing that. . . . Everything that is happening in her life is dovetailing with the monster magazines in an interesting way—the ways that we deal with fear, the ways that we deal with our own challenges. We externalize them through the device of horror."

And monsters are only one set of metaphors through which Ferris's characters understand the world: Mama's backwoods superstitions; her brother Deeze's overactive eroticism; the fashion sense of Kare's schoolmate Franklin;

FIGURE 5.1. Kare's sparse bedroom reveals the character's lack of resources to follow her passion for monsters. Emil Ferris, *My Favorite Thing Is Monsters* (2017). © Emil Ferris. Courtesy of Fantagraphics.

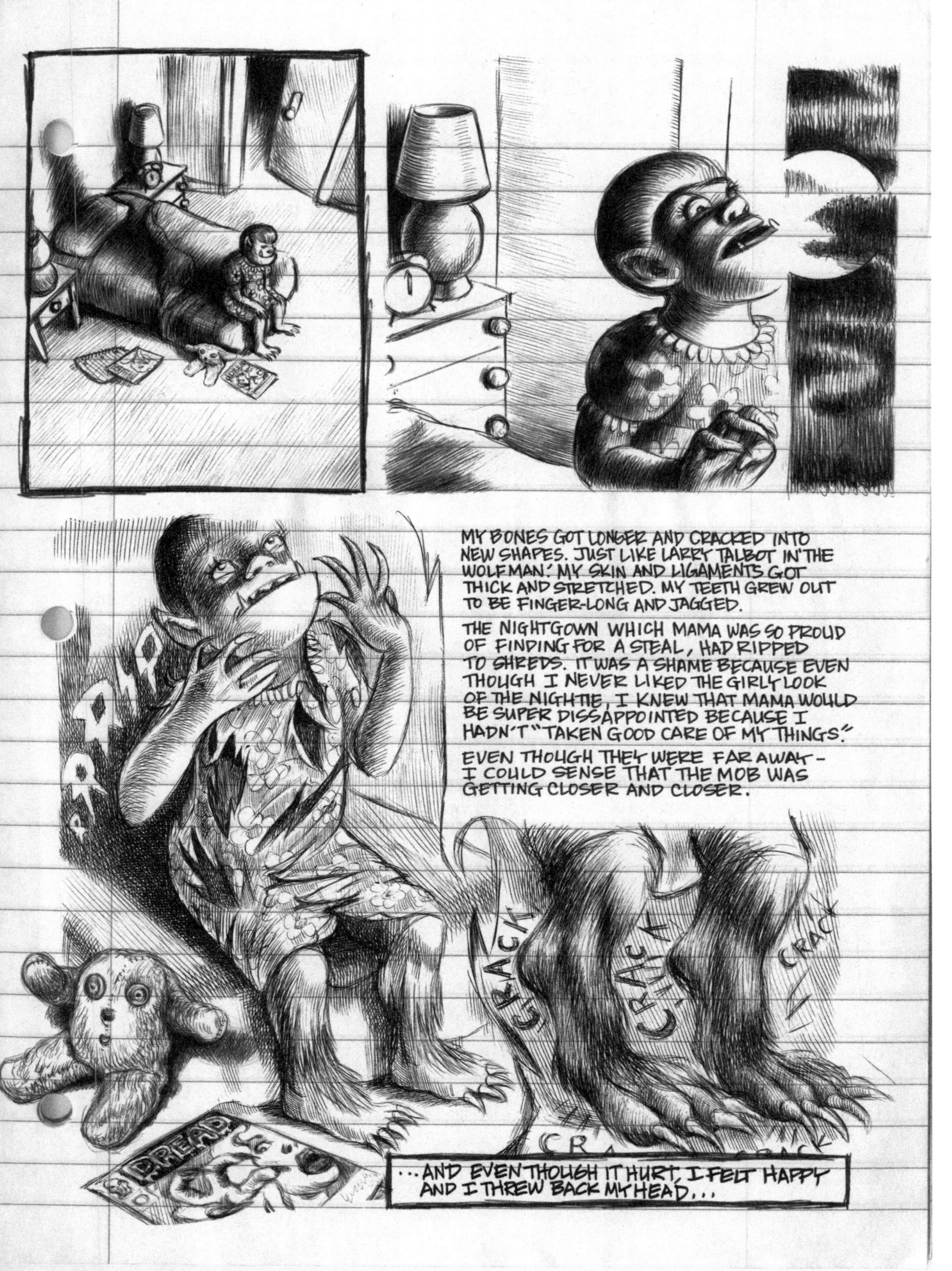
MY BONES GOT LONGER AND CRACKED INTO NEW SHAPES. JUST LIKE LARRY TALBOT IN "THE WOLFMAN." MY SKIN AND LIGAMENTS GOT THICK AND STRETCHED. MY TEETH GREW OUT TO BE FINGER-LONG AND JAGGED.
THE NIGHTGOWN WHICH MAMA WAS SO PROUD OF FINDING FOR A STEAL, HAD RIPPED TO SHREDS. IT WAS A SHAME BECAUSE EVEN THOUGH I NEVER LIKED THE GIRLY LOOK OF THE NIGHTIE, I KNEW THAT MAMA WOULD BE SUPER DISSAPPOINTED BECAUSE I HADN'T "TAKEN GOOD CARE OF MY THINGS."
EVEN THOUGH THEY WERE FAR AWAY - I COULD SENSE THAT THE MOB WAS GETTING CLOSER AND CLOSER.
CRACK
CRACK
CRACK
DREAD
...AND EVEN THOUGH IT HURT, I FELT HAPPY AND I THREW BACK MY HEAD...

her neighbor Anka's fairy tales—each represents an alternative frame for deciphering a confusing time in their lives. Kare muses, "If a person could see through a glass eye, would the world look more breakable?" (n.p.). And there are moments where Ferris explores what happens when different characters view the same phenomenon through conflicting interpretive frames: Deeze and Kare both witness clouds of smoke rising from a burning ghetto following the Martin Luther King shooting, but one sees a busty young woman and the other, Godzilla.

Across this chapter, I will explore more fully what kind of "things" monsters are or at least might be for the artist and for her protagonist. I will begin by thinking a bit more about the transformative work that went into the production of this graphic novel, understanding it in relation to Emil Ferris's physical and economic struggles to produce this work in the first place, and, not unlike my earlier discussion of Deitch and Darger, paying attention to her resources. I want to situate Kare's story in the context of the 1960s monster culture, showing the ways that, as a young girl raised in poverty, she is and is not able to participate in the material practices that took monsters off the screen and into the lives of their most passionate fans. From there, I will consider how monsters function as a resource for survival and resistance within the context of a culture often hostile to people like Kare (or Ferris)—that is, queer women of color. This discussion helps us to better understand the protagonist's close identification with monsters and how they function as an interpretive frame she maps onto the people around her. Building on this idea of monsters as an interpretive frame, I conclude with some thoughts about what I see as an antimaterialist impulse shaping this work—an interest in things that cannot be seen or bought, things that matter without being matter.

Monsters, Misfits, and Artists

Kare collects impressions, images, and memories that she records in her sketchbook, which is also the means by which Ferris tells her story. Everything in the book, thus, passes through Kare's subjectivity. We are encouraged to see the world not only through her eyes but also through her pen. The result is first-person address, not simply on the level of the text but also of illustrations.

FIGURE 5.2. The Dracula bank is one of the few signs that Kare was able to tap into the growing consumer goods surrounding the Universal monsters in the mid-1960s. Emil Ferris, *My Favorite Thing Is Monsters* (2017). © Emil Ferris. Courtesy of Fantagraphics.

HUH?!
THEY RISE!

She draws what matters to her. That Kare draws her room almost totally devoid of possessions suggests their relative unimportance to her, just as drawing herself as a junior werewolf tells us how her fantasies shape her identity. She does draw, again and again, the covers of the various monster comics whose metaphors she lives by, but she only rarely draws the magazines themselves as part of her object world and then only a few of them at a time, never accumulated into stacks as other collector-artists might depict them. The paintings she admires at the Art Institute are no less "hers" than the monster magazines she owns: they both have the same status as her "things." She also deploys monsters as visual analogies for her friends, neighbors, and family; horror provides a vocabulary through which to process her experiences. We see her as someone who does not simply embrace stories as given, but actively transforms them into her own personal mythology.

There is an interesting paradox here: the magazine covers are something Kare reproduces in the process of learning how to draw, but they are something Ferris fabricates as pastiches following broad genre conventions. These drawings simultaneously display the character's subjectivity and the artist's virtuosity. As one critic puts it, "[W]hile it's highly unlikely that a 10-year-old would have Ferris' skill with a pen, the sketchbook conceit gives the book a youthful spontaneity and emotional rawness. . . . The technical prowess on display in MFTIM is incredible, and the materials Ferris uses send a message that says it's possible to create fine art with everyday resources like ballpoint pens and notebook paper" (Sava 2017, n.p.). The book's format is designed to resemble a young girl's sketchbook. Its pages are lined and sized to resemble a sheet of notebook paper. At the edges, she has drawn punch holes and spiral binding. The images are produced with a BIC pen, or in some cases, Magic Marker. Similarly, Carol Tyler draws the images and writes the text that constitutes *Fab4 Mania* on recycled paper from her father's plumbing company, using stickers or drawings to, sometimes imperfectly, cover over the corporate logo and mark the pages as her own. Both of these women call attention to the lack of resources their characters can access, as well as their need to define these works as their own through other expressive means.

Sometimes, Kare seems to have been compelled to draw even when she could not access her sketchbook: for example, she doodles monsters on the

FIGURE 5.3. *My Favorite Thing Is Monsters* represents itself as the contents of its protagonist's sketchbook. Emil Ferris, *My Favorite Thing Is Monsters* (2017). © Emil Ferris. Courtesy of Fantagraphics.

FEBRUARY 14, 1968 TODAY OUR UPSTAIRS NEIGHBOR MRS. ANKA SILVERBERG DIED UNDER MYSTERIOUS CIRCUMSTANCES. SHE WAS SHOT IN THE HEART IN HER LIVING ROOM BUT SHE WAS FOUND LYING IN HER BED WITH THE COVERS ARRANGED NEATLY - JUST LIKE SHE'D TUCKED IN FOR THE NIGHT.
MR. SAM SILVERBERG (ANKA'S HUSBAND AND A DRUMMER) TOLD THE POLICE THAT WHEN ANKA DIED HE WAS AT A GIG IN PEORIA. MR. S. CLAIMED THAT HE'D NEVER BEFORE SEEN THE GUN USED TO KILL HIS WIFE.
SHE WAS THE MOST BEAUTIFUL WOMAN I EVER SAW...
KAREN, REMEMBER THAT YOU PROMISED TO DESTROY THE DRAWING AFTER YOU FINISH
UH...SURE THING MRS. S.
SHE WASN'T ACTUALLY BLUE... BUT SHE ALWAYS LOOKED AS IF SHE MIGHT START CRYING AT ANY MINUTE.
TUT CAT
ANKA ALWAYS WORE THESE.
IN HER LIFETIME ANKA SILVERBERG HAD DODGED MANY MANY BULLETS... SO WHY WOULD SHE CHOOSE TO END HER LIFE BY STANDING IN THE PATH OF ONE? BUT BECAUSE THEY FOUND THE FRONT AND BACK DOOR BOLTED FROM THE INSIDE THE POLICE DECLARED HER DEATH A SUICIDE... BUT I DON'T BELIEVE IT!

front and back of a failed math exam and then tapes them into her album. Another picture (figure 5.3)—a portrait of Anka and her cat, Tut—was drawn on a nicer grade of paper and paper-clipped into the sketchbook, along with a note suggesting that she had promised to destroy the drawing once it was finished. Readers may find themselves tempted to lift the attached image to see what may lie underneath, because the drawings on the original page tantalize us with only partially visible images and incomplete texts. Sometimes, the images are perfunctorily sketched and at other times carefully refined, suggesting her time constraints or her emotional state as she underwent the depicted experiences. As the girl writes, "The best way through hard times is to draw your way through" (n.p.), a philosophy that reflects the author's own struggles to produce this work.

As I am writing this, *Monsters* has been out for just a few months; a second volume, yet to be published, will complete what ultimately will be a nine-hundred-page plus opus. A full understanding of this graphic novel will only be possible when the work is completed, but the book filled such a crucial gap in my analysis here that I could not wait. I read the book for the first time and wrote the first draft of this chapter all within the same week. Ferris has received off-the-charts reviews, mostly focused on the book's visual storytelling. Alison Bechdel (*Fun Home*), for example, wrote the back-cover blurb: "Once you enter Emil Ferris's spectacular eye-popping magnum opus, there is no turning back. Her werewolf-girl protagonist's spiral-bound school notebook is a visual phantasmagoria of neural pathway-altering proportions. Through noir Chicago streetscapes, a freakish but lovingly cross-hatched cast of characters, meticulously envisioned covers of horror comics, and all-around virtuosic drawing chops, the heroine unravels a baroque mystery whose plot pulls you forward as insistently as the images demand that you linger."

Monsters was Ferris's first graphic novel and as far as the comic world was concerned, she came out of nowhere, following a remarkable struggle to complete this epic work. Disabled as a child, Ferris developed her drawing skills as a way of connecting with other children: "I had scoliosis and most of the days of my life were spent unable to do the things other children did. So I drew. That's how I dealt with not being able to run or not being able to play like most kids did. Then I realized that the kids were very interested in my sketchbooks and my notebooks. They wanted to spend time looking over them, pouring over them. Those were probably the first graphic novels I ever wrote" (Dueben 2017, n.p.). Drawing became a means of making a living and supporting her child, as she spent her early career doing illustrations for advertisements or designing toys for McDonald's and various Japanese companies. Bitten by a mosquito, she contracted West Nile fever, which had devastating consequences: "I was paralyzed from the waist down. I was barely able to talk. I'd had extensive brain damage. For months afterwards the pain felt like raccoons were gnawing on my withered legs. The neurologist told me I would not walk again, but as an artist the worst revelation was about my right hand. . . . Now—with a hand that shook and was too weak to hold a pen—I could no longer draw" (Ferris 2017b, n.p.). She shared with *Chicago* magazine readers a self-portrait she produced by duct taping a pen to her hand and allowing her young daughter to guide her path based on the artist's verbal instructions. But she fought her way back to create art again—in this case, intricate, beautiful art, and a great abundance of it, though it took the better part of a decade to complete this project. She had to survive economically when she was no longer able to pursue her commercial work, sometimes homeless while she continued to draw.

Rosemarie Garland-Thomson (2011) has reclaimed the powerful concept of the "misfit," a term closely associated with monsters, in order to discuss some of the social and material constraints imposed on the lives of disabled people:

> People with disabilities have historically occupied positions as outcasts or misfits as, for example, in the roles of lepers, the mad, or cripples. . . . People with disabilities become misfits not just because of social attitudes—as in unfit for service or parenthood—but in material ways. Their outcast status is literal when the shape and function of their bodies comes into conflict with the shape and stuff of the built world. The primary negative effect of misfitting is exclusion from the public sphere—a literal casting out—and the resulting segregation into domestic spaces or sheltered institutions. (594)

Monsters represents the culmination of Ferris's personal struggles to rethink the relationship between her body and her environment, to reskill herself into new ways of producing art, and to reclaim a space for herself within the public sphere. This is what makes the virtuosity of this comic feel like such a moral victory.

Accommodating the world to one's own distinctive physicality might be understood as another transformative process, an act of resourcefulness that comes from looking at the world through a misfit's eyes. Knowing how

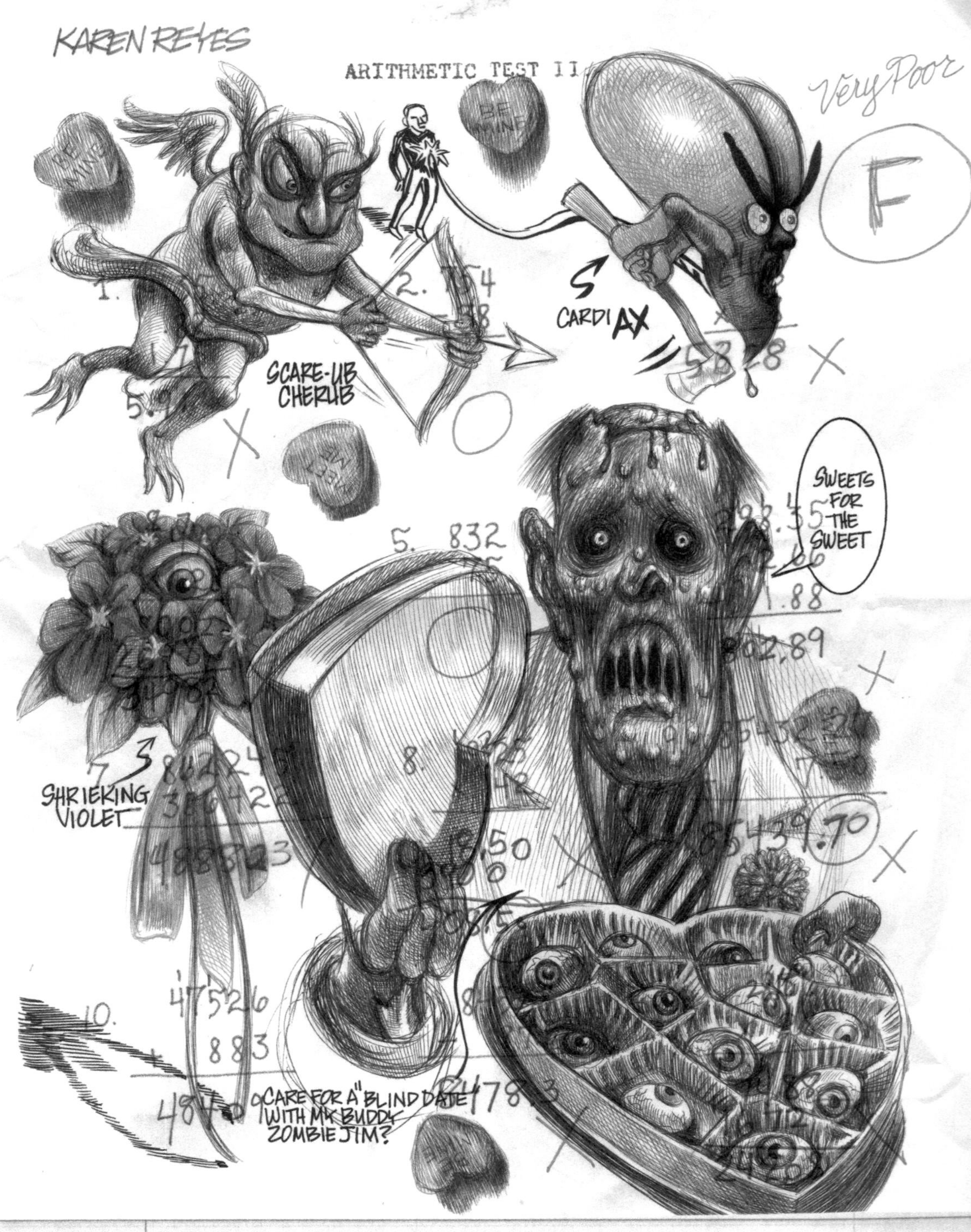
KAREN REYES
ARITHMETIC TEST II
Very Poor
F
CARDI AX
SCARE-UB CHERUB
SWEETS FOR THE SWEET
SHRIEKING VIOLET
CARE FOR A "BLIND DATE" WITH MY BUDDY ZOMBIE JIM?

physically difficult it often was for her to construct these images makes the artist's attention to detail that much more impressive. Just as the sketchbook conceit conveys Kare's urge to create regardless of her poverty, it also allows Ferris to experiment with new forms of graphic storytelling: "I loved comics, but I was always frustrated by the stories. I always wanted more text. I always felt like I had to really study those drawings and I felt like there could be more equity between text and image and they could work differently together. I wanted to slow it down" (Dueben 2017, n.p.). Drawing as Kare gave Ferris the freedom to break many sequential art conventions, rejecting any notion of a grid or panel structure and, for the most part, of word balloons in favor of text written in and around her images. Sometimes a drawing may command our attention as an individual image, sometimes it operates within a larger sequence, and sometimes we see multiple images sketched on the same page as if the artist was doodling on scrap paper (figure 5.4), but rarely does Ferris seek the closure Scott McCloud identifies with sequential art. The eclecticism of her visual language reflects the perspective of a child experimenting with technique and subject matter, trying out different approaches much as she is trying on different identities and, in the process, trying to work through on paper the shifting line between liberating fantasy and crushing reality. I've already discussed the ways that comics artists incorporate still life techniques into their work, but Ferris also deploys other techniques including portraits, architectural details, and street art where the artist stealthily captures the faces, expressions, and gestures of unknowing strangers. She imagines the covers of Kare's monster magazines and does precise reproductions—in colored ballpoint pen no less—of the paintings her protagonist admires, ignoring divides between high and low culture. She describes her often overstuffed pages:

> It was a matter of freedom and generosity. I needed freedom and I wanted to give the reader the most expanded, articulated and visually dense experience I possibly could. So many things that wouldn't fit into boxes. . . . I knew what the canon was, but it was somewhat hard for me to be that constrained. . . . I was opening worlds that I saw in my head for them [her readers] and hoping that the visions would catch hold, engage and

FIGURE 5.4. Kare often has to appropriate and reuse everyday materials as expressive resources. Emil Ferris, *My Favorite Thing Is Monsters* (2017). © Emil Ferris. Courtesy of Fantagraphics.

> communicate the story, even though (and maybe even because) it was getting created very much against the lines. (Brown 2017, n.p.)

Her search for how to accommodate things that don't "fit" within material and artistic constraints results in a transformation of comics storytelling and the discovery of new and monstrously beautiful forms. Figure 5.4 suggests the ways Ferris and, through her, Kare draw—literally and figuratively—outside the lines: recycling math homework into art supplies, rereading Valentine iconography through the lens of horror magazines, drawing figures at least partially on top of other drawings, creating no coherent relationship between the represented action, and leaving it unclear how this page fits into the larger exposition of her core narrative. Ferris's technique captures Kare's artistic and social awakening, just as the narrative uses the figure of the monster to work through her conflicting responses to her experiences. Kare has not yet developed a stable perspective, learning to see the world anew day by day.

Monster Culture

Ferris defines Kare in terms of her passion for monsters, situating her narrative in 1960s "monster culture." David J. Skal (1993) describes monster culture as a set of viewing rituals and material practices shared by many of the period's young fans:

> In Monster Culture, the participatory rituals surrounding the movies were every bit as important as the films themselves. The rites included the shared witnessing of the antics of horror hosts; an explosion of fan magazines that were read, reread, and traded among the cognoscenti; and even the creation of plastic model effigies. Most important, monsters materialized in the living room for the first time—not just reflected light in the movie theatres, but now a light *source*, a glowing electronic fireplace around which a generation could huddle and shudder and share. (266–267)

Monster culture began with the sale of old B-movies to local television stations as syndication packages in the late 1950s and early 1960s, as programmers were searching for low-cost, bulk content to fill the airwaves and as television was shifting from a technology enjoyed by elite early adopters toward a moment when most American household owned at least one set. Moving monster movies to television fundamentally altered their status: norror films had been viewed as adult entertainment in the 1930s (Berenstein 1996) and had targeted the teens going to drive-ins in the 1950s, but now they were sometimes after-school entertainment. As they were being domesticated, the Universal monsters were being reframed as good clean fun for school children. Kevin Heffernan (2004) recalls: "For the young horror fan, the kiddie matinee was only one component of an explosion of horror-related media and merchandising in the mid-sixties. This included Aurora plastic model kits, trading cards, LP records of old radio horror shows, 8mm home-movie versions of the Universal classics, monster magazines, and reprints of fifties horror comics" (212).

The reconstruction of 1930s and 1940s horror films as children's amusements was assisted by more goofy versions of these characters in comics (*Casper the Friendly Ghost*), sitcoms (*The Munsters, The Addams Family*), animated films (*Mad Monster Party*), and novelty songs ("Monster Mash"). Forrest J. Ackerman, himself a longtime horror fan, brought his expertise and his considerable collection of old photographs to the task of editing a monthly *Famous Monsters of Filmland* magazine, and his publisher James Warren built on its success by publishing a range of similar titles, such as *Creepy* and *Eerie*. As Matt Yockey (2013) has described, Ackerman modeled a particular fan subjectivity: a respect for the older films and the people who produced them, a fascination with the "classic" monsters who were read sympathetically as misunderstood creatures, and a DIY mentality that translated those fascinations into drawing pictures, making models, producing amateur films, developing costume and makeup, and creating monster collages from *Famous Monsters* images (Jenkins 2013a). These young fans did not fear the monsters; they wanted to possess and be possessed by them.

Bob Rehak (2013) describes the period in terms of the emergence of new "object practices" as the screen images were "materialized," turned into artifacts that could be purchased and displayed (29); this moment, he suggests, paves the way for the action figures of the 1980s and the profusion of media tie-in products at San Diego Comic-Con or at local specialty shops today. The Universal monsters were a potent entry point into these "object practices" because of their cross-generational appeal: parents could share with their children beloved media narratives of their own misbegotten youth, taking pride in being more permissive than their own parents had been. A 1965 *Famous Monsters* editorial by a Mrs. Terri Pinckard argued that "Monsters Are Good for My Children," making the case that these films helped youth to process real-world horrors: "As a child learns of the outside world, he learns of real-life things to be afraid of. The violence in the South, the murder of our President, these are all things our children cannot be protected from, must not be protected from. . . . How much better to have her dream of a Frankenstein than of Buchenwald" (Worland 2007, 139–140). But not all parents were this accepting, given that the moral panic Fredric Wertham generated around horror and crime comics had occurred less than a decade before and left a lasting impression on many parents.

If this monster culture was cross-generational, most accounts assume it was rigidly gendered: Rehak (2013) suggests both its focus on "the violent and disgusting" and its emphasis on "making and building" (33) made it "boy culture." But many girls were active participants in monster culture. Natasha Ritsma (2013) provides a nuanced reading of *Famous Monsters*, recovering the stories of female monster fans to question dominant assumptions about domestic containment often ascribed to this period. Film scholar Vivian Sobchack (1994) shared personal memories of her monster fandom:

> Both my sister and I loved horror films especially—at that time, before *Psycho*, often set in the Carpathians, or at least not in Brooklyn, and remote from our quotidian life. Nonetheless, they still seemed close enough to fire our imaginations. . . . Insofar as my mother confirms my recollection, the wolf men, the Frankenstein monster and his bride, Dracula and his daughters, never invaded my dreams, but my more susceptible sister almost always had nightmares on Saturday nights. In contrast, I never found those early horror films all that horrible or really scary, although I did find them incredibly poetic, and I almost always identified with the monsters, whatever their gender (assuming they had one). . . . I was very young and gloried in a sense of my own difference and its power. (n.p.)

Across a series of interviews, Emil Ferris has shared her own account of the 1960s monster culture, which, like Sobchack, she stills sees as central to her subjectivity: "My father was an artist and there were a lot of comics available to me. He had an enormous collection and I was not foresworn from reading horror comics—thankfully. I loved horror. . . . As a very small child I would stay up on Saturday night and drink as much Coca-Cola as I could so I could make it through the two features (Dueben 2017, n.p.). Ferris suggests that her Latina heritage—in particular, the richly decorated death carts she saw in New

Mexico during her early childhood—"primed" her for these monster movies: "I would weep for them. Their lives were so tortured and yet they were so forlorn and beautiful like New Mexico, like outsiders, like the people I loved most" (Tumey 2017). The fictionalized Kare embodies Ferris's own memories, offering a fuller depiction of the female monster fans of the 1960s than could be reclaimed from the brief references in old monster magazines: "There are a great many things within *My Favorite Thing is Monsters* that are TRUE and DID HAPPEN. How much is me? A great deal. Karen is very much an honest part of me. All I wanted to be as a child (and still want to be) was/is a monster" (Brown 2017, n.p.). Her last sentence pulls us into the space of desire and fantasy, where her book places its emphasis.

Ferris is also interested in the viewing rituals and material practices associated with monster fandom. Kare stays up late to watch monster movies on television with her mother and brother. She phones her friend Missy, and they talk through the movie as they are watching it. Her brother regularly buys her monster magazines with titles such as *Dread, Terror Tales, Ghastly,* and *Spectral,* and she carefully reproduces their covers into her sketchbook. Such practices are mildly transgressive (especially for a girl): the nuns force the schoolgirls to watch a film depicting monster comics as the gateway to hell. When Missy's mom is alarmed at her daughter's fascination with vampires, she blames Kare's "hillbilly" mother, echoing Wertham: "I really should not be surprised as people of your class never protect their kids from bad influences" (n.p.).

The Dracula effigy in figure 5.2, seen in only one panel, offers us a tenuous link to the era's many tie-in products. The fact that it is Dracula rather than the Wolf Man, Kare's preferred identity, suggests that perhaps Kare did not select this particular item herself: one might speculate that it was a gift from the more affluent Missy, who is obsessed with vampires. Read in this way, the toy suggests the imperfect fit between mass culture and personalized fantasies; some have to make do with what they can get their hands on, as opposed to collectors who leave no stone unturned in pursuing the exact objects they desire.

Though Rehak associates the "object practices" related to monsters with boy culture, Kare also embraces the DIY ethos, making do with—but also actively transforming—whatever materials she has at hand. Much as Carol Tyler recalls making her own representations of the Beatles' instruments to hang on her wall, Kare and Deeze create their own monster-themed Valentine cards on the kitchen table, using noodles and red food coloring to represent a bloody ventricle, but Kare gets into trouble because her cards are "too weird and too gory" (n.p.) compared with others' store-bought ones. After Kare and Missy have been pushed apart, Kare recalls making monsters by transforming that most iconic of dolls (figure 5.5): "[W]e used a black marker to dye a Barbie wedding dress for Missy's 'Countess Alucard.' I painted on the bloody fangs and the pretty blue shadows under her eyes. With my Barbie we cut her hair and cut up some clothes and covered her in glue and dryer lint" (n.p.). Erica Rand (1998) has documented lesbian narratives about abusing, dismembering, or otherwise transforming Barbies in the service of other, less traditional, female fantasies. Kare values the transformed Barbie doll not for what it is but for what it stands for—in this case, her self-perceptions as a girl who wants to be a werewolf, a token of her lost friendship with Missy, and a hint at her queer desires.

We might describe such practices as transformative use. "Transformative use" is a legal term introduced in a 1994 US Supreme Court decision clarifying fair use. A derivative work is "transformative" if it uses a source work in new or unexpected ways. The term has been embraced within fandom studies because it speaks to the ways that certain classes of consumers have to work harder to transform popular mass media narratives into their own imaginative resources. Most often, fandom studies research has focused on female spectators of television series and films that explicitly targeted male viewers—a category that would include Kare's beloved monster movies—but the term can also be extended to think about the creative work performed by minority spectators confronting a mostly white media culture, queer fans in a culture of prescriptive heterosexuality, or, for that matter, low-income fans in an increasingly commercialized culture. Her queer vision is suggested by the

FIGURE 5.5. Kare and Missy transform their Barbies into monsters in support of their horror film–inspired fantasies. Emil Ferris, *My Favorite Thing Is Monsters* (2017). © Emil Ferris. Courtesy of Fantagraphics.

ways that her appropriations of heterosexual romantic icons turn out wrong, becoming the object of horror for others, even if they are personally satisfying. Ferris explains, "Monsters are beings who must remain occult (hidden) and disguised, and yet also fluidly transformative" (Brown 2017, n.p.).

Comics critic Lily Hoang (2017) suggests that *Monsters* may itself be understood as a transformative work, given how actively and creatively it engages with monster movie narratives: "*My Favorite Things Is Monsters* is, to stake out an appropriate metaphor, a Frankenstein's patchwork monster: a beast with a constitution borrowed from various places but transformed into something overwhelmingly, gloriously its own" (n.p.). Paul Tumey (2016) references Ferris's cultural bricolage, describing *Monsters* as "a sort of *Harriet the Spy* meets Anne Frank monster mash-up, with a dose of *Where the Wild Things Are* thrown in for good measure and wrapped around dozens of other symbols and stories" (n.p.). Beyond her own storytelling techniques, Ferris is preoccupied with the ways culture can be read from the margins. Finally, as the Frankenstein metaphor above suggests, monsters are liminal figures, whose existence challenges any reality they enter.

Monsters as Meaning Machines

In *Skin Shows: Gothic Horror and the Technology of Monsters* (1995), Judith Halberstam writes: "Monsters are meaning machines. They can represent gender, race, nationality, class and sexuality in one body. . . . Monsters and the Gothic fiction that creates them are therefore technologies, narrative technologies that produce the perfect figure for negative identity" (21–22). In Halberstam's account, the monster invites these multiple and conflicting identifications, holding at a distance those things the culture fears in order to enable "the invention of human as white, male, middle-class and heterosexual" (21–22). What might it mean for Kare and other marginalized youth to adopt that "negative identity," identifying with the misfit monster in the face of pressures toward normalization? Kare is brown not white, female not male, poor not middle-class, and queer not heterosexual.

The monster, for her, embodies a particular intersectional identity through which she can escape, at least temporarily, constraints her society imposes upon her. In a recurring dream, she imagines herself being chased by a mob of local townspeople, waving torches, pitchforks, irons, and other household appliances (figure 5.6). She calls them the M.O.B., which stands for "Mean, Ordinary, and Boring" (n.p.). She fears that, someday, they will turn her into one of them: "[I]t isn't the jobs they do—like fry cook, nurse or farmer that

FIGURE 5.6. Kare's nightmare of being pursued by the M.O.B. (Mean, Ordinary, and Boring). Emil Ferris, *My Favorite Thing Is Monsters* (2017). © Emil Ferris. Courtesy of Fantagraphics.

makes them the M.O.B. No! It's the fact most of them believe only in what they can see, smell, taste, touch, hear or buy" (n.p.). The M.O.B. may accuse her of seeing things that are not there, but she's convinced that seeing things in the bright light of "reality" may not be all that it is cracked up to be: "If you've ever stood and waited in the florescent glare of the Goldblatt's Basement while your mom and a ton of other ladies tear through stuff like dented coffee pots and misspelled day-of-the-week panty sets (Twosday, Wendsday) then you've seen first hand the way 'light' just shows how sweaty and messed up human life really is" (n.p.). Ferris depicts the M.O.B. across a two-page spread, forcing the reader to look them in the eye, and see there the fear, the anger, the anxiety that lead them to try to contain that which they do not understand. Their dress, their tools, could not be more mundane, but the image also captures what it is like to be hunted because you are different, because you reject the trappings of the straight, mundane, and normative life. Spatulas and mops may seem a peculiar substitute for the torches that townspeople carry in traditional monster films, but they embody the roles Kare hopes to escape in her own life. And insofar as the spiral rings of her notebook represent the character's lack of resources, as well as her experiences of compulsory education, they also convey something of the forces she is fighting against across this book. She may see herself as a monster, but the forces Kare confronts are something even worse.

What constitutes a monster shifts across the book but Kare (and through her, Ferris) consistently deploys the monster as an imaginative resource for making sense of the powerful forces that are imposing themselves on her world. As these meanings become unmoored from any particular material object, everything and anything can become the raw material for the monster as a "meaning machine" (Halberstam 1995). Kare has much to work through and monsters give her much to work with. Like the monsters she admires, Kare and the people around her have multiple and fluid identities that make them hard to pin down. As Kare narrates, "Mama is one half Irish from Appalachia and part American Indian from who-knows-where. She calls herself 'a hillbilly gypsy.' Her grey eyes are like a combination of Dublin fog and the smoke from peace pipes" (n.p.). Kare's father was Mexican, an identity he maps onto Deeze, Kare's brother, who is named "Diego Zapata" after two Mexican heroes, one an artist, the other an activist. Mama and Kare can pass as white, but Deeze looks more like their father, attracting racist jeers when he walks into the diner where his mother and sister have been casually eating.

And Kare's few friends are similarly marginal, outcasts from a culture working overtime to force them to conform, misfits in a world whose contours do not meet their needs. As one writer explains: "Rather than make friends at school, Karen would rather participate in an imaginary monster coalition. Even standing before a mirror, she must be aggressively jarred before she can recognize herself as a human girl. There is safety in being a monster. To see oneself as a monster is to preemptively accept alienation. Before Karen can be rejected, she becomes self-rejecting, making herself into someone who does not belong because she cannot belong" (Hoang 2017, n.p.). Each child embodies one or more of the kinds of otherness that the monster performs for our culture.

At times, it seems her entire neighborhood is populated by monsters, displaced and dispossessed peoples from around the world who are riding what Deeze calls "the Royal Shaft Express" (n.p.). As Kare explains: "Most of the Spanish people in Uptown came here from countries where they were kept poor—despite working hard. A lot of the black people came up from the South to escape lynching and other horrible things. . . . Deeze says that the white people from Appalachia—who everybody calls 'hillbillys' were starving in the South—even though their hard work made mining companies rich. But the first people who rode 'The Royal Shaft Express' were the Indians" (n.p.). Everyone around them is running away from something and everyone has had the experience of being read as a monstrous other from the perspective of a more powerful group.

"I look like inny monster to you?" (n.p.) Sandy, the poor white girl, asks Kare when they first meet—the wrong question, since Kare reads everyone as one sort of monster or another. Her father, who abandoned his family, is depicted as the Invisible Man, because her mother tells people that he is "out of the picture," having "just disappeared one day" (n.p.). Mama identifies as a "hillbilly gypsy" who understands the world through "ordinary everyday portents, marvels, bodements, harbingers, signs, omens and curses" (n.p.); diagnosed with cancer, she wears a scarf around her head to mask the consequences of her chemo. A local gangster, who can nurture one moment and threaten the next, is Doctor Jekyll, his shuffling henchman becomes the Creature, and Mr. Silverberg, a withered old man who mourns his lost love, is the Mummy.

Across a book where she encounters racism, homophobia, and classism, learns how Anka survived the Nazi concentration camps, and confronts sexual violence, Kare discovers that the world is full of monsters who adopt different moral and ethical stances: "[T]he bad monsters want the world to look the way

DEAR NOTEBOOK - I'LL TELL YOU STRAIGHT - IN MY OPINION THE BEST HORROR MAGAZINE COVERS ARE THE ONES WHERE THE LADY'S BOOBS AREN'T SPILLING OUT AS SHE'S GETTING ATTACKED BY A MONSTER. THOSE COVERS GIVE ME SOMETHING WORSE THAN THE CREEPS. I THINK THE BOOB COVERS SEND A SECRET MESSAGE THAT IT IS VERY DANGEROUS TO HAVE BREASTS - AND CONSIDERING WHAT MAMA IS GOING THROUGH, MAYBE THE MAGAZINES KNOW STUFF THAT WE DON'T...

they want it to. They need people to be afraid . . . They don't live in their lair and mostly mind their own biz . . . I guess that's the difference . . . A good monster sometimes gives somebody a fright because they're weird looking and fangy . . . A fact that is beyond their control . . . But bad monsters are all about control . . . They want the whole world to be scared so that bad monsters can call the shots . . ." (n.p.). The world offers Kare many reasons to be fearful: "I have come to believe that love is actually the weirdest monster out there and if you think love doesn't rip people to bloody shreds, you're dead wrong" (n.p.). For Kare, growing up requires distinguishing good monsters from bad.

In her classic essay "When Women Look" (2002), Linda Williams describes the different ways in which men and women look at the monster: for the male, through a lens of male dread about sexual difference, which Williams links to castration anxiety—but for the woman, a "recognition of their similar status as potent threats to a vulnerable male power" (65). Reflecting back on her own experiences as a monster fan, Vivian Sobchack (1994) arrives at a similar place, writing about such B-films as *The Wasp Woman* and *The Leech Woman*: "I do remember the nameless pleasure I felt when each of the female characters—'transformed' from scared to scary by extraterrestrial contact or special serum—was suddenly empowered to carry out excessive acts of vengeance. . . . Thus, as I watched these women, like the boys, my highly conventionalized disgust and fear was *of* them, not *for* them. Nonetheless, unlike the boys, I think I sensed the pleasure of their revenge" (n.p.). Kare's fascination with monsters similarly allows her to express her ambivalence about growing up in a culture where being female is shaped by arbitrary constraints. As she notes, the persistent message of the monster magazine covers (which often depict women bursting out of their tops as the monster leers at them) is that it can be dangerous to have breasts (figure 5.7). Here horror films are just another vehicle telling her how she is supposed to act as a woman, but horror can also become a vehicle for pushing back. When a group of her male classmates try to rape her underneath the El tracks, Kare uses her monster fantasies to imagine taking unrestrained revenge against her attackers: "This is just another reason why being a human girl stinks compared to being a monster. When I'm a monster I won't have to keep my mouth shut. No, I'll open my mouth and use my rows of long sharp teeth to rip up guys like Jerry" (n.p.). I am monster—hear me roar.

FIGURE 5.7. Ferris's pastiche of 1960s horror film magazine covers. Emil Ferris, *My Favorite Thing Is Monsters* (2017). © Emil Ferris. Courtesy of Fantagraphics.

...HORROR THEATRE PLAYED THE MOVIE, 'DRACULA'S DAUGHTER' AND THERE WAS THIS ONE PART WHERE COUNTESS DRACULA KIDNAPS THIS WOMAN NAMED JANET...
I THINK THAT THE COUNTESS ALMOST...
...KISSED HER...
OH KAREN, YOU ARE FAR FAR BRAVER THAN I EVER WAS!
THAT WAS THE NIGHT WE CUT OUR FINGERS AND BECAME...
BLOOD SISTERS
AS I HUNG UP MY DETECTIVE COAT IN THE CLOAK ROOM I REMEMBERED HOW I'D WAITED TILL MISSY WAS ASLEEP. I'D SAID, "YOU ARE BEAUTIFUL" AND THEN...
..I LOVE YOU KARE...I LOVE YOU SO MUCH...
I THINK SHE MEANT IT BECAUSE SHE SAID IT FROM HER ASLEEP SELF NOT HER AWAKE SELF...

And Kare is not the book's only character who sees the monstrous female as an empowered position. In a flashback to Anka's experiences growing up in a Weimar brothel, she tries to explain the story of Medusa to her friend and mentor, Dolly, but the more worldly girl sees something else in the mythology of the snake-haired harpy—male fear of women's sexuality: "So Perseus went to HER house, where she was minding her own business and he CUT HER HEAD OFF! . . . Medusa scared men because when they looked at her they got hard. . . . What you don't understand is how much power Medusa had . . . even just her head was powerful . . . When a man does that, it's to take her power . . . to divide her from her power" (n.p.).

Here, again, Ferris suggests that women could become empowered by embracing their inner monsters, rejecting the limits and labels a male-dominated culture imposes upon them. Ferris describes monsters as a third term within gender binaries that restrict human potential: "I didn't ever want to be a woman. I mean, it just did not look like a good thing, nor did being a man, because it felt like they were being victimized by the same system. It didn't give them much more latitude than they gave women, in many ways. They were being constrained to behave in these ways that weren't authentic and didn't allow them to realize their full personhood, either. Being a monster seemed like the absolute best solution" (Thielman 2017, n.p.).

On NPR's *Fresh Air*, Ferris linked her evolving understanding of her sexuality as a young lesbian to a much discussed sequence in *Dracula's Daughter*, when the vampiress hires a young female model, brings her back to her apartment, has her remove her top, and then proceeds to drain her blood. For the first time, Ferris saw an on-screen representation of her own desires, though her era's technology did not allow her to hold onto this moment of recognition: "It was a time when you couldn't replay things but if I could have done it, I probably would have replayed that moment a thousand times" (Gross 2017). In *Monsters in the Closet* (1997), Harry M. Benshoff argues that *Dracula's Daughter* works to contain this homoerotic moment, situating the Countess in a heterosexual subplot, and even describing her desperation to find a cure for her troubling urges. But not all audience members got the message. The original ad slogan for the film, after all, was "She gives you that weird feeling" (Worland 2007, 67). Ferris restages this moment in *Monsters*, mapped onto Kare's relationship with Missy. The two girls watch *Dracula's Daughter*

FIGURE 5.8. Watching *Dracula's Daughter* surfaces the two girls' feelings toward each other. Emil Ferris, *My Favorite Thing Is Monsters* (2017). © Emil Ferris. Courtesy of Fantagraphics.

during a sleepover and Missy wonders: "Do you think that a girl could become the bride of Dracula's daughter?" Kare responds, "If they love each other then why not?" (n.p.). After watching horror films, the two girls pull their sleeping bags close enough to hold hands (figure 5.8). Later, they "cut [their] fingers and became blood sisters" (n.p.), and in a groggy state, express their affection for each other. The fleeting romantic connection between these two girls is suggested by the repeated heart motif here—at the bloody meeting point between their pricked fingers and at the intersection between their two sleeping bags. And Kare draws her friend at this moment as a vampire, a monstrous match for her werewolf persona, suggesting the ways their fantasy lives are now interwoven. But when Missy's mother learns about the feelings the film aroused, she ensures that this night was "the last sleepover we ever had" (n.p.). Missy's mother (at home) and what Kare calls "the pink mob" (at school) conspire to push Missy into compulsive heterosexuality and normative femininity: "Over the next few weeks I heard that all of Missy's monster magazines got replaced by hair and beauty mags. Her board games, like Haunted House, got replaced with the Mystery Date Game" (n.p.). Kare frames a binary choice: "She used to like monsters so me and her were best friends, but now she likes boys instead (a bad mistake)" (n.p.). Kare imagines herself protecting and nurturing a part of Missy—the part that liked monsters more than she liked boys—whereas she pictures that same aspect "in a coffin, in a crypt, staked, and hungry, and all alone" (n.p.) within Missy herself. When the mother takes away her monsters, something dies inside Missy.

Near the end of this first volume, Missy reaches out to Kare again to rekindle the friendship. When Kare goes to Missy's birthday party, she finds the others playing spin the bottle (another marker of compulsory heterosexuality) and her room is decorated with flowers and Monkees posters (normative femininity), though she still keeps a monster magazine hidden under her pillow. Kare relies on her own monster fantasies as they cope with the snooty and dismissive mothers at Missy's party: "If I had the bite I'd transform and then I'd feast on them like they were two pieces of stale bitter birthday cake" (n.p.). Here her monster fantasies offer her a vehicle for channeling her anger against the imposition of straight norms upon the queer little world that Missy and Kare created for themselves. Kare's horror over Missy's "cure" intensifies her own struggles against gender and sexual norms, first signaled by her distaste for the school's Valentine's Day celebration and the "sappy" cards her classmates give each other. She finds the day "pathetic" because it has no room for monsters.

Kare finds herself doodling during class, imagining her own monsters who might do right by the day, and, in the process, she rejects the heterosexual imperative these rituals perform. Hearts, candy, flowers are transformed into figures of disgust and dread (figure 5.4).

Frustrated by the persistence of Kare's monster fantasies in the face of their mother's impending death, Deeze forces Kare to confront her own reflection, reminding her that she is "a girl" and "not Larry Talbot three quarters the way to being the fucking Wolfman!" (n.p.). For the only time in *Monsters*, Ferris offers a realistic portrait of her protagonist, rather than depicting her as the she-wolf that she imagines herself to be. Kare comes out to her brother as a girl who likes girls and will never be normal in the sense that he demands. Deeze's response is accepting, but also tenuous, urging her not to burden her dying mother with this information and expressing concern about "every Uptown asshole who'll think he's doing you a favor by . . . um . . . trying to be your boyfriend if you get my drift" (n.p.). Both Kare and Deeze recognize, in this moment, the real dangers she confronts as a sexual outlaw, not quite a monster, but someone that the M.O.B. is going to be pursuing nevertheless.

Yet the intersectional identities associated with the monster do not stop with its associations with gender and sexuality. Around the edges of Kare's story, readers encounter other characters who similarly horrify the M.O.B. Kare imagines Franklin, a black boy from her school, as a sympathetic version of Frankenstein's monster. As she describes him, "He has a whole bunch of bad scars, he wears Taboo perfume, and he never speaks at all" (n.p.). Franklin is too big for his age and sometimes acts as Kare's protector from the bullies. He explains his disfigurement to Kare as the result of being attacked by an angry dog (an image that evokes a particular history of racialized violence in the book's 1960s context), but Kare imagines him as something "assembled in a lab" (n.p.). Later, however, we get other hints that the violence directed against Franklin's body may not have simply been motivated by racism. When Kare, Franklin, and Sandy run away to the Art Institute, Franklin finds himself fascinated with the paintings—particularly portraits of aristocratic women—and offers a running commentary on their fashion accessories and their gender performance. In each case, Ferris redraws these famous paintings so that Franklin has morphed into their female subjects—a means of queering the art world even as the two friends make the paintings their own (figure 5.9). At one point, as he is looking at a portrait of a Christian martyr who is literally holding his own tongue, Franklin's remark hints at violence that might have been directed against him as a queer youth of color: "You wore your best coat into the wrong neighborhood, too, huh? And then you just could not stop yourself from offering style advice to boys with knives" (n.p.). Ferris again demonstrates her virtuosity through these elaborate pastiches of classical works: she goes beyond the typical art student trick of learning by copying the masters, making transformative use of these resources much as Kare pulls everything she touches toward her creature-of-the-night fantasies. Franklin, literally and figuratively, sees himself in these paintings.

When the kids exit the museum, they learn the news of Martin Luther King's death. Franklin's own sense of loss is cut short, though, when his solidarity with black America is questioned by a stranger on the subway: "His kind isn't for civil rights . . . Not unless it's the Civil Right to wear a damned dress or stick his business where God never intended it to go. . . . This faggot ain't my brother . . . No one can convince me of that!" (n.p.). Just as Missy's story sees reinforcing gender norms as a means of punishing sexual deviation, Franklin's story suggests that queer youth do not gain admission into the black community just because they have been subjected to racism.

Ferris uses this gentle giant to illustrate the choices people make about how to respond to cruelty and tragedy in their lives: "[T]here is something ennobling, empathic about choosing not to pass cruelty on but there is this other thing, too. I'm thinking of people whom I've known who were broken by life and then engaged to re-form themselves (and this is the heart of the monster ideology to me) in order to be more extraordinary and more powerful within themselves" (Tumey 2017, n.p.). Here, again, she adopts an intersectional perspective—seeing race, gender, and sexuality working together to discriminate who belongs. Conceptualizing Franklin as a monster seems to be Kare's way of addressing the ambiguities about different forms of exclusion—as a black youth in a mostly white school, as a transgender youth in a culture shaped by homophobia—but also the possibility of inclusion in an intersectional community of monsters that dares to claim its own territory despite the opposition of the M.O.B.

Monsters is also attentive to the ways that class differences can create misfits and outcasts. When Sandy asks Kare what kind of monster she resembles, Kare responds that she reminds her of "a vampire or a ghost or a zombie" (n.p.). She sees Sandy as "skin and bones" (n.p.), with an insatiable hunger. Sandy comes from a white trash background in rural Kentucky, raised in a "holler," orphaned

FIGURE 5.9. Franklin maps himself into the paintings at the Art Institute of Chicago. Emil Ferris, *My Favorite Thing Is Monsters* (2017). © Emil Ferris. Courtesy of Fantagraphics.

FRANKLIN UNDERSTANDS CLOTHES IN THE SAME DEEP WAY THAT I UNDERSTAND MONSTERS...
UH OH! THE PAINTER KNEW THIS SISTER. HE WAS BOASTING! JUST LOOK AT THAT SLEEVE! FUR LINED WITH SOFT SOFT SATIN, SCANDALOUS! AND ANOTHER THING, YOU CAN TELL THE PAINTER THOUGHT THIS WOMAN WAS SEXY BECAUSE SHE WAS SMART! LOOK AT HER HAND POISED AGAINST HER CHEEK THAT WAY. THIS SISTER WAS A WILD THINKER!
PORTRAIT OF A WOMAN, JEAN-LEON GEROME, 1851
WHEN A GIRL WEARS A HAT THAT LOOKS LIKE A FANCY WRAPPED PRESENT, YOU CAN BE SURE THAT SISTER HAS A FEW SURPRISE PACKAGE IDEAS IN HER HEAD.

when her labor organizer parents were killed by mining company thugs, forced to wear a handmade knockoff of the official school uniform, and dismissed by the other kids as unworthy of their attention. When Sandy invites Kare to her birthday party, Kare finds that there are no adults around, that no other kids came; the two celebrate together in an empty closet in the girl's unfurnished bedroom. Sandy is quite literally one of those kids nobody sees—and as the story continues, there are hints that she may be a ghost or an imaginary friend, since Kare is the only person who acknowledges her existence. Sandy, however, seems to lack the creative resources from which Kare finds a way to create a bountiful fantasy life in the face of her lack; Sandy must make do with fantasies she borrows from others and this may be why she leaves so little footprint on the world.

Throughout, Kare is fascinated by the "undead," suggesting that the undead do not struggle with self-esteem issues. But later, the term takes on new significance as she watches her mother wither away from her cancer. Being "undead" means "showing death who's boss" (n.p.), she declares at one point, and, at another, she observes, "Monster ALWAYS beats cancer" (n.p.). As her mother's death approaches, Kare intensifies her search for a "maker" whose bite might give her immortality, imagining turning her mother and brother into "a tribe of monsters with our own lair and everything" (n.p.). If sometimes she imagines the monster's bite as a tool of vengeance against the boys who try to rape her or the upper-class mothers who patronize her, she also imagines the bite as a gift that might allow her to hold onto those she loves. These passages about pain and illness carry a particular punch because of what we know about the author's own health issues. When her mother dies, Kare is crushed that her fantasies failed to protect her: she feels rejected by the monsters who never transformed her into the "undead," imagining them as dismissing her as a "WANNABEast" (n.p.), much as she has been shunned by her classmates. Kare fantasizes about going on a rampage, staking vampires, smashing the Wolf Man's head with a silver wolf-headed cane, shooting the Invisible Man, reburying the Mummy, and burning Frankenstein's monster. As the first book comes to a close, Kare's worlds (both real and imagined) seem to be coming apart around her, and we can imagine, from what we know of the history of Chicago in 1968, this seeming sense of disruption and upheaval will extend to the political realm in the second book of this still evolving narrative.

Throughout, Ferris explores what it might mean to think of "monsters" as, in Halberstam's sense, "a meaning machine" or "narrative technology" the culture uses to manage difference. Jeffrey Jerome Cohen (1996) tells us that the monster is born at a "metaphoric crossroads" and exists "only to be read" (4); "the monster is difference made flesh, come to dwell among us" (7). How a culture imagines and responds to its monsters tells us much about how it processes difference, though Cohen acknowledges that such difference may be as much the object of desire and pleasure, at least temporarily, as the focus of horror and dread. We can engage with monsters, he says, because we know the movie will eventually end and everything will be put back into its proper place again. But Ferris raises the prospect that the monster may persist beyond any given story, that the monster becomes a "thing," a discourse people deploy to process everyday experiences, and when this happens, nothing need go back to normal ever again.

For Ferris, embracing what she calls "the monster ideology" is a means of resisting the othering process and constructing an empowered identity. Far from a celebration of the universal child who finds freedom through play, *My Favorite Thing Is Monsters* sees imagination as a resource—a survival mechanism—in the hands of a girl who is brown, poor, lesbian, and dealing with her mother's cancer, her father's desertion, her brother's criminality, and everything else people throw at her. Ferris has said that the book began with a single image—a lesbian werewolf hugging a transgender Frankenstein—and the rest of the story took shape around how to find a path to such solidarity and support. By the time the book was released, one month into Donald Trump's presidency, she saw this story as having political urgency: "When I started on this—years and years ago—we were living in a different time. . . . I was wondering, Why am I doing this? I'm talking about the rise of fascism. I'm talking about racial inequality. I'm talking about the lack of representation for children who are lesbian and gay and trans. . . . Is this just a history lesson that I'm making? I thought it's good to be reminded that these are important topics. Now, though, I'm a little astonished. It has all come back" (Mouly and Bormes 2017, n.p.). In particular, she cites Trump's demeaning language toward women, and expresses her hope that young girls may discover the monster metaphor as a means of deconstructing and deflecting that hostility.

What Can't Be Touched

For Ferris and her protagonists, thinking about oneself as a monster is a transformative possibility, a way to reclaim a space for difference (whether understood in relation to gender, sexuality, race, class, or disability and illness). Ferris explains why she has been drawn to the Wolf Man story as a means of exploring horror's relationship to social marginalization. Curt Siodmak, the

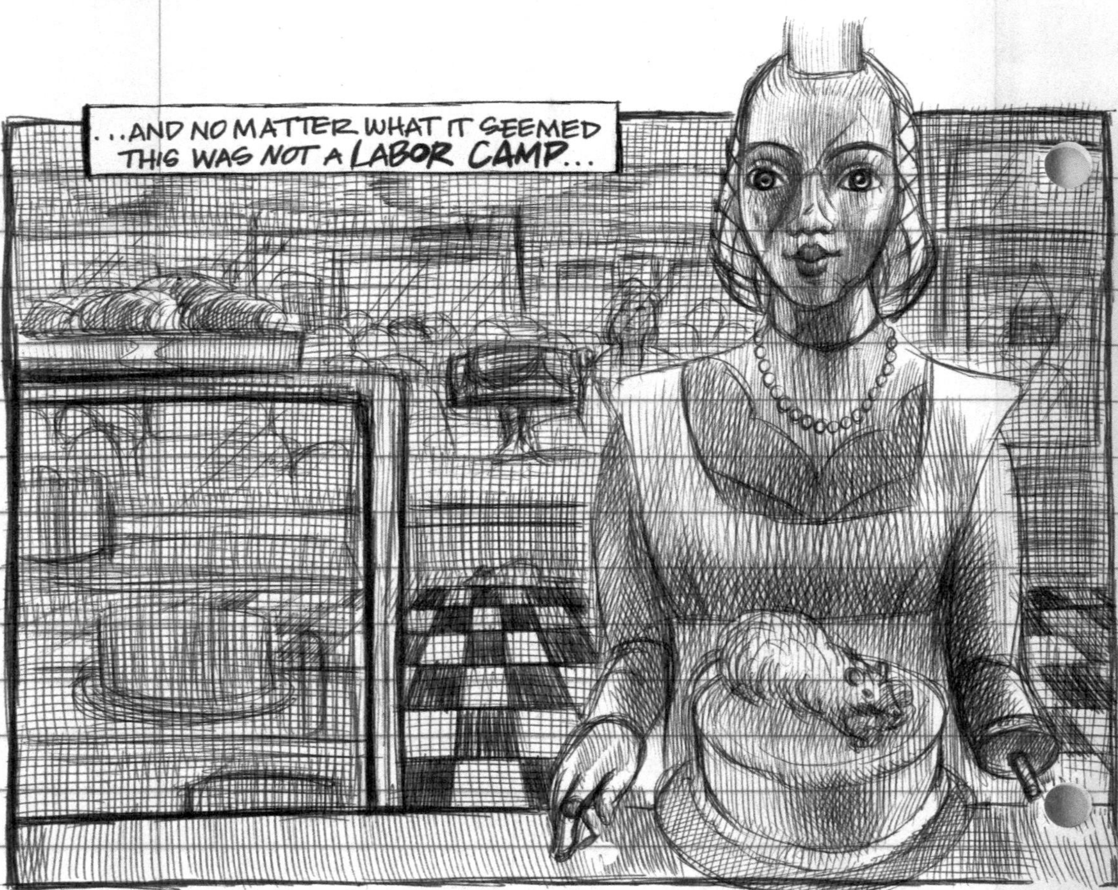

. . . AND NO MATTER WHAT IT SEEMED THIS WAS NOT A **LABOR CAMP** . . .

screenwriter of *The Wolf Man* (1941), was a Jewish refugee from Nazi Germany. Among his contributions to the werewolf mythology was the pentagram, the cryptic mark that the old gypsy woman sees in Larry Talbot's hands as she foretells his fate. As Ferris explains, "He [Siodmak] said that the appearance of the pentagram was something that he had assimilated from having to wear the star. . . . The star was this symbol of the coming mark that was on you and you were going to be destroyed" (Dueben 2017, n.p.).

This story connects Kare's experiences in 1960s Chicago with Anka's coming-of-age story as a young Jew and a child prostitute during Hitler's rise to power. Anka's stories help her to comprehend and repel the destructive forces around her. Sonja, the brothel's cook, deploys stories from classic mythology and old-world fairy tales to share insights that may allow Anka to survive the rough life ahead: "The brothel was transformed into Mount Olympus and when cruel Zeus rose from the ground like a giant mist and strode through the garden, Sonja would beg me to hold still as a rock so that Zeus wouldn't see me and take a fancy to me" (n.p.). And as she leaves the brothel, Anka finds other stories also help her navigate Berlin: "The only things I had left after Schultz put me out were all the books that I'd stolen from his library. . . . I took the characters from my books with me everywhere I went. Mrs. Haversham understood how it felt to be jilted and Gregor Samsa warned me to expect the unexpected" (n.p.). These became, like Kare's monsters, the metaphors she lives by.

As she makes her way, Anka learns to distrust the realm of material things. The powerful men she encounters are collectors—"The Big Doctor" decorates his quarters with statues and prints of rabbits, Schultz has his books and also classical statues. When Anka and the other Jewish women are separated from the men at the gates of a work camp, they are paraded past shopfronts displaying shoes and contemporary fashions, baked goods, and even books. At first, these displays promise kindness and opportunity, until Anka realizes that the people inside are all mannequins and that the displayed goods are overrun with rats (figure 5.10): "I knew at that moment that no matter what it seemed this was not a labor camp" (n.p.). The mannequin in the window becomes a monstrous other, lacking one of its hands, a pole impaling its head, its lips pursed together like a Gill-man out of water, its eyes looking outward with a fixed stare, even as a rat crawls atop the cake she is meant to display. If this window

FIGURE 5.10. Anaka distrusts the shop window façade as she is being lead into a German work camp. Emil Ferris, *My Favorite Thing Is Monsters* (2017). © Emil Ferris. Courtesy of Fantagraphics.

display is meant to pass as an ideal life, then who needs this stuff? One cannot help connect this moment of shock and dread to Kare's own dismissal of the cheapjack materialism of the consumer lifestyle.

Stories provide the tools we need to see past things and to reject the categories by which the "M.O.B." imposes its "reality" upon our lives. If writers like Seth sentimentalize the material world, wallowing in the dust as it were, Ferris wants to get rid of the "things" in order to confront the memories and feelings that they often substitute for, seeing materiality in terms of constraints on our capacity to imagine the world differently. Deeze similarly offers his sister the gift of narrative possibility when he teaches her how to look at art not with her eyes but with all of her senses, to crawl up inside the paintings and look at the world from the inside out, and, above all, to form interpretations that serve her ends rather than allowing meanings to be imposed on her. As Deeze explains, "Any person who sees this painting gets to end the story any way that he or she wants to" (n.p.).

Ferris's choice to depict Kare without much reference to her material belongings reflects the author's recognition of what it is like to do without and her protagonist's distrust of people that "believe only in what they can see, smell, taste, touch, hear or buy" (n.p.). Rather, Ferris reclaims the transformative potential of things—like monsters—that cannot be seen with the eyes but only with the imagination. These resources—the possessions of the dispossessed—can never be taken away. And with these resources, one may just be able to escape, transform, or simply endure the humdrum things with which others are content to fill their lives.

Moving Forward

Across the past four chapters, I've considered what it might mean to think about certain contemporary graphic novels as "collecting stories"—that is, as stories by, for, and about collectors. Comic artists had to be collectors initially, in order to maintain access to the history of their disposable medium. The emergence of the graphic novel, with all that it means in terms of shifting the status of the comics medium, has resulted in a new value placed on personal expression and everyday life stories, and in this context, comics creators display their personal obsessions and fascinations on the page. Collecting has always involved processes of meaning management, self-fashioning, world building, and storytelling. In *Projections: Comics and the History of Twenty-First Century*

Storytelling (2012), Jared Gardner uses Seth and Deitch to illustrate broader tendencies in the medium:

> Archives are everywhere in the contemporary graphic novel, although almost inevitably not the ordered collections of the academic library or a law firm. These are archives in the loosest, messiest sense of the word—archives of the forgotten artifacts and ephemera of American popular cultures, items that were never meant to be collected. Indeed, it is their ephemeral nature, their quality as waste products of modern mass media and consumer culture, that constitutes the perverse pleasures for those who collect, organize, and fetishize them. These are collections organized by invisible grids, by individual desires, by accident of geography or inheritance. And yet, these archives are far from the random gleamings of the packrat or hoarder. Their exploration and the disciplines and skills required lie somewhere between "data mining" and "dumpster diving," between analysis and scavenging. (150)

Gardner identifies several key aspects of the "archives" that inform the contemporary graphic novel. First, these collections do not observe traditional cultural hierarchies (collecting materials that once would have been discarded) or disciplinary boundaries (materials that do not fit within established bodies of knowledge).

Second, these collections take shape around "individual desires," even as they cluster at intersections between personal and collective memories. If these collecting practices and interests were totally idiosyncratic, these books would not have the same appeal. Yet because comics readers are often themselves fascinated with the broader histories of popular media, the materials these books explore are recognizable, even if our collecting impulses are directed toward different configurations of interests.

And third, these collections are "messy" or "loosely" defined. Across these chapters, we've seen examples of collectors with focused interests—from Simon's collection of novelty postcards of oversized objects in *Clyde Fans* to Pam's collection of black cats in *Alias the Cat!* Seth's stories often focus on collectors who share enough common interests that they actively compete over desired objects, and he also depicts collecting as an active pursuit for "finds," including the desire—upon discovering an artist whose work speaks to him—to gather as many examples of that artist's work and to learn as much about her (well, mostly him) as possible.

On the other end of the spectrum, we have the example of the Talbots' cabinet of curiosities, where each object is selected according to different criteria, where each represents a source of wonder, and where no single interpretive frame can encompass the whole. Here we are much closer to Gardner's "packrats" and "hoarders," yet we've also seen that the objects in *Alice in Sunderland* reflect local histories and geographies, and thus the possibilities are not infinite or endless. Kim Deitch's works fall somewhere in between: his protagonists often start out wanting to better understand a particular possession (a Waldo doll, a Sunshine bottle cap, an obscure children's program), but their investigations push them beyond their original goals. For both Deitch and Talbot, then, the line between collecting and accumulating meaningful objects is more of a continuum than a sharp divide: both explore how individuals and cultures negotiate those shifting motives and expanding contexts in our everyday choices about what stuff to keep.

Of the three, Deitch is most likely to depict collecting as not fully under his own control. As Gardner writes, "the pleasures and dangers of this archival research lead Kim closer, with each connected thread, to an elusive truth (about Waldo? About his own art?) but further and further from reason. The archive soon becomes a source of madness, as each media form (film, newspapers, tapes, magazines, antique phonebooks, etc.) lead him deeper and deeper into a labyrinth from which he seems unlikely to emerge" (163).

Yet, for the most part, people use their possessions as a source of social and cultural distinction, as they define themselves through what and how they collect. Russell W. Belk and Melanie Wallendorf (1994) describe what motivates collecting more generally: "Some of the identity work that goes on through collections involves striving for personal completion and perfection. Completing the collection, in a sense, completes the individual; the person who has a whole collection feels more like a whole person. Similarly, a representative collection confers on the collector a sense of being well rounded" (240). Collecting always involves display and explication: collectors show off their possessions to those they think may be impressed by their expertise. We've traced a range of different artistic practices through which earlier collectors shared their finds with the world (cabinets d'amateur, wonder cabinets, Victorian women's albums, etc.) and we might understand contemporary comics as borrowing, consciously or not, from these earlier forms of expression.

When read alongside these other collecting stories, *My Favorite Thing Is Monsters* seems an odd fit—a work whose protagonist shares the knowledge and mentality of a collector but lacks the resources to pursue collecting in the same way. Monsters are understood here not as "things" (material objects) but as a "thing" (a passion or interest). The interpretive frame has come unmoored from the physical objects upon which it might have been cathected in the hands of the collector, existing in her drawn images, in her fantasies, but not in material culture. Kare translates this interest into diverse activities, from retrofitting her Barbie dolls to copying the covers of her favorite horror comics. Like the other collector protagonists, Kare constructs her identity in relation to earlier forms of popular entertainment—in this case, the Universal monster movies of the 1930s and 1940s—but she uses those materials less for nostalgia than as metaphors for making sense of issues she and her friends confront—ways of working through their social exclusion on the basis of gender, sexuality, race, class, or illness. Compared to the highly materialistic perspectives represented by the male collectors, Ferris adopts an anti-materialist viewpoint, distrusting those characters who collect things in favor of those who place a greater value on social relations.

Understanding collecting in these terms prepares us for the next section, "Object Lessons," where we explore the work of several other female graphic storytellers who see "stuff" as embedded in family relations rather than as something that reflects purely personal and idiosyncratic interests. Collecting has historically been a means by which individuals exerted control over their material environment; not surprisingly, collecting as a practice has involved more men than women, since they have had greater control over the resources to collect (both in terms of funds and space) and because they have had greater freedom over their own choices and activities. While Deitch and Talbot represent their wives as sharing their interests and, more recently, Bryan Talbot has collaborated with his wife, Mary Talbot, there are very few examples of female comics creators who represent collections within their works. More often, female graphic artists tell stories about inheritance and family history, about what gets passed down (materially, emotionally) across generations, about hoarding and culling rather than about collecting and accumulating. An anthropological approach to material culture yeilds its greatest insights when it explores what materials matter to what people by what criteria. Collecting is one way people define what matters to them—a process that, as we have seen, involves active searching, careful appraisal, proud display, and knowing explication of materials that circulate through our life world. Yet other criteria enter the equation as graphic artists represent the processes of inheriting and culling materials not of one's own selection.

OBJECT LESSONS

6

Scrapbooks and Army Surplus

C. Tyler's *You'll Never Know*

One night, Carol Tyler received a call from her usually taciturn ninety-year-old father, Chuck, a World War II veteran, wanting to spill memories of long-ago experiences that previously fell into "the category of 'leave it the hell alone' or 'it's none of your goddamn business'" (n.p.). Her mother, Hannah, most often shared the family news, so Tyler was surprised that her father was on the phone, even before he blurted, "Rivers of blood!" (n.p.). That provocative phrase sent her racing for a pad and pencil to record his recollections. This call triggered an extended project, as Tyler captured her father's memories first with a video camera, then as a scrapbook, and finally through a trilogy of graphic novels. Chuck's story needed to be preserved for the next generation through whatever media she could get her hands on. As she sat him down in front of her video camera, Tyler rearranged her parents' living room, tacked an American flag on the wall, and displayed various artifacts on the coffee table.

C. Tyler,* the artist, re-creates the coffee table display—Chuck's medals,

*Throughout this chapter, I will use "Carol Tyler" to refer to the autobiographical character as represented within the graphic novels and "C. Tyler" to refer to the artist who created them. The author says she chose a more gender-neutral variant of her name for these books in hopes that they might reach more male veterans, though the rest of her works before and since were published under "Carol Tyler."

insignias and badges, his dog tags, some newspaper clippings—in *A Good and Decent Man*, the first of three volumes. While the books were published individually in hardcover as *You'll Never Know*, they were renamed for the paperback edition as *Soldier's Heart*, which is also the title of the third volume. I am sticking with the original title of the series throughout this discussion, while reserving *Soldier's Heart* to refer to the final installment. On the surface, Carol's patriotic display of her father's wartime memorabilia (figure 6.1) represents the heroic ideals of the "greatest generation," the men who survived the Depression and marched off to "make the world safe for democracy."

Yet this display only captures part of Chuck's story, just as old photographs of Chuck clowning with his pals represent only one slice of military life. Why has Chuck spent so much time avoiding the subject, boxing away any reminder of his World War II experiences? Why does he grimace with pain, curse out his daughter, and shut down the video camera? And why is he suddenly unable to contain the memories anymore?

The stuff on the coffee table evokes some memories, but masks others that C. Tyler feels shaped her father—and through him, his family—for decades to follow. She hopes that "that stuff on the table will provide a clue" (n.p.), but her father wants to put these things back where they belong. *You'll Never Know* is, as Tyler told one interviewer, about "the stuff that gets passed down to the next generation," with stuff here meant to describe both material culture (the "O.D. anomalies" [for "olive drab" (n.p.)] or toxic chemicals stored away in the basement) and the emotional baggage, equally toxic, that Chuck passed down to her generation.

FIGURE 6.1. An assemblage of medals and other paraphernalia suggests the heroic ideals of the "greatest generation." C. Tyler, *A Good and Decent Man* (2009). © C. Tyler. Courtesy of Fantagraphics.

A parallel scene occurs in the second volume, *Collateral Damage*, involving a box of old photographs and birth announcements that provoke Hannah to talk—for the first time—about the death of her first daughter, Ann. Shortly after the birth of Carol's own daughter, Julia, Carol and her sister are helping her mother prepare for a garage sale, going through "goofy luau things from the 50s" and "a 50 gallon drum full of old prom dresses," each hinting at previously unknown aspects of their parents' lives (n.p.). When they find a lingerie box, carefully tied shut, her mother is at first repelled and then agrees to open it. "Ann's stuff" has been closeted for the past forty-five years. Hannah's hands are reflexively thrown up to shield herself as the box's contents are dumped onto the table. Much like Chuck's war memories, Hannah's thoughts and feelings spill forth, as she recounts the horrible accident—her toddler pulled a pot of boiling water off the stove and scalded herself, but she died choking on her own vomit while lying on her back in a hospital bed. And then, her mother asks the girls to dispose of the contents: "I'll always have Ann in my heart. I don't need this box" (Tyler 2010, n.p.).

C. Tyler reproduces the cards and notes sent to her mother on Ann's birth, subsequent birthdays, and death (figure 6.2). Though more than a hundred pages apart in the final consolidated volume, this composite image of aggrieved motherhood contrasts explicitly with Chuck's war memorabilia (another example of flipability)—each a sentimental reconstruction of their generation's

FIGURE 6.2. These birth announcement cards—for a now dead daughter—express the feminine ideals of her mother's generation. C. Tyler, *Collateral Damage* (2010). © C. Tyler. Courtesy of Fantagraphics.

masculine and feminine ideals that mask more painful memories. In both cases, Tyler has painstakingly copied the particulars, trying to hold these things in the reader's memory even as her parents shove them aside: the artist's obsession confronts the older generation's repression. But, for all of the care in their reproduction, these objects have a different status than the collections discussed in other chapters. Though people can collect army surplus or old greeting cards, these items here might be better described as personal effects, offering clues about Tyler's family's history and insights about her own life.

Throughout this chapter, I will discuss C. Tyler's graphic novel as a project in what Annette Kuhn has called "memory work," a process of analysis by which conflicted family relationships and painful memories are recovered through close engagement with old photographs and artifacts. In particular, I am interested in scrapbooking and comics making as part of a larger tradition of women's creative expression within the domestic sphere. Over time, scrapbooks moved from public history (grounded in archiving newspaper clippings) to personal memory (grounded in preserving keepsakes and family photographs). Tyler reverses this process, using her graphic novel to disclose events, reframing personal memories as public discourse, and thus situating these experiences within the shared history of the generation that participated in World War II. Throughout, I discuss this project in relational terms: making comics is framed as both an interruption—and an extension – of her gendered obligations as daughter, mother, and wife. But, to be clear, this project does not simply reproduce the heterosexual American middle-class family, but rather critiques the social repression and domestic containment that defined her parents' generation, exploring how institutional sexism and homophobia acted upon the postwar family, and the war's aftereffects on subsequent generations.

Ken Chin describes *You'll Never Know*: "[Tyler's] autobiographical comics display a shocking, unruly wholesomeness: they are visually and morally beautiful, suffused with a scrap-doodle amateurism and palpable maternal love. . . . Tyler mitigates the directness of heart with a dynamically pesky drawing style, splattering each panel with the democratic debris of life" (as quoted on the back cover, Tyler 2012). The term "debris" here conveys a destructive force as life gets in the way, families can damage each other, and artifacts from the past are often caught in the line of fire. Chin's references to her "wholesomeness" and "scrap-doodle amateurism" are misleading, since they continue a history of dismissing women's art as domestic craft, whereas Tyler's artfulness comes in creating intimacy with her readers, inviting us to read her works as pouring spontaneously from the heart rather than emerging through meticulous planning and systematic development. Throughout, Tyler shows a mastery over what Will Eisner (2008b) described as expressive anatomy, the broad-strokes gestures that allow a cartoonist to shorthand the emotional state, the personality, the moral qualities of her characters: each character is instantly recognizable panel by panel, despite being represented at varied ages and life stages, because something in their core posture remains the same.

If men often read collecting as self-fashioning, the "graphic women" (C. Tyler, Joyce Farmer, and Roz Chast) whom I discuss across this chapter and the next are more interested in what gets passed down—for better or worse—from one generation to the next. Emil Ferris is a transitional figure between the two groups—in some senses, sharing the pop culture fascinations that inspired the male artists, but using such materials as resources to make sense of herself, her family, her friends, and her community. As with the other women, she treats stuff as relational rather than purely personal: emotional or social belonging is more important than the belongings themselves.

Born in 1951, C. Tyler came to *You'll Never Know* after several decades of working on autobiographical comics. Hillary Chute (2016) describes Tyler's husband, Justin Green, and his 1972 work, *Binky Brown Meets the Holy Virgin Mary*, as having "set the space for comics to be a realm of the intensely personal—a space to reveal, through words and pictures, what one might consider the purview of the especially private" (153–154). Tyler also discloses family secrets as part of her creative process—in this case, examining the sometimes cryptic signs that express and mask the ways her father was touched by the war. Tyler also benefited from the mentorship of R. Crumb and especially Aline Kominsky-Crumb, who embraced Tyler as part of their circle early in her career. The first generation of underground comics artists had been a boys' club, and their concerns—though countercultural—reflect the radical men's adolescent fantasies. As women entered underground comics, their own work was every bit as frank and transgressive but embraced different subjects—paralleling the concerns of second wave feminism.

Feminist consciousness-raising sessions held in living rooms in the 1960s and 1970s created a context where personal narratives were read for signs of patriarchy at work: such stories were compared and contrasted so that participants came to understand their shared conditions as women and recognize the power dynamics within the family as mirroring those within the society. As Kathie Sarachild writes in a 1978 essay on the successes and limits of the feminist consciousness-raising movement, "Analyzing our experience in our personal lives and in the movement, reading about the experience of other people's struggles, and connecting these through consciousness-raising will keep us on the track, moving as fast as possible toward women's liberation" (n.p.). She notes that many men were threatened by women getting together to share stories about their family lives and reflecting on their social conditions: "Whole areas of women's lives were declared off limits to discussion. The topics we were talking about in our groups were dismissed as 'petty' or 'not political.' Often these were the key areas in terms of how women are oppressed as a particular group—like housework, childcare and sex" (n.p.).

Feminist underground comics represented another space where women were reflecting on their own lives and exchanging stories—in this case, graphic stories—that spoke to experiences not being represented elsewhere in their culture. As Sarachild notes about consciousness-raising, the goal was not therapeutic—not simply about women having their say, getting things off their chest—but political, identifying shared issues feminists might mobilize around to change the lives of women.

Often, like the members of these consciousness-raising groups, female underground comics creators formed collectives that brought multiple perspectives (diverse in life experiences, though most often, white) together around a shared theme, like sexuality or reproductive rights. These collectives, also like the feminist consciousness-raising groups, constituted a support network for their participants. Tyler was a member of the Twisted Sisters, a collective of "bad girl" artists, including, among others, Kominsky-Crumb, Carol Lay, Debbie Drechsler, Mary Fleener, Phoebe Gloeckner, Diane Noomin, and Julie Doucet. Publishing two collections of material created over almost twenty years (Noomin 1991, 1994), the Twisted Sisters talked about growing up female, their romantic and sexual entanglements, their conflicted feelings toward their bodies, traumatic experiences (rape, sexual molestation, harassment), and more mundane aspects of their everyday lives. In drawing this parallel, I do not mean to suggest that all of these women necessarily saw their work in feminist terms—some did, some did not. When I shared the first draft of this essay, C. Tyler suggested that her relationship to feminism was "a toughy," since she had not set out to produce feminist comics, but only wanted to open a space within comics where women could tell their own stories, wherever that took them: "I knew comics was a boys game and wanted my work to be assessed on basic standards of excellence" (personal correspondence, 2018). But in expanding who produced comics, these female collectives changed the kinds of stories comics told, and in telling autobiographical stories that acknowledged the particulars of women's lives, issues of gender inequalities necessarily surfaced, much as they had done through feminist consciousness-raising. After all, the personal is political.

Tyler's two previously published books, *The Job Thing: Stories about Shitty Jobs* (1993) and *Late Bloomer: Stories* (2005), include works that depicted her own personal journey through failed relationships and dead-end jobs, the discomforts of pregnancy and the indignities of motherhood. Tyler's earlier stories were female centered, but with *You'll Never Know* she shifted her attention onto men's lives. Speaking at USC, she summed up this project: "It was clearly not going to be a book about war, but it was going to be a book about relationships. Relationship is everything" (Jenkins 2013b, n.p.).

During this same talk, Tyler discussed how her artistic ambition had been repeatedly deferred in favor of caregiving and cheerleading within the family, as making comics had to be fit into the smallest crevices of her everyday life. She shared the circumstances under which she completed the trilogy's final volume, while confronting health crises in the lives of her mother, father, sister, daughter, even the family dog: "I had a deadline, but I also had people falling off cliffs all around me and tragic things happening. There were times when I couldn't breathe but I was dipping the pen. I was fully aware of the fact that this was the last time I was going to be watching *The Nutcracker* together with my mom but I was dipping the pen, lettering part of the book" (Jenkins 2013b, n.p.).

Feminist economics has sought to direct attention onto the ways that reproductive domestic labor—the work women do to sustain their families—is unevenly distributed (with women doing the lion share) and consistently undervalued. As Weisinger (2012) argues, "In the case of housewives, an entire economy is built upon the idea of free labor and care: the informal economy. Housewives do not get reimbursed for taking care of children, shopping, cleaning, cooking, etc. These are elements of support that are deemed necessary in order for the male counterpart of the family unit to be able to work and provide for the family financially and to be able to develop in the formal economy, which is the ultimate definition of success in our society" (3). Producing comics—especially independent comics, especially graphic novels—constitutes precarious labor, a form of economic and creative risk, since producing a graphic novel can require years of work before any payment is received. It is a drain on family resources (both time and money) that is less often allowed women in our culture than it is men. Many of the female artists discussed here struggle with a similar set of binds, wanting to care for their families and wanting to create, ending up postponing their creative work until children are raised, or trying to work on the side, borrowing time from caregiving to express themselves.

Throughout her work, Tyler acknowledges the competing demands that sucked her time and energy over the past few decades. She dedicated *Late Bloomer* (2005) to "anyone who has deferred a dream due to raising children or caregiving, or has experienced a significant setback from emotional hurt, physical or mental illness, pain, injury or loss, or any other blind-side interruption that has impeded the achievement of a goal" (9). Several comics depict Carol drawing under a deadline, as her daughter yanks on her arm. By contrast, Justin, her husband, is shown in *You'll Never Know* with his own studio, protected from the family crisis du jour—and for much of the book, he has abandoned his family to chase after another woman. Tyler never lets us forget the ways that she has had to negotiate making comics against other responsibilities, while Seth or Kim Deitch often depict themselves as self-absorbed, hanging out with other cartoonists, and prioritizing these interests above their romantic partners. Carol doesn't get to be a collector; she's too busy picking up after everyone else.

During her USC talk, Tyler shared that, while she struggled with learning how to read in her early schooling, drawing has always been a central part of her identity, even if she had to scrounge for materials with which to make her marks, cutting open discarded grocery bags or sketching on the backs of junk mail envelopes. She described herself sitting underneath the family dinner table, drawing to stay out of family disputes: "I ended up just watching the world, observing. . . . I would be listening to the family doing its thing and I would just zone out, which is what I guess I am still doing" (Jenkins 2013b, n.p.). Cut off from words (both written and spoken), she turned her attention to pictures: drawing granted C. Tyler a voice. Comics making was once again embedded within the family; her observation skills and mimicry allowed her to critique the gender dynamics shaping her world.

In this chapter, I will draw on two different vantage points to understand the family secrets that surface across these three graphic novels—on the one hand, reading *You'll Never Know* in relation to the larger social and cultural history of the scrapbook; on the other, reading each of the core characters through the stuff that C. Tyler chose to represent on her pages (her father's tools, her mother's crafts, and the army surplus exchanged across generations). Both represent resources through which C. Tyler can perform "memory work," that is, reconstruct and reframe family history with a critical eye that helps us to perceive what cannot be directly shown and what often went unsaid in her relations with her father and mother.

Comics and Scrapbooks

Today, scrapbooking is a hobby most often associated with women, though historians are quick to note that, in earlier eras, all kinds of people produced scrapbooks for all kinds of reasons. Even today, scholars argue, gendered assumptions shape how we define what counts as scrapbooking: men who collect stamps, coins, or baseball cards are generally not described as scrapbooking, whereas women who accumulate candy wrappers, canned goods labels, advertising and fashion images, or movie star pinups are less likely to be described as collecting.

In practice, the history of scrapbooking is hard to extract from the history of collecting. The owners of wonder cabinets often maintained books where they recorded information or sketched their possessions and, in some cases, included images of objects they aspired to own. Even these earliest books must have resembled comics, since they combined sketches and texts, images and words. The commonplace book evolved from these early notebooks as people copied and preserved texts—quotations and poems primarily—that spoke to them, a practice soon encouraged as moral education, especially for young girls.

With the rise of cheap printed matter, scrapbookers displaced hand-copied texts with printed texts "gleaned" from periodicals. As Ellen Gruber Garvey (2013) recounts: "As they scissored in and scissored out, amassing and excluding, scrapbook makers imposed their will on what they read. They created a version of the newspaper that preserves only what they considered worth preserving, and organized the material within their own structure of arrangements and juxtapositions" (9). Because these scrapbooks were built mostly from public records, they often focused outward, toward events that impacted the community.

Scrapbookers were especially excited by the introduction of color printing, a technological shift that paved the way for the Yellow Kid and the other brightly colored Sunday funnies. As Jessica Helfand (2008) writes: "Many nineteenth-century albums were a virtual ode to chromolithography, consisting of pages that basically celebrated the thrill of the colored fragment. Many examples contained trade cards, token-of-affection cards, chromolithographs, and embossed prints, exemplifying the Victorian propensity to create decorative, non-narrative pages" (4). So again we see a potential connection between the history of scrapbooks and the history of American comics, as graphic elements become more dominant within the scrapbook. Something similar occurred because of the rise of low-cost, readily available photographs—the mass-produced carte de visite and, later, amateur snapshots enabled by Kodak's Brownie, the first camera for a broad consumer market. And the introduction of cellophane tape in 1930 made it easier to attach other physical materials to the pages: "Fragments of cloth from wedding gowns were included in bridal books, while new mothers included gentle locks from their baby's first haircut. Debutantes saved news clippings, farmers saved weather reports, high school girls saved gum wrappers, and everyone, it seemed, saved greeting cards" (xvii).

Helfand's examples are feminine, and with good reason, since the role of the scrapbook shifts during this period from capturing public history to recording personal memory, thus coming to center on the domestic sphere where women's lives were so often contained. As the introduction to *The Scrapbook in American Life* explains: "In form, many scrapbooks more closely resemble the junk drawer found in kitchens and desks. Some scrapbooks spend their entire existence unbound, in shoe boxes or other staging areas, awaiting the day when the gatherer becomes the compiler" (Ott, Tucker, and Buckler 2006, 12). The scrapbook offers a rich metaphor for women's lives—disrupted or interrupted, never allowed to be completed, fragmented, hidden from view, difficult to decipher without inside knowledge, built from salvaged resources, and often focused on domestic life.

Multimodality and Juxtaposition

As scrapbooks became multimodal, as representations coexisted on the same page with the objects themselves, scrapbookers experimented with different formal practices: "From perfunctory clippings to annotated images, the materials sequestered in the pages of these books would grow more varied, and their placement would begin to suggest a more dynamically nuanced relationship to the picture plane. Physical space, once rigid, would achieve a new authenticity as something decidedly more abstract, and with the advent of film, would come to reshape our visual perceptions of chronology, sequence, memory, even reality itself. Pages in scrapbooks would begin to exhibit new and unusual variations in texture and voice, mannerism and inflection" (Helfand 2008, 47). If considered at all, scrapbooks are primarily examined by social historians, which means there has been a focus on their contents but rarely on their formal or representational practices. Even a cursory consideration suggests that they were a site for visual experimentation and, in particular, for grassroots collage and remix practices, similar to the ones deployed by the Victorian women in their photo albums or Kare and her sketchbook. Consider, for example, the widespread practice of constructing "dreamhouses" or "dollhouses," producing a composite space from fragments selected from catalogs and advertisements (Gordon 2006).

Though she doesn't specifically reference scrapbooks, Hillary Chute (2010) discusses Alison Bechdel's *Fun Home* (2006) in terms of the ways the artist reconstructs her family history:* "Bechdel draws public and private photographs; her own diary entries; numerous maps; newspapers; many different kinds of books, including typeset pages from novels and dictionaries; childhood and adolescent drawings; poems; old cartoons; passports; police records; court orders; course catalogs; typed letters from her father and mother, and handwritten letters between her parents. She re-created absolutely everything in the book, reinhabiting the elements from her past to re-present them—and to preserve them, to publically re-archive them" (Chute 2010, 186). For Chute, it is important not simply that Bechdel has "re-archived" these materials, making them public, revealing certain family secrets along the way, but also that these materials have been copied by hand: "Instead of merely reprinting those materials, Bechdel re-creates them. She inhabits the past not only, in a general way, by giving it visual form, but further by the embodied process of reinscribing archival documents" (183). One might productively think of *Fun Home* as a commonplace book, representing an era when scraps of culture were reproduced "by hand" rather than cut from printed matter and pasted onto the page. This analogy seems particularly apt for talking not only about the family documents Bechdel redraws but also the many literary allusions she incorporates into this work.

**Fun Home* is one of the most important works in the feminist comics tradition and often the text most immediately recognized by non–comics readers. I struggled with whether to include an extended discussion here since my focus on material culture would yield some interesting insights into the father and his home decorating. But my desire to expand the canon of comic studies won out: much has already been written about Bechdel, so I put my energies into works that had not yet attracted this same critical engagement.

Bechdel and Tyler are not unique among the current generations of "graphic women" in taking inspiration from scrapbooks. Lucy Knisley's *Relish: My Life in the Kitchen* (2013) depicts her relationship with her mother through their shared interest in food, and incorporates recipes of dishes (ranging from chocolate chip cookies to California rolls) that figure prominently in her memories, displaying each core ingredient and diagramming their preparation. Earlier scrapbooks recorded family recipes and other domestic lore. Scrapbooks were not just multimodal but also multisensual: the scraps of cloth could be touched, the sprigs from Christmas trees carried scents. Tyler references the songs of her parents' generation, basing the project's original title around what Chuck and Hannah regarded as "their song," and Knisley evokes our sense of taste and perhaps a tactile sense as she reflects on foods that bonded her to her mother (as well as conflicts around cooking that sometimes pushed them apart). In *Dotter of Her Father's Eyes*, (2012), another father-daughter memoir, Mary M. Talbot and Bryan Talbot use, among other things, her father's lecture notes, his college report card, his ration book, his driver's license, his social security card, even some pressed flowers to construct our impressions of this difficult man, a Joyce scholar. In each case, these graphic artists were inspired by the visual practices of earlier generations, and a richer formal understanding of scrapbooks might be a key to appreciating their work.

You'll Never Know as Scrapbook

You'll Never Know directly and explicitly links itself to this scrapbook tradition. The book was reproduced in the shape of a traditional scrapbook, giving the graphic design a strong horizontal emphasis, unlike the vertical structure of most other contemporary comics. Tyler uses a different material for each of the volumes' covers: wood, specifically old-growth walnut, taken from a supply in her father's workshop, for *A Good and Decent Man*; lace to reflect the focus on her mother and daughter for *Collateral Damage*; and, finally, granite for *Soldier's Heart*, which deals, in parts, with public monuments. On top of these foundations, the artist places documents and artifacts that capture some of her key concerns. The first book reproduces (again, drawn by hand and blown up to a much larger size) her father's military identification photograph, held in place by photo album corners (figure 6.3); the second volume depicts a military patch, a pressed flower, her own portrait as a child, and a pencil (figure 6.4). By the third volume—as she shared with us at USC—she was exhausted and ended up with a quick sketch of her father, a gesture that also suggests the

ways that the scrapbook aesthetic has by this point been more fully absorbed into her practices as a cartoonist (figure 6.5). Strikingly, these elements are all missing in the single-volume paperback edition. Here the cover has one sepia-colored drawing inspired by a photograph of her father in uniform, and the inside flap has a map depicting the route of several hours she frequently traveled from her home to her parent's house.

The scrapbook analogy works on multiple levels in *You'll Never Know*. At the most basic, the narrative centers around Carol's efforts to assemble a scrapbook to document her father's World War II experiences. This project drives the book's events and Tyler uses the scrapbook as her primary means of recounting Chuck's military experiences. The scrapbook segments have a regimented structure—two panels per page, each numbered, each dated using a vintage stamp, and each provided a handwritten caption on lined paper (figure 6.6). Much like Bechdel, Tyler painstakingly reproduces actual photographs, but she also reconstructs

FIGURE 6.3. The cover mimics the grain of her father's old-growth walnut lumber. C. Tyler, *A Good and Decent Man* (2009). © C. Tyler. Courtesy of Fantagraphics.

FIGURE 6.4. The lace cover suggests the increased importance of Carol's mother, Hannah, and the other women in her life. C. Tyler, *Collateral Damage* (2010). © C. Tyler. Courtesy of Fantagraphics.

FIGURE 6.5. The marble cover suggests monumental conceptions of World War II. C. Tyler, *Soldier's Heart* (2012). © C. Tyler. Courtesy of Fantagraphics.

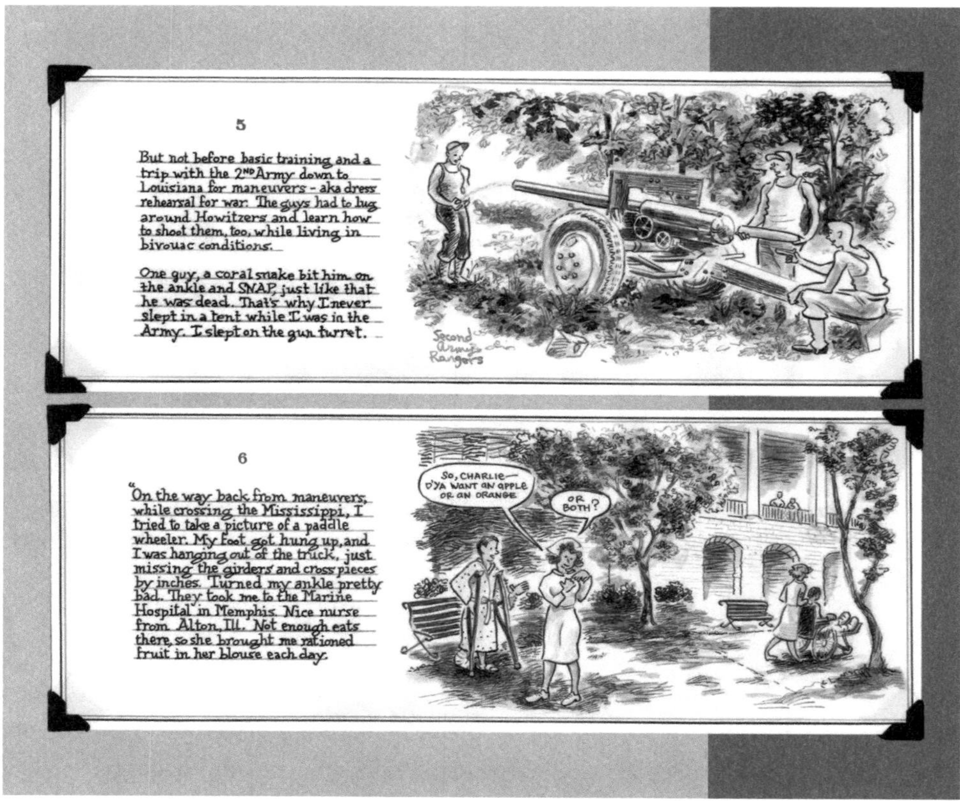

FIGURE 6.6. Tyler retells her father's war years experiences through the pages of a scrapbook. C. Tyler, *A Good and Decent Man* (2009). © C. Tyler. Courtesy of Fantagraphics.

imagined events. While written in the third person, the captions often capture her father's voice, excited as he sets off to war, enchanted when he first encounters an attractive redhead whom he will woo and win, matter-of-fact in describing conditions he encounters through various assignments or discussing how he becomes a conduit for black market goods, and breaking down before undescrible horrors. Tyler has shared that these sections draw much more directly on the recordings she made of her father's narrative, so they legitimately capture the sound of his voice.

Tyler's use of the scrapbook to tell her father's story is period appropriate. A therapeutic discourse surrounded scrapbooks for GIs during World War II—volunteers, mostly women, were encouraged to help wounded men to construct scrapbooks as a means of working through traumatic experiences. As Helfand (2008) notes, such projects often served a propagandistic purpose, reshaping what got remembered and shared with the people back home: "Pressed for time, concerned for their future, worried about forgetting (or worse, about remembering), midcentury soldiers used a peculiar subgenre of memory books which are almost unbearably cheerful. Here, goofy headings (HIGHLIGHTS AND FURLOUGHS) mask what would likely have been much more complex, even turbulent recollections, resulting in what was, in retrospect, a virtual epidemic of nostalgic amnesia. Publishers thus reframed memory as fiction, trading veteran dysphoria for a kind of plucky optimism" (130). Scrapbooks were commercially produced with generic categories instructing veterans which stories were worth recording (and, by extension, what was best left unsaid). Helfand reproduces one example titled *My Buddy Book* (1942), its cover featuring men from the various services marching side by side. Inside, there are pages dedicated to "Me the guy my friends know," "Some of my new friends," "Just a few pleasant memories," "My dates," "Officers I know," and "Guys on my 'good' list," each suggesting ways of maintaining the sense of fraternity and adventure some men associated with their war years (131). Tyler writes about "one scrapbook album of army pictures, carefully mounted photos with no dates or information. I never knew what they recorded specifically. No text. Maybe that's what intrigued me. A parallel world where my Dad looked like he was having fun. So different from the pained and distant guy I experienced" (Tyler 2009). The scrapbook shares only what the compiler wants to share (figure 6.7) and her father wanted to remain a closed book, even to his own family. So part of her project involves adding text, rendering the memories more explicit so they can be passed down. Tyler understood this project in both personal and public terms:

> When I started this new thing about my dad, I was thinking about the ancestors I don't know yet—possible grandchildren, so they can have this knowledge about the family, and know me a little bit. . . . It's not really just for the family, because I knew that . . . I was up against the clock, because a lot of people are losing their dads and grandpas who had served in World War II. And I knew that there was a new generation of warriors coming up that were dealing with the issues that my dad has been plagued with. I really talk about that more and more—the effects of mental illness and anxiety and what that does to families. So I knew that the audience would be part military, part people my age that have dads, people who are grandchildren—everybody, really. . . . Because none of those guys came back and talked about their experiences, and they were all damaged by it. All of them. They all carried this stuff when they came back that they gave to us children. (Heater 2009, n.p.)

FIGURE 6.7. Her father's scrapbook, like those of many World War II vets, masks the horrors of the war behind happy-go-lucky images. C. Tyler, *A Good and Decent Man* (2009). © C. Tyler. Courtesy of Fantagraphics.

Much of the controversy surrounding autobiographical comics has centered around how artists negotiate borders between private and public, what it means to share with the world things that would once have remained behind closed doors, recognizing that there are intense generational differences about what is appropriate to expose. The more Tyler emphasizes the processes by which her parents boxed their emotional lives, the more powerful become those moments when those repressed feelings surface.

Scrapbooks as Counterhistory

Helfand's account of veterans' scrapbooks suggests a process designed to repress painful memories and replace them with more joyful ones. On the other hand, as Ellen Gruber Garvey (2013) notes, scrapbooks could also function as tools for counterhistory, especially for those who do not fit as comfortably within their society's official truths. In *Writing with Scissors*, Garvey discusses how the African American community archived news clippings that acknowledged lynching and other racialized violence, knowing that these events would be quickly written out of accounts created by white-dominated institutions. In some cases, they scribbled in the margins or wrote directly over texts, challenging their representations of events. Garvey describes these scrapbookers as "using juxtaposition as a mode of critique," suggesting that the compilers developed and taught some basic media literacies in getting at masked truths.

C. Tyler hints at such counterhistory throughout *You'll Never Know*: first, when she encounters a World War I monument while walking her dog and juxtaposes the war memorial with the text of Wilfred Owen's antiwar poem "Dulce et Decorum Est," and later, when Chuck, seeing the faces of the dead while visiting the World War II memorial in Washington, states, "That's what they should call this place: Death Everywhere" (n.p.). Here, the efforts to sanitize and memorialize war ("died for one's country") are met with vivid images of its human costs. In the first case, Tyler challenges visuals with texts (the poem) and in the other, several pages of graphics overwrite the memorial's white marble.

In *Family Secrets: Acts of Memory and Imagination* (1995), Annette Kuhn suggests that conflicted truths shape practices, such as domestic scrapbooks and family photograph albums, as, for example, people cut their exes out of photographs or remove pictures from their albums altogether. Focusing on a few images from her own family album, Kuhn describes her mother's efforts to bend Annette's childhood memories by the ways her photographs are cropped, captioned, and contextualized, just as the mother had sought to determine how the daughter dressed and acted before the photographs were even taken: "[If] a photograph can be the site of conflicting memories, whose memory is to prevail in the family archive? . . . Family photographs may affect to show us our past, but what we do with them—how we use them—is really about today, not yesterday" (14–15, 19). Kuhn's writing reintroduces the daughter's voice into the equation, describing how certain images "cloak, occlude and subvert—as well as create—identities" (69).

You'll Never Know positions the father's scrapbook within a larger narrative about how those events impacted several generations of the Tyler family. If *Family Secrets* is the daughter's revenge on a controlling mother, *You'll Never Know* represents a daughter standing up to a bullying father and yet also paying tribute to him and his generation. The scrapbook project began as a labor of love. But she also has other motives for undertaking this work, since the project distracts her as her marriage hits rock bottom. Chuck verbally abuses Carol and her mother when he discovers that Carol has removed his photographs and documents from his house so she can work on them between trips ("It's my stuff, that's all"). He is further outraged when she uses his tools and supplies to construct a wooden cover, feeling a loss of control over resources by which he defines his mastery. But the father finds his own reasons to value the project. After talking with some fellow veterans, he believes that the government may have shortchanged him for a wartime injury: "To Hell with memories: the army owes me money!!"

Regardless of their motives, Chuck and Carol set out together to document his experiences and perhaps repair his faltering memory, visiting archives in Saint Louis and Washington, DC, and consulting with military experts. Yet this search is an exercise in frustration: many pertinent records were sunk at sea, some destroyed by fire, and whatever survives is often inaccessible due to bureaucratic obstacles and snafus that cannot be overcome given their limited time at each facility. Because his plumbing skills were valued during the war, the father moved between units, and so he cannot find anyone else who might have shared memories or even whom he recognizes from their time together. Even if they cannot document what happened to his body during the war, C. Tyler does demonstrate how Chuck was impacted by his traumatic experiences, suffering from "soldier's heart" (an archaic Civil War–era term for posttraumatic stress disorder). Early on, Tyler introduces what will be one of the book's key conclusions: "not all scars are visible." And that's why it becomes all the more important to capture the fleeting moments of pain on her father's face, his emotional outpouring when he visits the World War II memorial, the various mechanisms by which he deflects questions, and the ways he translates emotional lack into relentless labor. While such intimate moments may cross the thresholds of what her father would object to sharing, they represent how men of his generation were imprinted by militarization, mandatory heterosexuality, and masculine repression.

Here, too, the scrapbook analogy is appropriate for describing the book's eclectic visual style and digressive narrative strategies. As one essay notes, "Scrapbooks shuffle and recombine the coordinates of time, space, voice and memory. What could be more emblematic of the fractured narratives of modernity than scrapbooks?" (Ott, Tucker, and Buckler 2006, 16). If the scrapbook pages adopt a fixed grid structure that reflects the author's attempts to order and re-present her father's memories, the rest of the book uses a hodgepodge of different artistic styles to convey the chaos that her father left in his wake. If the scrapbook is her father's story, these other pages are Carol's story, though her own goals are often sacrificed to other demands on her attention: her daughter's psychological issues, her on-again/off-again relationship with her husband, her father's struggles with cancer, her mother's stroke, not to mention a succession of family dogs and a few family gatherings along the way. Comics critic Sean Collins (2009) has complained about the book's digressive structure and "ramshackled" artwork:

> Her comics' landscape layout and dashed-off line and lettering (complete with blue-pencil guidelines) evoke a mid-tier slice-of-life webcomic; they're pleasant and likeable, but they make this very serious and personal project feel slightly airy and inconsequential. They're not helped in this regard by their presentation as a supplement to the actual scrapbook she's putting together for her father, nor by her presentation of herself in an always slightly humorous fashion even when literally prostrated by her husband's infidelity and departure. Transitions and juxtapositions, too, feel under-considered, from the cuts to and from her own life story to this volume's abrupt cut-off point. (n.p.)

Again, we should distrust terms like "dashed-off" or "under-considered" as a male critic's denial of Tyler's artistic agency. But beyond that, I would argue such a structure gives artistic expression to the conflicting demands on attention many women confront. One might understand these digressions in another sense. Kuhn (1995) describes the sequencing of images in a family album as akin to "a classical narrative: linear, chronological," whereas she describes women's experience of everyday life as "more characteristic of the open-ended narrative form of the soap opera than of the closure of classical narrative" (19). This graphic novel's digressive structure is a refusal of ideological closure, rejecting the shutting down of memories and emotions performed by the original scrapbook, where every detail has been sequenced and date stamped. Tyler rejects the old adage, no doubt repeated by her father, "a place for everything and everything in its place," insisting that we recognize the interconnections between seemingly unrelated events.

Tyler's books are constructed through scraps, both literally and figuratively. Some of what gets presented here—for example, the collages of military badges and greeting cards, an invitation to her parent's wedding anniversary—are traditional subject matter for scrapbooks of the postwar era. In many cases, Tyler redraws these materials. She told her USC audience that incorporating actual photographs into her graphic memoir would be like "putting Oreos in a salad," that the materials would not mix well since they represented different ways of seeing (Jenkins 2013b, n.p.). But, in fact, there are several places where she does incorporate materials from other sources directly into her book: for example, an autobiographical essay her father wrote as a high school student and a technical drawing of the same vintage depicting the Panama Locks, both attached with what looks like masking tape in *A Good and Decent Man*, or a newspaper clipping reporting on her sister's death in *Collateral Damage*. Or consider a segment in *Soldier's Heart* the author entitles "Prairie Trek by Truck with Hannah and Chuck," where she compresses a road trip to Saint Louis into a series of partially transcribed conversations jotted down on a notepad, with the instructions to the reader to "slow down, especially after each sentence. Put some miles between them" (n.p.) and to "listen to the songs" her father had playing on the radio. And there are places where Tyler breaks the flow with beautiful full-page images, one depicting the ornaments on the family Christmas tree, another offering an Edward Hopper–like image of a gas station on a cold winter's night.

Perhaps the most poignant moment comes when she convinces her mother to draw a picture for the book. Though her hand is unsteady and her mental process is slowed by her stroke, the mother finds a graphic solution to sum up her family. In Hannah's picture, "out of war came my children" (n.p.), each child's life is depicted as what she describes as "stars in bloom," with their birth dates carefully recorded alongside each bloom. The bloom representing her lost daughter sheds tears, drawn with pencil. Her inclusion of her mother's drawing in her own graphic novel suggests how scrapbooks have classically been understood as vehicles for shared family memories, as much or more than they are vehicles for personal expression. This is C. Tyler's graphic novel (defined here as autobiographical), but she cannot help but incorporate expressive practices associated with the other family members.

Memory Work

There's another sense in which we might think of *You'll Never Know* as a scrapbook. Tyler told my students about the many notebooks she had compiled through the years, jotting down her observations about the people around her, and about a pad she kept next to her phone when she was in the most intense phases of her child-rearing, where she would jot down her scattered thoughts and toss them into a box to sift through later (Jenkins 2013b, n.p.). Over the years that mothering dominated her life, she accumulated a massive amount of material. I imagine her sifting through the scraps, like her notes about the Saint Louis trip, trying to decide what to incorporate into this particular project. This book, then, is built from meaningful fragments spanning fifty years or more in her family's history, all of which she is now sharing with her readers.

Kuhn (1995) describes her own autobiographical project in *Family Secrets* as "memory work":

> Memory work has a great deal in common with forms of inquiry which—like detective work and archeology, say—involve working backwards—searching for clues, deciphering signs and traces, making deductions, patching together reconstructions out of fragments of evidence. . . . Bringing the secrets and the shadows into the open allows the deeper meanings of the family drama's mythic aspects to be reflected upon, confronted and understood at all levels. This in turn helps in coming to terms with the feelings of the present, and so in living more fully in the present. (4, 7)

Truths cannot be read directly from the photograph, however much it seems to capture a moment of reality, because the photograph has been constructed and reconstructed over time: "You will get nowhere, for instance, by taking a magnifying glass to it to get a closer look: you will see only patches of light and dark, an unreadable mesh of grains" (13). Kuhn's description of reading an image through a magnifying glass no doubt captures some of what occurred as Tyler redrew old photographs from her family history. Yet this is only one step in a process that, for Kuhn, involves an active interrogation and recontextualization of such images to recover the gender dynamics that shaped the performance of self. Such moments are always constructed and staged, no matter how casually and no matter how much the conventions of the family photograph have been naturalized.

Hillary Chute (2010) describes this process as embodiment, writing in regards to *Fun Home*: "The pathos that itself underwrites the project of painstakingly learning to copy a dead father's handwriting is striking, as is her effort to pin it down correctly and reproduce it visually in her narrative" (186). The same could be said for Tyler's efforts to recreate a photograph of her dead sister, whom she never knew, or for that matter, to recall and draw from memory "what was on the coffee table in my house in 1965" (Jenkins 2013b, n.p.). Such memory work is never simply reproductive; it always, as Kuhn insists, involves acts of interpretation. Minor details are "evidence . . . to be solved, like a riddle; read and decoded, like clues left behind at the scene of a crime" (13). And linking individual experiences into a larger conceptual framework allows artists to identify those forces that imposed particular conceptions of masculinity and femininity on postwar American life.

Processing Things

If the scrapbook metaphor encourages us to recover family secrets, C. Tyler's work also encourages us to tap broader social knowledge as we scan the mise-en-scène for clues about who these people are and how they have lived their lives. Elaine Freedgood (2010) has discussed "the idea in things" as it emerges from the detailed discussion of everyday objects in nineteenth-century realist literature, suggesting that there has been a devaluing of descriptive details in more modernist texts. Today, "thing culture" survives "only in those marginal or debased forms and practices in which apparently mundane or meaningless objects can suddenly take on or be assigned value and meaning: the flea market, the detective story, the lottery, the romantic comedy—in short, in any cultural site in which a found object may be stripped of its randomness" (8). If we ignore her literature professor condescension, we might add to this list the scrapbook and the graphic novel. Freedgood identifies a range of strategies by which literary critics might engage with descriptions of "things" in realist novels: as creating a "reality effect," their particularity suggesting a real time and place; through metonymy where the part stands in for something larger, representing a lifestyle, identity, or cultural process; and, finally, as a metaphor with its symbolic meaning abstracted from material history. Of these, Freedgood argues that critics have neglected metonymy for metaphor, focusing on interpreting things abstractly rather than engaging with what they might tell us about the people who owned them. Each of these levels of analysis sheds light on the role of "things" in C. Tyler's graphic narratives.

Chuck's Tools

Consider, for example, a full-page depiction of her father's home workshop in *A Good and Decent Man*. This image works on all of the levels discussed above, and then some (figure 6.8). For starters, the drawing's attention to detail displays the artist's virtuosity. But the accompanying text shifts focus from the artist to her father: "A person's workshop can be a reflection of who they are and Dad's is clean, purposeful, and authentic. He's got every power tool, every hand tool there is, as well as many obscure but critical parts needed to complete even the most obsolete tasks" (Tyler 2009, n.p.). The caption, "C. W. Tyler's Tennessee shop, for example, circa 1970s," makes its own bid for the "reality

FIGURE 6.8. Tyler lovingly reconstructs her father's workshop, circa 1970s. C. Tyler, *A Good and Decent Man* (2009). © C. Tyler. Courtesy of Fantagraphics.

effect." C. Tyler is carefully cataloging Chuck's actual possessions, and each has a story behind it. She confirmed as much (Jenkins 2013b, n.p.), suggesting that her siblings dig out this illustration when they want to refer to specific things that the family used to own. Some objects will figure in subsequent chapters—for example, the airplane propellers that Chuck disastrously deploys as a fan to cool his living room; C. Tyler mentions here the "old-growth walnut that's been carefully dried for 30 years" around which centers the book's most intense father-daughter dispute. Other evocative objects—for example, a hand-cranked ice cream churner—may bring back specific memories for readers of her generation. Tyler told one interviewer, "We are a family of interesting personal artifacts. No Tiffany lamps or Civil War buckles, but yes, the kayak Dad built from scratch when he was 8 is still hanging up in his workshop, coated with decades of 'old-growth walnut' sawdust" (Lorah 2009, n.p.). And the kayak is depicted here. Chuck, quietly working off to the side, his clothes blending into the background, his capped head slumped over his tools, becomes simply one more element here, given no more stress than the buzz saw or the lawnmower. Chuck belongs in this space, just as everything here belongs to him.

C. Tyler draws each and every object in her father's workplace with precision, with light pouring into the workshop from seemingly every direction. By comparison, in her depiction of her own work space, the artist and her drawing table are well lit, but her surroundings are lost in murky shadows (figure 6.9). Some details, such as a Beatles board game, are partially visible, but most are obscured, and few depicted objects figure elsewhere. While she uses the dim images to suggest her accumulated clutter, she is not interested in illuminating these possessions. (Only with the publication of her subsequent book, *Fab4 Mania*, do we get a sense of the personal importance the Beatles held in her life.)

During her USC talk, Tyler shared photographs of core tools of her craft—her pen tips, her pencil sharpener, her hand-mixed inks. Like her father, she values the right tool for the right job (Jenkins 2013b). In a 1991 single-page comic (Tyler 2005, n.p.), she refers to "adult children of plumbers and pipefitters" as if they were patients in a twelve-step program, depicting a woman who loses her job because she stops to wrestle with a dripping faucet. The compulsion to work with their hands unites father and daughter. By comparison, Bechdel in *Fun Home* uses interior decoration to contrast her values with those of her father: "My own decided preferences for the unadorned and purely functional emerged early. I was Spartan to my father's Athenian, Modern to his Victorian, Butch to his Nelly, Utilitarian to his Aesthete" (14–15). Surrounded by her father's "curatorial onslaught," she protests: "I grew to resent the way my

FIGURE 6.9. Tyler reveals fewer details of her own life in this murky rendering of her work space. C. Tyler, *A Good and Decent Man* (2009). © C. Tyler. Courtesy of Fantagraphics.

father treated his furniture like children and his children like furniture" (14), a passage suggesting how realistic details can become metonymous and then metaphorical within the same passage.

Apart from anchoring the reality of her personal narrative, Tyler clearly intends her depiction of his workshop to portray her father as constantly working with his hands. Again, the text offers clues as to how readers might link this space to his larger life-narrative: "The guy can do anything! I've seen it with my own eyes!" (Tyler 2009, n.p.). On the very next page, there is another full-page drawing, capturing Carol's memory of coming home from school and discovering the family house being lifted off the ground by a giant crane so her father and his buddies can lay a new foundation. In *Collateral Damage*, her father, seventy-five years old and battling cancer, insists on building his own home, roping his extended family into the process: "Over the next few months, it kinda went like this: go for some chemo, then come home and get busy with some drywall. Few days later, go for another treatment, come home and get busy again. . . . This was the deal at Camp Chemo" (Tyler 2012, n.p.).

Chuck's work ethic masks a pathology that drives him to keep working no matter what else is going on in his life. Refusing to accept human frailty, he bullies family members into working, even when they are sick or dealing with trauma. *Soldier's Heart* depicts the final chapters of her father's wartime experience, when he found himself in a military hospital after getting blasted by a German howitzer: "His mind was blown for weeks: no memory, no communication—catatonic from a concussion, coupled with a condition called 'battle fatigue'" (Tyler 2012, n.p.). Chuck is taunted by fellow soldiers, suggesting that he is "soft." Chuck pushes out of bed to demonstrate his hard-body masculinity: "he could not risk having the label follow him home to 'ruin' his life there, so despite the shakes, the memory lapses . . . he mustered a solution" (Tyler 2012, n.p.). He demands to be put back to work removing frozen corpses from the nearby battlefield, shoveling up "random parts of human bodies. . . . Careful! Some parts may break off while being detached from the ice with your abrupt shovel. Try not to break them. . . . But they snap when I hoist 'em up onto the beds of the deuce-and-a-halfs, cold hard beds. . . . Like lumber, they 'clunk' and 'thok' for days overlapping old as the ages" (Tyler 2012, n.p.). This sequence reveals Chuck's stoicism, demonstrating how servicemen policed each other's performance of masculinity: "What a job he does! That Tyler! Processing the dead so efficiently while burying the whole goddamn mess of war under tons of mental concrete" (Tyler 2012, n.p.).

Throughout, Tyler uses metaphors drawn from construction materials, such as the comparison of dead bodies to lumber or the reference to "mental concrete" in the above passages, to describe what she sees as broken about her father's masculinity. Going back to the depiction of her father's workshop, Tyler's text directs our attention to some rusty cans and gunky jars, "chemicals that have been outlawed by the EPA" (n.p.). She returns to these substances in a segment she labels "The Tale of Mr. Tox-eek!" (figure 6.10). Here she labels and catalogs the deadly substances—asbestos, lead paint, rat poison, muriatic acid, arsenic, DDT, etc.—that her father kept in his workshop for decades: "Truth is any self-respecting 'boy mechanic' type, raised in the 1920s, was bound to have a collection like this, amassed over the years, saved during the depression, the war years and beyond, because God knows it might come in handy—you never know when you might need 50 gallons of hydrochloric acid" (Tyler 2010, n.p.). Each mismatched container seems to have been recycled, including a Coke bottle whose logo has been blocked out with electrical tape and whose content is now unknown to all. Tyler draws a thick cloud of gas swirling above the noxious substances. But, for all of the realism motivating these details, she also is drawing an implicit connection to her father's "tox-eek" masculinity—as all of

FIGURE 6.10. The toxic materials Chuck assembled reflect his corrosive personality. C. Tyler, *Collateral Damage* (2010). © C. Tyler. Courtesy of Fantagraphics.

the corrosive feelings he has bottled inside him come gurgling up in moments of misdirected rage or as he spits out homophobic ("cocksucker") and misogynistic ("squats-to-pee") taunts.

In the "Camp Chemo" segment, Tyler draws a blueprint of her father's aging yet still "strong and steady" body, depicting his internal organs as pipes and faucets (figure 6.11). On one side, the blueprint maps the "plan," which includes such stages as "add ostomy bag" and "reattach colon." On the other side, she captions body parts—"lungs clear, despite years of cigs, cigars and asbestos," "meat and potatoes processing center," and "painful army-damaged knees" (n.p.). Her father's body is another construction project (like the half-completed cottage in the background), as he fights cancer and builds a new house all at once. Even if some parts need to be replaced, nothing here suggests anything as vulnerable as human emotion. Apart from the reference to the army, her father's body is autonomous, untouched by other people.

FIGURE 6.11. A blueprint captures the mechanistic way Chuck thinks about his own body in the wake of his chemotherapy. C. Tyler, *Collateral Damage* (2010). © C. Tyler. Courtesy of Fantagraphics.

Hannah's Crafts

Apart from the segment dealing with the loss of her daughter, Hannah remains marginal, mostly a character in other people's stories, offering terse reactions to Chuck's various antics and outbursts. Hannah's presence is felt, if not always heard, through the ways Tyler links her mother to the family's seasonal rituals. For example, one segment, "Christmas in the Air," deals with the intense undertaking of addressing and sending Christmas cards to the many friends the couple acquired over cross-country moves. Tyler describes this task as a "project" similar to the various home repairs Chuck undertakes, though her father would have rejected such comparisons. Chuck gets angry about the intensity with which Hannah embraces this task: "Mom found such pleasure in her annual card ritual, and he seemed kind-of jealous of the fun she was having, of her elan—something in him couldn't allow that. Too much joy and not enough grind" (Tyler 2010, n.p.). Chuck seals the holiday cards behind the drywall he was constructing in the living room—an act that provides him with a means, however blunt, of putting his wife back in her place.

This story about Christmas cards prepares readers for the later collage of greeting cards representing Hannah's repressed memories of Ann's life and death. More than that, readers can recognize the mother's presence in holiday decorations, even when the depicted action and dialogue do not direct attention to them. *Collateral Damages* conveys the passing of her parents' later years through images of the couple, sitting in arm chairs, looking out the window, and watching television, while seasonal knickknacks appear along the window ledge. Tyler draws her father's full body, including his ever present red suspenders, relaxing in his easy chair; the dog is also shown sprawled on the floor or crouching beside Chuck's chair to be stroked; but Hannah is mostly obscured, apart from her red hair, suggesting the limited role she plays in this particular narrative. Jack-o'-lanterns, Christmas trees and presents, and Easter baskets and bunnies signal the cyclical succession of holidays (figure 6.12) and assert the mother's hidden role in shaping the domestic environment. In conversation (Jenkins 2013b), Tyler discussed her mother's artistic temperament, while noting that nothing encouraged Hannah to pursue those interests outside of her duties as a wife and mother. This explains why Tyler was so determined that her mother draw for the book. Following her mother's stroke, Tyler depicts her own heroic efforts to keep the holiday spirit alive, bringing out sparklers and Lady Liberty hats for a Fourth of July picnic. Her mother's indifference is read as a symptom of her declining mental acuity: "Gone were

FIGURE 6.12. Hannah's personality emerges most vividly here through the images of holiday decorations. C. Tyler, *Collateral Damage* (2010). © C. Tyler. Courtesy of Fantagraphics.

many intangibles like modesty, the ability to relish evanescence, or to declare 'I'm tickled pink!' and really mean it. She could tell you the bank balance or work a crossword puzzle, but the sizzle had fizzled" (Tyler 2010, n.p.). Still later, she describes Chuck "cuss decorating" the Christmas tree when Hannah is too incapacitated.

Army Surplus

In one episode, Carol stops by an army surplus store in search of a specific military patch: "Sgt. Smith's is an old Texaco Station with buzzing fluorescents and few customers. It's an oddly calming place" (Tyler 2010, n.p.). She decides, under the circumstances, to keep her "anti-war sentiments" to herself, but the good Sarge admires a M-43 liner, which she has decorated with her own patches, including florals, a California flag, a Buddhist peace symbol, and a red criss-cross to evoke her father's suspenders (figure 6.13). Tyler's fascination with the surplus store is suggested by the attention she pays to incidental details (such as the stacks of goods on the shelves or the POW flag on the wall), her redrawing of the insignia she is purchasing, her diagramming and cataloguing of the patches on his jacket, and the multiple renderings of the jacket itself, abstracted from its physical surroundings and treated as "a stylish addition to the olive-drab collection." By comparison, the human figures are much more cartoonish, reduced to a few broad gestures (her frumpy hair, the clerk's oversized hands).

As the sequence continues, she recounts how Chuck's much-coveted Ike jacket, worn in the European theater, was destroyed in a fire that burned down her grandfather's home in the late 1940s, but somehow the liner survived for her to reclaim as part of her personal identity. Read on a metonymic level, his willingness to let her appropriate this artifact to express her countercultural values suggests the close father-daughter bond. And, on a metaphoric level, Chuck himself might be read as "army surplus," used—and used up—by the military, and then dumped into the civilian world with little regard for his future value.

Tyler depicts the army surplus store as part of the support system that GIs of her father's generation created for themselves, a place where they can find others who know what the war was like without having to put it into words. The fact that we see Carol there, but not Chuck, says something about his estrangement from that support system. The army surplus store is also, as Carol's own story suggests, a place where the younger generation went to find resources for acts of adolescent rebellion as the meaning of military garb shifted through the years. How youth of her generation appropriated and assigned new meanings to World War II artifacts was a recurring example in the discussion of subcultures and resignification within the British cultural studies tradition. Stuart Hall ([1981] 2009) wrote about British youth reclaiming the swastika: "Every now and then, amongst the other trinkets, we find that sign which, above all other signs, ought to be fixed—solidified—in its cultural meaning and connotation forever: the swastika. Yet there it dangles, partly—but not entirely—cut loose from its profound cultural reference in the twentieth-century history" (517). Carol recalls discovering Iron Crosses among her father's things and reclaiming them as a "Carnaby Street" fashion statement with little sense of their historical associations. Her sputtering father erupts, "We fought and

FIGURE 6.13. Carol's visits to an army surplus store cement an unlikely bond across generations. C. Tyler, *Collateral Damage* (2010). © C. Tyler. Courtesy of Fantagraphics.

died! People got killed!" (Tyler 2012, n.p.). By the time we see Carol visiting the army surplus store, she has already been reading up for her scrapbook project, impressing the Sarge with her mastery of "army trivia." Sarge—himself from a different generation than her father—appreciates the ways that she has incorporated patches associated with her own life and values onto her father's jacket, whereas Tyler's artwork suggests a deep respect for the particulars of military uniforms.

The idea of army surplus surfaces again in her description of a holiday gift exchange: "He really liked the presents I got him: chocolate covered peanuts, French cognac and a sweater, actually an authentic WWII G.I. issue, olive drab wool sweater. When he opened the box, he lurch-grabbed it, with a look of pained desperation. Then he pressed it against his ribcage, fighting back tears again with that contorted 'screwed-on-wrong' look . . . And he gave me this HEART he'd carved for mom while in Dijon, out of an aircraft windshield" (Tyler 2012, n.p.). This is one of the book's few passages suggesting that their shared fascination with his World War II experiences brought them any closer understanding of each other.

Her father's scrapbook later provides a bit more backstory on the psychic weight the two gifts bear. During a sequence about the Battle of the Bulge and its aftermath, the scrapbook recounts the brutal struggle "to survive, hunker down, stay warm and try not to catch a bullet," which Tyler illustrates with her father and another GI huddled around a fire and shivering (n.p.). "Goddamn why'd I lose my sweater," Chuck grumbles, suggesting how poignant it is when his daughter gifts him a similar-issue sweater. Tyler also explicitly links the plexiglass heart to the concept of "soldier's heart." While in the hospital, her shell-shocked father confused one of the nurses for his beloved wife, Hannah, or as he calls her, "Red," and made the heart as a gift for her, a gesture of affection that led the other patients to label him as "soft," thus pushing him back into the field. These gifts communicate more than Carol could have understood or her father could acknowledge at the time.

Pulling Things Together

If we want to understand what goes unsaid between the central characters here, we need to learn to follow their stuff, with these material objects intended to be read on both literal and figurative levels. Stuff occupies space within the Tyler household, with the space allotted to Chuck or Justin a reflection of their male privilege within the family, or with the mother's holiday decorations a means of making her presence felt even when her voice has been silenced. Tyler is interested in the exchange of stuff (the sale of army surplus goods, the gift exchange that creates bonds between father and daughter) and stuff may become the focus of conflicts (as when Chuck drywalls Hannah's Christmas cards out of jealousy over the pleasure she takes in this task, or when father and daughter clash over the appropriate treatment of German war medals). Such things matter, perhaps all the more when feelings cannot be expressed in any other way. And this brings us back to the two images with which I opened this chapter—the displays of her father's war memorabilia and the cards and gifts that signaled the birth and death of the sister that Carol never knew. These two panels crystalize many of the central themes and relationships in the book as they suggest the traumatic memories that shaped (and were in turn repressed by) both of her parents.

You'll Never Know is filled with such family secrets, the things people must forget to get through the day, the things that get obscured by more public-facing narratives. Underground comics, especially autobiographical comics, involve confession and disclosure, a refusal to accept limits on what can or should be said, an insistence on dragging painful or embarrassing truths into public view. This autobiographical impulse reflects the consciousness-raising focus that shaped the feminist movement in C. Tyler's youth, as women discovered that the domestic sphere was where they must fight many of their battles if they were going to claim greater control over their lives.

As the book's title suggests, there is much we will never know about Chuck Tyler and other men of his generation, what they experienced during the war and how it touched them in ways that the era's masculinity offered few outlets to express. *You'll Never Know* is a critique of those various mechanisms of repression and how the refusal to acknowledge pain and suffering led to psychological and sometimes physical violence within the family. C. Tyler uses practices associated with scrapbooks as women's writing to reframe her father's narrative and surface many things he could not or would not say about himself. And she uses everyday objects—tools, holiday decorations, and army surplus—that function on both literal and metaphorical levels to shed light on the family's dynamics, often communicating relationships and feelings that the characters themselves do not know how to put into words. Throughout, C. Tyler struggles with the complexities and contradictions of her relationship with her father—a man she clearly loves, admires, and emulates, even as she raged over his negative impacts on her life.

As such, *You'll Never Know* demonstrates the power of "memory work" to articulate what cannot be read directly from family photographs or other mementos. Kuhn (1995) explains: "Memory work is a conscious and purposeful performance of memory; it involves an active staging of memory; it takes an inquiring attitude towards the past and its (re)construction through memory; it calls into question the transparency of what is remembered; and it takes what is remembered as material for interpretation" (157). Thinking of memory as "performance" acknowledges the embodiment Chute (2010) found in Bechdel's redrawing old photographs by hand. One of Tyler's greatest strengths as a comics artist is her ability to convey the personalities of her characters through their postures, gestures, and facial expressions, often rendered in fairly broad line drawings. But it also explains the gifted mimicry C. Tyler displayed during her USC talk as she impersonated each family member's personalities, including Chuck's foul mouth and tight-lipped grumbling. These bits of spontaneous performance capture and reproduce scraps of experience, just as the scrapbook itself gathers and preserves meaningful materials from its subject's life. Her focus on scraps extends to a fascination with physical objects, whether her father's tools and supplies, her mother's holiday decorations, or the army surplus that passes between father and daughter. And of course, comics themselves are built from juxtaposed fragments that add up to more than the sum of their parts. It's scraps all the way down, but those scraps have an additive effect. Through the careful analysis of those bits and pieces, we can construct a portrait of a life and, in turn, surface those things left unsaid, those things shared with others of Chuck's generation, and those things shared across generations among family members. In the next chapter, I consider the work of two other "graphic women," Joyce Farmer and Roz Chast, as they also reflect on the nature of inheritance and the process of letting go—of life, of loved ones, of accumulated possessions.

7

Sorting, Culling, Hoarding, and Cleaning

Joyce Farmer's *Special Exits* and Roz Chast's *Can't We Talk about Something More Pleasant?*

New Yorker cartoonist Roz Chast translated her experiences caring for her elderly parents into the graphic memoir *Can't We Talk about Something More Pleasant?* (2014). Chast discussed the problems she encountered in dealing with the stuff her parents had accumulated:

> They never threw anything away, and it was not like there was anything "valuable." It was mostly just old, beat up luggage and typewriters . . . an old rexograph machine, bajillions of old bed slippers and umbrellas and shoes and towels. . . . Just detritus of decades. And when I was going through the stuff I would think, "I want to keep this, and I want to keep that," and it was very surreal, very bizarre. And then at a certain point, it was like, "I don't want anything. I want the photo albums and a few things off the wall." And I started putting stuff in garbage bags because I thought maybe I could do this myself, and I filled up a few of them and I had not even done one percent. Finally I just wound up paying the super to empty it, and it was horrible in some ways. . . . I just could not do it. (Fresh Air 2014, n.p.)

We have reached a logical endpoint for this book's exploration of the problem that stuff represents in the early twenty-first century. Going through used bookstores and yard sales or sniping on eBay is one matter, but having to process and dispose of other people's clutter is something different. Here different conceptions of value set our priorities about what to keep—valuing some objects because of what they mean to us and others because of what they meant to the people in our lives. Different siblings desire different objects because they remember their parents at different phases of their lives, or engaged in different activities. As the previous chapter suggested, women often bear the responsibility for preserving family history and the burden of culling unwanted stuff. In this context, sorting and culling constitute a caregiving obligation women (mostly) perform as they help relatives prepare for their final days. As Chast explains: "I think about something a friend of mine who had gone through something similar said, which was that if you don't think your children will be interested, don't keep it. And he's absolutely right. I feel much more conscious of how much stuff I have now and what are my kids going to do with my stuff once I die" (Fresh Air 2014, n.p.).

This chapter considers Joyce Farmer's *Special Exits* (2014), alongside Roz Chast's *Can't We Talk about Something More Pleasant?* (2014), two autobiographical comics exploring the transitions and disruptions associated with aging and death, depicting the challenges associated with inheritance and hand-me-downs. McCracken (1988b) would discuss such processes as "divestment rituals." When people let go of objects: "an attempt will be made to erase the meaning that has been invested in the good by association. Individuals in moments of candor will suggest that they feel 'a little strange about someone else wearing my old coat.' With still greater candor they confess that they fear the dispossession of personal meanings. . . . [Divestment rituals] suggest that the meaning of goods can be transferred, obscured, confused, or even lost when goods change hands" (87). The decision to outsource the labor of sorting through the deceased's belongings short-circuits these divestment rituals, perhaps because the emotions are too raw in a death's immediate aftermath, perhaps because those who inherit them are already more distanced than their original owners. But the emotions this process stirs up can be hard to settle again.

Literary scholar James Krasner begins his essay "Mess and Memory" (2010), recounting experiences similar to Chast's:

> When my parents passed away and my brothers and I were left to clean out the house, we expected the worst. . . . Each grubby, broken toy, each

> battered box of school art projects or tacky souvenirs, stopped us in our tracks. I would turn a corner to find one of my brothers standing, staring abstractedly at a grimy action figure or a bent cufflink, sometimes smiling, always stalled and entranced. After two days we fled, overwhelmed by the number and intensity of unexpected ghosts raised by these soiled and useless items. We hired a cleaning company: people to whom such speaking objects were mute, people who could disinterestedly claw through and dispose of them without being touched by the memories they carried. (41)

Such moments create practical challenges, which is why so often, as in both of these stories, the tasks get offloaded onto more disinterested professionals.

Divestment rituals are highly generative: they kick up memories, they inspire stories, yet they pose problems of representation since these micro-narratives swamp narrative goals and clutter story structure. If masculine narratives often prioritize plots over characters, emotions, or environments, one strategy of feminist authorship requires greater attention to meaningful details (Schor 1987), mapping the associations formed between memory and mess. Interestingly, both authors discussed here had previously been associated with short works—in Chast's case, cartoons in the *New Yorker*, and in Farmer's case, covers and short stories in feminist underground comics. Both were stretching to construct longer, book-length narratives and both started by listing individual incidents that could be spun off into shorter works, before realizing that they had enough material for a stand-alone book. So their plots are loosely conceived, mostly organized around the life processes depicted, with each incident unfolding across one or two pages at most. Each book has a fragmented and digressive structure. The details that command our attention are often "grubby" and "grimy," "broken" and "bent," but the memories they evoke are also often bittersweet.

This chapter examines two works by female authors that deal with clearing away junk and encrusted memories. In both cases, the moments of death, while acknowledged, are treated as matter-of-fact outcomes of a much longer process of physical and mental decay. Grief for a lost parent is displaced onto sorting and letting go of their material traces. I am interested in how sorting and culling are performed formally, in terms of these graphic memoirs' narrative and visual strategies, but also conceptually, as the authors make sense of these life processes.

As I explore *Special Exits* and *Can't We Talk*, I ask what they suggest about the relationship between mess and memory: things become extensions of people's identities, relationships, life courses, choices, and values. What means a thing when everything else is said and done? Keep in mind that however visceral our responses may be to what these works depict, notions of clutter, rubbish, and mess are social constructs. "There is no natural relation to our objects," writes Scott Herring in *The Hoarders* (2014), a book that challenges normative understandings about what constitutes appropriate relationships with the material world: "What counts as an acceptable material life? Who decides? Why is one material life commended while another is reviled? Who calls these shots? Under what historical circumstances?" (17).

The literature on hoarding almost always includes a chapter specifically focused on the elderly, as their ability to maintain lifelong standards gives way as their bodies give out; seniors come to accept living under conditions previously unimaginable and viewed with horror by their loved ones. At the same time, these final years are often spent laying memories to rest, as people edit their lives, passing things to friends and family, or, alternately, taking comfort in accumulated memorabilia. Often these relationships to stuff end with death or with some health emergency that results in the senior being placed into an institutional environment, frequently over their own objections. Such abrupt departures leave many unresolved matters for their offspring to confront, often under conditions of emotional distress. People are frequently unprepared for what they will confront, given our tendency to turn the subject to "something more pleasant." These two works are not easy reads for that reason.

This chapter takes the sorting of inherited things, the cleaning away of messes, as its central structuring principle. First, I consider the brief passage where Chast discusses how she dealt with the clutter she inherited following the death of her mother and father, as the artist shifts modalities between photographs, cartoons, and text. Next, I consider the ways that these works tap shared knowledge among those who do housework to describe the cleaning away of dust, grease, and grime, as the elderly's relationship to household and bodily cleanliness shifts in their final days. Then, I will discuss "happy objects," those things that give affect and meaning to people as they sift through their memories and appreciate their remaining days. And I will deal with various forms of the abject—parts of the body that are shed and must be discarded—and, finally, with the cremated remains themselves. I deal with these various kinds of stuff in terms of the obligations they impose on family members who must help their parents close out their lives. Along the way, I will also consider hoarding and culling as two different ways of making meaning and ascribing value to accumulated belongings. I admire how directly and unflinchingly these two works deal with aspects of death and bodily decline that often go undiscussed in our culture, taking advantage of the freedom that alternative comics have claimed for themselves to shock and discomfort their readers. Given the intensity of emotions surrounding so many of the experiences depicted here, both artists are surprisingly unsentimental, modeling what it takes to let go of people you love and the things they have gathered over their lifetimes.

Clearing Out "The Old Apartment"

Roz Chast goes through her parents' old apartment in chapter 10, more than two-thirds of the way through her graphic memoir. By this point, readers have met her small, fearful father and her oversized, domineering mother. This particular set of comic stereotypes has a long history in the *New Yorker* going back at least to James Thurber. Chast's characters seem constantly jittery, their postures defensive, their eyebrows arched, their eyes and mouths open wide, and she draws them with what feels like a nervous, unsteady hand. There is something almost hypnotic about the ways that her images jiggle before our eyes. Chast's representation of this relationship brings a different subjectivity to the table than Thurber's notoriously misogynistic images of the battle between the sexes; Chast is much more sympathetic about the forces that shaped her parents. She doesn't pull any punches about how her own "wounds"—as someone who grew up in this somewhat dysfunctional family—shaped her choices as a caregiver or the ways her parents were unprepared for their next life stage.

Can't We Talk opens with a carefully posed family photograph, showing her mother and father reading to Roz as a young girl, before rendering a more cartoonish version, as Roz, now an adult, initiates an awkward conversation about their contingency plans. This shift between modalities—between the photograph and the cartoon—prepares us for similar shifts in "The Old Apartment." Throughout, Chast creates an unstable relationship between text and image, one less modeled on the comic book tradition than on the *New Yorker*'s mix of prose and cartoons. Many anecdotes are self-contained and boxed off like one-page cartoons. In some cases, prose dominates, with images reduced to illustrations. Some images function as diagrams with captions, others have word balloons. A few pages borrow from the scrapbook tradition, including photographs of her parents at various ages.

Yet, regardless, all of these chapters advance the core narrative, moving inevitably toward her parents' respective deaths: "By 2002, they were 90, and it was hard not to notice that every time I came to see them, the grime had grown thicker. The piles of newspapers, magazines and junk mail had grown larger and they themselves had grown frailer. . . . Something was coming down the pike!" (20). But, in chapter 10, as Krasner might have predicted, the narrative halts with very little time (mostly at the start and finish of the sequence) spent in telling us what happened; instead, Chast displays objects found while cleaning her parents' space. Early on, she signals her discomfort with this invasion of privacy, having shown little interest in her youth in exploring her parents' stuff when they were out, and suddenly finding herself given permission "to rifle through all the drawers, all the closets: everything." But she quickly acknowledges that there were no amazing finds here: "There was no buried treasure. No Hermès scarves, no Chanel purses. No first editions, no Braque etchings. No heirloom china. (My mother believed in plastic plates—they were lightweight and didn't break.) It was pretty much old junk. But it was our junk, and the thought of never seeing it again was troubling. So I took some photos" (108). Chast surrounds her characters with overstuffed but nondescript furniture, dime-store lamps, tacky wall paper, and yes, plastic place settings: many will have already concluded that little here is worth keeping.

For Chast, the key sensual experience is seeing rather than touching or holding these objects, a shift from the thing to its representation. And, for the next ten pages, Chast shares the most extended photographic sequence in the entire work. Some of the photographs focus on individual (but mundane) objects—such as a stapler—and more often, she photographs an assemblage—her mother's glasses, all from "before my time"; a "museum" of her father's Schick shavers (109); an assortment of "random art supplies" (110) or a drawer full of pencils and pens. Some things defy explanation—"Why was there a drawer of jar lids?" (115). In one image, Chast "arranged" her mother's purses on her bed (112). But from here, she captures the cluttered gestalt—her parents' bedroom "how they left it" (112), her parent's "work stations," her own childhood bedroom. She takes readers inside their refrigerator, medicine cabinet, and the "crazy closet," where they threw everything they didn't know what to do with. It is hard to explain the fascinations of someone else's medicine cabinet, in this case mostly containing consumer products decades beyond their use-by dates, yet each shared image invites us to be nosy. Chast leaves it to her readers, by and large, to provide some cognitive structure to the jumble of objects. These objects are defamiliarized; readers look at them without comprehension much as her father, suffering growing dementia, stares at a toaster, unable to remember how it works.

Sometimes, Chast directs attention to items that figure in earlier chapters. For example, she flags the location where her father stored his old checkbooks (figure 7.1). Chast recounts her father's paranoid fantasies that a neighboring couple might break into their apartment for these checkbooks, which he imagines might pose a "temptation" to strangers. Chast recounts, "The 'bankbooks' were a collection of canceled and uncanceled bankbooks dating back to at least the 1960s. . . . Many of them were from banks that didn't even exist anymore" (71). Apart from the emotional upheaval they caused, the bankbooks caused Chast problems in settling the estate—small amounts of money scattered across institutions that had changed names and management over the years. Elsewhere, Chast describes her mother's obsession with the free gifts she gets from making deposits, even though those gifts remain unopened and unused.

Then, for one page (figure 7.2), she shifts from photographs to drawings inventorying "what I rescued and decided to keep." Each item is in its own box, offering an impression of order, curation, and display. Her captions provide a bit more context for how these items relate to her personal history: "a bird picture I liked as a child," "some silver pins I associated with my mother," or "a piece of Indian pottery my mother once told me was valuable" (119). Some objects embody particular traits and practices she associates with

FIGURE 7.1. Her parents' old checkbooks are only one of the many items Chast photographs as she goes through the stuff they left behind. Roz Chast, *Can't We Talk about Something More Pleasant?* (2014). © Roz Chast. Courtesy of Bloomsbury.

her parents—"a book demonstrating embroidery stitches my mother made in some long-ago home-ec class," "My father's beloved reference books, all heavily annotated by him, and stuffed with 'relevant' magazine and newspaper clippings"—while some are not linked to any specific memory—"an evening bag of my mother's which I never saw her use. It was extremely out of character for her" (119). At some places, the captions raise unresolved questions: Chast kept "almost all of the photograph albums"—so why not all of them? And, yes, she notes, almost as an aside, she kept the bankbooks that had been such a burden. Why does she shift to drawings at the moment she identifies particular objects she saved? Some have noted the intimacy achieved when the same artist writes and draws the book. As Hillary Chute (2010) writes, "the subjective mark of the body is rendered directly onto the page and constitutes how we view the page" (11). Perhaps the goal here is to create a stronger emotional bond as Chast shifts from her parents' undifferentiated accumulation toward objects that carry personal significance. Perhaps the goal is to make these objects seem more generic, given what Scott McCloud tells us about the ways iconic or cartoonish images are more open to multiple identifications than more photorealistic images might be. The photographs document a specific moment of time, whereas we can imagine that the cartoons were drawn sometime later, reflecting back on the experiences.

And the prose carries the weight for the rest of the chapter, though still she makes lists rather than recounting events or describing responses. She describes three "tattered, decomposing cardboard cartons tucked away on the top of a closet" that contained her parents' correspondence, including various letters they exchanged while separated during World War II (120). As she notes, "the letters became more affectionate [during their courtship] but there was—I'm half sorry and half relieved to say—nothing racy" (120). She does provide a belated explanation for one treasured keepsake—"a bracelet my father brought back from New Guinea, where he was stationed during WWII, made from New Guinea coins" (119)—through a fuller context of his wartime experiences: "In 1945, he was sent to New Guinea, and the letters continued, with descriptions of the heat and mud and mosquitoes and warnings not to go into the jungle because of headhunters and cannibals" (120). Then even this level of description breaks down. Chast lists the things she discards:

> I didn't want my 6th grade-graduation autograph book, my mother's piano, the console organ, any clothes, any linens, anything from the

FIGURE 7.2. Chast shifts from photography back to cartoons as she depicts those meaningful objects she salvaged from her parents' apartment. Roz Chast, *Can't We Talk about Something More Pleasant?* (2014). © Roz Chast. Courtesy of Bloomsbury.

> kitchen. I didn't want any of the falling-apart furniture that was ugly even when it was new. The knickknacks could all go to hell, along with my grade-school notebooks. I left thousands of books and records and manual typewriters and appliances and grimy liqueur glasses that were probably last used in 1963. Lamps and radios, galoshes, costume jewelry, goodbye. Is it possible there was something amazing hiding in the wreckage? Yes. Do I wish I had had unlimited time to comb through everything? Kind of. But where would I have put all the stuff? (121)

The list becomes increasingly random, reflecting her disassociation from all this junk. Babette Bärbel Tischleder (2014) identifies a similar list-making tendency in Jonathan Franzen's *The Corrections*:

> One could indeed consider the list as the literary equivalent to still life painting; both aesthetic forms assemble its elements in an order of equal coexistence, which is defined by the absence of cause and effect or the logic of the event. . . . The heterogeneity of enumerated items defies categorization and hierarchy, and they often lack definite biographical links or clues. . . . Divided by commas rather than propelled by verbs, the congestions of words hinder the flow and pace of narrative progression for paragraphs and even pages at a time. In short, the reader is made to sense the blockage in the dramatic action, the traffic jams of things that hold up the narrative drive, the speed bumps of clutter that slow down our reading. (254–255)

Tischleder offers a critical frame for thinking about the list that connects my discussion of Chast's book back to chapter 1's consideration of how graphic novels relate to the still life. Chast's *New Yorker* cartoons often rely on similar lists, graphs, and catalogs. While she emerges from a tradition associated with single-panel gags, few of the works brought together in her collection *Theories of Everything* follow such a simple structure. Instead, most involve complex displays of visual information. She charts the evolution of ice cream products, she catalogs the offerings of the pill-of-the-month club, she showcases the specialized magazines at her local newsstand, she breaks down the canned goods required to produce an American Thanksgiving feast, she identifies "passive-aggressive birthday gifts," and she maps layers of debris underneath Manhattan. "Do you ever feel like you have too much stuff?" she asks in the opening of "The Tragedy of Prosperity," and its central panel showcases several dozen hair products. *Can't We Talk* incorporates these same techniques within a more extended and more personal narrative. Here her emphasis shifts from reading details for satirical insights into a culture of accumulation toward deploying details for insights into actual people who touched her life.

Mess and Meaning

In *Mess* (2015), his memoir of his struggles to overcome his hoarding impulses, Barry Yourgrau maps a classic distinction between collectors and hoarders:

> Hoarders amass, without sharp selectivity. They have no compunction about owning multiples of the same thing, as opposed to unique items to complete a set. They don't take public pride in what they have, are generally burdened and shamed. Not only don't they display their objects to others, they don't engage with their acquisitions themselves in much more than a perfunctory way. . . . Hoarders are powerless before their possessions; there's an inertness about them—both hoarder and hoard. (196–197)

The collection is kept pristine, removed from everyday use, protected from the elements, and preserved for future generations. Collections are bagged, boxed, shelved, cataloged, and classified, or at least the collector has the ambition to order, discipline, and display their holdings. The hoard rots, unsorted, often mulched with household garbage, and left to be dealt with someday. If romantic accounts of collecting talk about "dust," hoarders are associated with grime, gunk, and filth, rancid foodstuffs and decaying matter, vermin and bugs. Scott Herring (2014) writes about "material deviance in modern American culture," arguing that moral panics around elderly hoarders are often defined in relations to more normative assertions about optimal aging. He notes that gerontologists often talk about the value of seniors holding onto and spending time with a few cherished items to remember key moments from their life. But hoarding, Herring suggests, represented the pathologized manifestation of these same tendencies, "the promise of an optimal life soiled by the damaged world of goods." He continues, "In lieu of reminscentia, rubbish. In place of a cherished possession, living spaces riddled with useless items" (128).

Our contemporary understandings of "good housekeeping" emerged over several hundred years of moral discourse, economic shifts and technological innovations promising to benefit the women most often expected to perform domestic labor, but as Susan Strasser (1982) documents, such technological breakthroughs almost always were met with intensified standards of cleanliness. In a world where women's social contributions were defined around their performance as caretakers and homemakers, women policed each other's performance, reading homes for evidence of inappropriate shortcuts or other transgressions against their society's codes of material conduct. Strasser documents the industry of writers such as Harriet Beecher Stowe's sister Catherine Beecher, who wrote comprehensive manuels on domestic economy, "coloring her advice with a coherent theory about women's place and the function of women's work" (xv). This historic imprint remains firm despite decades of feminist critique. Household labor is still gendered and the messiest tasks remain "women's work." Given this history, we should not be surprised that when "graphic women" represent domestic life, they often pay attention to the labor required to clean up after family members.

Roz Chast describes the accumulation of grime in her parents' old apartment: "It's not ordinary dust, or dirt, or a greasy stovetop that hasn't been cleaned in a week or two. It's more of a coating that happens when people haven't cleaned in a really long time. Maybe because they're old, and they're tired, and they don't see what's going on. It covered everything. The cookie jar . . . chairs . . . knickknacks . . . silverware . . . books." Chast discusses this buildup as a breakdown in household routine. Her mother had told her many times, "You have to dust! If you don't, the dust gets into the interstices of the furniture and breaks it all apart!!!" But now, Chast tells us, "It was clear that she had stopped worrying about that" (15). For Chast, forced to witness the lowered standards of hygiene, the temptation is to pick up a scrub rag and battle this sludge, but such intervention is unwelcome: "What are you doing that for? I want that exactly where it is," her mother says. "Don't touch that." Her father chimes in: "Don't upset your mother." Chast concludes, "I wasn't great as a caretaker, and they weren't great at being taken care of" (16). Seth depicts the materiality of everyday goods (for example, the tiny fragments left behind by shattered Christmas ornaments) with nostalgia and melancholy—signs of a world passing away before his eyes—but for Chast, her parents' grime produces guilt and shame, in part because she feels some responsibility for ensuring the quality of their lives. Walter Benjamin can celebrate the clouds of dust when he unpacks his bookcase, but he doesn't have to chase dust bunnies with a Porta-Vac.

Grant McCracken (1988a) writes about the physical and symbolic properties associated with patina:

> Furniture, plate, cutlery, buildings, portraiture, jewelry, clothing and other objects of human manufacture undergo a gradual movement away from their original pristine condition. As they come into contact with the elements and the other objects of the world, their original surface takes on a surface of its own. As these objects are minutely dented, chipped, oxidized and worn away, they begin to take on "patina." . . . The surface that accumulates on objects has been given a symbolic significance and exploited for social purpose. . . . Its function is not to claim status but to authenticate it. Patina serves as a kind of visual proof of status. (32)

Grime, like patina, marks a movement away from the "original pristine condition." It is also a "surface" that accumulates on objects and authenticates their wear, but grime is not patina: it does not enhance status, it does not create symbolic value. Rather, grime destroys value and damages social status. Objects marked by patina are destined for the antique store; objects covered with grime are heading to the dump. Grime offers "visual proof," but, in this case, of moral failure or pathological disorder.

Joyce Farmer depicts herself throughout *Special Exits* doing basic household tasks, vacuuming kipple, washing dishes and scrubbing counters, disposing of garbage bags of hoarded materials, mopping unsanitary spills, buying groceries, and otherwise caring for her father and his second wife during their declining years. If Chast and Franzen use list making as literary clutter, Farmer crams her pages with tightly framed panels that provide little breathing room. The air is clogged with dust and cat hair, and many of her compositions show mounds of stuff in the background (figure 7.3). Yet there is a particularity about the things Farmer draws, unlike the more generic belongings Chast depicts in her work: each doll, here, is distinctive, as are the hats and the old cathedral clocks she dusts in this sequence. *Comics Journal*'s Paul Karasik (2011) writes that Farmer's "scratchy drawings" initially flustered the "comics snob" in him, but eventually won him over:

> I picked the book up between thumb and forefinger like a curious lab specimen and set it on my night table. Then the thing snuck up and bit me on the ass. It is moving without being sentimental. Real without being

> pedantic . . . Farmer's panels are chock full, reflecting and amplifying the claustrophobia. . . . At first glance, her decision to stick to a fairly rigid grid appears monotonous. But it is, in fact, a brilliant move that allows every small sidestep off of that grid to take on a deliberate meaning. More importantly, the grid serves like a metronome for these lives tick, tick, ticking away. (n.p.)

Farmer's drawings are "scratchy" in two senses—they seem scratched out on the page and they give the images such a vivid texture that they make readers feel itchy. Farmer and her contemporaries in the women's underground comics movement rejected anything that might be read as "cute" or "pretty," embracing "the ugly" as part of a general refusal to play by the rules of traditional femininity. Sara Ahmed (2010) writes that feminists often experience traditional family life as "an affect alien," one who refuses others' definitions of what is good or pleasant, or in this case, beautiful, rather than consent to their definition of the social order: "She might even kill joy because she refuses to share an orientation towards certain things as being good" (39). Karasik's initial disavowal of work that did not meet his standards was somewhat predetermined, since his standards reflect an art form that was for the most part produced by and for men and thus shaped by "an orientation towards certain things" not necessarily shared by these pioneering female artists. Joyce's messy, cluttered, overwrought visual style is a conscious strategy for conveying a particular experience of the domestic space.

Whereas Chast localizes the disposal of her parents' effects into one chapter, this process spreads across *Special Exits*, as Laura helps Lars and Rachel find some order and meaning in what remains from their life together. Early on, the couple discusses the prospect of moving to an assisted living facility but decides that the challenges of shutting down their house would be too great: "How could we pack up so much stuff? You'd have to sell your dolls. I'd have to get rid of my rocks and books. . . . We either have to make some big changes or we have to make the best of it" (6). They feel "stuck" because of their accumulated stuff, though the conversation overlooks the degree to which this labor will get passed down to their daughter, who sooner or later will have to confront this problem. Throughout, Laura and her father conspire to reclaim some spaces for him to pursue his own interests and hobbies. Their tight little quarters have become progressively dysfunctional as a consequence of the stepmother's hoarding. "There's a table in here somewhere" (17), the father

FIGURE 7.3. Farmer's scratchy visual style captures the clouds of dust and cat hair she confronts in cleaning her elderly father's house. Joyce Farmer, *Special Exits* (2011). © Joyce Farmer. Courtesy of Fantagraphics.

mumbles as the two survey a dining room completely overrun by Rachel's sewing projects. "Where can we put all of this stuff?" But Rachel pleads from the wings, "Don't throw anything away" (17). Laura's father opens the door to the spare bedroom and shows her "the way I save things around here," tossing another garbage bag of assorted stuff onto the pile. Laura blows various particulates off an old photo album, before breaking down in a sneezing fit: "It's at least eleven years since this room has been cleaned. Your beautiful dolls are covered with spider webs and cat hairs." Rachel shouts from her permanent place on the sofa, "Well, I aim to get in there and dust one of these days" (20). Lars and Rachel do not want Laura coming by regularly because she has a life of her own, and they do not want her to hire a maid service because "we don't want strangers in the house." She has to overcome their resistance, convincing them to part with things they no longer need but which might be of value to someone else. As Rachel gradually goes blind, Laura and Lars reclaim more of the cluttered space, though not without guilt. "Are we shameless?" Laura asks during one cleaning session, and her father responds, "Maybe, but it's hard to walk around all of this stuff. I have to live here too," before he suggests that the accumulation reflects the ways her early life experiences shaped her: "Go easy on her. You don't know what it was like to be so poor" as a child. Lars warns, "We can't throw anything valuable away. If she ever recovers, she'll never forgive us" (66). They move bags of her fabric to the garage and, when it fills, Laura takes them home to trash, recycle, or keepsake.

If such passages illustrate the intense labor involved in clearing away someone else's stuff, *Special Exits* also includes vivid representations of the health consequences of living in squalor. Ching, her father's beloved Siamese cat, bites, claws and scratches, spits and screams. In one especially distasteful segment, Laura's arm breaks out in hives, which she at first believes to be scabies, but later discovers are the results of mites from the cat who lay their eggs under human skin and create infection when they are unable to hatch. The problem, predictably enough, requires ever more rigorous cleaning of the cat and her environment. In another sequence, Lars finds an army of ants crawling out of his microwave. He tries to spray insecticide on the area but fumbles with the can, spraying his own hand instead. Interrupted by Rachel's calls from the other room, he forgets to wash, resulting in swollen, blistered, and peeling hands.

An especially poignant moment (figure 7.4) comes as Laura is scrubbing the woodwork and Rachel has one of her few flashes of lucidity. "Is there dirt in the

FIGURE 7.4. Ink stains in the doorstop conjure up a lifetime of memories for those whose perspective has been shaped by housework. Joyce Farmer, *Special Exits* (2011). © Joyce Farmer. Courtesy of Fantagraphics.

middle of the doorjams?" Rachel asks. Laura is surprised to hear such a question from a blind and disabled woman, long disinterested in her environment. "When Lars reads the paper he gets newsprint on his hands. Then he walks around and hangs onto everything. I never could keep up the cleaning of it" (76). Here the ink smudge constitutes a sign of Lars's repeated behavior across their lifetime together and, just as importantly, a sign of Rachel's affectionate observation. Such marks remain in her memory, even if she no longer can see her surroundings.

Historian Carlo Ginzburg (1986) writes: "Man has been a hunter for thousands of years. In the course of countless chases he learned to reconstruct the shapes and movements of his invisible prey from tracks on the ground, broken branches, excrement, tufts of hair, entangled feathers, stagnating odors. He learned to sniff out, record, interpret, and classify such infinitesimal traces as trails of spittle" (102). Hunting, like other professions, Ginzburg suggests, requires a particular way of reading the world that needs to be taught to novices. Ginzburg's discussion extends from the direct passing along of such knowledge to the ways it can be shared through representations—in particular, pictographs and, subsequently, phonetic writing, each of which represents further abstraction from the direct and multisensory knowledge involved in sniffing out an animal in the wild. Ginzburg's references to hunters reading animal droppings and soothsayers reading their entrails comes in an essay that also deals with the ways art historians use certain stylistic choices (such as how artists draw fingers, noses, ears) to identify fake works, or historians trace various clues through the archive. Coming across this passage again in the process of writing a book about graphic storytelling, I am reminded of the affordances of comics, which combine pictographic and phonetic writing, as a means of teaching us how others "read" the world.

Can't We Talk and especially *Special Exits* consider what it means to read the world as someone who performs housework, including learning to read family members' bodies for medical symptoms and their environments for smudges and other traces of repeated behaviors. Derf Backderf's *Trashed* (2015), a graphic memoir of the author's time working as a garbageman in 1980s small-town Ohio, teaches another professional epistemology—what it is to read the world through what people dispose. Garbage collectors scavenge for goods that still have some value (for example, one coworker's "find" of *Starlog* magazines evokes the male collectors in Seth's stories). A coworker shouts "porn alert" as the trashmen uncover a stash of erotic magazines and videos, a situation that turns awkward when the recent high school graduate realizes who owned this trash: "Wanna know the porn habits of your math teacher?" (76). Here and elsewhere, trash still retains some connection to previous owners, even when they imagine that they have erased all traces. "Why do people put that stuff out on the curb like that? Do they think we won't notice?" the former student asks, and his coworker responds, "More likely they don't think about us at all! We don't exist. Trash disappears—like magic" (76).

Other garbage is read as symptomatic of larger social and economic conditions. In the late 1980s, the trashmen confronted the aftermath of foreclosures, signs of the larger economic downturn. The banks were supposed to clear away whatever was left behind when homeowners were forced to vacate their residences, often on short notice, but huge piles were left at the roadside. Even the most hardened trash collectors are touched by a shoebox full of family photographs, including images of a child's birthday party, hastily abandoned under these circumstances (figure 7.5). They are even tempted to hold onto them, fearing the photos may have been thrown away by mistake, until they feel overwhelmed by the scale at which such foreclosures are taking place. A more hardened worker explains, "Think of the economy as a giant digestive tract, and we're here at the rectum of the free market to clean it all up" (203). There is no point in the life cycle of material goods when owners are fully and completely disassociated from their belongings. The trashmen speculate about what kind of people would dump such objects or, in some cases, what sort would possess such things in the first place. Such representations call into question the idea of indifferent garbagemen carting away family belongings.

FIGURE 7.5. Garbage collectors read the traces of stories from what people discard. Derf Backderf, *Trashed* (2015). © Derf Backderf. Courtesy of Harry N. Abrams.

Meaning clings to objects, whether in the form of mental associations or smudges on the door frame. Imagine the transfer of meaning expanding until it gets mapped onto every object that enters the house, and one comes close to the psychology of hoarding. In "Mess and Memory" (2010), James Krasner writes: "Hoarding amounts to an excessive faith in the power of material objects to convey memories. This same faith makes cleaning out any long-inhabited space painful for us. . . . Standing still in the semidark of the attic, we strain to recall some past moments while others burst upon us unbidden, and it occurs to us that if we do discard the object, the memory may never come again" (54). What others perceived as "undifferentiated matter" (55) represents the offloading of personal memories onto material artifacts, which the hoarder preserves and protects for fear of losing parts of themselves. Rachel has lost her sight, lost control over her bodily functions, lost her mobility, and lost much of her consciousness as mind and body are shutting down, but she will fight fiercely to hold onto her mess, which encapsulates her decaying memories. Her mess is all that remains of the person she once was.

"Happy Objects"

On the other hand, some objects really are cherished, really do need to be preserved, because they express something fundamental about their owners. In her essay "Happy Objects" (2010), Sara Ahmed discusses how objects enter or exit from "our near sphere, the world that takes shape around us, as a world of familiar things" (32). She maps the choices we make about objects that make us happy: "To experience an object as being affective or sensational is to be directed not only toward the object, but to 'whatever' is around that object, which includes what is behind the object, the conditions of its arrival. What is around an object can become happy: for instance, if you receive something delightful in a certain place, then the place itself is invested with happiness, as being 'what' good feeling is directed toward" (33). She explores how ordinary objects get charged with happiness but are often difficult for people to recognize from the outside looking in. Recognizing the emotional disposition of objects shapes the choices we make about our belongings: "The bodily horizon could be redescribed as a horizon of likes. To have our likes means certain things are gathered around us. . . . Those things we do not like we move away from" (32). Ahmed's focus on the "bodily horizon" seems an apt phrase for thinking about the clearing away of stuff in *Special Exits*: Rachel's declining mobility, vision, and mental acuity limit how far beyond her physical body her consciousness extends, and as this happens, Lars and Laura are reclaiming what once constituted her near sphere.

The best-selling book *The Life-Changing Magic of Tidying Up*, the central text of an international "decluttering" movement, offers an account of "happy objects." Marie Kondo, the book's author, counts on our bodies to "know" what we want:

> The best way to choose what to keep and what to throw away is to take each item in one's hand and ask: "Does this spark joy?" If it does, keep it.

> If not, dispose of it. . . . Don't just open up your closet and decide after a cursory glance that everything in it gives you a thrill. You must take each outfit in your hand. When you touch a piece of clothing, your body reacts. Its response to each item is different. . . . Are you happy wearing clothes that don't give you pleasure? Do you feel joy when surrounded by piles of unread books that don't touch your heart? Do you think that owning accessories you know you'll never use will ever bring you happiness? (41)

There is no place for sentimentality in her anti-clutter regime: she recommends going through family albums, weighing each picture separately, and culling those that do not represent the desired self: "It is not our memories but the person we have become because of those past experiences we should treasure. . . . The space in which we live should be for the person we are becoming now, not for the person we were in the past" (118). For the most part, Kondo treats these as individualized choices, reflecting a bias toward the single lifestyle over the consequences of such a selection process in the context of the family. She does advise, "Don't let your family see," because of parents' relationship to objects they have given their children: "Despite knowing that they should rejoice at their child's independence and maturity, parents can find it very painful to see clothes, toys, and mementos from the past on the rubbish heap, especially if they are things they gave to their child" (48). She does not consider the reverse: having children edit their parents' possessions.

By contrast, Farmer depicts the decisions about what to keep and what to discard as an ongoing social negotiation among her three primary characters—the father, the stepmother, and the daughter. What gives one family member pleasure may be meaningless to another: Rachel is reluctant to get rid of anything, claiming more than her share of the space, effectively blocking Lars from enjoying his own "happy objects." Across his life, Lars has acquired a range of interests: he collects stamps, coins, and rocks; he has built model trains; he enjoys reading. As his own end approaches, he works back through each of these hobbies, trying to discover what still holds his attention and can help him pass the long, lonely hours. Lars and Laura's excavations into the mess uncover items that require explanation, the passing down of family history. For example, Laura has repaired two antique cathedral clocks that belonged to Lars's Danish grandparents. Lars stumbles upon negatives of photographs he took on a Europe trip decades before: he had developed the film but did not have the funds to get his pictures printed. Laura starts getting them printed a few at a time, so that he can enjoy his memories. Some objects are difficult to discard—for example, some uranium ore Lars mined decades ago creates challenges, given it is illegal to simply dump the substance. And other items he abandons painlessly, handing a rare teddy bear to his addled wife, knowing she may soil it: "I don't care. If it gives her comfort, it makes us both happy" (111). When Rachel passes, Lars spends more time in bed, rereading favorite books, sorting his coins, replacing a portrait of his mother-in-law with a painting of a dancing girl from his bachelor years. Lars's broad grin, twinkling eyes, or chuckling reveal that he has stumbled onto a "happy object."

Rachel's relations to the object world are seen as more problematic: she's the one who hoards while the others have to clear away her mess. Her primary hobby was collecting—and sewing clothing for—baby dolls. Many panels show Lars or Laura admiring a large display cabinet overflowing with dolls and their accessories. At one point, Laura notes, "Someone told me that doll collectors often had no children of their own, were born poor, and married well," and Lars passes it off as a joke, suggesting that other than his being rich, "the description fits" (67). While Farmer makes no effort to explain Lars's stamp collecting, say, there is a persistent need to trace Rachel's obsession back to her father's abandonment: he gave Rachel her first doll. As she becomes more addled, she forgets, insisting that she has only ever had that one doll, as the others have vanished not only from her bodily horizon but from her memory as well.

After Rachel's death, when Lars and Laura are going through her hope chest, her most private cache, they discover a bundle of letters that Rachel's father wrote her mother, suggesting a history of continued contact and interest in his daughter's life. And they even find some affectionate letters between Rachel and her father, written the same year as his death, further undercutting her narrative about their relationship. As Lars explains, "She would have thought it disloyal to dispute Louise's version of the separation" (155). Laura felt that these letters should be shared with Rachel's nieces, but she later learned that her sister burned them because she did not think her daughters would be interested, a painful reminder that different relatives do not place the same value on family history.

If there are happy objects, there are also unhappy objects, objects that produce displeasure because they recall traumatic past events, but nevertheless touch their owners so deeply that there is no simple way to discard them. Rachel pushes back when Lars brings an old walker and commode from the garage, not simply because she rejects the necessity of such items, but because she is distressed that these are hand-me-downs from Lars's mother, who judged her harshly. Rachel shares the story of returning from her honeymoon to find Lars's first wife's clothes still in the closet: "That hurt my feelings like nothing before or since!" She ultimately had to clear them away so that she could unpack her own things (70). Recalling the same incident, Lars confesses that when she threatened to move back to her mother, he decided against putting her name on the title for their house, fearing that she might contest his ownership. Rachel's dispossession explains why she clings so fiercely to her belongings and fights for control over her own space within the home she was never allowed to call her own. Here Farmer explains Rachel's insecurity not in terms of her father's abandonment in a distant past, but rather the ongoing inequalities in her marriage.

What Remains

The stuff most closely linked to the body is often the stuff that produces the greatest distaste among others, the stuff that takes a strong stomach to confront when family members are tasked with cleaning out the old apartment. Here we move beyond domestic knowledge or sentimental attachments to a more intimate knowledge of bodily waste, and here we move deeper into the matters that are rarely discussed in polite company. Underground comics have always sought to shatter taboos, so it may be no surprise that a veteran of the underground comics movement might also be willing to depict things that people do not like to discuss, let alone depict.

By the time Joyce Farmer published *Special Exits* in 2014, she was herself seventy-three years old. While she had been working as a comics artist and editor since her involvement in the underground comics movement in the early 1970s, *Special Exits* was her first book-length project, having taken more than a decade to produce, and, much like C. Tyler and *You'll Never Know*, following long delays as a consequence of her personal obligations. She had been a contributor to *Wimmen's Comix*, an important anthology series, which has gained greater visibility in recent years as its collected output has been edited into a hardbound edition. She is best known for having co-edited another feminist anthology, *Tits & Clits*, with Lyn Chevil. *Tits & Clits* maps cultural divides within American feminism, reflecting what has been called the emergence of sex-positive feminism in response to the feminist anti-porn movement. But Farmer also describes the book as a reaction against sexism in male-produced underground comics: "We started looking at ourselves and our sexuality and we decided that our idea of sex had a lot to do with birth control and menstruation and sanitary pads going flop on the ground when you didn't want them to, tampon loss, not having a tampon when you needed it" (Dangerous Minds 2010). Farmer received hostile responses when she shared her first issue with the *LA Free Press* and other underground newspapers; one male reviewer, she recalls, insisted that "a vagina was something to put things into and not have anything come out of."

Farmer's cover art captures the gender and sexual politics of the 1970s and 1980s. *Tits & Clits* 3, published in 1977, features women of diverse ages and races marching on the US Capitol, waiving their dildos and vibrators high and proud, and chanting, "We shall overcome!" This image (figure 7.6) with its overtones of female solidarity—the three women have linked their arms together—suggests women's assertion of their right to sexual pleasure outside of compulsary heterosexuality or the reproductive mandate. Farmer's cover for *Tits & Clits* 5, published in 1979, depicts men and women checking each other out on the beach, each wearing skimpy swimwear (figure 7.7). The men eyeing the women's breasts are thinking "oranges & grapefruit" and "papayas & cantaloupes," while the women, returning the objectifying gaze, imagine "Polish sausage & dumplings" and "Vienna sausage & prunes." This reversal of perspective directs attention to fundamental inequalities in representation, particularly the objectification of women's bodies, which the comic seeks to address. Farmer's cover for *Tits & Clits* 6 (figure 7.8), published in 1980, depicts a naked woman, glowing in the aftermath of passionate sex, still straddling her male lover: "Hey! That was great! Uh . . . What did you use for birth control?" Here, the joke hinges on the different consequences sex carries for women: "There's many factors to sex that men don't pay any attention to, and women have to pay exquisite attention to, or we pay heavily" (Campbell 2011). *Tits & Clits* ultimately shut down amid the anti-porn hysteria of the early Reagan years. Though there is nothing pornographic about her images, Farmer incorporates sensual details. In figure 7.7, she shows the women's nipples and buttocks, the men's genitalia, pressing against the fabric of their bathing suits, not to mention one woman's extended tongue as she is about to take a lick of her ice cream cone. Here and in figure 7.8, the men's bodies are covered in dense, tangled hair, intended to contrast with the women's smooth skin. The women's direct stares break with long-standing traditions in pinup pictures of women's more demure glances. In each case, we are meant to read the image from the perspective of her female characters, with the men often possessing the

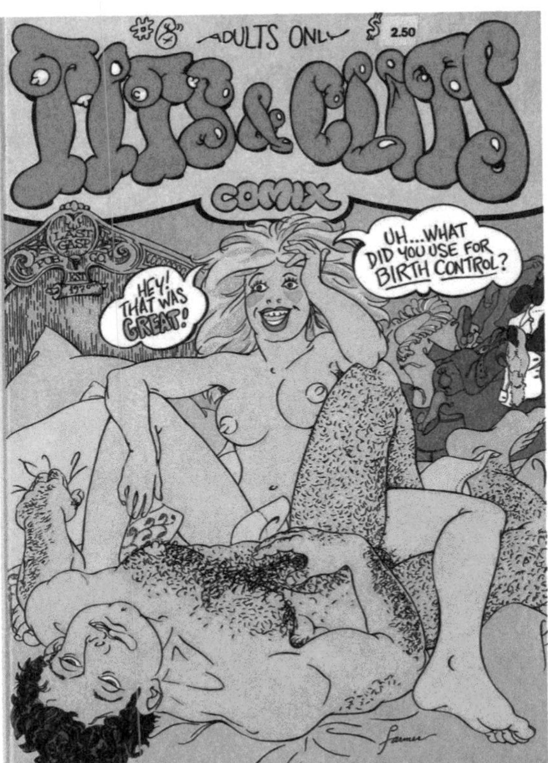

FIGURES 7.6–7.8 (CLOCKWISE FROM TOP LEFT). Cover for feminist underground comic conveys sexual openness and female solidarity; reverses the male gaze as women reduce men to their body parts; and imagines a world where men have primary responsibility for birth control. Joyce Farmer, *Tits & Clits* 3 (1977), *Tits & Clits* 5 (1979), *Tits & Clits* 6 (1980). © Joyce Farmer.

quality that Laura Mulvey famously called "to-be-looked-at-ness." Her female characters are muscular and their faces positively glow. Read together, these three covers offer a glimpse of the iconography and ideological agenda of this generation of feminist artists as they pushed back against restraints on sexual and artistic expression.

Special Exits reflects the concerns of an author at a very different life stage. Her focus has shifted from menstruation to menopause, from sexually active young bodies to decaying old ones, but there are important continuities in the underlying political commitments. Consider, for example, a moment when Laura is giving Rachel a sponge bath, a repeated routine, and the older woman, in a moment of uninhibited playfulness, tugs on her sagging old tits with a look of dazed pleasure (figure 7.9). Here Rachel becomes a transgressive, unruly woman, in keeping with the underground tradition, recalling in particular the carnivalesque representations of mature women's bodies found in the work of Roberta Gregory (*Bitchy Bitch*), a contributor to *Tits & Clits*. Another key moment comes when a black neighbor and her children seek refuge, escaping from an abusive relationship. Learning about her unwanted pregnancy, the deeply religious Rachel, often shown watching televangelists, surprises Laura by recommending Planned Parenthood, acknowledging that sometimes abortion is the only solution. Farmer had produced a 1973 underground comic, *Abortion Eve*, specifically designed to help women think through their choices in regard to abortion and has more recently said that she wants to devote her creative skills to confronting global population growth.

But at a more fundamental level, *Special Exits* reflects Farmer's fight to get the medical profession to respect the dignity of seniors: "I was outraged over the care they were given late in life, because they were turned from people with their own private lives that they loved and lived, into being medical fodder for the medical community. They were deprived of their personalities and privateness and were treated like old fools, and I resented that for them" (Dangerous Minds 2010). As she discusses her motives for writing the book, Farmer explains how she has evolved from a focus on the sexual objectification of women's bodies to the medical objectification of aged bodies. *Special Exits* vividly depicts Farmer's struggles with the medical profession, their bureaucratic procedures, their casual disregard for the particulars of their patients' situations, the physical harm that befell her blind stepmother when a nurse forgot to secure a bedrail, the various ways Farmer had to advocate for what Rachel required to survive. Thankfully, the book has become a required text for

FIGURE 7.9. Joyce Farmer incorporates some of the bawdy body humor of her underground work into the representation of the aged. Joyce Famer, *Special Exits* (2011). © Joyce Farmer. Courtesy of Fantagraphics.

a growing number of nursing programs, because it has so much to teach the healing professions.

Farmer brings the underground comic era's frankness about what comes out of bodies to a consideration of the process of decomposition. She is unflinching in her depiction of the various blisters, bruises, bedsores, and burns her parents experience throughout the aging process. She carefully documents the progressive shedding of identity: Rachel's wedding ring keeps sliding off her withered fingers; Lars discards old clothes that will never fit him again or buys a new suit knowing that most likely he will be buried in it; Rachel's long hair gets cut to avoid tangles; Laura buys adult diapers for her father and gets chastised at the hospital for failing to cut Lars's toenails. Much of the imagery centers around what Julia Kristeva (1982) describes as the abject, that is, the human reactions of repulsion and disgust brought about by the potential collapse of boundaries between the self and the other, between the body and the object world. Dead and dying bodies, Kristeva suggests, offer a painful reminder of our own mortality and materiality:

> A wound with blood and puss, or the sickly, acrid smell of sweat, of decay, does not signify death. In the presence of signified death—a flat encephalograph, for instance—I would understand, react, or accept. No, as in true theater, without makeup or masks, refuse and corpses show me what I permanently thrust aside in order to live. These bodily fluids, this defilement, this shit are what life withstands, hardly and with difficulty, on the part of death. There, I am at the border of my condition as a living being. My body extricates itself, as being alive, from that border. Such wastes drop so that I might live, until, from loss to loss, nothing remains in me and my entire body falls beyond the limit—cadere, cadaver. (3)

In our culture, death may be the ultimate obscenity (that which is off scene, something we don't depict, something we don't talk about) because we always want to talk about something more pleasant.

In both *Special Exits* and *Can't We Talk,* moments of death occur when the caretaker protagonists are out of the room. There is nothing here like the naked male bodies with gaping wounds Alison Bechdel depicts during the embalming room scenes in *Fun Home,* a book that Hillary Chute (2010) describes as "drenched in death" (195). Chast depicts herself sitting quietly alongside her mother's corpse, shortly after her death, drawing her one last time, and includes several more realistic sketches of her corpse (figure 7.10). There is a quiet beauty in this depiction of death, a willingness to look directly, without sentimentality, at the body in its final moments. Here, as in Chast's other drawings, she seems preoccupied with the most mundane aspects of her surroundings—the lamp, a trash can, a vent. In *Special Exits,* Laura returns to the hospital to find her mother's bed empty, her belongings in a plastic bag, before anyone notifies her what has happened. And her father passes away in his sleep, in his own home, when she has gone to deal with some banking issues. Both deaths occupy only a few panels, not even the entire page, as compared to the extensive images of her cleaning away their material possessions.

By this point, readers have already witnessed that ongoing process by which the aged shed parts of their bodies. Laura finds one of Rachel's teeth in her fouled blanket; Lars matter-of-factly drops it into a little chest: "I have a collection. This one's from the washing machine. That one I stepped on. It doesn't seem to matter that they fall out. . . . All her molars are gone now with this last

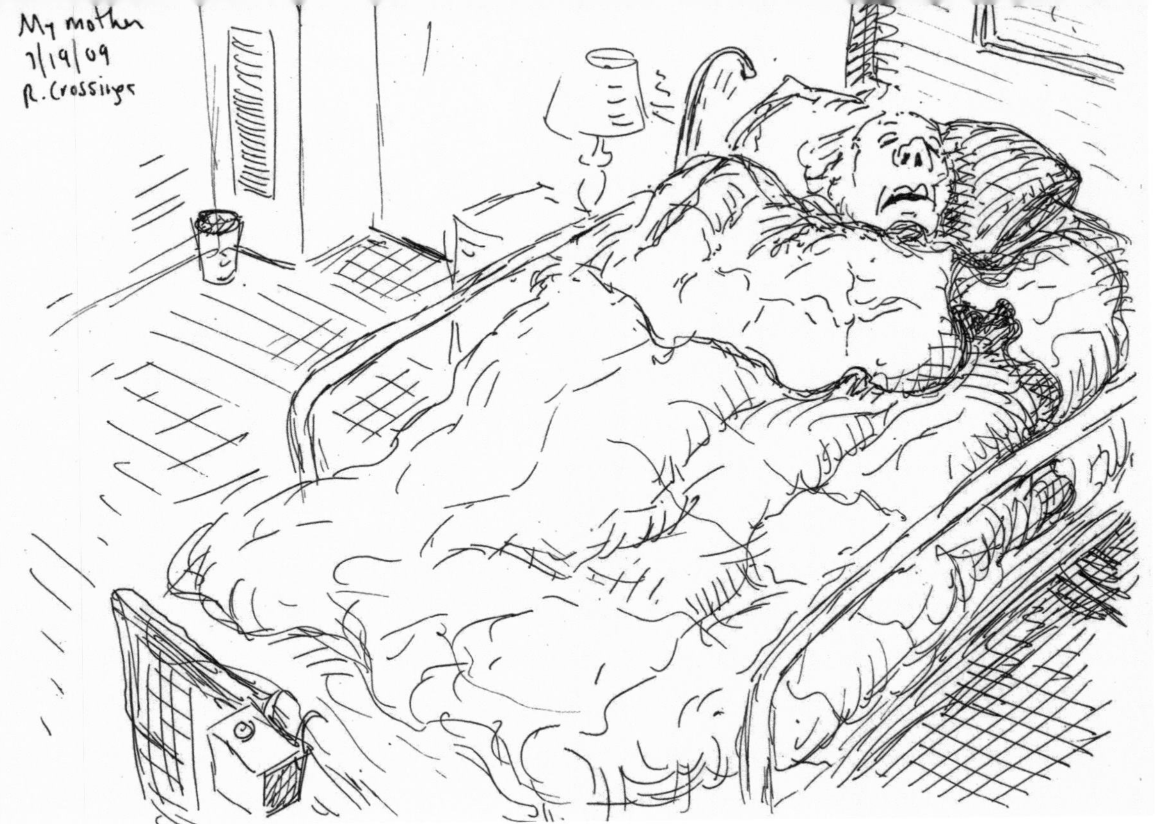

FIGURE 7.10. Roz Chast shares a sketch she produced at the bedside of her deceased mother. Roz Chast, *Can't We Talk about Something More Pleasant?* (2014). © Roz Chast. Courtesy of Bloomsbury.

one" (125–126). In another scene, Laura and Lars discuss how he deals with the messes Rachel makes now that she is unable to get off the couch to go to the bathroom. He allows her to pee into a ratty old towel and then tosses it into the washing machine; he does the same for her poop, "the washing machine doesn't care. I just put those towels through twice. . . . Things get worse in such small increments that you can get used to everything" (85). Lars's normalized reactions to the soiled towels exist alongside Rachel's affectionate recollection of her husband's ink smudge on the door frame as the small costs of the things we do for those we love, but for someone coming in from the outside, such stories still evoke abjection, a profound disgust with human filth. Such details separate people who are caregivers (most often female) from those readers (most often male) for whom this is an alien experience.

In her final pages, Chast offers yet one more cataloging of her possessions:

> On the floor of my closet, along with shoes, old photo albums, wrapping paper, a sewing machine, a shelf of sleep t-shirts, an iron, a cartoon of my kid's childhood artwork, and some other miscellaneous stuff, are two

> special boxes. One holds my father's cremains. The other holds my mother's. My father's box is inside a navy blue velvet drawstring bag, which I placed inside of the ancient Channel 13 bag that he took everywhere. My mother's box is inside a maroon velvet drawstring bag. It is "en plein air." . . . Inside each of the velvet bags is a white cardboard box. Inside the cardboard box is a black plastic box, plus a certificate that assures you that the person enclosed was cremated in the "official" way. When you break the seal of the black plastic box, first there are a bunch of packing peanuts. Then you can pull out a plastic bag with a finely milled grayish powder which weighs around five pounds. In case you cannot believe what you are looking at, each bag has a tag on it. Until I figure out a better place for them, they're staying in the closet. (224–226)

Her parents, in the end, have turned into more stuff, which Chast has to store or dispose, the perfect conclusion to a work so preoccupied with the disposition of her parents' things and the settling of their affairs.

Putting Things to Rest

Across this book, I have explored the processes by which the artists and their characters map their identity and manage their memories through the stuff they collect or accumulate. We have moved from a focus on collecting, understood as a creative project of self-fashioning through which people surround themselves with objects they have selected as particularly evocative or meaningful, toward a focus on the moment of letting go of loved ones and their belongings, a process of cleaning away stuff that has outlived its meaningfulness, not to mention its usefulness. Just as Seth shows us the moment when a postcard collection loses its interest, Farmer and Chast take us to the place where even a parents' ashes become just more junk stashed in a closet.

We use our stuff to define who we are, what we value, and what aspects of ourselves we display to others. This is true of collectors (Seth, Kim Deitch) and discriminating accumulators (Bryan Talbot) who curate their belongings. It is true even for those who lack stuff (Kare in *My Favorite Thing Is Monsters*), who have to make do with what they can make themselves. It is also true for hoarders (such as Rachel in *Special Exits*), who often have trouble restricting this production of meaning to a small subset of their possessions, but, instead, see their identities as saturating everything they touch. And it is also true for family members dealing with someone else's stuff (as Joyce Farmer and Roz Chast did). When, like C. Tyler, we seek to represent important figures in our lives, we often display their most precious objects (her father's tools, her mother's holiday decorations). We are defined by our possessions, our belongings, our stuff.

At a time when more and more artists see themselves as "worldbuilders" as much or more than as storytellers, representations of objects assume greater prominence. These threshold objects render the worlds (both real and imagined) that matter to these artists visible, even tangible, to their readers, connecting their protagonists' experiences with our own material lives. If we also collect rocks or baby dolls, old comics or postcards, cats or monsters, if we share the mental frames that collectors place around these materials, then we will share a sense of kinship with these authors and their works will speak to and for us. The artist may tap local knowledge, allowing us to display our own expertise or draw comparisons with our own treasures. But they may also speak to us in a more generalized way: stories about sorting through our deceased parents' stuff do not require us to identify with particular object choices, but rather speak to shared experiences of loss and grief.

By this point, I hope my readers appreciate the value of this particular approach—situated at the intersection between material culture and visual studies. Though my focus is on contemporary graphic novels, I have located comics in relation to a history of practices such as still life paintings, cabinets d'amateur, cabinets of curiosities, sketchbooks, and scrapbooks, all of which told stories through "the medium of stuff" (99), as Daniel Miller (2010) suggests. Certainly, comics add something to these traditions in their ability to juxtapose images within a narrative context that encourages readers not only to scan them closely but also to move back and forth across their pages. What is striking here may ultimately not be traits that are specific to comics, but the capacity of graphic novelists to raid the entire history of visual representation for techniques that can be meaningfully deployed to tell their stories or render their worlds. Stylistic choices are never random: though male critics have sometimes described female-produced comics as amateurish, this has more to say about those critics' resistance to alternative styles and the historical links of women's expressive practices to the realm of domestic craft than it has to do with these women's artistic agency. I fear that sometimes comics studies has been more preoccupied with issues of decoupage than they are with what's in the frame. My approach here has required us to follow the stuff, pulling details from the background of panels that may speak to larger material practices.

Coming back to where I began, comics *are* stuff, comics display stuff, and comics tell stories about stuff. Miller suggests that stuff gains its power because we don't notice or reflect upon it much of the time: "Stuff has a quite remarkable capacity of fading from view, and becoming naturalized, taken for granted, the background or frame to our behaviour. Indeed, stuff achieves its mastery of us precisely because we constantly fail to notice what it does. Things act much more commonly as analogous to the frames around paintings than the paintings themselves" (155). Yet here I am applying these methods to look at "the paintings themselves," or at least the drawings. What's depicted here has been consciously "framed" for our attention and, in many cases, I have been interested in the ways different artists have displayed their virtuosity through their representation of the material world. I have explored moments where readers are invited to become more self-conscious about their relationship to stuff. Some elements linger in the "background" when we first read these books, but the artists made great efforts to track down, reference, and reproduce these elements within their panels. Most stories deal with moments when the characters themselves are hyperconscious about their material surroundings—moments of acquisition or divestment. Miller acknowledges such moments—for example, when dealing with the transfer of belongings across generations:

> We don't expect people to keep objects pertaining to their parent's long decline through Alzheimer's or incapacitation through illness. Indeed they retain a few photos from the wedding, the holidays, the moments when the relationship came closest to its ideal. Deceased males are often memorialized by other males through items of technology: tools of their trade as a carpenter, their cricket bat or their best fly-fishing rod. These are objects which help fuse the memory of the specific ancestor with the idealized conceptualization of a man, especially the working man. A woman is more likely to be recalled through the tokens of her love and care, that equally make her the generic woman. . . . So people have both an economy of relationships that pares things down to a few key objects and also use this to transform the memory of that relationship from a more actual to a more idealized component. (151)

At such moments, people select what stuff to keep and what memories to attach to that stuff.

The artists producing these comics make similar decisions, selecting what to draw and what to ignore, what stories to tell and what props might support those narratives. Such moments defamiliarize routine relationships with objects, forcing their readers to think about what and how materials matter. My analysis of these specific artists and graphic novels is intended to surface the implicit and explicit reflections they offer about our relationship with stuff. Often these artists may start with a simple nostalgia or a collector's passion, but along the way, these elements accrue more meaning. As William Davies King (2008) suggests, "Collecting is a way of linking past, present, and future. Objects from the past get collected in the present to preserve them for the future" (27). Telling stories about collecting (and, even more so, inheritance) thus situates their authors and readers in time, looking backward at who they have been, sideways at who they have become, and forward at who they might be.

Miller's example suggests how gender shapes the association of people and objects: gender enters both in terms of the gender of the person being remembered and the gender of the person holding onto the objects (the ways normative masculinity discourages certain forms of sentimentality). Such gender differences also shape the kinds of stories male and female writers share about their relationships to stuff. In many female-authored narratives, meaningful objects are embedded in family relationships, whereas the male-authored stories are more likely to either focus on self-definition through collecting (as in Seth's works) or public history (as in Bryan Talbot's *Alice in Sunderland*). One could argue that I have cherry-picked my examples to reach this conclusion, which, in practice, I have actively resisted every step along the way. I would be happy to see the counterexamples or alternative readings. To me, Emil Ferris's work is perhaps the most interesting in this regard, because *My Favorite Thing Is Monsters* shares so much with the male-centered collecting stories (its protagonist's passionate interests in a particular category of popular culture, an interest she shared with many male collectors during this period). Yet her narrative situates that passion in relation to the other people in her protagonist's life (her troubled brother, her dying mother, her absent father, her friends who are each struggling with their own issues of identity). The same could be said of Carol Tyler's *Fab4 Mania*, which appeared as this book was wrapping up: Tyler captures her own teenage fascination with the Beatles, drawing on materials she herself had preserved as keepsakes (such as radio station playlists, collector cards, record albums, and the diary that she adapted for her core narrative). Like Ferris, she made up for a lack of economic independence by creating what she could not buy, making her own representations of her favorite rock stars.

We might consider why male and female artists are pulled in such highly gendered directions, what this suggests about the current moment in comic history, as more women are producing comics (than at any prior point in history) and more women are reading comics (than at any point since the late 1940s, when males and females read comics in more or less equal numbers). I have discussed the different routes by which male authors and female authors get the opportunity to produce graphic novels—the different support networks, the degree to which, as C. Tyler recounts, these "graphic women" are often making comics in and around family demands on their attention. If this is the case, will different stories about stuff emerge as more younger women enter comics, straight from arts schools and professional training programs, determined to make comics and eager to speak to an expanding female readership who desperately want to see their experiences reflected on the page?

8

"Contemptible Collectibles"

Confronting the Residual in Jeremy Love's *Bayou*

In *Special Exits*, as Lars and Laura are going through Rachel's stuff following her death, they turn their attention to a chest that she has never allowed anyone to examine before: this is where she keeps her secrets and they feel like they are invading her privacy just opening its lid. Some of what they find thrills them—such as an old quilt produced by Rachel's grandmother. Some debunks Rachel's self-representation—a stack of old letters undermines her narrative of being abandoned by her father as a girl. And some are things they probably didn't want to find; in particular, Laura pulls out a statuette of a Klansman (figure 8.1). Lars offers a somewhat matter-of-fact explanation: "She showed me that once. It belonged to her first husband" (154), but both characters get quickly distracted by the cache of letters. Laura lowers the troubling object from the frame and it never resurfaces again. What are readers to make of this object, which, surely, offers us a counternarrative to Rachel's life as profound as what they discover reading the old letters? This object implicates Rachel (or at least her first husband) in a culture of white supremacy that contradicts our perceptions of Rachel's kindness when she offers refuge and maternal advice to the black single mother who lives next door.

RACHEL WOULD NEVER LET ANYONE LOOK IN THIS CHEST, BUT NOW IT'S TIME TO GO THROUGH IT.
OK, DAD.
WHAT TINY STITCHES ON THIS QUILT!
PROBABLY BY HER GRANDMOTHER. RACHEL NEVER WORKED IN RED AND WHITE.
LOOK AT ALL THESE LETTERS! 1914, 1916... AND PHOTOS OF A MAN. HER FATHER, I'M SURE.
?
1885
SHE SHOWED ME THAT ONCE.
IT BELONGED TO HER FIRST HUSBAND.
YOU MIGHT WANT TO READ THESE. (COUGH) THEY'RE FROM HER FATHER TO HER MOTHER AFTER HE LEFT HOME. ONE LETTER A WEEK FOR TWO AND A HALF YEARS.
WHAT?
Dear Louise, I miss you and the children Rent due $0 inclose $1.50 More next Ti Kiss the chil me. All my Lewis
Laredo Tex. Dear Louise A good week here is $5.00 I'm mighty tir With love to and David and Rachel. Lewis
Dear Louise Weatherford I'll be home Christmas. Kisses from husband. Lewis xxx ooo
Oklahoma Louise I'm sorry out of work cold weather. $1.00 inclosed for a dress for Rachel Kiss her for me. All my love. Lewis
L. G. Hoffman New Orleans Mrs Lewis Hoffman Spfld, Missouri
Lewis G. Hoffman
"YOU HEARD WRONG ABOUT ME. SOME PEOPLE LOVE TO GOSSIP. KISS RACHEL AND DAVID FOR ME."
"ONLY ONE DOLLAR THIS TIME. HAPPY BIRTHDAY, DEAR WIFE. I'M SENDING YOU A GOLD WATCH. I MISS THE CHILDREN, PLEASE LET ME COME HOME. ALL MY LOVE, LEWIS."

Such fleeting moments of revelation are not unique in the comics we have considered. I could point to similar moments when artists direct attention—always briefly, often for a single panel—on racialized and racist objects from earlier eras. In *Clyde Fans*, for example, Seth depicts Simon's encounter with a novelty salesman who offers him what the busker acknowledges is a "revolting trifle," a celluloid watermelon that opens up to reveal a "little pickaninny" inside: "Yes, to men of our intelligence, this is a tawdry thing—but you would be surprised at how many I move" (148). And indeed, when we see Simon later, he's holding this same racist toy (figure 8.2) (129). Simon's expression is hard to read—shame? Loneliness? Contemplation? And given the relentless narration across the work, the absence of any text in this sequence seems shocking. Simon seems to be at a loss for words.

FIGURE 8.2. This "revolting trifle" hints at a history of material practices around racial stereotypes within which comics artists and readers have been complicit. Seth, *Clyde Fans* (2019). © Seth. Courtesy of Drawn & Quarterly.

FIGURE 8.1 (OPPOSITE). Lars and Laura discover something they would rather not have found while going through Rachel's things after her death. Joyce Farmer, *Special Exits* (2011). © Joyce Farmer. Courtesy of Fantagraphics.

Look Away, Dixieland!

Such objects represent ideology congealed; they capture a particular moment in time, locking down a set of values an individual might have possessed at some unspecified moment in the past. Such objects raise nagging questions: Why and how have those objects survived? Why were they stashed away in a chest, a closet, an attic? What meanings do they preserve? Have the feelings and memories those objects express dissolved over time even as the things themselves remain unchanged? What happens when these items get passed from one generation to the next? Do we throw them away? Do we sell them on eBay and perpetuate their circulation? Do we reread them as kitsch and camp? Do we hold them at arm's length as if they had nothing to do with us and as if we will catch their stank if we bring them too close? How do they alter our impressions of the people we knew?

Bill Brown (2015) identifies similarly uncomfortable elements in the mise-en-scène of Spike Lee's 2000 film, *Bamboozled*: "I want to draw your attention to those objects in the movie that are generally designated Sambo art, Negro memorabilia, or black collectibles: Aunt Jemima cookie jars, the Jocko hitching posts, the canisters and salt and pepper shakers, the hot-pad holders, most infamously the Jolly Nigger bank" (251). Here Brown indicates a whole class of objects that many (mostly white) might prefer to forget and others (mostly people of color) find difficult to ignore. Such objects were widespread in the first decades of the twentieth century, part of the emergence of mass media and consumer culture. When Seth or Deitch feel nostalgia for this era of popular culture, they often bracket overtly racist items, though they also acknowledge them as something they cannot get rid of quite so easily and, in some cases, they are the very thing (like *Spooktown*, "beloved racist kid's humor comic," in *Wimbledon Green*) that collectors are drawn toward.

Scholars such as Kenneth W. Goings (1994) and Patricia Turner (2002) have traced the histories of such artifacts, which were "cheap, mass-produced and much more likely to be sold in discount variety stores than in department stores, which catered to the middle and upper classes," made from "paper, chalkware, lead, ceramics, various metals, and later, plastics," and thus more likely to be possessed by lower- or working-class whites than by their more upscale contemporaries. Such products depended on "the broad image, the stereotype" because there could be little attention paid to nuanced details (Goings 1994, 12–13). Goings sees this targeting of lower-class whites as reflecting both taste and ideology—part of a larger attempt to draw a wedge between poor whites and blacks so that they could not be united around shared class interests. Turner (2002) goes further in her discussion of what she calls "contemptible collectibles": "They are about the ways in which, even after the institution of slavery was over, American consumers found acceptable ways of buying and selling the souls of black folk" (11). Goings and Turner trace the recurring stereotypes that were reproduced through these cheap household objects (just as Bryan Talbot traces the materialization of local legends and folk tales in *Alice in Sunderland*). Race myths were perpetuated not only through cheap bric-a-brac but also through greeting cards, brand logos (many of which—such as Aunt Jemina or Uncle Ben—persist to the present day in altered forms), comics, and animated cartoons. Because of this intertextual context, because of the ways images reflected larger mythologies, a simple icon may carry a more complex shared history. Goings, for example, provides an entry point for contextualizing the racist toy that Seth depicts in *Clyde Fans* (figure 8.2):

> The figures, usually children, but sometimes adult males, are shown to be almost savagely biting into watermelon, attacking it like animals brought to a trough to feed. Several associations were made with these images. The bright, primary (read primitive) colors were thought to be attractive to African-Americans. There were also fondly repeated tales of slaves stealing into the watermelon patch during the dead of night, only to be caught by the master. The reason they were caught was that while their dark skin provided camouflage at night, the whites of their eyes, like those of a wild scavenger (such as the raccoon), gave them away. (39–40)

Turner notes that such picaninny toys were often valued far more by white America than the lives of actual black children, who were "underclothed, overworked, underfed" (16). Images of black children romping in cotton fields and watermelon patches suggested, Turner argues, that "if they had been given a chance, they would have chosen to spend their days in the field rather than in a schoolroom" (16). Such toys concretized ideology into something you can hold in your hands, something you might chuckle over with others who shared your beliefs and values (37) and something that can perpetuate stereotypes that hurt and humiliate.

There is no simple way to separate such racist objects from the history of comics and animation, even as there has been an effort since the 1960s to strip overtly racist works from the archives of cartoons still being circulated.

Someone drew these caricatures, someone told these stories, and more often than not, they were produced and reproduced by cartoonists, who often picked up extra money doing other commercial jobs—drawing greeting cards, advertisements, magazine covers, perhaps even designing the objects themselves. As racial attitudes shifted after World War II, as civil rights groups spoke out against more overt forms of white supremacy, the design of such objects shifted accordingly: "The exaggerated nature of many of the earlier collectibles was now being replaced by more restrained stereotypes—but stereotypes nevertheless" (Goings 1994, xvii). Many of the most beloved characters in cartoons and comic strips—Mickey Mouse, Felix the Cat, Pogo—smoothed over stereotypes, making traces of the minstrel show more acceptable to a general audience. Leonard Rifas (2010) writes: "Cartoonists often defend the stereotypes in their work by saying that the art of cartooning fundamentally relies on simplification, generalization, distortion and exaggeration. Caricatures become racist stereotypes, though, when instead of exaggerating an individual's particular features to bring out his or her unique humanity, the cartoonist suppresses the individuality of a person's appearance to bring the portrait into conformity with a preexisting racial stereotype" (33). As these characters evolve from generic prototypes to distinctive personalities, they reverse that trajectory—more individualized, less beholden to stereotypes. Yet contemporary cartoonists are haunted by that legacy, which may be why they incorporate these fleeting moments when racist caricatures from the past are put on display alongside other household objects. Whereas the archaic might refer to materials or practices that are no longer culturally relevant, Raymond Williams (1977) tells us, "the residual, by definition, has been effectively formed in the past, but it is still active in the cultural process, not only and often not at all as an element of the past, but as an effective element of the present." Williams stresses that such elements persist "because they represent areas of human experience, aspiration, and achievement which the dominant culture neglects, undervalues, opposes, represses, or even cannot recognize" (123). Characters in graphic novels pull such figures from a previous generation's hope chest with shock and surprise, inviting readers to ponder how they got there (not just in the chest, but in the graphic novel itself).

Rifas (2010) has explored the efforts of underground comics artists to exorcise these residual elements from American cartooning: as they took advantage of their creative freedom to break old taboos and challenge persistent stereotypes, they often began by amplifying controversial images rather than moving beyond them: "After a long struggle, African Americans had largely succeeded in driving the images derived from the 'minstrel' tradition from mainstream comics. The old stereotypes had a disturbing half-familiarity when comix resurrected them in the form of parodies, satires and homages" (33). The underground comics artists sought to recontextualize such images, which may or may not have been the effect, but, either way, they were reproducing and recirculating them.

These objects remain evocative—for some, they provoke nostalgia, for others, they raise questions that cannot be resolved. Goings (1994) writes of his own relationship, as a black scholar, to the racist artifacts he studies:

> Even now, in the last decade of the twentieth century, these objects are still seductive. When I see Aunt Jemima and Uncle Moses resting on my shelves, I think of them as people. I try to imagine what their lives were like, and who they would be if they were alive today. In my imagination, I see Aunt Jemima not as a cook but as a fighter for freedom in the mold of Angela Davis or Shirley Chisholm. Uncle Moses I imagine not as the faithful butler but as an activist and orator in the mold of Malcolm X or of Medgar Wiley Evers, the courageous NAACP field secretary who was assassinated in 1963. Then I come back to reality and America in the 1990s and realize that Aunt Jemima would probably still be cooking and Uncle Moses serving—living their lives, as we all try to do, with dignity and self-respect. (xiv)

Here we see a particular fantasy of toys being brought to life, so that the objects might evolve with the times, might awaken to their political situation and thus serve a different agenda. Goings reclaims an empowering fantasy from what many would see as a cabinet of horrors, even if he has trouble sustaining it in the face of the country's slow progress in racial relations.

As Brown (2015) notes, Spike Lee's *Bamboozled* similarly depends on the fantasy that such objects might become animated, through here they are treated with uncanny dread: "[T]he collectibles become a mute chorus, sitting in judgement and pained by the recapitulation of the history they are witnessing in the new millennium" (258). The film's black protagonist, Delacroix, has revived the minstrel show in contemporary popular media, enriching his coffers and damning his soul. Brown describes how the closing credits sequence revitalizes such figurines: "Multiply animated—by their own mechanism, by the film, by the music—each figure, whether gorgeous or grotesque, seems caught, frantically dancing or fiddling, bouncing or swinging, swallowing pitched balls, grinning and smiling, unable to stop" (269). Spike Lee, known as one of several prominent black collectors of such materials, acknowledges that most of the objects he brought to life in *Bamboozled* came from his own collection (D'Arcy 2001).

Old Times There Are Not Forgotten: *Bayou* and *Song of the South*

Jeremy Love's webcomic *Bayou* (2010, 2011) draws inspiration from stories of the old South, tapping demons from the racist imagination to construct a distinctive mythology—a brutal and fantastical reconstruction of the Jim Crow era. Love has described what inspired the comic's creation:

> I never really felt connected to African mythology until I started reading Joel Chandler Harris' Uncle Remus tales. Seeing how elements of African mythology were interwoven with American folklore was the spark. What led me to the Uncle Remus tales was Disney's *Song of the South*, a film I've always had mixed feelings about. I felt I as an African American creator could reclaim that mythology. . . . I could mash up elements of the Civil War, blues, African mythology, Southern Gothic and American folklore and show how they form a tapestry that is the American South (Hogan n.d., n.p.).

Love was the first winner in a new talent competition that DC Comics ran as part of the launch of their short-lived Zuda platform, an attempt by the major publisher to enter the webcomics space. *Bayou* was also the first of the Zuda Comics to be published in a print format, with two volumes published in 2010 and 2011. Although a third volume was promised, it has—as of the time of writing—not appeared; as a consequence, the series ends abruptly, not allowing us to fully understand where Love was ultimately going with this attempt to construct a classic fantasy story, along the lines of *Alice in Wonderland* or *The Wizard of Oz*, but set in Charon, Mississippi, in 1931, and centered around the adventures of a young black girl.

To understand the ways that Love reworks earlier mythologies, I will trace the trajectory of the Uncle Remus stories upon which *Song of the South* is based. The white author, Joel Chandler Harris, had assembled trickster stories about

Br'er Rabbit and his brethren that had circulated among slaves in the plantation South and rendered them in a minstrel show dialect, surrounded with a frame story about the benevolent black storyteller Uncle Remus, for a mostly white readership. These stories had gained enormous popularity in both the North and the South in the early twentieth century. Many of these stories could trace their roots back to trickster tales that the slaves carried with them from Africa and revised to reflect their new realities in North America. For the slaves, these stories were empowerment fantasies. As Lawrence Levine (1977) writes, "The white master could believe that the rabbit stories his slaves told were mere figments of a childish imagination. . . . Blacks knew better. The trickster's exploits, which overturned the neat hierarchy of the world in which he was forced to live, became their exploits; the justice he achieved, their justice; the strategies he employed, their strategies. From his adventures they obtained relief; from his triumphs they learned hope" (114). But these trickster tales are more than that, they also were vehicles by which slaves taught their children how to survive in a white man's world—"the dangers of acting rashly and striking out blindly . . . the futility of believing the sincerity of the strong . . . the necessity of comprehending the ways of the powerful" (115). In the hands of a white author, and framed to meet the emotional needs of a white child, these same stories offered reassurance that the South was able to work through its own problems. As Goings (1995) writes, "The Uncle Remus stories were helpful in creating the illusion that race relations were progressing smoothly in the South and that the North need not worry about its colored brethren in Dixie. . . . Race relations cast in a comedic form were much easier to believe and accept than the real thing" (9–10).

Produced after the end of World War II, Walt Disney's *Song of the South* reflected the broader trends Goings traces—downplaying the more grotesque aspects, reducing the reliance on dialect humor, but continuing to reproduce the same old stereotypes. While many fans defend the film as a reflection of its times, Jason Sperb (2012) argues that *Song of the South* was contentious from the start, denounced by many contemporary critics as old-fashioned and racist. Disney resituated the stories into some vaguely defined moment of reconstruction, offering an idealized representation of white-black relations that does not acknowledge the actual conditions black people confronted. James Baskett was the first black actor to receive an Academy Award, an honorary Oscar praising the dignity he had brought to his portrayal of Uncle Remus, but none of the black performers were allowed to attend the film's Atlanta premiere. The film's live-action segments have been critiqued for their reproduction of familiar stereotypes—the warm hearted "Uncle," the tart-tongued "Mammy," and the happy-go-lucky "pickaninny"—though the film has some potentially progressive elements—the interracial and cross-class friendships; the representation of adult sexuality between Remus and Aunt Tempy (Hattie McDaniel, given much greater depth than allowed her in *Gone with the Wind,* her other iconic mammy role); and the mutual respect between Remus and the boy's grandmother (Brode 2006).

Following several decades of protests from the NAACP and other civil rights organizations, the Disney corporation withdrew the film from future circulation, a policy they have maintained since the feature was last released in the 1980s. But as Sperb (2012) notes:

> Many generations were less dependent on the sporadic rereleases of the film than on the continuous circulation of *Song of the South*–related books and records in the pre–home video, pre-Internet age. Brer Rabbit and Brer Fox, and in particular the story of the "Tar Baby," were fixtures in children's texts produced by several companies. In the Golden Books, children could read the tales of Brer Rabbit every night. Thanks to Capitol and Disneyland Records, Uncle Remus's voice continued to materialize on numerous records that compiled both his stories and his singing. (103)

Sperb describes a process of "transmedia dissipation," suggesting that the company's distancing of itself from the film proper has not precluded Disney from profiting from these assets across other media, including the resurfacing of the Uncle Remus characters in the Disneyland Splash Mountain attraction and of the animal characters in *Who Framed Roger Rabbit?* Sperb also stresses the persistence of the material artifacts: "It may be tempting to think of these pieces of memorabilia as ephemeral or fleeting—nostalgic fragments of a past time. But we should not be so quick to dismiss their durability. They remained in circulation for years, passed from friend to friend, family member to family member" (103).

Uncle Remus, Br'er Rabbit, and the "Tar Baby" play central roles in Love's *Bayou,* alongside a range of other racist stereotypes from early twentieth-century material culture and popular music. Love brings to Uncle Remus much of the political context that critics have found missing in the original Disney film. As Na'amen Gobert Tilahun (2016) writes: "*Bayou's* stunning artwork doesn't shy away from the harshness of life for African-Americans in the south during the 30s, creating a disturbing effect that leaves the reader in awe of the visuals while recoiling from what they can contain. The blending of the mundane racist world of the time with the spirit world and the influences they have on each other is an extremely important part of the work" (n.p.).

If *Song of the South* is focused around Johnny, a young white boy who is befriended by a young black boy, Toby, and a poor white girl, Jenny, *Bayou* depicts the risks Lee and her family face as a consequence of her unsanctioned friendship with a white upper-class girl, Lily. When Lily disappears and is believed to have been raped and murdered, Lee's father is accused of the crime and awaits in a prison cell as a lynch mob gathers outside. Believing that Lily may have been snatched by a monster the two girls had seen lurking in the swamps, Lee overcomes her own fears of diving into the brackish waters and goes in search of another world below. Rather than being welcomed by bluebirds and butterflies, Lee's ankles are grabbed by the Golliwog, a demonic figure with kinky hair, coal black skin, haunting yellow eyes, and a big red mouth; she encounters the "strange fruit" of lynched black bodies hanging from the trees and gets pursued by a bloodhound dressed in a confederate uniform. Lee is rescued and mentored by Bayou, a lumbering, good-natured black "monster," who has been beaten into submission by the evil Bossman. At one point, Lee challenges Bayou to stand up for himself rather than accepting whatever punishment the Bossman imposes: "Look at you! You a big ol' monster with arms like tree trunks! You can whup just about anything in the whole wide world! Whatchoo got to be scared of some Bossman fo'?" (n.p.). Bayou represents unrealized black potential that needs to be awakened before blacks can stand up for their rights. As Mother Sister says in volume 2, "Maybe the time for singing hymns and waitin' for manna from heaven is over" (n.p.). Lee is also assisted by a guardian angel, the spirit of Billy Glass, a young black boy lynched for whistling at a white woman.

Critical accounts of *Bayou* (Whitted 2012; Young 2015) have emphasized its vivid construction of a Southern landscape. In the most developed analysis of the comic to date, Hershini Bhana Young links Love's visual practices to the nineteenth-century moving panorama tradition; abolitionist presentations of such panoramas invited a particular reading of Southern spaces—including the "Dismal Swamp"—in terms of differing degrees of control exerted upon black bodies. Young writes: "Page after page gives itself over to the landscape, where water, rocks and trees constitute both the text and the narrative in such fulfilling ways that one barely notices how sparse the words become. . . . It would be easy to give oneself over to the horrible beauty of a global South saturated by plantation economics and the relationships it engendered" (274). The swamp, in these accounts, provided a refuge from the slave catchers but also was a site of pursuit and capture. Love evokes this story tradition when he recounts the saga of Lee's great-grandfather Enoch, the child of an escaped slave and a Choctaw warrior, who was raised in an old Spanish fort, hidden away in the Everglades: "Injuns, Choctaw, Seminole and negroes who run off from slavery. That was a safe place for them. They made a good life for themselves in that swamp" (n.p.). My approach, however, stresses how Love repurposes, reframes, and revitalizes the stereotypical constructions of blackness that were reproduced so often in early twentieth-century material culture.

The Golliwog (figure 8.3) is the first of many such mythological creatures Lee encounters. The Golliwog first appeared in a children's book, *The Story of Two Dutch Dolls*, written by Florence Kate Upton in 1895, where the character is described as "a horrid sight, the blackest gnome" (Pilgrim 2012). Upton based the character on a minstrel doll she had remembered fondly from her own childhood. Having failed to copyright her story, the character was reproduced widely, a popular prototype for rag dolls marketed in the United States, the United Kingdom, and across Europe. Today, original Golliwog dolls produced by the German company Steiff are especially valued by collectors, going for as much as $15,000 in good condition. Such dolls are storied objects—not simply objects that represent or embody racialized stories but also objects that encourage their possessors to perform certain scripts or repertoires of actions associated with those narratives. Robin Bernstein (2011) notes that the Golliwog and other minstrel show–associated dolls "provide especially effective safe houses for racial ideology because dolls are emblems of childhood that attach, through play, to the bodies of living children. . . . Dolls are crucial props within the performance of childhood because they are contrivances by which adults and children have historically played innocent" (19). Bernstein recognizes that black girls rarely, if ever, would have owned such playthings, which were objects for the amusement of white children. Here the Golliwog represents a hideous monster that literally drags black people down, a shadowy figure who lurks in the murky swamp water. If the Golliwog's broad grin once signaled a happy-go-lucky character, here, it takes on sinister dimensions, not unlike the Joker in the Batman comics: a figure whose emotional responses have been stilted, or perhaps a character taking great pleasure in tormenting the young girl within his grasp.

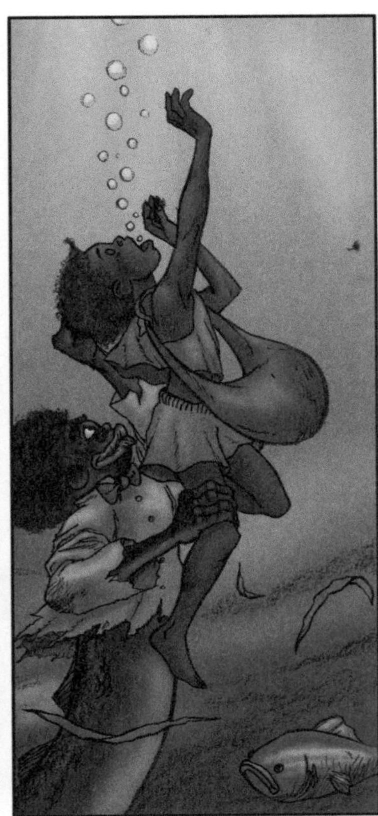

FIGURE 8.3. The monstrous Golliwog originated in a children's book and became a popular toy. Jeremy Love, *Bayou, Volume One* (2010). © Jeremy Love. Courtesy of Jeremy Love.

Lily was eaten alive by Cotton-Eyed Joe. Folklorists have traced the figure of Cotton-Eyed Joe back to pre–Civil War black folk music traditions, where his "cotton eyes" may have indicated a black child with blue eyes, the offspring of miscenegenation. In *Bayou*, Cotton-Eyed Joe's father, Bossman, is the root of most of the evil Lee confronts across the book, and depicted as the afterlife personification of General Douglass M. "Hellhound" Bogg, the Confederate general whose statue towers over the streets of Charon (figure 8.4). Like the smaller figurines and dolls discussed earlier, such statues have become a persistent problem in contemporary American culture, fortifying residual ideologies, whether more overt forms of white supremacy (as mouthed by the neo-Nazis in Charlottesville in 2017) or the nostalgic and sanitized "lost cause ideology." Lee and the other sympathetic characters are watched and sometimes attacked by Jim Crows, black birds whose name evokes a character from the minstrel tradition and later associated with the segregationist and discriminatory policies of the American South.

The incorporation of the Uncle Remus characters into this mythological

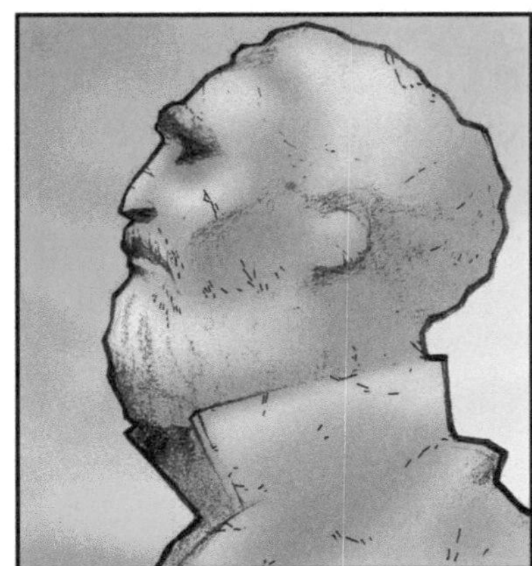

FIGURE 8.4. The statue of a Confederate general, Douglass M. "Hellhound" Bogg, looms over the town. Jeremy Love, *Bayou, Volume One* (2010). © Jeremy Love. Courtesy of Jeremy Love.

stew reflects Love's "mixed feelings" toward the source material. Uncle Remus (figure 8.5) is modeled after James Baskett—somewhat anachronistically, given that the Disney film was not produced for more than a decade after this story is set. Remus enters near the end of volume 2, sent as a treacherous emissary—in effect, a propagandist—to convince Lily that she has misunderstood the situation, that she is listening to and aligning herself with the wrong people. But when Lee refuses to stop looking for her white friend, Remus transforms into a giant black bird, much like the crow costumes black performers were required to wear in some minstrel show performances. Here Love suggests the longstanding criticisms of Remus as an Uncle Tom figure.

Br'er Rabbit constitutes a more ambivalent figure: Lee and Bayou rescue him against his will from a chain gang and seek his help in trying to track down Lily, given that he knows so many stories. Br'er Rabbit comes across as a feckless scamp who has impregnated bunnies up and down the Natchez Trace, who looks after himself above all else, who is full of ruses (all traits associated with his origins in the trickster folk-tale tradition). As Bayou explains, "Rabbit is a low down dirty rascal, but he gonna help muh friend, Miss Lee" (n.p.). Ultimately, he can't provide the information they seek: "I lost dem stories in a dice game in Nawlins to Brer Fox" (n.p.). Volume 2 ends with Lee, Rabbit, and another animal companion, a crossdressing Coon, hopping a train toward the City in search of Brer Fox, but not before the book offers its own version of the Tar Baby story. Here Tar Baby is a 1920s blues singer who "beguiles" the many men who frequent her riverboat dive; Rabbit, one of her many lovers, is a musician who plays the same club. Rabbit dies in a knife fight with Stagolee; Tar Baby and others are swept away in a flood when the levee breaks, sending them all into the afterlife. Tar Baby, we discover, was Lee's mother and Rabbit might have been her illegitimate father: "Dat nappy headed-pigmeat, her hide is black like Tarbaby but she got da eyes of Bruh' Rabbit" (n.p.). When Stagolee resurfaces, he threatens to end Rabbit: "No deals, no tricks, no Briar Patch, no Laughing Place . . . No Escape from Hell" (n.p.). His references to the Briar Patch and the Laughing Place evoke two of the most popular sequences in *Song of the South*, again anchoring his version of the Remus stories to Disney's retelling.

FIGURE 8.5. Love's depiction of Uncle Remus draws on the image of James Baskett, who played the part in Walt Disney's *Song of the South*. Jeremy Love, *Bayou, Volume Two* (2011). © Jeremy Love. Courtesy of Jeremy Love.

Love's appropriation and remixing of these racially charged archetypes invites comparison with the works of Kara Walker, who has remained a controversial figure in the art world because of her play with elements reproduced from the racist imaginary of the late nineteenth and early twentieth centuries. Raised in Stone Mountain, Georgia, not far from the meeting grounds of the Ku Klux Klan, she uses her art to work through the disturbing images she encountered as a child. Walker is known for cut-out silhouettes and large panoramas of the antebellum South. Her images are childlike in their simplicity and brutal in their representations of atrocities (both the violence that slaveholders imposed on black bodies and black fantasies of uprising and resistance). Speaking of her own relationship to the found materials that inspire her work, Walker explains: "The whole gamut of images of black people, whether by black people or not, are free rein in my mind. Each of my pieces picks and chooses willy-nilly from images that are fairly benign to fairly charged. . . . The audience has to deal with their own prejudices or fears or desires when they look at these images. So if anything, my work attempts to take those 'pickaninny' images and put them up there and eradicate them" (Shaw 2004, 103). Critics, including some prominent black writers and artists, argue that Walker is naive and reckless if she believes that she can evoke such stereotypes without negative consequences, and one can imagine the same argument might be made about Love's *Bayou*. Yet refusing to acknowledge that history, locking all of those racist texts in a vault, or hiding the memorabilia in a chest offers no better remedy for the hurtful memories they evoke, if the case of *Song of the South* is any indication. As Jason Sperb notes, despite (or perhaps because of) Disney's decision not to circulate the title, fan enthusiasm remains high for a text that many adults recall fondly (but often imperfectly) from their childhoods. These Disney buffs experience *Song of the South* as something robbed from them, a forbidden object, an arbitrarily chosen scapegoat for Hollywood's past sins. They point to much more overtly racist sequences in other Disney films, such as the black crows in *Dumbo*, the Siamese cats in *Lady and the Tramp*, or the "Red Men" in *Peter Pan*, all of which the studio continues to market and sell, even if they are less likely to turn these racialized characters into plush toys than they were in the past. Sperb notes that the Disney corporation, rarely noted for its tolerant attitudes toward copyright infringement, has done little to police the underground circulation of bootleg *Song of the South* prints, even as it also spreads less offensive elements of the film through self-promotion. And the company continues to release the film outside the North American market, having no problems reproducing black stereotypes across Asia or Latin America.

Advocates of the ban note that Disney films are put back into circulation not as texts grounded in particular historical periods, but as timeless classics for "children of all ages," consumed without much regard for when or why they were first produced. For Disney to rerelease the film in the US would be to acknowledge its association, to endorse *Song of the South* as a Disney film. Sperb (2012) worries that the intensity of the critical backlash against *Song of the South* has diminished over time, the longer the film has been hidden from view—but not the intensity of its supporters, who continue to petition for its rerelease. Ultimately, he concludes, "*Song of the South* is a much more interesting and provocative film when people cannot see it. . . . Releasing the film again would bring the film back from the realm of myth, where it has been built up into so much more than it really is" (232).

In his classic essay "Should We Burn Babar?" (1995), Herbert Kohl asked what should be done with beloved works from the past that contain and convey racist, sexist, and colonialist agendas. For some, such works provoke nostalgia and delight, and for others, pain and humiliation. Kohl interrogates Jean de Brunhoff's stories about Babar the Elephant as texts associated with French colonialism. He concludes that the modern world is better off without such texts:

> I wouldn't ban or burn *Babar*, or pull it from libraries. But buy it? No, I see no reason to go out of one's way to make *Babar* available to children, primarily because I don't see much critical reading going on in the schools and children don't need to be propagandized about colonialism, sexism or racism. There are many other cute and well-illustrated, less offensive animal tales for young people. I believe *Babar* would best be relegated to the role of collector's item, an item in a museum of stereotypes. (18)

Jeremy Love's remixing of the Uncle Remus stories, his reanimation of old rag dolls, offers the critical perspective that Kohl fears is missing from contemporary American education. Whereas *Song of the South* constructs a "timeless" or at least temporally ambiguous version of the "old South," one that blurs the line between slavery and sharecropping, Love focuses attention on his story's historical context. Whereas *Song of the South* imagines a "colorblind" friendship between white and black children, *Bayou* sees Lee's friendship with Lily as ultimately putting the entire black community at risk. Love introduces questions of power and violence that remain unstated in the Disney film. His artwork sometimes has the simplicity and beauty of a classic children's book, but it acknowledges brutal truths about adult society that would violate prevailing myths of childhood innocence. Love maps a black girl's pursuit of the truth as she learns to see past racist baggage, discovering ways to stand up for herself and demand justice for others. Br'er Rabbit and the other animal characters introduce whimsy in this story, but that does not mean that they are not implicated in *Bayou*'s Jim Crow–era mythology. Love promises his readers no happy endings.

Love may well be playing with fire, as Walker's critics suggest about her works, in bringing these painful representations into what looks like and follows the narrative conventions of a classic children's story, yet the implication is that there is no way to protect the innocence of black children in a society still unable to accept the basic truth that black lives matter. Love suggests that such caricatures have consequences in terms of how black people are treated when he shows the picture of Lee's father, Calvin Wagstaff, that appeared in the *Yazoo Herald* following his arrest: a drawing that looks more like a racist

WEATHER FORECAST — High 83, Low 74, Partly Cloudy, Humid

THE YAZOO HERALD

LATE EDITION

June 18, 1933

NEGRO HELD IN KIDNAPPING

TRAGEDY ON THE BAYOU

Special Commentary by Jack Barbour

In the northwest corner of our great state of Mississippi, along the Yazoo river, is the hamlet, Charon. Nestled on the great alluvial plain, where cotton is king, Charon is the very definition of "salt of the earth". From the majestic plantations and mansions to the north, the sprawling cotton fields, and the haunting bayou's in the south, there is one of the last bastions of Southern grandeur.

The town was renamed from its original moniker, Clarksville, after the War Between the States. It was there, in the waning days of the epic conflict, that General Douglass Matthew Bogg made his last stand against Sherman's Northern marauders. Bogg fought so fiercely that a Yankee writer likened him to Charon, the ancient Greek figure who ferried dead souls into Hades.

Refusing to surrender, General Bogg fought to the

MASSIVE SEARCH UNDERWAY FOR MISSING WHITE GIRL

VOLUNTEERS POUR IN FROM SURROUNDING COUNTIES

A comprehensive search is underway all around Yazoo County for Lily Ann Westmoreland, age 10. The search is centered around the town of Charon. Volunteers from surrounding delta counties have poured in to assist local sheriff deputies.

Authorities did not comment on the health of the missing girl, but sources indicate sexual molestation. A negro suspect has yet to provide information on her whereabouts or condition. Sources inside the Sheriff's department site "damning eyewitness and physical evidence" as the cause for arresting the negro man, Calvin Wagstaff on suspicion of kidnapping and rape.

Miss Eugena Westmoreland, Lily's

PRIME SUSPECT: SHARECROPPER CALVIN WAGSTAFF, 33, NEGRO

YAZOO COUNTY BASEBALL TEAM OPTIMISTIC ON

'PRETTY BOY FLOYD' KILLS FOUR G-MEN IN KANSAS CITY

FBI AGENTS WERE UNARMED

Four law enforcement officers and a criminal fugitive were shot dead at the Union Station railroad depot in Kansas City, Missouri yesterday morning. According to the official FBI report, the Kansas City Massacre occurred as the result of the attempt by Charles "Pretty Boy" Floyd, Vernon Miller, and Adam Richetti to free their friend, Frank Nash, a federal prisoner. At the time, Nash was in the custody of several law enforcement officers who were returning him to the U.S. Penitentiary at Leavenworth, Kansas, from which he had escaped three years earlier.

However all of the men alleged to be involved denied involvement. Floyd, in particular, went so far as to write to a newspaper denying involvement in the massacre.

A green Plymouth was parked about six feet away on the right side of Agent Caffrey's car. Looking in the direction of this Plymouth, Agent Lackey saw two men run from behind a car. He noticed that both men were armed. at least one of them

FIGURE 8.6. This newspaper sketch reduces Lee's father to a racialized stereotype. Jeremy Love, *Bayou, Volume One* (2010). © Jeremy Love. Courtesy of Jeremy Love.

FIGURE 8.7. This postcard of a lynching erases the humanity of the victim of white mob violence. Jeremy Love, *Bayou, Volume One* (2010). © Jeremy Love. Courtesy of Jeremy Love.

stereotype than any recognizable human being (figure 8.6). This image begins the process of dehumanization that allows the townsfolk to engage in lynching without regard to the human costs of their actions. Consider the ways that Love's re-creation of a lynching postcard erases Bobby Glass's face while creating individualized portraits of the men who murdered him (figure 8.7). In both cases, Love wants such images to shock and disturb us even as he suggests the banality with which such images were treated within white Southern society for so many decades (Allen 2000).

Both images represent the exercise of white power to construct how people of color are viewed and are meant to be read in contrast with Love's own more rounded and particularized treatment of the book's black characters. Both examples suggest that Love's reproduction of black stereotypes fits within a larger consideration of how the representational codes of our culture determine the ways we see black bodies. And this brings us back to the core questions: What are we to do with all of this stuff? What role do artifacts and materials from the past play in our contemporary consciousness? What do we keep and what do we discard?

Some have argued that *Bayou*'s relationship to stuff is different from the other cases discussed across this book. This is debatable, since the stereotypes and myths that Love builds his narrative around have persisted into the contemporary era, to a large degree because they were rendered in material form—because they were turned into lawn jockeys, cookie jars, and comic strips, because Disney spread *Song of the South* across so many things that it could never be fully withdrawn from circulation. Such objects often get passed from one generation to the next. All of these material practices preserve these myths as a residual element in our culture: we recognize them because we have seen them someplace before, and often, for guilty white readers, we recognize them because we have some of that same stuff stashed away some place, hidden from view, but still formative influences on how we understand American racial politics. Love restores those characters to life, translating residual objects into living subjects, much as Waldo represents a "transitional object" that has taken on a life of his own across Deitch's stories. Love counts on his readers to know where these stereotypes come from and does not represent, for example, the Golliwog dolls directly on his pages. Love abstracts the myths from the objects that reproduce them, much as Kare reads monsters as a frame she can map onto the world, even in a context of material lack. Yet Love is nevertheless deeply influenced by the stuff that previous generations left behind.

Epilogue

Unpacking *My* Comics

Now I put my hands on two volumes bound in faded boards which, strictly speaking, do not belong on a bookcase at all: two albums with stick-in pictures which my mother pasted in as a child and which I inherited. . . . There is no living library that does not harbor a number of booklike creations from fringe areas. They need not be stick-in albums or family albums, autograph books or portfolios containing pamphlets or religious tracts; some people become attached to leaflets and prospectuses, others to handwritten facsimiles or typewritten copies of unattainable books; and certainly periodicals can form the prismatic fringes of a library

WALTER BENJAMIN, "Unpacking My Library" ([1931] 1969, 66)

Walter Benjamin—the self-proclaimed collector—takes us on a tour of his "prize objects," his books—as they lay in stacks on the ground, "the air saturated with the dust of wood, the floor covered with torn paper" (59), newly unpacked from a move. The books need to be organized and shelved before he can control "the spring tide of memories" they evoke. I am fascinated by what Benjamin shares about the "booklike creations from fringe areas" that populate his possessions but, "strictly speaking, do not belong on a bookcase at all." For Benjamin, these include two sticker books that date back to his mother's childhood and set him on the path toward collecting other "picture books" across his lifetime. For someone else—Emil Ferris, say, or C. Tyler—these might include sketchbooks or scrapbooks that helped to inspire their own creative journeys. For me, those "booklike creations" would include comics—lots and lots of comics.

As I am wrapping up this book, I am confronting one of the quintessential problems of the early twenty-first century: I have too much stuff. In particular, I have way too many books for my bookshelves; one shelf recently collapsed under the weight and so I am in a process of shuffling the pieces, moving some books between my home and my office, putting others into storage. My parents taught me better than to throw out a book. Many of the books I drew upon in writing this book are stacked in a pile against the back wall—Daniel Miller's *Stuff*, Bill Brown's *Other Things*, Grant McCracken's *Culture and Consumption*, not to mention other related titles that I never ended up citing and a few I never even read. I am moving them back to my USC office to make room for the books for my next writing projects. In this case, I am repacking my library. I am giving away more than a hundred books to my students and colleagues in anticipation of incorporating these titles, which I have come to possess in the process of writing the one you now hold in your hands.

Benjamin tells us that the "most praiseworthy method" of acquiring books is "writing them oneself" (61), but I always find that writing books, at least as an academic, requires acquiring massive numbers through other means. Then again, reading books as an academic also results in more books, since we often get paid for reviewing manuscripts with other books from the press's catalog. The more interdisciplinary you are in your thinking, the more books you need to own. And so books accumulate, requiring periodic attention to their disposal. Things pass into our hands and out again. They move us, they get moved with us, and we move them between different shelves—or between home and office—as we reprioritize and recategorize our possessions.

My equivalent of Benjamin's mother's sticker books would be my father's original paperback editions of Walt Kelly's *Pogo* comics circa the 1950s. I do not recall a time when those books were not in my life; my memories of them as printed objects far precede my reading of their contents. As a native Atlantan, my father had a particular investment in *Pogo* (as did I) because of its South Georgia setting. My dad kept them in a special place next to his bed. I remember him lying there flipping through them with a big boyish grin. I have acquired the contents of those books in other forms since: a different selection of *Pogo* with commentary from Kelly, which I gave to my father as a Christmas present once; hardbound copies with detailed annotations and commentary (a byproduct of Art Spiegelman's "Faustian deal"); other volumes in the series that I have found in the used book sections of various comic shops. I have also added several books of critical commentary by comics scholars and I have supplemented them with other collectible and ephemeral items tied to *Pogo* that I have tracked down on eBay and stumbled upon in secondhand shops and garage sales.

But I still recall which ones belonged to my father and touching them brings back my memories of him, as I hold them in my hands, contemplating their well-worn covers and yellowing pages. These *Pogo* books (and my taste for comics more generally) are my cultural inheritance—we were so unalike in so many ways and our relationship was difficult at times, but one of the things my father and I shared was our love of these particular comics.

After my parents died, I found, hidden in the attic, a drawing of Pogo that my mother had done on the back of an old cardboard box. I have since found the drawing in the background of family photographs and so I now know that she must have created it in the mid-1950s and that it once hung in my father's study when he was an undergraduate at Georgia Tech. I had the drawing framed and it hangs on the wall of my USC office. Not far away but separated by several bookcases are two full-color pages from the *Chicago Tribune*'s Sunday supplement, original printings of Winsor McCay's *Little Nemo in Slumberland.* I bought these at the Sunday Press Books table at San Diego Comic-Con, as they were selling off the originals they had used to produce the recently published full-size reprints of McCay's work, which I also own. My "finds" as a collector coexist with the things I inherited from my mother and father.

My grandfather—my father's father—also collected comics—in this case, a bundle of comics depicting biblical stories clipped out of the *Atlanta Journal.* When he shared them with me, I was more interested in *Little Orphan Annie, Alley Oop, Henry,* and *Blondie,* the funnies that were on the backside of these more sanctified texts. Different collectors can bring different interpretive frames to the same objects.

I also still have two very distinct collections of comics from my own childhood. On the one hand, there are about a hundred *Classics Illustrated* comics, which my mother had lovingly stored all of these years, alongside more than a decade's worth of *National Geographic.* These were the comics she valued, the ones she bought for me when I was home sick from school; reading these comics was how I was first exposed to many of the great works of the Western canon. On the other hand, there are the comics I bought myself with my allowance—mostly *Dennis the Menace, Richie Rich,* and *Uncle Scrooge,* a few superhero books, some 1960s issues of *Mad* and *Famous Monsters of Filmland* mixed indiscriminately into the stack. The *Classics Illustrated* titles are almost pristine whereas the others have been read—and loved—to death. Few have covers, many have lost their staples, all are tattered and torn. The wear and tear suggests what happens when you turn various groups of preteen boys loose upon fragile, floppy comics on rainy summer days trapped inside a lake house. My mother tended to trash them when they became too dingy and battered, but these I salvaged. There is hardly anything left, but I refuse to part with them, even if I have replaced their content with better and more contemporary editions. As Leah Price (2012) reminds us, "Texts survive in proportion as books decay. . . . The more readings a work undergoes, the more reprintings are likely to be produced but the least likely any given copy is to survive" (225). In these cases, I value the texts enough to purchase the reprintings, but I value the particular books, with all of their embedded memories, even more.

I have filled more and more bookcases with comics—and books about comics—as my obsession with the medium has grown through the years. And at the foot of the bookcase there are long boxes filled with newly purchased comics which exist in a purgatory space, owned but not yet possessed. I won't shelve them until I have read them and perhaps not even then. I have become more discriminating as shelf space has dwindled, and my ability to hold onto every printed object that has passed through my hands starts to look more and more like hoarding.

And so it goes. Every comic book evokes memories, associations, feelings, meanings, too intertwined to be fully recounted here. Each work has a story behind it—not all as central to who I am as the ones I've shared above—but important to me as a collector: stories about how I acquired them, about why they matter in the history of the medium, about who I was and where I was when I first read them. And to get rid of these books would be to slice off and dispose of parts of myself. Benjamin talks about collecting books as a means of managing the "chaos" of memories, creating order out of disorder, but what happens when the collection itself becomes more disordered and chaotic? At what point does pride in possession give way to shame? Writing *Comics and Stuff*—yet another one to toss onto the pile—has held at bay these anxieties as long as could be hoped. Working through these texts has helped me to contain my own uncertainties, but they now all come rushing back upon me in the end. What do we do when we run out of shelf space, when all the closets are full, when we can't afford any more storage units? Sooner or later, our stuff will engulf us.

I undertake this homage to Benjamin's "Unpacking My Library" as a reminder that comic (and other) books are also stuff. Books have weight, both symbolically and literally. Books mediate relationships—such as the love of cartoons that has passed across generations in my family. Things published as books last longer than things published on newsprint. And books exist in dialogue with other aspects of material culture: movies, records, figurines, and the like.

As Price (2012) suggests, we "do things with books": they are "bought, sold, exchanged, transported, displayed, defaced, stored, ignored, collected, neglected, dispersed, discarded" (19). Price is writing about Victorian literature, fascinated by how often these various operations are described and narrated in the pages of nineteenth-century novels, reflections of a proliferation of low-cost print culture that threatened to overwhelm our ancestors just as it threatens to engulf us now. The democratization of book ownership meant that more people would come to possess books and that the wealthy would have more books than they knew what to do with. Writers such as Anthony Trollope and Charles Dickens, and cartoonists for *Punch* and other British humor magazines, had much to say about what people did with books, just as contemporary graphic novels have much to say about what we do with all of the stuff that comes in and out of our lives through collecting, accumulating, and inheriting, but also sorting and culling.

As we have seen, our own moment of cultural and economic churn leaves artists and readers alike reflective about what kinds of stories could—or should—be put on the pages of a graphic novel. People are going through past works, trying to decide what should be passed down, sometimes discovering forgotten treasures, sometimes stumbling onto things we wish we had not found. Surrounded by all of those texts, it can sometimes be hard—at least for those of us who constitute the cultural dominant—to notice what's missing, what stories are not being told, what voices are not being heard. We need to knock over some of the stacks and question what previous generations have thrust upon us. How do we respond when we discover overtly racist stereotypes created by even some of the most admired and beloved figures in comics history—Will Eisner, say, or Walt Kelly (Soper 2017)? I find myself wanting to make excuses and exceptions, to deny what I see, but I cannot unsee it. Despite such knowledge, I cannot bring myself to burn *Pogo* and I cannot disown or dispossess my father's old Walt Kelly books, because those stories, those characters, those pictures are too much a part of me, too much bound up with the history of my family, my generation, and my region, to distance myself from them. And yet I am still working through my increasingly conflicted feelings about what they might have meant to people with histories different from my own. We need to unpack our libraries in a different sense.

These debates parallel discussions in the culture at large about what should be done with the symbols and traces of the Confederacy, what monuments need to be taken down, what flags redesigned, what streets renamed, issues that are forcing themselves upon us with greater urgency and intensity. Should white America hold onto things that evoke fond memories of their childhoods but perpetuate stereotypes hurtful to others? Should such works be hidden or destroyed, erasing aspects of the past that provide a context for today's civil rights struggles? Should such works be reserved for collectors, locked in a vault, put in a museum, or studied in the classroom, but withheld from children susceptible to their influence?

People are anticipating works that will emerge in the future when comics become less of a boys' club, when more women overcome the obstacles to producing comics, when more artists of color tell their stories through this medium. As they do so, they also will have to decide how to respond to inherited materials from earlier generations of comics creators, who brought different identities, meanings, and memories to their work. Readers respond differently to these images, ascribing different meanings and motives to them, reading them in relation to alternative subjectivities, when they recognize that such stereotypes are being reproduced by a black artist like Jeremy Love, just as monsters take on intersectional meanings in the hands of Emil Ferris. But however aggressively Love mines and reframes such stereotypes, he cannot exhaust their hold upon our culture.

If we understand comics as "stuff," then we need to understand that comics are subject to the same cultural practices that surround other material culture—we map our meanings and memories onto them; they become evocative objects that help us think about our place in the world; these belongings help us articulate when and where we belong. They may be "happy objects" or sad, but they persist because they are meaningful not just in the past but also in the present and perhaps, we imagine, in the future. If we get rid of the objects, those meanings persist; those memories are apt to get attached to a different object rather than disappear altogether. If reformers attack symbols and do not address underlying attitudes, they ensure that those unmoored meanings and memories persist, often in an even more intense form, precisely because they have shattered the horcrux that once contained them.

As we bring comics into the twenty-first century, we still have a lot of stuff to talk about.

ACKNOWLEDGMENTS

This project was launched during a sabbatical spent at Microsoft Research New England and I am grateful for the insights and encouragement I received while I was there from Andrea Alarcon, Nancy Baym, Sarah Brain, Kevin Driscoll, Tarleton Gillespie, Mary L. Gray, and Lana Swartz, among others. Thanks also for support I have received through the years from the USC Visions and Voices Program and the Annenberg Innovation Lab. The earliest inspiration for thinking about comics in relation to stuff came from my former MIT colleague Sherry Turkle, who included my reflections on comics in her "evocative objects" project—this had a slow gestation (more than a decade), but it has finally emerged fully formed. I first worked through some of this material as a lecture presented as part of a tribute to Kristin Thompson hosted by the University of Wisconsin–Madison Communication Arts Department.

The comics studies world is small and supportive. Thanks for encouragement and insights I gained along the way from Jorn Aherns, Bart Beaty, Scott Bukatman, Hillary L. Chute, Ramzi Fawaz, Moritz Fink, Sam Ford, Jared Gardner, Dan Goldman, Charles Hatfield, Clifford V. Johnson, Mimi Pond, Billy Proctor, Greg Smith, Nick Sousanis, Daniel Stein, Bryan and Mary Talbot, Carol Tyler, William Uricchio, Rebecca Wanzo, and Matt Yockey.

Thanks also to my USC colleagues and students who have shared their insights with me through the years: Soledad Altrudi, Sarah Banet-Weiser, Samantha Close, Larry Gross, Joan Joda, Shawna Kidman, Josh Kun, James Lee, Geoffrey Long, Nancy Lutkehaus, Colin Maclay, Tara McPherson, Mauricio Mota, Christine Panushka, Gabriel Peters-Lazaro, Erin Reilly, Howard A. Rodman, Rox Samer, Andrew Schrock, Vanessa Schwartz, Sangita Shresthova, Jonathan Taplin, Virginia Wright Wexman, and Holly Willis.

In addition to the PhDs, I also thank all of the MDs who kept me pulled together and on the mend during a particularly difficult chapter of my life.

I want to acknowledge the labor of Ritesh Mehta, who did some of the initial spadework for this project many years ago, and Yomna Ali, who helped proof and fact-check a later draft. But, above all, I want to thank Jocelyn Areté Kelvin, my assistant, who has proofed and formatted everything here, helped to assemble the images, and provided enormous insights, at first timidly, then with more confidence. She is wise well beyond her years.

ACKNOWLEDGMENTS

Portions of this research have been presented at the Billy Ireland Cartoon Library and Museum at the Ohio State University, the USC Visual Studies Research Institute, the USC School of Cinematic Arts Graduate Caucus, the USC Sidney Harman Academy for Polymathic Study, the Los Angeles Times Festival of Books, the Society for Cinema and Media Studies conference in Atlanta, the Lewis Carroll Society of North America, King Juan Carlos University, and the University of Göttingen.

Chapters were also taught as part of my USC classes on comics and graphic storytelling; fandom, participatory culture, and Web 2.0; medium specificity; and humanistic approaches to communication.

I have been working with Eric Zinner for almost twenty-five years now. His deft editorial insights have informed nine of my books. The great team at NYU Press treat their writers right. I especially wish to thank Dolma Ombadykow.

Having written so many acknowledgements through the years, it is hard to keep finding new ways to express how much debt I owe to my wife of more than thirty-six years, Cynthia Jenkins, and my son, Charlie Jenkins. If it is possible, we have grown even closer in the past few years. Your spirit runs through everything I do.

LIST OF FIGURES

INTRODUCTION

CHAPTER 1. HOW TO LOOK AT STUFF

CHAPTER 5. "MONSTERS" AND OTHER "THINGS"

CHAPTER 6. SCRAPBOOKS AND ARMY SURPLUS

REFERENCES

Acland, Charles R., ed. 2007. *Residual Media*. Minneapolis: University of Minnesota Press.

Ahmed, Sarah. 2010. "Happy Objects." In *The Affect Theory Reader*, edited by Melissa Gregg and Gregory J. Seigworth, 29–51. Durham, NC: Duke University Press.

Allen, James. 2000. *Without Sanctuary: Lynching Photography in America*. Santa Fe: Twin Palms.

Altman, Rick. 2008. *A Theory of Narrative*. New York: Columbia University Press.

Anderson, Steven F. 2011. *Technologies of History: Visual Media and the Eccentricity of the Past*. Lebanon, NH: Dartmouth University Press.

Arnold, Andrew D. 2002. "The Transgressive Comix of Kim Deitch." *Time*, September 27. http://content.time.com.

Backderf, Derf. 2015. *Trashed: An Ode to the Crap Job of All Crap Jobs*. New York: Abrams ComicArts.

Bakhtin, Mikhail. 1984. *Rabelais and His World*. Bloomington: Indiana University Press.

Bal, Mieke. 1994. "Telling Objects: A Narrative Perspective on Collecting." In *The Cultures of Collecting*, edited by John Eisner and Roger Cardinal, 97–115. London: Reaktion Books.

Balzer, Jen. 2010. "'Hully Gee, I'm a Hieroglyphe'—Mobilizing the Gaze and the Invention of Comics in New York City, 1895." In *Comics and the City: Urban Space in Print, Picture and Sequence*, edited by Jörn Ahrens and Arno Meteling, 19–31. New York: Continuum.

Banet-Weiser, Sarah, and Manuel Castells. 2017. "Economy Is Culture." In *Another Economy Is Possible: Culture and Economy in a Time of Crisis*, edited by Manuel Castells, Sarah Banet-Weiser, Sviatlana Hlebik, Giorgos Kallis, Sarah Pink, Kirsten Seale, Lisa J. Servon, Lana Swartz and Angelos Varvarousis, 4–33. London: Polity.

Baudrillard, Jean. 1996. *The System of Objects*. London: Verso.

Bazin, André. 1960. "Ontology of the Photographic Image." *Film Quarterly* 13, no. 4 (Summer): 4–9.

Beaty, Bart. 2011. "Selective Mutual Reinforcement in the Comics of Chester Brown, Joe Matt, and Seth." In *Graphic Subjects: Critical Essays on Autobiography and Graphic Novels*, edited by Michael A. Chaney, 247–259. Madison: University of Wisconsin Press.

Beaty, Bart. 2012. *Comics versus Art*. Toronto: University of Toronto Press.

Beaty, Bart, and Benjamin Woo. 2016. *The Greatest Comic Book of All Time: Symbolic Capital and the Field of American Comic Books*. New York: Palgrave McMillan.

Bechdel, Alison. 2006. *Fun Home: A Family Tragicomic*. Boston: Houghton Mifflin.

Belk, Russell W., and Melanie Wallendorf. 1994. "Of Mice and Men: Gender Identity in Collecting." In *Interpreting Objects and Collections*, edited by Susan M. Pearce, 240–253. London: Routledge.

Belk, Russell W., Melanie Wallendorf, John F. Sherry, Jr., and Morris B. Holbrook.1990. "Collecting in Consumer Culture," in *Highways and Buyways: Naturalistic Research from the Consumer Behavior Odyssey* , ed. Russell W. Belk, 3–95 (Provo, UT: Association for Consumer Research), as quoted in Susan M. Pearce, "The Urge to Collect" (1992). In *Interpreting Objects and Collections* (1994), edited by Susan M. Pearce, 157–159. London: Routledge.

Bender, Hy. 1999. *The Sandman Companion*. New York: Vertigo.

Benjamin, Walter. (1931) 1969. "Unpacking My Library: A Talk about Book Collecting." In *Illuminations*, translated by Harry Zohn, edited by Hannah Arendt, 59–67. New York: Schocken Books.

REFERENCES

Benshoff, Harry M. 1997. *Monsters in the Closet: Homosexuality and the Horror Film*. Manchester: Manchester University Press.

Berenstein, Rhona J. 1996. *Attack of the Leading Ladies: Gender, Sexuality and Spectatorship in Classic Horror Cinema*. New York: Columbia University Press.

Berger, John. 1972. *Ways of Seeing*. London: Penguin.

Bernstein, Robin. 2011. *Racial Innocence: Performing American Childhood from Slavery to Civil Rights*. New York: New York University Press.

Blom, Philipp. 2002. *To Have and to Hold: An Intimate History of Collectors and Collecting*. Woodstock: Overlook Press.

Bloom, John. 2002. "Cardboard Patriarchy: Adult Baseball Card Collecting and the Nostalgia for a Presexual Past." In *Hop on Pop: The Politics and Pleasures of Popular Culture*, edited by Henry Jenkins, Tara McPherson, and Jane Shattuc, 66–87. Durham, NC: Duke University Press.

Brode, Douglas. 2006. *Multiculturalism and the Mouse: Race and Sex in Disney Entertainment*. Austin: University of Texas Press.

Brooker, Will. 2004. *Alice's Adventures: Lewis Carroll in Popular Culture*. New York: Continuum.

Brooks, Peter. 1995. *The Melodramatic Imagination: Balzac, Henry James, Melodrama and the Mode of Excess*. New Haven, CT: Yale University Press.

Brown, Bill. 2003. *A Sense of Things: The Object Matter of American Literature*. Chicago: University of Chicago Press.

Brown, Bill. 2009. "Thing Theory." In *The Object Reader*, edited by Fiona Candlin and Raiford Guins, 124–138. New York: Routledge.

Brown, Bill. 2015. *Other Things*. Chicago: University of Chicago Press.

Brown, Chester. 1992. *The Playboy*. Montreal: Drawn & Quarterly.

Brown, Hillary. 2017. "The Holocaust, Art, Chicago & Sickness: A 3,500-Word Interview with *My Favorite Thing Is Monsters* Mastermind Emil Ferris." *Paste*, February 23. www.pastemagazine.com.

Brower, Steven. 2012. "Jack Kirby's Collages in Context." *Print*, April 17. www.printmag.com.

Bryson, Norman. 1990. *Looking at the Overlooked: Four Essays on Still Life Painting*. London: Reaktion Books.

Bukatman, Scott. 2012. *The Poetics of Slumberland: Animated Spirits and the Animating Spirit*. Berkeley: University of California Press.

Bukatman, Scott. 2014. "Sculpture, Stasis, the Comics, and Hellboy." *Critical Inquiry* 40, no. 3 (Spring): 104–117.

Burch, Noël. 1990. *Life to Those Shadows*. London: British Film Institute.

Bute, Michael. 1997. *A Town like Alice's*. Sunderland: Heritage Publications.

Campbell, Josie. 2011. "Farmer Discusses *Special Exits*." *Comic Book Resources*, February 8. www.cbr.com.

Cardinal, Roger. 1994. "Collecting and Collage-Making: The Case of Kurt Schwitters." In *The Cultures of Collecting*, edited by John Eisner and Roger Cardinal, 68–96. London: Reaktion Books.

Chamberland, Luc. 2015. *Seth's Dominion*. Montreal: National Film Board of Canada.

Chast, Roz. 2014. *Can't We Talk about Something More Pleasant?: A Memoir*. New York: Bloomsbury.

Chute, Hillary. 2010. *Graphic Women: Life Narrative and Contemporary Comics*. New York: Columbia University Press.

Chute, Hillary. 2016. *Disaster Drawn: Visual Witness, Comics and Documentary Form* Cambridge, MA: Belknap.

Chute, Hillary L. 2017. *Why Comics?: From Underground to Everywhere*. New York: Harper.

Clowes, Daniel. 1998. *Ghost World*. Seattle: Fantagraphics.

Cohen, Jeffrey Jerome. 1996. "Monster Culture (Seven Theses)." In *Monster Theory: Reading Culture*, edited by Jeffrey Jerome Cohen, 3–25. Minneapolis: University of Minnesota Press.

Collins, Sean T. 2009. "Comics Time: You'll Never Know, Book One: A Good and Decent Man." *Attention Deficit Disorderly* (blog), December 30. http://seantcollins.com.

Crafton, Donald. 1994. *Before Mickey: The Animated Film, 1898–1928*. Cambridge, MA: MIT Press.

Danet, Brenda, and Tamar Katriel. 1994. "No Two Alike: Play and Aesthetics in Collecting." In *Interpreting Objects and Collections*, edited by Susan M. Pearce, 220–239. New York: Routledge.

Dangerous Minds. 2010. "Special Exits: Joyce Farmer." Video, 25 min. *Vimeo*, December 6. https://vimeo.com/17512623.

D'Arcy, David. 2001. "Black Market." *Guardian*, March 29. www.theguardian.com.

Daston, Lorraine, and Katharine Park. 2001. *Wonders and the Order of Nature*. Brooklyn: Zone Books.

Deitch, Kim. (1972) 1989. "The Cult of the Clown." In *Beyond the Pale!*, 43–52. Seattle: Fantagraphics.

Deitch, Kim (1976) 1989. "Teddy Beariana." In *Beyond the Pale!*, 65. Seattle: Fantagraphics.

Deitch, Kim. (1977) 1989. "TV and Me." In *Beyond the Pale!*, 79–84. Seattle: Fantagraphics.

Deitch, Kim. 1989. *Beyond the Pale!* Seattle: Fantagraphics.

Deitch, Kim. 1990. "Karla in Kommieland." In *Raw* 2, no. 1, edited by Art Spiegelman and Françoise Mouly. New York: Pantheon.

Deitch, Kim. 1992a. *A Shroud for Waldo*. Seattle: Fantagraphics.

Deitch, Kim. 1992b. *All Waldo Comics*. Seattle: Fantagraphics.

Deitch, Kim. 2005. *Alias the Cat!* New York: Pantheon Books.

Deitch, Kim. 2006. *Shadowland*. Seattle: Fantagraphics.

Deitch, Kim. 2008a. *Deitch's Pictorama*. Seattle: Fantagraphics.

Deitch, Kim. 2008b. "The Sunshine Girl." In *Deitch's Pictorama*, 4–81. Seattle: Fantagraphics.

Deitch, Kim. 2008c. "The Cop on the Beat, the Man in the Moon and Me." In *Deitch's Pictorama*, 167–197. Seattle: Fantagraphics.

Deitch, Kim. 2010. *The Search for Smilin' Ed!* Seattle: Fantagraphics.

Deitch, Kim. 2011a. "Mad about Music: My Life in Records, Television." *Comics Journal*, June 30. www.tcj.com.

Deitch, Kim. 2011b. "Mad about Music: My Life in Records, Cartoon Tunes." *Comics Journal*, September 9. www.tcj.com.

Deitch, Kim. 2013. *The Amazing, Enlightening and Absolutely True Adventures of Katherine Whaley*. Seattle: Fantagraphics.

Deitch, Kim, and Simon Deitch. 2002. *The Boulevard of Broken Dreams*. New York: Pantheon Books.

Desjardins, Mary. 2006. "Ephemeral Culture/eBay Culture: Film Collectibles and Fan Investments." In *Everyday eBay: Culture, Collecting, and Desire*, edited by Ken Hillis and Michael Petit with Nathan Scott Epley, 31–44. New York: Routledge.

Dick, Philip K. 1968. *Do Androids Dream of Electric Sheep?* New York: Del Rey Books.

REFERENCES

Douglas, Mary. 1966. *Purity and Danger: An Analysis of Concepts of Pollution and Taboo*. New York: Routledge Classics.

Dueben, Alex. 2017. "*My Favorite Thing Is Monsters*: Author Talks 2017's Buzziest Graphic Novel." *Comic Book Resources*, March 25. www.cbr.com.

Duffy, Damian. 2010. "Introduction." In *Black Comix: African American Independent Comics Art and Culture*, edited by Damian Duffy and John Jennings. New York: Mark Batty.

Duffy, Damian, and John Jennings, eds. 2010. *Black Comix: African American Independent Comics Art and Culture*. New York: Mark Batty.

Duncan, Randy. 2012. "Image Functions: Shape and Color as Hermeneutic Images in *Asterios Polyp*." In *Critical Approaches to Comics: Theories and Methods*, edited by Matthew J. Smith and Randy Duncan, 43–54. New York: Routledge.

Ehrenreich, Barbara, Elizabeth Hess, and Gloria Jacobs. 1992. "Beatlemania: Girls Just Want to Have Fun." In *The Adoring Audience: Fan Culture and Popular Media*, edited by Lisa A. Lewis, 69–83. New York: Routledge.

Eisner, Will. 2008a. *Comics and Sequential Art: Principles and Practices*. New York: W. W. Norton.

Eisner, Will. 2008b. *Expressive Anatomy for Comics and Narrative*. New York: W. W. Norton.

Farmer, Joyce. 1973. *Abortion Eve*. Laguna Beach, CA: Nanny Goat Productions. http://www.ep.tc/eve/01.html.

Farmer, Joyce. 1977. *Tits & Clits* 3. Laguna Beach, CA: Nanny Goat Productions.

Farmer, Joyce. 1979. *Tits & Clits* 5. Laguna Beach, CA: Nanny Goat Productions.

Farmer, Joyce. 1980. *Tits & Clits* 6. Laguna Beach, CA: Nanny Goat Productions.

Farmer, Joyce. 2011. *Special Exits*. Seattle: Fantagraphics.

Ferris, Emil. 2017a. *My Favorite Thing Is Monsters*. Seattle: Fantagraphics

Ferris, Emil. 2017b. "The Bite That Changed My Life." *Chicago Magazine*, February 8. www.chicagomag.com.

Fiske, John. 1992. "The Cultural Economy of Fandom." In *The Adoring Audience: Fan Culture and Popular Media*, edited by Lisa A. Lewis, 30–49. New York: Routledge.

Formanek-Brunell, Miriam. 1998. "The Politics of Dollhood in Nineteenth-Century America." In *The Children's Culture Reader*, edited by Henry Jenkins, 363–392. New York: New York University Press.

Freedgood, Elaine. 2010. *The Ideas in Things: Fugitive Meaning in the Victorian Novel*. Chicago: University of Chicago Press.

Fresh Air. 2014. "A Cartoonist's Funny, Heartbreaking Take on Caring for Aging Parents." *Fresh Air*, May 8. www.npr.org.

Frost, Randy O., and Gail Steketee. 2010. *Stuff: Compulsive Hoarding and the Meaning of Things*. Boston: Mariner Books.

Gardner, Jared. 2012. *Projections: Comics and the History of Twenty-First-Century Storytelling*. Stanford, CA: Stanford University Press.

Garland-Thomson, Rosemarie. 2011. "Misfits: A Feminist Materialist Disability Concept." *Hypatia* 26, no. 3 (Summer): 591–609.

Garvey, Ellen Gruber. 2013. *Writing with Scissors: American Scrapbooks from the Civil War to the Harlem Renaissance*. Oxford: Oxford University Press.

Geraghty, Lincoln. 2014. *Cult Collectors: Nostalgia, Fandom and Collecting Popular Culture*. London: Routledge.

Ginzburg, Carlo. 1989. *Clues, Myths and the Historical Method*. Baltimore: Johns Hopkins University Press.

Glenn, Joshua. 2010. "Kim Deitch—Q&A." *Hilobrow*, July 3. http://hilobrow.com.

Goings, Kenneth W. 1994. *Mammy and Uncle Mose: Black Collectibles and American Stereotyping*. Bloomington: Indiana University Press.

Gordon, Beverly. 2006. "Scrapbook Houses for Paper Dolls: Creative Expression, Aesthetic Elaboration, and Bonding in the Female World." In *The Scrapbook in American Life*, edited by Susan Tucker, Katherine Ott, and Patricia P. Buckler, 135–154. Philadelphia: Temple University Press.

Gordon, Ian. 1998. *Comic Strips and Consumer Culture, 1890–1945*. Washington, DC: Smithsonian Institute Press.

Grainge, Paul. 2011. "Introduction: Ephemeral Media." *Ephemeral Media: Transitory Screen Culture from Television to YouTube*. London: British Film Institute.

Gravett, Paul. 2008. "Bryan Talbot: An Artistic Wonder from Wearside." www.paulgravett.com/articles/article/bryan_talbot.

Green, Justin. 1995. *Binky Brown Sampler*. San Francisco: Last Gasp.

Gross, Terry. 2017. "In *Monsters*, Graphic Novelist Emil Ferris Embraces the Darkness Within." *Fresh Air*, March 30. www.npr.org.

Gunning, Tom. 1986. "The Cinema of Attractions: Early Film, Its Spectators, and the Avant Garde." *Wide Angle* (Fall): 63–70.

Halberstam, Judith. 1995. *Skin Shows: Gothic Horror and the Technology of Monsters*. Durham, NC: Duke University Press.

Hall, Stuart. (1981) 2009. "Notes on Deconstructing the 'Popular.'" In *Cultural Theory and Popular Culture: A Reader*, 4th edition, edited by John Storey, 508–518. London: Pearson Longman.

Hatfield, Charles. 2004. "The Presence of the Artist: Kim Deitch's Boulevard of Broken Dreams vis-à-vis the Animated Cartoon." *Imagetext* 1, no. 1. www.english.ufl.edu/imagetext/archives/v1_1/hatfield/index.shtml.

Hatfield, Charles. 2005. *Alternative Comics: An Emerging Literature*. Jackson: University Press of Mississippi.

Hatfield, Charles. 2012. *Hand of Fire: The Comics Art of Jack Kirby*. Jackson: University Press of Mississippi.

Heater, Brian. 2009. "Interview: C. Tyler." *Daily Cross Hatch*, December 23. http://thedaily-crosshatch.com.

Heer, Jeet. 2010. "Inventing Cartooning Ancestors: Ware and the Comics Canon." In *The Comics of Chris Ware: Drawing Is a Way of Thinking*, edited by David M. Ball and Martha B. Kuhlman, 3–13. Jackson: University Press of Mississippi.

Heffernan, Kevin. 2004. *Ghouls, Gimmicks and Gold: Horror Films and the American Movie Business, 1953–1968*. Durham, NC: Duke University Press.

Helfand, Jessica. 2008. *Scrapbooks: An American History*. New Haven, CT: Yale University Press.

Herring, Scott. 2014. *The Hoarders: Material Deviance in Modern American Culture*. Chicago: University of Chicago Press.

Hillis, Ken. 2006. "Auctioning the Authentic: eBay, Narrative Effect, and the Superfluity of Memory." In *Everyday eBay: Culture, Collecting, and Desire*, edited by Ken Hillis and Michael Petit with Nathan Scott Epley, 167–184. New York: Routledge.

Hoang, Lily. 2017. "Monster, Monster, on the Wall." *Los Angeles Review of Books*, April 9. https://lareviewofbooks.org.

Hodder, Ian. 2012. *Entangled: An Archeology of the Relationships Between Humans and Things*. Malden, MA: Wiley-Blackwell.

REFERENCES

Hoffman, Eric, and Dominick Grace. (2013) 2015. "Interview with Seth." In *Seth: Conversations*, edited by Eric Hoffman and Dominick Grace, 145–221. Jackson: University Press of Mississippi.

Hogan, John. n.d. "Jeremy Love's American Style." *Graphic Novel Reporter*. www.graphicnovelreporter.com.

Holland, Stephen L. n.d. "Page 45's Bryan Talbot Interview." *Page 45*. www.page45.com.

Honig, Elizabeth Alice. 1999. *Painting and the Market in Early Modern Antwerp*. New Haven, CT: Yale University Press.

Inkstuds. 2007. "Kim Deitch Part 3," August 2. www.inkstuds.org.

Jenkins, Henry. 1992. *What Made Pistachio Nuts?: Early Sound Comedy and the Vaudeville Aesthetic*. New York: Columbia University Press.

Jenkins, Henry. 2013a. "I Was a (Pre)teenage Monster." *Journal of Fandom Studies* 1, no. 1: 87–100.

Jenkins, Henry. 2013b. "Scrapbooks, Army Surplus, Comics and Other Stuff: A Conversation with C. Tyler." Video, 88 min. *YouTube* (USC Annenberg), April 16. www.youtube.com/watch?v=-pBWS-Zji7o.

Jenkins, Henry. 2015. "Archival, Ephemeral, and Residual: The Function of Early Comics in Art Spiegelman's *In the Shadow of No Towers*." In *From Comic Strips to Graphic Novels: Contributions to the Theory and History of Graphic Narrative*, edited by Daniel Stein and Jan-Noël Thon, 301–324. Berlin: Walter De Gruyter.

Jenkins, Henry. 2017. "'Man without Fear': David Mack, Daredevil, and the 'Bounds of Difference' in Superhero Comics." In *Make Ours Marvel: Media Convergence and a Comics Universe*, edited by Matt Yockey, 66–104. Austin: University of Texas Press.

Jennings, Dana. 2017. "First, Emil Ferris Was Paralyzed. Then Her Book Got Lost at Sea." *New York Times*, February 17. www.nytimes.com.

Karasik, Paul. 2011. "Review: Special Exits." *Comics Journal*, July 15. www.tcj.com.

Kartalopoulos, Bill. 2010. "Auguries of Brilliance: The Kim Deitch Universe." Introduction to *The Search for Smilin' Ed!*, edited by Kim Deitch, 1–10. Seattle: Fantagraphics.

Kashtan, Aaron. 2018. *Between Pen and Pixel: Comics, Materiality and the Book of the Future*. Columbus: Ohio State University.

King, William Davies. 2008. *Collections of Nothing*. Chicago: University of Chicago Press.

Knisley, Lucy. 2013. *Relish: My Life in the Kitchen*. New York: First Second.

Kohl, Herbert. 1995. *Should We Burn Babar?: Essays on Children's Literature and the Power of Stories*. New York: New Press.

Kondo, Marie. 2014. *The Life-Changing Magic of Tidying Up: The Japanese Art of Decluttering and Organizing*. Berkeley, CA: Ten Speed Press.

Krasner, James. 2010. *Home Bodies: Tactile Experience in Domestic Space* (including "Mess and Memory," 41–61). Columbus: Ohio State University Press.

Kristeva, Julia. 1982. *Powers of Horror: An Essay on Abjection*. New York: Columbia University Press.

Krysa, Danielle. 2014. "Introduction." In *Collage: Contemporary Artists Hunt and Gather, Cut and Paste, Mash Up and Transform*, edited by Danielle Krysa, 10–12. San Francisco: Chronicle Books.

Kuhn, Annette. 1995. *Family Secrets: Acts of Memory and Imagination*. London: Verso.

Kuznets, Lois Rostow. 1994. *When Toys Come Alive: Narratives of Animation, Metamorphosis and Development*. New Haven, CT: Yale University Press.

Langer, Mark. 2011. "Polyphony and Heterogeneity in Early Fleischer Films: Comic Strips, Vaudeville, and the New York Style." In *Funny Pictures: Animation and Comedy in Studio-Era Hollywood*, edited by Daniel Goldmark and Charlie Keil, 29–50. Berkeley: University of California Press.

Lemonnier, Pierre. 2012. *Mundane Objects: Materiality and Non-Verbal Communication*. Walnut Creek, CA: Left Coast Books.

Levine, Lawrence W. 1977. *Black Culture and Black Consciousness: Afro-American Folk Thought from Slavery to Freedom*. Oxford: Oxford University Press.

Levitz, Paul. 2014. *Will Eisner: Champion of the Graphic Novel*. New York: Abrams.

Lorah, Michael C. 2009. "A Father and Daughter: Carol Tyler on You'll Never Know." *Newsarama*, February 26. www.newsarama.com.

Love, Jeremy. 2010. *Bayou, Volume One*. New York: Zuda.

Love, Jeremy. 2011. *Bayou, Volume Two*. New York: Zuda.

Marks, Laura U. 2000. *The Skin of the Film: Intercultural Cinema, Embodiment and the Senses*. Durham, NC: Duke University Press.

Marrone, Daniel. 2016. *Forging the Past: Seth and the Art of Memory*. Jackson: University Press of Mississippi.

Matt, Joe. 2002. *Fair Weather*. Montreal: Drawn & Quarterly.

Matt, Joe. 2007a. *Spent*. Montreal: Drawn & Quarterly.

Matt, Joe. 2007b. *The Poor Bastard*. Montreal: Drawn & Quarterly.

Mauriès, Patrick. 2002. *Cabinets of Curiosities*. London: Thames & Hudson.

Mazur, Dan, and Alexander Danner. 2014. *Comics: A Global History, 1968 to the Present*. London: Thames & Hudson.

Mazzucchelli, David. 2009. *Asterios Polyp*. New York: Pantheon Books.

McCloud, Scott. 1993. *Understanding Comics: The Invisible Art*. Seattle: Tundra.

McCloud, Scott. 2000. *Reinventing Comics: The Evolution of an Art Form*. New York: William Morrow

McCracken, Grant. 1988a. "'Ever Dearer in Our Thoughts': Patina and the Representation of Status before and after the Eighteenth Century." In *Culture & Consumption: New Approaches to the Symbolic Character of Consumer Goods and Activities*, edited by Grant McCracken, 31–43. Bloomington: Indiana University Press.

McCracken, Grant. 1988b. "Meaning Manufacture and Movement in the World of Goods." In *Culture & Consumption*, 71–92.

McCracken, Grant. 2005. "Living in the Material World." In *Culture and Consumption II: Markets, Meaning, and Brand Management*, edited by Grant McCracken, 3–5. Bloomington: Indiana University Press.

McCulloch, Joe "Jog." 2004. "Kim Deitch—An Appreciation and Review." *Jog-The Blog*, July 16. http://joglikescomics.blogspot.com.

Medhurst, Andy. 2007. *A National Joke: Popular Comedy and English Cultural Identities*. London: Routledge.

Miller, Bryan. (2004) 2015. "An Interview with Seth." In *Seth: Conversations*, edited by Eric Hoffman and Dominick Grace, 68–76. Jackson: University Press of Mississippi.

Miller, Daniel. 1998. *Material Cultures: Why Some Things Matter*. Chicago: University of Chicago Press.

Miller, Daniel. 2008. *The Comfort of Things*. London: Polity.

Miller, Daniel. 2010. *Stuff*. London: Polity.

Mitchell, W. J. T., and Art Spiegelman. 2014. "Public Conversation: What the %$#! Happened to Comics?" *Critical Inquiry* (Spring): 20–35.

Moon, Fábio, and Gabriel Bá. 2011. *Daytripper*. New York: Vertigo/DC Comics.

Moon, Michael. 2012. *Darger's Resources*. Durham, NC: Duke University Press.

Mouly, Françoise, and Genevieve Bormes. 2017. "A Graphic Novel about a Young Girl, a Murder, and the Allure of Monsters." *New Yorker*, February 10. www.newyorker.com.

Muensterberger, Werner. 1994. *Collecting: An Unruly Passion: Psychological Perspectives*. New York: Harvest.

Nelson, Victoria. 2001. *The Secret Life of Puppets*. Cambridge, MA: Harvard University Press.

Nickel, Douglas R. 2002. *Dreaming in Pictures: The Photography of Lewis Carroll*. New Haven, CT: Yale University Press.

Noomin, Diane. 1991. *Twisted Sisters: A Collection of Bad Girl Art*. New York: Penguin.

Noomin, Diane. 1994. *Twisted Sisters 2: Drawing the Line*. Northampton, MA: Kitchen Sink Press.

Onion, Rebecca. 2008. "Reclaiming the Machine: An Introductory Look at Steampunk in Everyday Practice." *Neo-Victorian Studies* 1, no. 1 (Autumn): 138–163.

Orwell, George. 1941. "The Art of Donald McGill." *Horizon*, September 24. www.orwell.ru/library/reviews/McGill/english/e_mcgill.

Ott, Katherine, Susan Tucker, and Patricia P. Buckler. 2006. "An Introduction to the History of Scrapbooks." In *The Scrapbook in American Life*, edited by Susan Tucker, Katherine Ott, and Patricia P. Buckler, 1–28. Philadelphia: Temple University Press.

Pamuk, Orhan. 2010. *The Museum of Innocence*. New York: Vintage Books.

Pamuk, Orhan. 2012. *The Innocence of Objects*. New York: Abrams.

Pearce, Susan M. 1992. "The Urge to Collect." In *Interpreting Objects and Collections*, edited by Susan M. Pearce, 157–159. London: Routledge.

Perkins, V. F. (1972) 1991. *Film as Film: Understanding and Judging Movies*. London: Da Capo Press.

Pilcher, Tim, and Brad Brooks. 2005. *The Essential Guide to World Comics*. New York: Collins & Brown.

Pilgrim, David. 2012. "The Golliwog Caricature." Jim Crow Museum of Racist Memorabilia, Ferris State University. https://ferris.edu/HTMLS/news/jimcrow/golliwog/homepage.htm.

Pond, Mimi. 2014. *Over Easy*. Montreal: Drawn & Quarterly.

Powers, John. 2017. "*My Favorite Thing Is Monsters* Is a Dazzling Graphic Novel Tour-de-Force." *NPR*, February 22. www.npr.org.

Pratt, Mary Louise. 1991. "Arts of the Contact Zone." *Profession*: 33–40.

Price, Leah. 2012. *How to Do Things with Books in Victorian Britain*. Princeton, NJ: Princeton University Press.

Raeburn, Daniel. 2004. *Chris Ware*. New Haven, CT: Yale University Press.

Rand, Erica. 1998. "Older Heads on Younger Bodies." In *The Children's Culture Reader*, edited by Henry Jenkins, 382–394. New York: New York University Press.

Rehak, Bob. 2013. "Materializing Monsters: Aurora Models, Garage Kits and the Object Practices of Horror Fandom." *Journal of Fandom Studies* 1, no. 1: 27–45.

Rifas, Leonard. 2010. "Race and Comix." In *Multicultural Comics: From Zap to Blue Beetle*, edited by Frederick Luis Aldama, 27–38. Austin: University of Texas Press.

Ritsma, Natasha. 2013. "Lurking in the Shadows: Famous Monsters of Filmland and Its Female Fans." *Journal of Fandom Studies* 1, no. 1: 47–64.

Robbins, Trina. 1993. *A Century of Women Cartoonists*. Northampton, MA: Kitchen Sink)

Rochberg-Halton, Eugene. 1986. *Meaning and Modernity: Social Theory in the Pragmatic Attitude*. Chicago: University of Chicago Press.

Rogers, Vaneta. 2008. "Behind the Page: Jeff Smith (Part Two)." *Newsarama*, February 26. www.webcitation.org/5s406drEH?url=http://forum.newsarama.com/showthread.php?t%3D148242.

Rotella, Carlo. 2007. "Pulp History." *Raritan* 27, no. 1: 11–36.

Sarachild, Kathie. 1978. "Consciousness-Raising: A Radical Weapon." In *Feminist Revolution*, edited by Kathie Sarachild, Carol Hanisch, Faye Levine, Barbara Leon, and Colette Price, 145–150. New York: Random House. https://web.archive.org/web/20110718193344/http://scriptorium.lib.duke.edu/wlm/fem/sarachild.html.

Sattler, Peter R. 2010. "Past Imperfect: 'Building Stories' and the Art of Memory." In *The Comics of Chris Ware: Drawing Is a Way of Thinking*, edited by David M. Ball and Martha B. Kuhlman, 206–222. Jackson: University Press of Mississippi.

Sava, Oliver. 2017. "*My Favorite Thing Is Monsters* Is a Brilliant, Eye-Opening Graphic Novel Debut." *A.V. Club*, February 24. www.avclub.com.

Schneider, Greice. 2016. *What Happens When Nothing Happens: Boredom and Everyday Life in Contemporary Comics*. Leuven: Leuven University Press.

Schor, Naomi. 1987. *Reading in Detail: Aesthetics and the Feminine*. New York: Methuen.

Schor, Naomi. 1994. "Collecting Paris." In *The Cultures of Collecting*, edited by John Eisner and Roger Cardinal, 252–275. New York: Reaktion Books.

Schwenger, Peter. 2006. *The Tears of Things: Melancholy and Physical Objects*. Minneapolis: University of Minnesota Press.

Seth. 1996. *It's a Good Life, If You Don't Weaken*. Montreal: Drawn & Quarterly.

Seth. 2005. *Wimbledon Green: The Greatest Comic Book Collector in the World*. Montreal: Drawn & Quarterly.

Seth. 2006. *Forty Cartoon Books of Interest*. Oakland: Buenaventura Press.

Seth. 2009. *George Sprott 1894–1975*. Montreal: Drawn & Quarterly.

Seth. 2010. "Dominion City." In *Palookaville* 20. Montreal: Drawn & Quarterly.

Seth. 2011. *The G.N.B. Double C.: The Great Northern Brotherhood of Canadian Cartoonists*. Montreal: Drawn & Quarterly.

Seth. 2013a. "Nothing Lasts, Part One." In *Palookaville* 21. Montreal: Drawn & Quarterly.

Seth. 2013b. "Sublime Neglect." In *Palookaville* 21. Montreal: Drawn & Quarterly.

Seth. 2014. "Nothing Lasts, Part Two." In *Palookaville* 22. Montreal: Drawn & Quarterly.

Seth. 2019. *Clyde Fans*. Montreal: Drawn & Quarterly.

Shaw, Gwendolyn Dubois. 2004. *Seeing the Unspeakable: The Art of Kara Walker*. Durham, NC: Duke University Press.

Siegel, Elizabeth. 2010. "Society Cut-ups." In *Playing with Pictures: The Art of Victorian Photocollage*, edited by Elizabeth Siegel, 13–36. Chicago: Art Institute of Chicago.

Sigler, Carolyn. 1997. *Alternative Alices: Visions and Revisions of Lewis Carroll's Alice Books*. Bowling Green: University of Kentucky Press.

Singer, Ben. 1995. "Modernity, Hyperstimulation and the Rise of Popular Sensationalism." In *Cinema and the Invention of Modern Life*, edited by Leo Charney and Vanessa R. Schwartz, 72–102. Berkeley: University of California Press.

Skal, David J. 1993. *The Monster Show: A Cultural History of Horror*. New York: Penguin.

Smart, Tom. 2016. *Palookaville: Seth and the Art of Graphic Autobiography*. Erin, ON: Porcupine's Quil.

Smolderen, Thierry. 2007. "Why the Brownies Are Important." *Coconino World*, December 6.
Smolderen, Thierry. 2014. *The Origins of Comics: From William Hogarth to Winsor McCay*. Jackson: University Press of Mississippi.
Soper, Kerry. 2017. "Walt Kelly's *Pogo* and the Politics of De/Re-racialization in Midcentury Comics." *Inks: The Journal of the Comic Studies Society* 1, no. 1: 4–26.
Sperb, Jason. 2012. *Disney's Most Notorious Film: Race, Convergence and the Hidden Histories of Song of the South*. Austin: University of Texas Press.
Spiegelman, Art. 1997. "Dirty Little Comics." Introduction to *Tijuana Bibles: Art and Wit in America's Forbidden Funnies, 1930s–1950s*, by Bob Adelman with Richard Merkin, 4–10. New York: Simon & Schuster.
Spiegelman, Art. 1998. *Comix, Essays, Graphics, and Scraps*. Rome: Le Centrale dell'Arte.
Spiegelman, Art. 2005. *Breakdowns:* Portrait of the Artist as a Young %@# *! New York: Pantheon Books.
Spiegelman, Art, and Françoise Mouly, eds. 2009. *The TOON Treasury of Classic Children's Comics*. New York: Abrams ComicArts.
Sobchack, Vivian. 1994. "The Leech Woman's Revenge: On the Dread of Aging in a Low-Budget Horror Film." Paper presented at the Scary Women Symposium, UCLA, January. https://web.archive.org/web/20190411224021/http://old.cinema.ucla.edu/women/sobchack/default.html.
Stallabrass, Julian. 2009. "Trash." In *The Object Reader*, edited by Fiona Candlin and Raiford Guins, 406–424. New York: Routledge.
Steedman, Carolyn. 2002. *Dust: The Archive and Cultural History*. New Brunswick, NJ: Rutgers University Press.
Stern, Lesley. 2004. "Paths That Wind through the Thicket of Things." In *Things*, edited by Bill Brown, 393–430. Chicago: University of Chicago Press.
Stewart, Susan. (1984) 1993. *On Longing: Narratives of the Miniature, the Gigantic, the Souvenir, the Collection*. Durham, NC: Duke University Press.
Strasser, Susan. 1982. *Never Done: A History of American Housework*. New York: Pantheon.
Straw, Will. 2007. "Embedded" Memories. In *Residual Media*, edited by Charles R. Acland, 3–15. Minneapolis: University of Minnesota Press.
Sutton-Smith, Brian. 1986. *Toys as Culture*. New York: Gardner Press.
Talbot, Bryan. 1978–1989. *The Adventures of Luther Arkwright*. Various publishers.
Talbot, Bryan. 1995. *The Tale of One Bad Rat* (four-issue miniseries). Milwaukie, OR: Dark Horse Comics.
Talbot, Bryan. 1999. *Heart of Empire: Or the Legacy of Luther Arkwright* (nine-issue limited series). Milwaukie, OR: Dark Horse Comics.
Talbot, Bryan. 2000. *Heart of Empire, or the Legacy of Luther Arkwright*. Seattle: Dark Horse Comics.
Talbot, Bryan. 2007. *Alice in Sunderland*. Milwaukie, OR: Dark Horse Comics.
Talbot, Bryan. 2009. *Grandville*. Milwaukie, OR: Dark Horse Comics.
Talbot, Bryan. 2010. *Grandville Mon Amour*. Milwaukie, OR: Dark Horse Comics.
Talbot, Bryan. 2012. *Grandville Bête Noire*. Milwaukie, OR: Dark Horse Comics.
Talbot, Bryan, and Mary Talbot. 2016. *The Red Virgin and the Vision of Utopia*. Milwaukie, OR: Dark House Comics.
Talbot, Mary M., and Bryan Talbot. 2012. *Dotter of Her Father's Eyes*. Milwaukie, OR: Dark House Comics.

Tamen, Miguel. 2001. *Friends of Interpretable Objects*. Cambridge, MA: Harvard University Press.

Tanselle, G. Thomas. 1998. "A Rationale of Collecting." *Studies in Bibliography* 51: 1–26.

Taylor, Diana. 2003. *The Archive and the Repertoire: Performing Cultural Memory in the Americas*. Durham, NC: Duke University Press.

Thielman, Sam. 2017. "Emil Ferris: 'I Didn't Want to Be a Woman—Being a Monster Was the Best Solution.'" *Guardian*, February 20. www.theguardian.com.

Thompson, Michael. 1979. *Rubbish Theory: The Creation and Destruction of Value*. Oxford: Oxford University Press.

Thompson, Michael. 1994. "The Filth in the Way." In *Interpreting Objects and Collections*, edited by Susan M. Pearce, 269–278. London: Routledge.

Tilahun, Na'amen Gobert. 2016. "*Bayou* by Jeremy Love & Patrick Morgan." In "People of Colo(u)r Destroy Fantasy!," special issue, *Fantasy*. www.fantasy-magazine.com.

Tinkcom, Matthew, Joy Van Fuqua, and Amy Villarejo. 2002. "On Thrifting." In *Hop on Pop: The Politics and Pleasures of Popular Culture*, edited by Henry Jenkins, Tara McPherson, and Jane Shattuc, 459–517. Durham, NC: Duke University Press.

Tischleder, Babette Bärbel. 2014. *The Literary Life of Things: Case Studies in American Fiction*. Frankfurt: Campus Verlag.

Tucker, Susan, Katherine Ott, and Patricia P. Buckler. 2006. "An Introduction to the American Scrapbook." In *The Scrapbook in American Life*, edited by Susan Tucker, Katherine Ott, and Patricia P. Buckler, 1–28. Philadelphia: Temple University Press.

Tumey, Paul. 2016. "*My Favorite Thing Is Monsters*." *Comics Journal*, October 28. www.tcj.com.

Tumey, Paul. 2017. "The Emil Ferris Interview: Monsters, Art and Stories (Part One)." *Comics Journal*, February 16. www.tcj.com.

Turner, Patricia. 2002. *Ceramic Uncles and Celluloid Mammies: Black Images and Their Influence on Culture*. Charlottesville: University of Virginia Press.

Tyler, C. 1993. *The Job Thing: Stories about Shitty Jobs*. Seattle: Fantagraphics.

Tyler, C. 2005. *Late Bloomer: Stories*. Seattle: Fantagraphics.

Tyler, C. 2009. *You'll Never Know: A Graphic Memoir, Book One: A Good and Decent Man*. Seattle: Fantagraphics.

Tyler, C. 2010. *You'll Never Know: A Graphic Memoir, Book Two: Collateral Damage*. Seattle: Fantagraphics.

Tyler, C. 2012. *You'll Never Know: A Graphic Memoir, Book Three: Soldier's Heart*. Seattle: Fantagraphics.

Tyler, Carol. 2018. *Fab4 Mania: A Beatles Obsession and the Concert of a Lifetime*. Seattle: Fantagraphics.

Wajda, Shirley Teresa. 2003. "'And a Little Child Shall Lead Them': American Children's Cabinets of Curiosities." In *Acts of Possession: Collecting in America*, edited by Leah Dilworth, 42–65. New Brunswick, NJ: Rutgers University Press.

Wall, Russell. 2014. *The Graphic Novel Man: The Comics of Bryan Talbot*. Video, 142 min. Digital Story Engine.

Wanzo, Rebecca. 2020. *The Content of Our Caricature: African American Comic Art and Political Belonging*. New York: New York University Press.

Watterson, Bill. 1989. "The Cheapening of Comics." Speech delivered at the Festival of Cartoon Art, Ohio State University, October 27. http://web.archive.org/web/20060210115506/http://hobbes.ncsa.uiuc.edu/comics.html.

Weisinger, Maya. 2012. "Housewifization." *Tapestries: Interwoven Voices of Local and Global Identities* 2, no. 1. https://digitalcommons.macalester.edu.

Weiss, Andrea. 1992. *Vampires and Violets: Lesbians in the Cinema*. New York: Penguin.

Whitted, Qiana J. 2012. "Of Slaves and Other Swamp Things: Black Southern History as Comic Book Horror." In *Comics and the U.S. South*, edited by Brannon Costello and Qiana J. Whitted, 187–213. Jackson: University Press of Mississippi.

Whitted, Qiana J. 2015. "The Blues Tragicomic: Constructing the Black Folk Subjects in Stagger Lee." In *The Blacker The Ink: Constructions of Black Identity in Comics & Sequential Art*, edited by Frances Gateward and John Jennings, 235–254. New Brunswick, NJ: Rutgers University Press.

Williams, Linda. 2002. "When the Woman Looks." In *Horror: The Film Reader*, edited by Mark Jancovich, 57–62. London: Routledge.

Williams, Raymond. 1977. *Marxism and Literature*. Oxford: Oxford University Press.

Wilson, Julie Ann, and Emily Chivers Yochim. 2015. "Mothering through Precarity: Becoming Mamapreneurial." *Cultural Studies* 29, nos. 5–6: 669–688.

Winnicott, D. W. 1971. *Playing and Reality*. London: Routledge.

Worland, Rick. 2007. *The Horror Film: An Introduction*. London: Blackwell.

Yockey, Matt. 2013. "Monster Mashups: At Home with Famous Monsters of Filmland." *Journal of Fandom Studies* 1, no. 1: 65–86.

Young, Hershini Bhana. 2015. "Performance Geography: Making Space in Jeremy Love's Bayou, Volume 1." In *The Blacker the Ink: Constructions of Black Identity in Comics & Sequential Art*, edited by Frances Gateward and John Jennings, 274–291. New Brunswick, NJ: Rutgers University Press.

Yourgrau, Barry. 2015. *Mess: One Man's Struggle to Clean Up His House and His Act*. New York: W. W. Norton.

Zinonos, Anthony. 2014. "Foreword." In *Collage: Contemporary Artists Hunt and Gather, Cut and Paste, Mash Up and Transform*, edited by Danielle Krysa, 7–9. San Francisco: Chronicle Books.

INDEX

ABOUT THE AUTHOR

HENRY JENKINS is Provost's Professor of Communication, Journalism, Cinematic Art, and Education at the University of Southern California. He is the author or editor of twenty books, including *Textual Poachers: Television Fans and Participatory Culture*, *Convergence Culture: Where Old and New Media Collide*, *Spreadable Media: Creating Meaning and Value in a Networked Society*, and *By Any Media Necessary: The New Youth Activists*. With Karen Tongson, he co-edits the NYU Press series Postmillennial Pop. He blogs at henryjenkins.org and co-hosts the *How Do You Like It So Far?* podcast.